DATE DUE

OCT 1 6 2006	
GAYLORD	PRINTED IN U.S.A.

The METAPHYSICS of St. Thomas Aquinas

"St. Thomas Aquinas looked *only* for truth; he had both power of intellectual intuition and power of articulate reasoning at their peak; his thought was steeped in being; it was wholly centered on the primordial grasping of the act of existence in things, and wholly striving toward the knowledge of the Prime Being, *Esse per se subsistens*. Humble and magnanimous, he started from sense experience, with full respect for it and for the slightest data of perceivable reality, and he discerned with infallible insight the invisible structures of a purely intelligible realm of being. As the philosopher of being he is without peer."

JACQUES MARITAIN*

* From a note to the author, April, 1958.

HERMAN REITH, c.s.c.

University of Notre Dame

The METAPHYSICS of St. Thomas Aquinas

THE BRUCE PUBLISHING COMPANY

MILWAUKEE

NIHIL OBSTAT:

Theodore J. Mehling, C.S.C.
Provincial, Priests of Holy Cross
Indiana Province

IMPRIMATUR:

✝ Leo A. Pursley, D.D.
Bishop of Fort Wayne
April 15, 1958

Library of Congress Catalog Card Number: 58–12070

© 1958 by The Bruce Publishing Company
MADE IN THE UNITED STATES OF AMERICA

53448

Foreword

Some contemporary non-Catholic philosophers view the whole philosophical system of St. Thomas as an archaism of no more than mere historical interest. Even among some contemporary "Thomists" it is thought that in the area of the philsophy of nature the teaching of St. Thomas has been outmoded and that a system more in harmony with the findings of contemporary science must be developed, if it is to meet the challenge of our times. But on the whole, even among the extremely liberal neo-scholastics, very few question the validity of the philosophical principles that have come to be known as the metaphysics of St. Thomas. For if any part of the philosophy of St. Thomas belongs to the *philosophia perennis*, it is his metaphysics.

It is not my intention to write an apology for the metaphysics of St. Thomas. His philosophy is its own best apology. There is no need to feel that it is out of tune with contemporary problems and with sound contemporary thought. If authority were of any value in philosophy, one could find many great philosophers of our day who look on St. Thomas as perhaps the greatest metaphysician of all times. As an example of the respect that is shown St. Thomas, one of the great minds of the present century paid this tribute to the undiminished vitality of his metaphysics:

> If I say that it [Thomism] is, in my opinion, the only authentic existentialism, the reason is not that I am concerned to "rejuvenate" Thomism, so to speak, with the aid of a verbal artifice which I should be ashamed to employ, by attempting to trick out Thomas Aquinas in a costume fashionable to our day. . . . I am not a neo-Thomist. All in all I would rather be a paleo-Thomist than a neo-Thomist. I am, or at least I hope I am, a Thomist.[1]

The present book is an attempt to restate as accurately as possible, in the manner and sequence found in the writings of St. Thomas, those

---

[1] Jacques Maritain, *Existence and the Existent*, translated by Lewis Galantiere and Gerald Phelan (New York: Pantheon Books, Inc., 1948), p. 1.

metaphysical principles that have become the natural foundation upon which our contemporary Christian philosophy has been built. To avoid the pitfalls of an interpretation that might turn the metaphysics of St. Thomas into a convenient eclecticism and thus destroy its character as philosophy, we shall make his writings our constant guide. If I fail to give an authentic interpretation of his teaching, it will be due to a lack of understanding rather than disagreement, for my only purpose is to present the metaphysics of St. Thomas.

I feel that the method of presentation is second only in importance to the content of his thought. Indeed, to separate the excellence of his pedagogical method from his doctrinal content is to distort St. Thomas, to give an inadequate view of him as a philosopher. I also feel that for the order of development of doctrine there is no better source than his *Commentary on the Metaphysics of Aristotle.* Here St. Thomas, as a skilled teacher, develops his metaphysics in a way that is best suited to the nature of the human mind. He begins with an introduction to the subject matter, in which he shows the nature and dignity of metaphysics; then he gives an exposition of the proper subject matter of this science, together with its divisions, properties, principles, and proximate causes; at the end he lifts the mind of the reader to the vision of the ultimate cause in which is found the origin and end of all things that pertain to the subject matter of the science.

Some historians of philosophy doubt that the various commentaries of St. Thomas on the works of Aristotle really represent his own views. With this I cannot agree. First of all, there is the inner criterion of agreement with points of view expressed in his other works, those universally accepted as expressing his own philosophy. In addition, one may cite the authority of a man who is recognized an an eminent historian of medieval philosophy, Father Chenu, O.P. As the following passage shows, he points out that the commentaries of St. Thomas are a true exposition of his own philosophy and theology:

> The commentator advances along a very narrow line between two purposes: he keeps to the text, it is true, and wants to penetrate it, but this is not for the sake of some kind of erudite historical interpretation, but rather to discover a witness to the truth. . . . The medieval commentator is plainly concerned not only with the letter of the text but also with the "intention" of the author. . . . Because of his reverence (for the original) he will develop more fully, in his exegesis, the principles and fragments of truth contained in the text. That is why Cajetan says: "Very often he [St. Thomas] adds an explanation to Aristotle the Philosopher, and not simply to Aristotle, and this in view of the truth" (Cajetan, in *Summa Theologiae,* II–II, q. 172, art. 4, ad 4). Hence the difference between him and a modern exegete, who abstains from making the thought of the author his own and does not say whether or not he accepts this as his own. The medie-

val commentator implicitly makes the content of the text his own; and if he does not accept it, he says so explicitly. As long as he does not say anything, he is presumed to accept it.[2]

In order that the reader may have the experience of working directly with a great teacher and in this way develop a philosophical habit of mind, I have put at the end of the book what seemed to me some of the most important texts relating to the metaphysics of St. Thomas. Since these passages will closely parallel the exposition in the first part of the book, the two parts should be read as constituting one exposition of the metaphysics of St. Thomas. The reading selections are taken from a wide range of St. Thomas' writings. Among the sources that are more strictly philosophical I have chosen passages from the *Commentary on the Metaphysics* and the short treatise *On Being and Essence*; from works that bridge his philosophy and theology I have selected passages from the *Disputed Questions: On Truth* and *On the Power of God*; from sources that are more specifically theological I have taken passages from the *Summa Theologiae*, the *Summa Contra Gentiles*, the *Commentary on the Sentences of Peter Lombard*, and the *Exposition of the Trinity of Boethius*.

St. Thomas was often called upon in his capacity as a teacher to help the members of his own religious order. His treatise *On Being and Essence* was written early in his carrer for his confreres. The beginner in philosophy and theology found in him a teacher who was sympathetic to his difficulties, aware of the pitfalls he might encounter, and willing to lead him slowly and carefully to the intellectual goal set for him. This purpose is evident in his Prologue to the *Summa Theologiae*. St. Thomas said that he would keep in mind that his readers were beginners in theology and that he would try to help them by avoiding many useless questions, articles, and arguments, and too frequent repetitions that create weariness and confusion. And in a letter attributed to St. Thomas, though its authenticity is not certain, he gives advice to Brother John of Piperno, who wanted to know how to become a scholar. It is advice from which both the beginner and the experienced teacher can profit, especially in a subject like metaphysics, where one must have humility, patience, a sense of order, purity of conscience, and a dedication to the intellectual life.

You have asked me, my friend in Christ, how you must study to acquire the treasure of knowledge. My advice to you is based upon this principle: you must go through the rivulets and not try to come at once to the sea, for we must necessarily go to the more difficult through the less difficult. Be slow to speak. Love purity of conscience. Pray often. Love to be in your room. Be kind to everyone. Do not inquire into the affairs of others

---

[2] M. D. Chenu, O.P., *Introduction a l'étude de St. Thomas d'Aquin* (Montreal: Institut d'Etudes Medievales, 1950), p. 77.

and do not be too familiar with anyone, for too great familiarity breeds contempt and gives occasion for leaving off study. Do not be interested in the sayings and doings of people in the world. Avoid, above all, needless running about. Imitate the saints and the just. Remember every good thing you hear and do not consider who says it. Understand what you read and hear. Have all your doubts settled. Labor to fill the storehouse of the mind. Do not inquire into things above you. If you follow this advice, you will bring forth good fruits in the vineyard of the Lord. You will be able to obtain what you desire. Farewell.

Acknowledgments

The author wishes to thank the following individuals and publishers for their kind permission to use copyrighted translations of the works of St. Thomas:

Ralph McInerny, Ph.D., of Notre Dame University, for selections from his translation of St. Thomas' *Exposition of the Trinity of Boethius;*

John P. Rowan, Ph.D., of Duquesne University, and the Henry Regnery Company for selections of his translation of St. Thomas' *Commentary on the Metaphysics* of Aristotle;

Doubleday and Company, for selections from the translation of the *Summa Contra Gentiles (On the Truth of the Catholic Faith):*

Translations by Anton C. Pegis (Book I); James F. Anderson (Book II); Vernon Bourke (Book III); and Charles J. O'Neil (Book IV);

Random House, Inc., for selections from Anton C. Pegis, *The Basic Writings of St. Thomas Aquinas;*

Henry Regnery Company, for selections from the *De Veritate* (*Truth*): translations by Robert W. Mulligan, S.J. (Volume I); James McGlynn, S.J. (Volume II); Robert W. Schmidt, S.J. (Volume III);

The Newman Press, for selections from the translation of the Dominican Fathers of the English Province of *On the Power of God;*

The Pontifical Institute of Mediaeval Studies, for selections from Armand Maurer's translation of *On Being and Essence.*

Contents

Foreword v

Acknowledgments ix

I. **The Need of Metaphysics** 1

Prescientific Metaphysics, 1
Metaphysics as a Science, 4
Value of the Study of Metaphysics, 6
Metaphysics Is Wisdom, 8
Metaphysics Is Directive Knowledge, 9
Metaphysics Is Certain Knowledge, 10
Metaphysics Is Universal Knowledge, 12
Metaphysics Is Liberal Knowledge, 13

II. **The Formal Subject of Metaphysics** . . . 17

Formal Subject of a Science, 17
The Relationship of Formal Subject and Formal Object, 19
The Orders of the Speculative Sciences, 21
Separation and the Object of Metaphysics, 23
Metaphysics and Logic, 26
Metaphysics and the Philosophy of Nature, 29
The Proper Subject of Metaphysics, 33
Metaphysics as Natural Theology, 36
Metaphysics Is a Distinct Science, 37

III. **The Analogy of Being and the Unity of
Metaphysics** 39

The Doctrine of Analogy, 41
The Mode of Signification and What Is Signified, 43
Divisions of Analogy According to Signification and Existence, 45
The Foundations of Analogous Terms, 48

xi

Comparison of Analogy Based on Simple Proportion and
    That Based on Proportionality, 53
Divisions of Proportionality, 54
Metaphorical Proportionality, 56
Analogy Based on Proper Proportionality, 56
The Causal Relationship in Analogy Based on Proper
    Proportionality, 56
Application of Analogy to the Subject of Metaphysics, 59
Summary, 60

IV.   **Substance and Accidents** **61**

Metaphysics Deals Primarily With Substance, 62
Various Notions of Substance, 64
A Descriptive Definition of Substance, 67
The Reality of Substance, 68
The Phenomenalist Rejection of Substance, 70
Analogical Character of Substance, 73
The Being of Accidents, 75
Predicable and Predicamental Accident, 76
The Analogy of Being in the Relationship of Substance
    to Accident, 77
The Relationship of Substance to Its Accidents, 81

V.   **Potency and Act; Essence and Existence** .   .   **83**

The Meaning of Potency, 84
The Reality of Potency as a Mode of Being, 85
The Meaning of Act, 88
Analogous Notion of Act, 89
A Comparison of Potency and Act, 91
Limitation of Act by Potency, 93
Essence and Existence, 96
Existence and the Individual, 102
Individuality and Subsistence, 105
The Act of Subsistence, 106
The Person: the Highest Form of Subsistent Being, 106

VI.   **The Transcendentals** **109**

Logical Ordering of the Transcendentals, 109
The Transcendental One, 111
Identity of Being With the Transcendental One, 112
Transcendental Truth, 115

The Basis of Transcendental Truth, 117
Transcendental Good, 120
The Kinds of Good, 121
The Common Good, 123
Transcendental Beauty, 125
The Contraries of Transcendental Unity, Truth, and
   Goodness, 129

VII.   The Metaphysical Principles of Knowledge and
the Causes of Being **141**

The First Principles, 142
The First Principle of Knowledge, 144
The Principle of Identity, 144
The Principle of Contradiction, 147
Defense of the First Principle, 147
The Principle of Sufficient Reason, 150
Causes in General, 152
The Four Species of Causes, 153
The Modes of the Causes, 156
The Principle of Efficient Causality, 158
The Principle of Final Causality, 164

VIII.   The Origin and End of All **172**

The Ontological Argument, 174
Five Ways to Demonstrate the Existence of God, 176
The First Way of Demonstration: From Motion in the
   Universe, 178
The Second Way of Demonstration: From Efficient
   Causality, 183
The Third Way of Demonstration: From the Contingency
   of the Universe, 185
The Real Distinction Between Essence and Existence, 187
The Fourth Way of Demonstration: From the Grades
   of Perfection in Things, 195
The Fifth Way of Demonstration: From the Ordering
   of Beings to Their End, 197
Conclusion, 199

READING SELECTIONS

I. **The Need of a Metaphysics** **200**

1. *What Is Metaphysics?* 200
   Saint Thomas, Commentary on the Metaphysics, Prologue

2. *Wisdom Considers Universal First Causes and First Principles,* 202
   A. Aristotle, Metaphysics, I, 2, 982a4–982b11.
   B. Saint Thomas, Commentary on the Metaphysics, I, lesson 2, nos. 36–51.

3. *The Nature and Goal of Metaphysics,* 208
   A. Aristotle, Metaphysics, I, 2, 982b11–983a23.
   B. Saint Thomas, Commentary on the Metaphysics, I, lesson 3, nos. 52–68.

II. **The Formal Subject of Metaphysics** . . . **215**

1. *The Division of Speculative Science,* 215
   Saint Thomas, Exposition of the Trinity of Boethius, q. 5, art. 1.

2. *The Kinds of Abstraction,* 221
   Saint Thomas, Exposition of the Trinity of Boethius, q. 5, art. 3.

3. *Metaphysics as a Divine Science,* 228
   Saint Thomas, Exposition of the Trinity of Boethius, q. 5, art. 4.

III. **The Analogy of Being** **235**

1. *No Univocal Predication Between God and Things,* 235
   Saint Thomas, Summa Contra Gentiles, I, Ch. 32.

2. *Not All Names Said of God and Creatures Are Equivocal,* 236
   Saint Thomas, Summa Contra Gentiles, I, Ch. 33.

3. *Names Said of God and Creatures Are Analogical,* 237
   Saint Thomas, Summa Contra Gentiles, I, Ch. 34.

4. *No Univocation in Names Said of God and Creatures,* 238
   Saint Thomas, Summa Theologiae, I, q. 13, art. 5.

5. *The Primacy of Predication in Names Said of God and Creatures,* 241
   Saint Thomas, Summa Theologiae, I, q. 13, art. 6.

6. *How Names Are Predicated of God and Creatures,* 242
   Saint Thomas, Commentary on the Sentences, I, d. 35, q. I, art. 4.

7. *Univocal, Equivocal, and Analogical Predication,* 245
   Saint Thomas, On the Power of God, q. 7, art. 7.

IV.   **Substance and Accidents** **251**

1. *The Primacy of Substance, 251*
   A. Aristotle, *Metaphysics*, VII, 1 and 2, 1028a10–1028b32.
   B. Saint Thomas, *Commentary on the Metaphysics*,
   VII, lesson 1, nos. 1245–1269.

2. *The Being of Accidents, 259*
   A. Aristotle, *Metaphysics*, XII, 1, 1069a18–1069a30.
   B. Saint Thomas, *Commentary on the Metaphysics*,
   XII, lesson 1, nos. 2416–2423.

3. *The Definition of Person, 262*
   Saint Thomas, *Summa Theologiae*, I, q. 29, art. 1.

4. *Substance, Essence, and Subsistence, 264*
   Saint Thomas, *Summa Theologiae*, I, q. 29, art. 2.

V.   **Potency and Act; Essence and Existence**   .   .   **267**

1. *The Division of Potency Into Active and Passive, 267*
   A. Aristotle, *Metaphysics*, IX, 1, 1045b27–1046a35.
   B. Saint Thomas, *Commentary on the Metaphysics*,
   IX, lesson 1, nos. 1768–1785.

2. *Various Views on the Nature of Potency, 273*
   A. Aristotle, *Metaphysics*, IX, 3 and 4, 1046b29–1047b30.
   B. Saint Thomas, *Commentary on the Metaphysics*,
   IX, lesson 3, nos. 1795–1814.

3. *Actuality and Its Various Meanings, 281*
   A. Aristotle, *Metaphysics*, IX, 6, 1048a25–1048b36.
   B. Saint Thomas, *Commentary on the Metaphysics*,
   IX, lesson 5, nos. 1823–1831.

4. *Potency and Actuality Compared, 284*
   A. Aristotle, *Metaphysics*, IX, 8, 1049b4–1050a3.
   B. Saint Thomas, *Commentary on the Metaphysics*,
   IX, lesson 7, nos. 1844–1855.

5. *Priority of Actuality Over Potency in Substance, 289*
   A. Aristotle, *Metaphysics*, IX, 8, 1050a4–1050b6.
   B. Saint Thomas, *Commentary on the Metaphysics*,
   IX, lesson 8, nos. 1856–1866.

6. *Priority of Actuality in Incorruptible Things, 293*
   A. Aristotle, *Metaphysics*, IX, 8, 1050b6–1051a3.
   B. Saint Thomas, *Commentary on the Metaphysics*,
   IX, lesson 9, nos. 1857–1882.

7. *Essence and Existence, 298*
   Saint Thomas, *On Being and Essence*, Ch. 1.

8. The Relation of Essence to Genus, Species, and
Difference, 301
Saint Thomas, On Being and Essence, Ch. 3.

9. Essence in Separate Substances, 303
Saint Thomas, On Being and Essence, Ch. 4.

VI. The Transcendentals **309**

1. Relation of the Transcendentals to Being, 309
Saint Thomas, Truth, q. 1, art. 1.

2. Transcendental Truth, 315
Saint Thomas, Truth, q. 1, art. 2.

3. The Transcendental One, 318
Saint Thomas, Summa Theologiae, I, q. 11, art. 1.

4. The One and the Many, 320
Saint Thomas, Summa Theologiae, q. 11, art. 2.

5. Unity and Number, 321
Saint Thomas, On the Power of God, q. 9, art. 7.

6. The Transcendental Good, 331
Saint Thomas, Truth, q. 21, art. 1.

7. The Relation of Good to Being, 336
Saint Thomas, Truth, q. 21, art. 2.

8. The Nature of Evil, 339
Saint Thomas, Summa Theologiae, I, q. 48, art. 1.

9. The Presence of Evil in Things, 342
Saint Thomas, Summa Theologiae, I, q. 48, art. 2.

10. The Cause of Evil, 343
Saint Thomas, Summa Theologiae, I, q. 49, art. 1.

11. God and Evil, 345
Saint Thomas, Summa Theologiae, I, q. 49, art. 2.

**VII. The Metaphysical Principles of Knowledge and
the Causes of Being** **347**

1. The Meaning of the Term "Principle," 347
A. Aristotle, Metaphysics, V, 1, 1012b34–1013a23.
B. Saint Thomas, Commentary on the Metaphysics,
V, lesson 1, nos. 749–762.

2. The Defense of the First Principle, 352
A. Aristotle, Metaphysics, IV, 3 and 4, 1005b8–1006a18.
B. Saint Thomas, Commentary on the Metaphysics,
IV, lesson 6, nos. 596–610.

3. *The Principle of Contradiction, 358*
   A. Aristotle, *Metaphysics,* XI, 5 and 6, 1061b34–1062b19.
   B. Saint Thomas, *Commentary on the Metaphysics,*
      XI, lesson 5, nos. 2211–2224.

4. *Causes in General, 364*
   A. Aristotle, *Metaphysics,* V, 2, 1013a24–1013b16.
   B. Saint Thomas, *Commentary on the Metaphysics,*
      V, lesson 2, nos. 763–776.

5. *Four Classes of Causes, 369*
   A. Aristotle, *Metaphysics,* V, 2, 1013b16–1014a25.
   B. Saint Thomas, *Commentary on the Metaphysics,*
      V, lesson 3, nos. 777–794.

VIII. The Origin and End of All **376**

1. *Evidence of God's Existence, 376*
   Saint Thomas, *Summa Theologiae,* I, q. 2, art. 1.

2. *Demonstrability of God's Existence, 378*
   Saint Thomas, *Summa Theologiae,* I, q. 2, art. 2.

3. *The Demonstration of God's Existence, 379*
   Saint Thomas, *Summa Theologiae,* I, q. 2, art. 3.

4. *Difficulties in Demonstrating God's Existence, 381*
   Saint Thomas, *Summa Contra Gentiles,* I, Ch. 12.

5. *The Argument From the Principle of Motion, 383*
   Saint Thomas, *Summa Contra Gentiles,* I, Ch. 13.

6. *God's Universal Governance of All Things, 390*
   Saint Thomas, *Summa Theologiae,* I, q. 103, art. 1.

7. *God's Continued Act of Creation, 392*
   Saint Thomas, *Summa Theologiae,* I, q. 104, art. 1.

Index **397**

Index of Readings **402**

The METAPHYSICS of St. Thomas Aquinas

CHAPTER **1**

The Need of Metaphysics

The Prescientific Metaphysics of Common Sense

A French philosopher of science, Emile Meyerson, once wrote: "Thinking metaphysically is as natural as breathing."[1] If, by "thinking metaphysically," he meant, among other things, having a lively curiosity about ourselves and the world around us, wondering about such things as the origin and destiny of the world and of people in it, accepting, perhaps without knowing why, the first principles of reason that underlie our whole social structure — if that is what he meant, we would undoubtedly agree with his statement. What Meyerson said is more than a statement of a man who was himself a great thinker; it is something that everyone has experienced for himself at some time or another. Indeed, it would be more correct to say that this kind of thinking is more natural than breathing, because breathing is something shared with many other kinds of beings on earth, but thinking is something specifically human, and all thinking is to some extent metaphysical, since there are certain fundamental metaphysical presuppositions at the bottom of it.

If the statement about everyone being a metaphysician is true because in some way this simply means acting like a human being, then a broader statement that everyone is a philosopher is also true, for the metaphysician is the philosopher *par excellence*. Therefore, if we want to see more clearly how man is a metaphysician, we should first of all find out what the more generic classification *philosopher* means. Who is a philosopher? In his *Commentary on the Metaphysics* St. Thomas takes up the etymology of the word and tells us how it was first used.

> The philosophers were men who were moved to philosophize because of wonder, and since wonder comes from ignorance, it is evident that they began to philosophize in order to escape ignorance. So it is clear that they pursued knowledge and sought it zealously, only for the sake of knowing and not because of some utility.

[1] *De l'explication dans les sciences* (Paris: 1927), p. 20.

1

From the name *wisdom* that was first used (for this inquiry) there has been a change to the name *philosophy*, though both names mean the same thing. The early sophists who undertook the study of wisdom were called *wise men*. But when Pythagoras was asked what he would like to be called, he refused to take the name *wise man*, as his predecessors had done, because this seemed to him presumption. He called himself a *philosopher*, that is, a *lover of wisdom*. Hence the name was changed from *wise man* to *philosopher*, and from *wisdom* to *philosophy*. This latter name is more appropriate, for he is recognized as a lover of wisdom who seeks it not for the sake of something else but for itself. On the other hand, a person who seeks something for the sake of something else loves that for the sake of which he seeks something rather than what he seeks.[2]

A philosopher is a person who wants to find an explanation of the things that he experiences — first of all in his own person and then in the world about him. He wants to understand for the sake of understanding; to him truth is its own reward. But he is a man who realizes that his intellect can never encompass the whole truth, the total explanation, and that is why he calls himself a *lover of wisdom* rather than a *wise man*. He realizes that what he discovers will never be a complete answer. Other men will come after him to add something significant to what he and others have said. They, too, will realize that the fullness of truth lies beyond them. They will see that wisdom can never be a personal possession: it can never be bought; it cannot be owned as one would own a house or automobile. Truth is by its nature independent of men's minds, for it is divine, as even the pagan Greek philosophers knew.

Among the Greeks as among medieval philosophers it was the metaphysician more than anyone else who pursued knowledge for its own sake and for that reason was more deserving of the title *philosopher*. Most men pursue knowledge because of some other goal. Thus it would appear that metaphysical knowledge is a rare achievement, acquired only by the few. Yet, as we have seen, metaphysical thinking is natural for *all* men. How explain this seeming paradox?

It seems that there are several senses to the term *metaphysics*. In one sense it is knowledge that is almost synonymous with *common sense*, which itself has several meanings that can be applied in different ways to the kind of knowledge that Meyerson said is naturally found in man. Common sense can mean, first of all, the kind of knowledge that is contrasted with technical or scientific knowledge; it is the understanding that comes from the use of our native intelligence in the ordinary affairs of life. Common sense can also mean, in its more technical psychological context, the knowledge of the central sense (*sensus communis*), one of whose functions is to make us aware of the existence of sensible

---

[2] St. Thomas, *Commentary on the Metaphysics*, I, lesson 3, nos. 55–56.

realities. Though this act of knowing cannot be called consciousness in the strict sense, it is at least a prereflexive consciousness that makes judgment and self-reflection possible. Through this power of the soul we are made aware of the activity of the physical world upon our sense faculties. But man cannot employ the various powers of his soul as though they could be isolated from each other. The unity of man is shown in the operations of any of his powers. Intelligence begins to operate as soon as the common or central sense makes us aware of the outside world. What man knows through his intelligence is not merely a sensation, but an embodied essence, an existing something. In this grasping of essence and existence in an object of sense experience man is first awakened intellectually and first begins to think metaphysically. At that moment the rudiments of the analogy of being that is at the heart of metaphysics are given. But this first judgment about reality is only the seed of metaphysics. Metaphysical truth has been planted in the soul; but, like seeds that are sowed by the farmer, some fall upon good ground and some do not; some begin to grow and then are destroyed by birds and drought; some continue to grow to mature life. St. Thomas says that this is the way it is with our knowledge of metaphysical principles:

> We must give a similar explanation of the acquisition of knowledge. For certain seeds of knowledge pre-exist in us, namely, the first concepts of understanding, which by the light of the agent intellect are immediately known through the species abstracted from sensible things. These are either complex, as axioms, or simple, as the notions of being, of the one, and so on, which the understanding grasps immediately. In these general principles, however, all the consequences are included as in certain seminal principles. When, therefore, the mind is led from these general notions to actual knowledge of the particular things, which it knew previously in general and, as it were, potentially, then one is said to acquire knowledge.[3]

The prescientific metaphysics of common sense is sufficient for our ordinary intellectual needs. However, if someone without formal training in metaphysics were to try to explain metaphysical principles to others, he would find that his knowledge is vague and that he does not understand the reasons for holding them. Thus metaphysical knowledge is paradoxical. It is the most commonplace insofar as its subject is found everywhere and its general principles are known by all men; but it is also the most difficult kind of human knowledge and therefore few men understand the significance of what they know. When the philosopher by profession investigates the principles and causes of being, he is working with a subject matter no different from that with which the ordinary man is acquainted. The

---

[3] St. Thomas, *Truth*, 11, art. 1, c. Translated by James McGlynn, S.J. (Chicago: Henry Regnery, 1952), Vol. II, p. 82.

fundamental truths of metaphysics are no different for the one than for the other. But to some extent it is the very proximity of the subject matter that makes metaphysical truths so hard for the untrained philosopher. In this domain we are, in the words of Aristotle, like bats that cannot see well during the brightness of the noonday sun; our minds are at home only in twilight reality.[4] We cannot look directly at being and say what it is — we can see it better by looking out of the corner of our intellectual eye when we fix our attention more directly on something else immediately ahead.

Metaphysics as a Science

There is, then, another side to metaphysical knowledge that is not the knowledge of common sense. This is metaphysics as a science. We should not be misled into conceiving of it in the frame of reference of contemporary natural science, for the term *science* has a much broader scope. In its general sense the name is applicable to such diverse areas of knowledge as theology, philosophy, logic, mathematics as well as to what we know as the empirical sciences. The contemporary notion of science usually implies the use of scientific method, in which mathematics plays an essential role and in which the knowledge derived from the combination of observation and mathematical analysis passes through stages of hypothesis and theory, until it has been confirmed by subsequent experiments and generally accepted, when it is given the name of *law*. The immediate goal of empirical science is not the understanding of reality by means of ultimate causes but a reasonable explanation of the phenomena that can be observed in nature. In the older meaning of the term, a meaning that might seem to a student of the empirical sciences too ambitious, *science* meant certain and necessary knowledge achieved through an understanding of the proper causes of a thing. In this context the purpose of science was not to explain phenomena but to understand the reality beneath phenomena. Where the name is applied to metaphysics, as distinguished from the metaphysics of common sense, it means an understanding of the principles from which metaphysical truths can be drawn with certitude and necessity.

Philosophers have regarded the science of metaphysics as difficult to attain. Part of the difficulty comes from the lack of training regarding the subject matter itself, for it is not the kind of thing that can be seen immediately by the naked eye. It is like the reality of the microscopic world of the biologist or physicist in comparison with the world of trees, animals, water, and stones with which we are familiar. (We shall take up

---

[4] *Metaphysics*, II, 1, 993 b 10.

this point in the following chapter where we deal more precisely with the subject matter of metaphysics.) Another part of the difficulty, however, stems from extraneous reasons such as preoccupation with the more immediately practical needs of life or lack of physical, moral, and intellectual maturity that prevents one from coming to grips with the problems of metaphysics. This does not mean that someone cannot learn metaphysics if he is leading a very busy life, or if he is still a young person. But it does mean that one will not have the leisure or stamina to make the effort, or, if he is young, will probably get only a superficial understanding of metaphysical truths. That is why St. Thomas suggests that metaphysics should be studied after one has achieved a certain measure of leisure and maturity, and after one has become acquainted with other intellectual disciplines. Here St. Thomas speaks with the authority of one who is experienced in teaching a great number of young people. In his *Commentary on the Ethics of Aristotle* he says:

> As far as wisdom is concerned, he [Aristotle] adds that young persons do not believe — that is, do not understand with their mind — the objects of wisdom or metaphysics, although they may speak them with their lips. But regarding mathematical entities, their essences are not hidden from them, because the definitions in mathematics concern things that are imaginable, whereas objects of metaphysics are purely intellectual. Now young people can easily grasp what falls under the imagination. But they cannot understand with their minds what transcends sense and imagination, because their intellects are not trained to such consideration owing to the shortness of their life and the many changes of their nature.

> Consequently, the fitting order of learning will be the following: first, boys should be instructed in logic, because logic teaches the method of the whole of philosophy. Second, they should be instructed in mathematics, which does not require experience and does not transcend the imagination. Third, they should learn the natural sciences, which although not transcending sense and imagination, nevertheless require experience. Fourth, they should be instructed in the moral sciences, which require experience and a soul free from passions, as is said in the first book. Fifth, they should learn metaphysics and divine science, which transcend the imagination and demand a robust intellect.[5]

Notwithstanding the difficulty of the task, it is the vocation of every man to seek, during the years that are allotted to him, an ever deepening understanding of metaphysical truths, for eventually his eternal happiness is to consist in attaining the transcendent truth that he has begun to love in the present life. A foretaste of the pleasure that awaits him can be enjoyed by the person who puts value on the intellectual life and makes efforts to grow in it. Not even the meagerness and obscurity of his effort will deprive him of this joy.

---

[5] St. Thomas, *Commentary on the Ethics*, VI, lesson 7, nos. 1210–1211.

Value of the Study of Metaphysics

St. Thomas has said in several places that one of the most important functions of the teacher is to point out at the beginning of any investigation the importance of the subject matter, because in this way he will make the student well disposed and eager to learn (cf. *Commentary on the Soul*, I, lesson 1, no. 2). In his *Exposition on the Liber de Causis* he does this by showing that the essential happiness of man will consist in the perfection of his intellect, and that the greatest natural happiness that a man can attain in this life will consist in the contemplation of the truths of metaphysics insofar as this leads to the knowledge of God. The fact that some people do not enjoy intellectual activity does not disprove his point, for men can be turned from their natural goal.

> The highest felicity of man consists in the best activity belonging to his highest power, that is, his intellect, in attaining the most intellectual object. Furthermore, since an effect is known through its cause, it is clear that a cause is in its nature more intelligible than its effects, although at times effects are better known to us than causes, because our knowledge of universal and intelligible causes has been gathered from the particular things which fall under the senses. Absolutely speaking, therefore, the first causes of things must be in themselves the highest and the most intellectual objects, since they are the highest beings and the highest truths, being for other things the cause of their essence and truth, as the philosopher makes clear in the *Metaphysics*. It remains, however, that such primary causes are less well known as far as we are concerned, for our intellect stands to them as the eye of an owl to the light of the sun, which, owing to its excessive clarity, cannot be perfectly perceived.
>
> It is proper, therefore, that the highest felicity that man can obtain in this life should consist in the contemplation of the first causes; for the little that can be known about them is more lovable and noble than everything that can be known about lesser things, as is clear from the words of the Philosopher in his *On the Parts of Animals*. And it is through the completion of this knowledge in us after the present life that man is made perfectly happy, according to the words of the Gospel: "This is eternal life, that they may know thee, the only true God."[6]

If the greatest happiness of man consists in knowledge, then the greatest degree of happiness will be found in the kind of knowledge that most completely fills the capacity of the intellect. At the beginning of his *Commentary on the Metaphysics*, St. Thomas outlines the various kinds of knowledge that men pursue and then shows how, in this life, metaphysics is supreme among them. The first and lowest of all is that which man shares with irrational animals, namely sense knowledge. Even though man is not precisely like an irrational animal in acquiring sense knowledge

---

[6] St. Thomas, *Exposition of the Liber de Causis*, preface.

and in the use he makes of it, this knowledge remains an experience in which the causes of the phenomena are not understood. Beyond sense knowledge man has the knowledge of remembered experience. He is able to profit from the assimilation of individual sensory experiences and come to a kind of reasoned prudence, without understanding the causes of things. More perfect than this experience is his knowledge of how to make things — this is called art. Art is primarily knowledge, not a manual skill. It is superior to experience because it deals more with the universal character of things and presupposes on the part of the artist a knowledge of causes, while experience remains a knowledge of contingent individual events. Mere knowledge of fact is not true understanding; consequently experience is not the kind of knowledge that is explanatory nor can it be taught.

Superior to art is scientific knowledge. St. Thomas advances several reasons to show why. First, a man of science is like an architect with respect to men in the building trades — he can give directions to others because he knows the reasons that are behind the arts and skills. For example, in the building of a ship he must direct the people who prepare the materials; he must direct the actual builders because he understands the reasons for the particular specifications that he has drawn up. His superiority comes, in the final analysis, because he knows the end that is to be achieved and the means of reaching it. Second, a man of science can teach others, whereas a man of experience can tell what happened to himself but cannot give precise instructions how anyone else should act. And the artist can give only very general directions because each work of art is something subjective. Science, on the other hand, prescinds more from subjective elements, since it deals with objective truth. Hence the scientist, if he has reached maturity in his science, can assist others in acquiring it for the very reason that it is not highly subjective. Third, a man of science can know some things with certitude, whereas the man of experience and the artist do not have absolutely universal norms of truth because they deal directly with singular, contingent things. The universal judgment made by the scientist abstracts from individual matter which is the principle of contingency.

The metaphysician qualifies for the name *man of science* because these three characteristics are found in his knowledge of reality. But the metaphysician also differs from other men of science. For one thing, he arrives at many truths in a way that differs from the methods of other sciences. In addition, the truths he attains are more excellent than those investigated in other sciences. Most sciences prove the truth of a proposition by means of a demonstration from previous knowledge, as, for example, in geometry where a theorem is demonstrated from axioms that were previously seen to be true. But the basic truths of metaphysics are prior to and superior to truths that are demonstrated. If science through demonstration is valid, there must be universal and certain knowledge that is known without demonstration, otherwise the mind would require an infinite series of unsustained propositions. St. Thomas proves this point in his *Commentary on the Posterior Analytics.*

> Not all science is demonstrative, that is, acquired by demonstration. It should be understood here that Aristotle takes *science* broadly for any certain knowledge, and not as opposed to *understanding*, as when it is said that science deals with conclusions, but understanding with principles. That certain knowledge of some things is had without demonstration, he proves thus: It is necessary to know the prior things from which demonstration proceeds. At some point these must be reduced to things that are immediately certain. Otherwise it would be necessary to say that between two extremes, that is, the subject and predicate, there would be an infinite number of middle terms in act; even further, that there could be no two things between which there would not be an infinity of middles. In whatever way middles are taken, there must be something immediate to what follows. But since those which are immediate are prior, they must be indemonstrable. Therefore it is evident that knowledge of some things must be had without demonstration.[7]

Metaphysics Is Wisdom

Metaphysics is superior to other particular sciences because it is a wisdom and has a regulative or directive function in relation to the particular sciences. In the popular mind a wise person is more than someone who knows a great many things. The adjective "wise" has the connotation of knowing how to direct others wherever there is a common striving for a goal. A "wise" businessman is one who has an over-all knowledge of the goal of the company and the most efficient means of reaching it. Therefore he can organize a business establishment so that it can do its job most efficiently and make the most profit. A "wise" military leader is one who knows with certitude the strength and weaknesses of his own position and those of the enemy, but above all, who is able to co-ordinate this knowledge and dispose his troops so that they can gain a final victory. With Aristotle, St. Thomas has set down the following characteristics of a wise man: (1) he is one who knows all things at least in broad outline, though he may not know all things in the individual detail; (2) he is one who understands difficult things over and beyond the ordinary understanding of men; (3) he is one who has greater certitude than most men possess; (4) he is one who better understands the causes of things; (5) he is one who is more liberally educated, because he prizes knowledge as a goal in itself rather than as an instrument for something else;

---

[7] St. Thomas, *Commentary on the Posterior Analytics*, I, lesson 7.

(6) he is one who has greater dignity because he is able to direct others. These are the characteristics that belong to the metaphysician and to the science of metaphysics.

We shall not take up all the points made by St. Thomas nor treat them in the order just given, because the listing is partially arbitrary, as Aquinas says, and the definition is a dialectical one, inasmuch as Aristotle "gathered this definition of wisdom from the opinions that men hold regarding a wise man and wisdom."[8] But we shall take up four of the things that are usually mentioned as characteristics of wisdom and apply them to metaphysics: Metaphysics is the basic *directive* science on the natural plane; it is the most *certain* of the sciences; it is the most *universal* of the sciences; it is the most *liberal* of the sciences.

Metaphysics Is Directive Knowledge

In the foreword to his *Commentary on the Metaphysics* St. Thomas compares the role of metaphysics to that of the ruler in the order of politics and to the soul in the order of life.

> As the Philosopher teaches in the *Politics*, when a number of things are ordered to a single goal, one of that number must be regulative or direc- tive, and the others regulated or directed. This indeed is evident in the case of the union of the soul and the body, for the soul naturally com- mands and the body obeys. So, too, within the powers of the soul, the irascible and the concupiscible, by a natural ordering, are governed by reason. Indeed, all sciences and arts are ordained to one thing, namely, the perfection of man, which is his beatitude. Hence, among them that one must be mistress of all the others which rightly lays claim to the title of wisdom. For it is the office of the wise man to order others.[9]

If a number of things tend to the same general end, there must be some kind of order among them. This implies a principle of order, a principle of unity. A heterogeneous plurality cannot conduct itself in an orderly movement to an end for the simple reason that there will always be interactions among many things, when all tend to the same end. If there is nothing to direct them, they will act at random and will interfere with each other, thus preventing the attainment of the goal or making it more difficult. If beings are different in kind, they will necessarily be on different levels of existence and have different kinds of operations.

Each thing operates and moves toward the end according to its own nature, it is true, but by the very fact that it is moving toward an end it participates in the perfection of the end. The causality of the end

---

[8] St. Thomas, *Commentary on the Metaphysics*, I, lesson 2, no. 36.

[9] St. Thomas, *Commentary on the Metaphysics*, Preface.

is found in different measure in all things that tend toward it; the end is the unifying principle. As in the example given by Aristotle, there is an ordered arrangement of causes in the art of shipbuilding. The superior cause of shipbuilding is the architect who directs the artisans who prepare the material and put it into a form; the architect himself is directed by the purpose of shipbuilding. He acts as the intermediary between the end and the means — it is his function to direct the means to the end.

The diversity that is found among things in nature and in the arts and crafts is also found in the order of science. The ultimate goal of all science is the attainment of truth in its highest form; and this in turn will be the ultimate happiness of man, as we have already seen. But there must be some intermediary in the order of science by means of which particular sciences all work harmoniously in the direction of the final goal. This directive science must be in contact with both the final end and the other sciences, as the architect is in contact with the purpose of shipbuilding and with the men who work under him. To act as an intermediary in the order of learning by which man achieves happiness is the role of metaphysics on the natural plan of human life, as it is of revealed theology on the supernatural plane of life.

As directive knowledge metaphysics is called *First Philosophy*. The name does not refer to the chronological order of learning, as we shall see, but to the priority that metaphysics enjoys with respect to other human sciences. Metaphysics has priority over other sciences because it, as the science of indemonstrable principles of being, is the guardian of the first principles of other sciences. In addition, metaphysics, as natural theology, is able to direct other sciences toward God, who is the origin and end of all things.

Metaphysics Is Certain Knowledge

The certainty of metaphysics, as compared with that of other sciences, is not immediately evident, for it seems that the kind of knowledge that comes closest to sense experience would be most certain for us. Also, there are some passages in St. Thomas where it is said that the greatest certitude is to be found in other sciences. For example, he says in his *Disputed Question on Truth*:

> Knowledge of the soul is most certain for this reason that each one experiences within himself that he has a soul and that the acts of the soul are within him.[10]

In his *Commentary on the Metaphysics* he says:

> Things that are immaterial by nature are not certain for us, because of

---

[10] St. Thomas, *Truth*, 10, art. 8, ad 8. McGlynn translation, Vol. II, p. 46.

a weakness in our intellect. . . . But mathematical beings are abstracted from matter, yet do not exceed the capacity of our intellect. Hence in this subject matter the greatest certitude is to be sought.[11]

Both these difficulties can be answered through a distinction that St. Thomas makes between subjective and objective certitude. He writes:

> Certitude can mean two things. The first is firmness of adherence, and with reference to this, faith is more certain than any understanding of principles and scientific knowledge. For the first truth, which causes the assent of faith, is a more powerful cause than the light of reason, which causes the assent in the intellectual habitus of first principles or in science. The second kind of certitude is the evidence of that to which assent is given. Here faith does not have certainty but science and the habitus of first principles do.[12]

When it is said that metaphysics is the most certain of the sciences, it is to be understood in the sense of knowledge that deals with objects that can cause greater certitude. Beings higher in the ontological order and therefore more universal in the order of causation offer greater objective evidence. Since metaphysics treats of immaterial substances, which are highest in the ontological order, it is objectively the most certain kind of human knowledge. However, the pre-eminence of the objects of metaphysics does not find a corresponding receptivity to the evidence on the part of the human intellect. That is why other sciences and less perfect forms of knowledge can be more certain subjectively. St. Thomas says:

> It may well happen that what is in itself the more certain may seem to us less certain because of the weakness of our intellect, which is dazzled by the clearest objects of nature, as the owl is dazzled by the light of the sun.[13]

And:

> Immaterial beings are in themselves most certain, because they are immobile. But things which are by nature immaterial are not most certain for us because of the weakness of our intellect.[14]

The certitude of other sciences could not be sustained without metaphysics, because the certitude of first principles is a presupposition in all the other sciences. The strength of a conclusion in mathematics, for example, can be no greater than the certitude of the principle of identity and of contradiction. But it is metaphysics that establishes the validity of the first principles. Since metaphysics does not go to any other science for its own principles but derives them by an analysis of its proper

---

[11] St. Thomas, *Commentary on the Metaphysics*, II, lesson 5, no. 336.
[12] St. Thomas, *Truth*, 14, art. 1, ad 7. McGlynn translation, Vol. II, p. 212.
[13] St. Thomas, *Summa Theologiae*, I, 1, 5, ad 1.
[14] St. Thomas, *Commentary on the Metaphysics*, II, lesson 5, no. 336.

object, it is the foundation of the certitude of all other sciences that take these first principles for granted.

> Particular sciences are posterior in nature to universal sciences, because their subjects add to the subject matter of the universal sciences, as is clear in the case of natural philosophy which adds to being as such, the subject of metaphysics, and to quantified being, the subject of mathematics. Therefore the science which treats simply of being and the most universal things is most certain.[15]

Metaphysics Is Universal Knowledge

The need for a universal science is established on the grounds that there are genuine problems that lie beyond the scope of the particular sciences. In the context in which we speak, *particular sciences* are those that have limited subject matter and that demonstrate propositions through a restricted set of causes and principles. For example, in the genus of mathematics algebra and geometry are particular sciences; and mathematics as a whole could be called a particular science with respect to other sciences such as biology, chemistry, and other natural sciences. In one sense metaphysics is a particular science, in that it studies its subject in a way that is different from that of any other science, but it is at the same time a universal science because it treats of all being and because its principles and causes are applicable to all the other sciences.

The particular sciences take many propositions for granted either because they are not in a position to discover the truth of these propositions by the method that is peculiar to them or because such things are sufficiently well known by common sense, even though they are not known analytically.

Although each science demonstrates through principles that are its own, these principles in turn depend on more general principles that are common to a number of sciences. The particular sciences do not demonstrate their own first principles, since any attempt would involve a circular argument — a science does not demonstrate its first principles but demonstrates *by means of them*. Whatever certitude there is, then, in the particular sciences ultimately comes from the truth of the universal principles established in a universal science. If there were no first science that is autonomous with respect to the universal principles, there would never be any subsequent certain demonstrations. This point is made by St. Thomas in his *Commentary on the Posterior Analytics:*

> Since the principles of a lower science are proved by the principles of a superior science, one does not proceed from the caused to the causes, but conversely. Whence such a process must be for these things that are

---

[15] St. Thomas, *Commentary on the Metaphysics,* I, lesson 2, no. 47.

prior and better known absolutely. Therefore, that must be better known which belongs to the superior science from which the principles of the inferior are proved, and the better known is that by which all else is proved while it itself is not proved by anything prior to it. Consequently, the superior science will be more truly science than the lower; and the supreme science, namely first philosophy, will be most truly science.[16]

Metaphysics Is Liberal Knowledge

Liberal knowledge or a liberal education is not easy to define. There are many points of view on what constitutes a liberally educated person. Some people equate liberal education with a broad or general education that takes in a cross-section of what an educated person of our time ought to know. Some, as Robert Hutchins does, take it to be an "education for freedom," that is, the kind of education that a person would need to judge wisely and responsibly the issues that confront a free man in a free society. Some of the more traditionally minded educators think of it as one in which knowledge is sought in order to perfect the mind rather than for some service to be rendered to the "more practical needs of life." Few today think of liberal education according to the etymology of the term. In earlier times a liberal education was one that was given to free men as opposed to that given slaves. Whatever the most accurate definition may be, we are here taking liberal knowledge and liberal education to mean primarily the pursuit of knowledge for the perfection of the mind and for the happiness of man. Since the attainment of knowledge is the greatest perfection of man and the source of his ultimate happiness, the kind of knowledge that best achieves this will be the most *liberal*.

Let us read a passage in which St. Thomas treats of this kind of knowledge.

That man is rightly called free who exists not for the sake of another but for himself. Slaves are for the sake of their masters; they work for their masters, and whatever they acquire, it is for their masters. But free men live for themselves, insofar as they work for themselves and acquire things for themselves. Now that science [metaphysics] which is pursued for itself is for that reason among all sciences the most free. Note that this can be understood in two ways. In one sense this can be said with respect to all speculative knowledge. Then it is true that only those are called liberal arts that are directed toward knowledge for its own sake, while other arts that are directed to some utility gained through activity are called the mechanical or servile arts. In another sense, this can be said above all for that philosophy or wisdom that treats of the highest causes, for of all the highest causes, the final cause is the greatest. Therefore, this science must consider the ultimate universal cause of all things. In

[16] St. Thomas, *Commentary on the Posterior Analytics*, I, lesson 17, no. 5.

this respect all other sciences are ordained to it as to the final cause. Hence it alone is in the truest sense "for its own sake."[17]

In brief, a man who is seeking knowledge for its own sake, as something in whose possession he can be happy, is on the way to being liberally educated. This purpose is contrasted with that inherent in the practical arts and the practical sciences. They serve some more immediate goal, perhaps to produce what is necessary to sustain physical life, or to achieve some physical comfort over and above the necessities of life. Liberal knowledge is of the same essence of that spiritual quality by which a man has freedom. Liberal knowledge is spontaneous and unhampered by the dictates of a temporal pragmatic goal. All speculative sciences participate in this quality of freedom to a greater or less degree. Hence we can speak of *pure mathematics, pure theoretical physics,* or *pure astronomy.* But metaphysics is, among all kinds of human knowledge, the purest and most free.

It is evident that no human knowledge can be completely liberal. It is a question of more or less, in the degree that it is analogous to the divine knowledge that is absolutely for its own sake, since it is identical with divine being. Man's knowledge cannot terminate solely in the perfection of man; it is directed toward truth that is beyond anything created. Hence no man can claim to be absolutely wise. Wisdom is connected with something higher and has value only as long as it is not isolated from its source. Nevertheless, we should not regret having only a borrowed wisdom. The dignity of the subject matter is such that the few truths man can learn only obscurely during his lifetime are to be esteemed than all that one can learn about the immediately practical goods in life. As Aristotle puts it:

> The scanty conceptions to which we can attain of celestial things give us, from their excellence, more pleasure than all our knowledge of the world in which we live; just as a half glimpse of persons that we love is more delightful than a leisurely view of other things, whatever their number and dimensions.[18]

One should not be discouraged, then, if he cannot attain this kind of knowledge in full measure — for that is impossible by the very nature of the object. He must not give up its pursuit entirely because he must occasionally or often have to put his mind to things that are ultimately less important but in the particular situation more necessary. We should take the advice of St. Thomas when he says:

> Even that science which is most liberal cannot be the possession of one's nature, but in many respects is a servant or handmaid, for human

---

17 St. Thomas, *Commentary on the Metaphysics,* I, lesson 3, nos. 58–59.
18 Aristotle, *On the Parts of Animals* I, 5, 644b33.

nature itself is in many respects a servant. Therefore the aforementioned science cannot be a human possession. Human nature is said to be a servant in that it is often subject to manifold needs. From this it happens that a man sometimes puts aside things that are to be sought for themselves to go after that which is necessary for life, as it is said in the *Topics*, Book III; that philosophizing is better than acquiring wealth although sometimes acquiring wealth is to be preferred, in order to take care of the needs of the poor. It is clear, then, that the wisdom that man seeks for its own sake cannot belong to him as his possession. To belong as a possession means that man can have it when he wants and exercise it as he wants. But man cannot freely employ the knowledge which he seeks for its own sake, because he is often impeded by life's needs. It is not under his arbitrary control, for man cannot perfectly acquire it. But the little that is had of it is worth more than all the other things learned in other sciences.[19]

What the ideal of the intellectual life shows is that it is not the immediately practical which is of paramount worth. Nevertheless, the immediately practical is extremely important in human life and cannot be neglected. The leisure and freedom from material cares which the intellectual pursuit seems to presuppose is rarely given to man. The cares and demands of life cut the majority off from what Boethius called the *consolation of philosophy*. Consequently there have been few great metaphysicians.

It is only fitting that in the natural order of learning metaphysics should occupy us last, for it deals with that which, although most perfect in itself, is most difficult for us. Thomistic philosophers always regarded this study as the natural crown of the intellectual life. The order of learning taught by St. Thomas assures one who observes it of arriving at the goal of the intellectual life, the possession of wisdom, even if in this life it is only a taste of the reality. Wisdom is knowledge sought pre-eminently for itself, and Aristotle, one of the greatest thinkers of the pre-Christian era, saw happiness as consisting principally in the contemplation of the objects of metaphysics. Not only was metaphysics conceived as the apex of the speculative sciences, it was also the reason for the practical sciences.

We must qualify the perfection of metaphysical knowledge by phrases such as "on the natural level of learning." The reason for the qualification is that there is a higher kind of wisdom on the supernatural plane. Although in metaphysics one arrives at some kind of knowledge of God, this knowledge is extremely limited and imperfect. And since only few men can devote themselves seriously to this study, and even then they are liable to error in their thought, the knowledge that man could attain by this means alone is very precarious. St. Thomas sees this as a potent argument for the necessity of divine revelation. (Cf. *Summa Theologiae*,

---

[19] St. Thomas, *Commentary on the Metaphysics*, I, lesson 3, no. 60.

I, q. 1, art. 1.) The metaphysician attempts to achieve knowledge of divine things by means of the natural light of reason. At any stage on this laborious passage, error is possible. St. Thomas observes that divine revelation is both a safeguard against these errors as well as a gratuitous richening of our knowledge of divine things. In truths held by divine revelation, the strength of the evidence is God Himself. We have then as Christians a body of supernatural truths which serves as an extrinsic norm and guide for the attainment as well as the development of those truths that can be known by the light of human reason.

CHAPTER **II**

The Formal Subject of Metaphysics

The Formal Subject of a Science

The subject of any science is a starting point of that science, the *terminus a quo*. Consequently the subject, at least within the framework of the science in question, must be easier to grasp than the properties that follow from it; and its properties must be easier to grasp than the conclusions that are demonstrated about it. The subject is a cause of knowledge since the conclusions are contained potentially in it, as a tree is contained in a seed, or a beam of light in a flashlight battery. It can happen at times that the subject of one science is derived as the property of another more fundamental science. But even in this case we must come to a property that is the first in that particular order. Thus the subject of a science is always the point of departure for that science.

> In those sciences that treat of certain properties of things it is possible that what is taken as the subject in one case is taken as the property of a prior subject. But this cannot go on to infinity. One must come to something first in a science that is to be taken as subject in an absolute sense and not as a property.[1]

Metaphysics, like any other science, has its own formal subject, method, and order. A science is an organically constructed body of knowledge in which the mind, through demonstration or analysis, proves the properties of its formal subject. The development of any science is like the growth of any natural organism. It starts from a unity that contains potentially the diverse properties that will actually exist at the end of the process, like the viable human being that exists after a full and natural period of growth. In the subject of a science there is a latent intellectual vitality that corresponds analogously to the vital force present in a zygote. Hence it is important to establish accurately at the very outset what the formal subject of each science is so that it can, as an

---

[1] St. Thomas, *Commentary on the Posterior Analytics*, I, lesson 2, no. 5.

intellectual conception, mature naturally and fully, since the formal subject is the principle from which the propositions belonging to the science originate.

Since the order of learning does not always correspond to the order of being, the priority of the formal subject in the order of knowing does not necessarily mean that it has causal priority in reality. That is why knowledge of common being (being as such), which is the formal subject and principle of metaphysics, comes at the beginning of metaphysics, and the knowledge of God, who is the principle of metaphysics in the order of reality, comes at the end. Since knowledge already possessed is the cause of subsequent knowledge insofar as the truth of a new proposition is seen in the light of the old, the formal subject of the science is said to cause new knowledge. This causality is effective provided that the movement of reason does not leave the framework of the formal subject. It is not possible to derive from one type of formal subject a conclusion proper to another science. Thus mathematics cannot prove a conclusion of metaphysics nor can metaphysics prove a conclusion proper to mathematics. The formal subject is, as it were, the pivotal point on which the science turns; all demonstrations radiate from it in the order of knowledge, though in the order of causal dependence apart from knowledge the same order may not prevail. The formal subject is a guideline that keeps clear the several lines of inquiry. That is why one engaged in a science must always be aware of the formal nature of his science, otherwise his conclusions may turn into some kind of intellectual hybrid.

The goal of any science is knowledge of the formal properties of a formal subject, that is, a knowledge that is peculiar to the subject of inquiry and within the framework of the inquiry. A science is capable of demonstrating with certitude only when it remains within this framework and treats of objects that belong to it specifically.

The formal object of a science is to be found in all of the three operations of the intellect, namely simple apprehension, judgment, and reasoning. But since a valid or true judgment is the goal of knowledge in respect to which simple apprehension and reasoning are means, the most complete sense of formal object is to be found in the judgments that are proper to a science. The total proposition, S is P, is the formal object in its fullest sense. It is a proposition in which the formal properties of the subject are made manifest and are seen to belong to the subject. Thus the formal subject and formal object are essentially correlative.

Judgment, however, can unite subject and object either in the order of essence (called an *essential judgment*) or in the order of existence (an *existential judgment*). For example, in the proposition, *a triangle is a three-sided polygon, the sum of whose angles is equal to 180 degrees,* a correct judgment is made in the order of essence. But in the proposition,

I, as a contingent being, am dependent on a necessary being, the judgment (based upon a posteriori reasoning) goes beyond the essential to the existential order. It is precisely on this diversity of judgment that one important formal difference between sciences like logic or mathematics, for example, and metaphysics is brought out.

The Relationship of Formal Subject and Formal Object

The term *subject* calls to mind its correlative, the term *object*. Science deals with things as they exist in formal relationship to the mind. It is true that the conclusions of a science are intended to reflect reality, and the purpose of a scientific investigation is to understand things as they really are,[2] but science as such is a quality of the intellect and not of the thing known.

The nature of a science is derived according to the following order: An intellectual habit, like any natural power, is specified by its operation, and the operation is specified by its object. But it is not an object taken in any sense of the term whatsoever, but precisely as an object, that is, as a *formal object*.

The word *object* has several analogous meanings. The principal meaning, however, comes from the relationship of something to an intelligence. An object is what is presented to the knower. Things become *objects* in the formal sense when this relationship is established. They are objects potentially before it is established.

The formality whereby a being is constituted an object of the intellect is not precisely identical with its actuality as an existing thing. It is by reason of the formality of a thing as an object that powers and habits are specified. It can happen that many objects considered materially, that is, as individual beings, can be brought together in one formally objective consideration; and on the contrary, one object considered materially can be the basis of several distinct formally objective considerations. For example, many material objects such as plants, animals, and men can be considered under one formal point of view as in biology. Or, on the contrary, one material object such as man can be the basis of such diverse intellectual disciplines as ethics, psychology, biology, medicine, and metaphysics.

When we speak of this formality of object we are not immediately concerned with the reality or entity as it has existence in reality, but with the object from the point of view of its relationship to a power. We do not consider this proportion or relation to the power as something

---

[2] Epistemology, or the critique of knowledge, is not a distinct science but a philosophical inquiry whose structure rests primarily on metaphysics as first philosophy.

existing merely in the thing, but as something with an objective relationship to this power. Though it is concerned with real beings, a cognitive power corresponds to the reality of the object precisely as related to the power. Hence, when we speak of an existing thing, we can consider it without reference to a power; or we can consider it *objectively*, that is, in reference to a cognitive power. Thus a being of the mind, like a genus or species in logic, even though it does not have existence outside the mind, can still be the object of the intellect and can specify it by reason of the *objective relationship* which it has toward the intellect. This is possible because it has a foundation in reality and is conceived after the manner of reality. Once we suppose the foundation in reality and the intellect's dependence on real being for its concept, there is a real proportion and relationship to the cognitive power. This is all that is considered in a formal object. Therefore a being of reason can terminate the act of the intellect as object just as well as a real being.[3] Even though as a being it is fictitious, it is not fictitiously proposed as an object of the intellect; it is a real intellectual object.

How can a real distinction of intellectual disciplines come from objects that are not really distinct? How can a distinction of reason as regards the real thing cause a real distinction among sciences? The answer is that a being does not specify the powers by reason of a distinction which it has in itself, but by reason of the various specific relationships that the being, as object, has to mind. This specification itself is real. Since the being is one in its entitative or ontological character, it does not cause the different specifications by reason of a distinction in itself, but by its virtue or capacity as an intelligible object. Thus, God, though the most unified being, is the cause of the greatest variety of knowledge. The object which is entitatively one is virtually multiple, and in this we have distinct *rationes formales*, that is, formal specifications.

In other words, powers are not specified by the objects taken materially, but formally, i.e., according to their relationship to the powers. If there are diverse formal objects there will be diverse disciplines corresponding to them, even though the object in its entitative or extramental character is only one; if there is a plurality of material objects, but only one formal object, there will be only one discipline to study them. Thus the nature

---

[3] A difficulty arises here because a being of reason has existence only by means of an act of the human intellect. Hence it would seem that it depends on the intellect, rather than that the intellect depends on it. A being of reason has *existence* not as real beings have existence, but only denominatively, i.e., by a relationship that is consequent upon the act of the intellect knowing the being of reason. Consequently, the intellect is not perfected and determined by mere actual existence, but rather by the objective relationship or proportion existing between the object and itself. It is this object with its relationship to the intellect that is the object, the terminus of the intellect.

of a science is not determined by the material object studied in it, but by the particular approach that the human mind takes with respect to this object. For example, a biologist, a physician, and a moral philosopher can study the same material object, let us say *man*, but they will actually be working in distinct sciences because they study man in different ways.

A material object is a potential object. The adjective *material*, in this context, connotes that out of which something is made. It is like the wood out of which various objects can be made. The formal object, on the contrary, is like the form or determining principle making the thing to be what it is. Just as the specific formality of the thing made depends on the nature of that which works with the wood, so the formal object depends upon the kind of intellectual operation that takes place. Note that *material object* is not the same as *corporeal object*, for it does not necessarily refer to corporeal beings. Thus spiritual things can be *material objects* of a science.

The Orders of the Speculative Sciences

There are different ways of designating the formal diversity of object. One can say that speculative sciences differ *by their modes of intelligibility*, *by their modes of relationship to matter*, or *by their definitions or principles*. Although all these differences amount to the same thing, we shall, as is more traditional, consider the subject of metaphysics from the aspect of its relationship to matter and compare it on this point to the subject of logic and natural philosophy. The different modes whereby the intellect grasps its object form the basis for the orders of the sciences. The differences arise for the mind precisely insofar as the objects are considered formally, that is, precisely as objects of knowledge and not as existent beings that are really differentiated and can be investigated in widely different ways. As St. Thomas tells us:

> Now we must understand that when habits or powers are distinguished according to their objects, they are not distingished according to just any differences of objects, but according to those which essentially character-ize the objects as objects. For instance, to be either an animal or plant is accidental to a sensible thing as sensible; and so the distinction of the senses is not taken from this difference, but rather from the difference of color and sound. Consequently, the speculative sciences must be distinguished according to the differences among objects of speculation precisely as objects of speculation. Now an object of this kind — that is to say, an object of a speculative power — possesses one characteristic on the side of the intellectual power and another on the side of the habit of science perfecting the intellect. On the side of the intellect it belongs to it to be immaterial, because the intellect itself is immaterial. On the side of the habit of science it belongs to it to be necessary, because science is of the necessary, as it is proved in the

Posterior Analytics. Now whatever is necessary, is as such immobile; for, as is said in the *Metaphysics,* everything which is moved, insofar as it is moved, can be or not be, either absolutely or in a certain respect. Therefore, separation from matter and motion, or connection with them, essentially belongs to an object of speculation, which is the object of speculative science. Consequently the speculative sciences are distinguished according to their disposition (*ordinem*) with reference to separation from matter and motion.[4]

This brings us to the question of what kind of intellectual vision it is that differentiates metaphysics from other speculative sciences that deal with the reality of the world of which we are a part.

The expression "abstraction from matter" or its equivalent is found consistently in the works of St. Thomas. His teaching on the orders of abstraction is integral to his system of philosophy. The various modes of abstraction are not made arbitrarily or chosen to give merely a logical pattern to his thinking. The division of the speculative sciences according to the orders of abstraction from matter is as applicable today as it was in the time of St. Thomas, and this for the reason that in final analysis intellectual knowledge is possible only by rising above the limitations of matter.

We have chosen only one text in which St. Thomas outlines the order of the speculative sciences, though there are numerous other passages in which he gives equivalently the same wording.[5]

Our text is taken from St. Thomas' *Commentary on the Trinity of Boethius.*

Now there are some objects of speculation which depend on matter with respect to their existence, for they can only exist in matter. And there is a distinction among these. Some depend on matter both with respect to their existence and their concept. This is the case with those whose definition contains sensible matter; as, for instance, it is necessary to include flesh and bones in the definition of man. Physics or natural science studies things of this sort. There are some objects of speculation, however, which although depending on matter with respect to existence, do not depend on it with respect to their concept, because sensible matter is not included in their definitions. This is the case with lines and numbers — the sort of things mathematics studies. There are still other objects of speculation which do not depend on matter with respect to their existence because they can exist without matter. That is true, whether they never exist in matter, e.g., God and the angels, or whether they exist in matter in some things and in others do not, e.g., substance, quality, being, potency, act, one and many, and the like. Theology or

---

[4] St. Thomas, *Exposition of the Trinity of Boethius,* q. 5, art. 1.

[5] For example, see: *Commentary on the Physics,* I, lesson 1, no. 2; *Commentary on the Metaphysics,* Preface; *Commentary on the De Sensu et Sensatu,* no. 1; *Summa Theologiae,* I, q. 88, art. 1, ad 2; I, q. 85, art. 1, ad 1 and ad 2; *Exposition of the Trinity of Boethius,* q. 5, art. 3.

divine science (so called because God is the principal thing known in it) deals with all these. It is called by another name "metaphysics," that is to say, "transphysics," because in the order of learning it comes after physics for us who must rise from sensible things to what is beyond the sensible. It is also called "first philosophy" insofar as all the other sciences take their principles from it and so come after it. It is impossible, however, for some things to depend on matter with respect to their concept and not with respect to their existence, for the intellect by its very nature is immaterial. So there is no fourth kind of philosophy besides the ones mentioned.[6]

The first remark that should be made with respect to the orders of abstraction is that they are not merely quantitatively different from each other, as though one could move continuously from one order to another. Hence the expression "degrees of abstraction" should be explained in such a way that the differences are seen in the order of qualitative modes rather than quantitative degrees. But even as qualitative modes the orders of abstraction do not have the unity of a common genus, but only an analogical unity.

Separation and the Object of Metaphysics

In several texts St. Thomas uses the word *abstraction* for all three modes, but in his *Exposition of the Trinity*, which we have quoted, he uses the word *abstraction* for the first two modes and the word *separation* for the third. This shift in expression is a key to understanding the subject of metaphysics.

In the case of those things which can exist separately, separation rather than abstraction obtains. Similarly when we say form is abstracted from matter, we do not mean substantial form, because substantial form and the matter correlative to it are interdependent, so that one is not intelligible without the other, because the appropriate act is in its appropriate matter. Rather, we mean the accidental forms of quantity and figure, from which indeed sensible matter cannot be abstracted by the intellect since sensible qualities cannot be understood unless quantity is previously known, as is clear in the case of surface and color. And neither can we understand something to be the subject of motion unless we understand it to possess quantity. Substance, however, which is the matter of intelligible quantity, can exist without quantity. Consequently, the consideration of substance without quantity belongs to the order of separation rather than to that of abstraction.

We conclude that in the operation of the intellect there is present a threefold distinction: One with respect to the operation of the intellect composing and dividing, which is properly called separation; and this belongs to divine science or metaphysics. There is another with respect to the operation by which the quiddities of things are formed, which is the

[6] St. Thomas, *Exposition of the Trinity of Boethius*, q. 5, art. 1, c.

abstraction of form from sensible matter; and this belongs to mathematics. And there is a third with respect to the same operation which is the abstraction of the universal from the particular; and this indeed belongs to physics and to all the sciences in general, because in every science we disregard the accidental and consider what is essential. And because certain persons, like the Pythagoreans and the Platonists, did not understand the difference between the last two and the first they fell into error, asserting that mathematics and universals are separate from sensible beings.[7]

The "separation" that distinguishes metaphysics from the "abstraction" proper to the other speculative sciences is said to be the act of a "negative judgment." Why is it so named? It is because the intellect in knowing metaphysical truth forms a negative proposition something like the following: "There is being not essentially connected with matter." Thus the judgment is cast in a negative form. However, it really expresses something positive — it asserts the *de jure* independence of being from matter. It does not say that all being must be independent of matter, but it does say that it is not necessary for being as such to exist in matter.

While emphasizing the nonabstractive mode of arriving at the subject of metaphysics, we should not suppose that when the philosopher of nature or the mathematician abstracts forms from matter the process consists in moving away from reality. As Gilson says: "To abstract is not primarily to leave something out, but to take something in, and this is the reason why abstractions are knowledge."[8] Thus in natural philosophy, the mind grasps what is intelligible in the world of physical reality. If abstraction were a mere prescinding from matter, it would be only a negation.

In order to get a clearer notion of the intellectual process by which one grasps metaphysical objects, let us illustrate the kind of abstraction found in the various speculative sciences. This will help us understand the difference between the *abstraction* of mathematics and of natural philosophy and the *separation* of metaphysical knowledge. Here we must keep in mind that propositions formed in metaphysics have a different bearing to existence than those formed in mathematics and the philosophy of nature. A composition in the order of essence is not the same as a judgment in the existential sense. For example, in the proposition: "A triangle *is* a polygon of three sides, whose angles are equal to 180 degrees," or "man *is* a rational animal," the verb *to be* does not have the same signification as it does in the judgment, "I *am* a substance capable of making decisions." When the mathematician is defining an axiom, or when the philosopher of nature is defining man he is not directly con-

---

[7] St. Thomas, *Exposition of the Trinity of Boethius*, q. 5, art. 3, c, *passim*.
[8] Etienne Gilson, *The Unity of Philosophical Experience* (New York: Charles Scribner's Sons, 1941), pp. 144–145.

cerned with the act of existence but rather with the intelligibility of the concepts with which he is dealing. Thus the function of abstraction is to make intelligible a statement about the objects proper to the science of mathematics or the philosophy of nature. But the metaphysician deals with the order of existing reality and includes a judgment about the act of existence. Hence, existence plays an integral part in the subject matter of metaphysics. How existence can be intelligible at all is another problem and cannot be understood apart from the transcendental properties of being that are treated in a later chapter. *To be* has a twofold meaning, propositional and entitative, as St. Thomas notes in the following text:

> *To be* is taken in two ways, as is made clear in Aristotle in the Fifth Book of the *Metaphysics* and in Origen's gloss on the opening words of the gospel of St. John. In one way it is a verbal copula signifying the composition in a proposition made by the mind. This kind of *to be* is not something actually existing but belongs to the act of the mind which composes and divides. Therefore this kind of being is attributed to everything about which a proposition can be formed, whether it is being or privation of being (as when one says that *blindness is*). In another way *to be* is the act of a being as it is a being and thus is predicated only of things that actually exist. Taken in this sense, it is predicated only of those things that are found in the ten genera of real being — it is on this basis of existence that beings are divided into ten genera.[9]

The subject of metaphysics is real being. It is not grasped in an abstraction of the first operation of the mind but in a judgment which affirms that the objects of metaphysical inquiry exist. In this act of judgment the intellect affirms that there are beings some of which actually do exist apart from matter and motion and that there are others which, though normally found in the world of matter and motion, are such that existence outside of matter does not imply a contradiction. Thus metaphysics has as its subject *being* that can be defined and can exist apart from the material conditions of time, space, and movement. The objects of natural philosophy and mathematics, on the other hand, cannot be defined without matter, and the actual existence of these objects always implies matter. This is how St. Thomas contrasts the objects of metaphysics with those of mathematics and the philosophy of nature.

> Those things are in the highest degree separated from matter which abstract not only from signate matter, as do natural forms taken univerally, of which natural science treats, but which abstract altogether from sensible matter — and not only according to reason (by definition), as mathematical objects do, but according to actual existence, as with God and the separated substances.[10]

When the term *separated substance* appears in the writings of St.

---

[9] St. Thomas, *Quodlibetalia*, IX, q. 2, art 2, c.
[10] St. Thomas, *Commentary on the Metaphysics*, Preface.

Thomas, it usually refers to the angels, but he also uses the term in reference to God and to the human soul. For example, in the treatise *On Being and Essence*, he says: "It remains for us to see in what way essence is in separated substances, namely, in the soul, in the intelligences and in the first cause."[11] But when St. Thomas uses the term *separation* to signify the intellectual process proper to metaphysics he makes it clearly understood that through this process we gain knowledge not only of things which actually do exist apart from matter, such as separated substances, but also of those which can be defined and can exist apart from matter, such as being, potency, act, unity, truth, goodness, and the like.

In summing up the difference between abstraction and separation, we may say that abstraction, as opposed to separation, is a process whereby the mind makes a judgment in which the intellectual content of the object is grasped by lifting it from those material conditions that surround it in the real order of existence. The mind must rise above these conditions in order to grasp a being under the objective formality proper to a given science. Thus in the science of nature the mind prescinds from the individual characteristics of matter, because science deals with universals. But it cannot leave out those sensible properties that characterize all things belonging to nature. Likewise, in mathematics, the mind rises above sensible properties, because these do not belong to a mathematical consideration. However, the mind cannot rise above all matter when engaged in mathematical speculation, as it cannot in the philosophy of of nature, since matter is at the heart of all objects that come under these sciences. It is of the essence of a metaphysical consideration, on the other hand, that the mind rise above all material conditions. Hence, the philosopher discovers that there are beings that do actually exist or can exist without matter; these will constitute the formal subject matter of metaphysics, and with these he enters formally into the science.

Metaphysics and Logic

We shall now try to see the formal subject and method of inquiry proper to metaphysics by comparing them with the formal subjects and methods of inquiry found in logic and the philosophy of nature. Too often the nature of metaphysics is misunderstood in its role as first philosophy because it is conceived as a kind of science of the first principles of logical thought rather than a science of the first principles of reality. And it is sometimes misconstrued in its role as ontology to be the generic knowledge of being under which the philosophy of nature would be placed as a specific difference. But to confuse metaphysics

---

[11] St. Thomas, *On Being and Essence*, Ch. 4.

with either logic or the philosophy of nature is to destroy its character as wisdom.

Logic is like metaphysics in several important points. St. Thomas says: "The subject of logic extends to all those things of which real being is predicated. Hence one concludes that the subject of logic is co-extensive with the subject of metaphysics that treats of real being."[12] Logic and metaphysics are equally broad in scope. Logic, like metaphysics, has being in general as its most universal concept. Logic goes beyond the limitations of the particular sciences and treats of any object knowable by man. It is a universal science. Like metaphysics it is said to belong to the third order of abstraction from matter, because, in a formal treatment of its subject, it completely prescinds from matter and motion.

Logic is said to belong to the third order of abstraction, an order that includes both metaphysics and supernatural theology. This statement contains a partially equivocal use of the expression "third order of abstraction." It certainly does not mean *separation* as St. Thomas uses it in the passage quoted from the *Exposition of the Trinity*, for the term *separation* cannot be applied in any proper sense to the beings of logic. A "separated" logical form would be the equivalent of the separated universal Platonic forms, conceived to have an existence apart from the world of sense. Thus the term *third order of abstraction* is applicable to logical concepts in that logic prescinds from any essential connection with matter. This is a negative notion of abstraction and applies only to the reflexive acts of the mind wherein it deals with beings of reason and not to acts of judgment about those beings that are separated in definition and existence from all matter.

In one sense it is true that logical entities exist and are defined without an essential reference to matter. But this is not the same as affirming that these are real beings, independent of matter and as such subject to intellectual investigation. Logical entities have no direct bearing upon matter — the relationship is irrelevant. Logic is in a state of neutrality as far as matter is concerned. For example, the notions of genus and species, of subject and predicate, the law of extension and comprehension, the square of opposition, and so on, have no necessary bearing on the realities that exist in matter. Logic may deal with a subject that exists in matter, as when it is used to demonstrate correctly in the philosophy of nature, but this does not affect the formal nature of logic itself. Again, the rules of logic can be applied to a metaphysical proof, in which case logic deals with beings that can exist without matter; but this application does not determine the nature of the science of logic. Logic is a neutral science. It is this condition of neutrality that makes it possible for logic to be a

---

[12] St. Thomas, *Commentary on the Metaphysics*, IV, lesson 4, no. 574.

universal science; it is not limited to any particular subject matter. Hence like metaphysics it is applicable to all being and can serve as a directive science.

Though logic has universal being as its object and is as extensive as metaphysics itself, the formal aspect under which it studies being is different from that of metaphysics. This is the point that St. Thomas makes in the following passage.

> It should be recognized that logic and first philosophy are concerned with common principles in different ways. For first philosophy is of common being because its consideration is of common things themselves, i.e., being and the parts and passions of being. And since reason must negotiate concerning all that is in things, and logic is of the operations of reason, logic will be of those things which are common to all, i.e., the intentions of reason, which are of all things. Not that logic is of common things themselves as subjects. For logic considers as its subjects: syllogism, enunciation, predicate or some such things.[13]

Logic and metaphysics are poles apart — as far apart as the shadow of reality is from the substance. Metaphysics deals with real beings that do actually exist apart from matter as God and the separated substances, or with being that can exist apart from matter, such as truth, beauty, unity, and the like. Logic, on the contrary, does not treat of the actual modes of existence apart from the mind but rather the modes of predication, as St. Thomas says in the following sentence: "The logician considers the mode of predication and not the existence of things."[14]

Logic is related to reality as a roadmap is to real cities and highways. A roadmap is a useful guide for the traveler for it tells him what he must do to go somewhere. The roadmap contains a sketch of the most direct routes as well as the side roads and what detours are to be avoided; it indicates the distances from one town to another. Logic, too, has its rules and directions to point out the direct and indirect ways to arrive at a conclusion, its warnings of possible errors on the way, and mistakes to be avoided. In short, logic is a roadmap of the mind in its trip to knowledge. But the beings of logic are no more real with respect to existence outside the mind than a roadmap is to the real pavement, the countryside, and the cities connected by the pavement.

In summing up, we can say that logic and metaphysics differ precisely because the one deals with abstraction while the other deals with separation. The being of logic is universal because it is gained through a negative abstraction. The logician does not care whether or not being is material or immaterial. That aspect of the question has no relevance for him. The being of the logician is immaterial in the same way that a series

---

[13] St. Thomas, *Commentary on the Posterior Analytics*, I, lesson 20, no. 5.
[14] St. Thomas, *Commentary on the Metaphysics*, VII, lesson 17, no. 1658.

in mathematics is infinite, namely as a negative conception. But the metaphysician positively asserts the existence of being that transcends the material order. He has looked into being and seen that material existence does not contain its deepest significance. This is why the realization of the actual existence of beings apart from matter is necessary for the metaphysician but irrelevant for the logician. Metaphysics also differs from logic in the ultimate conclusion of the science. When the science of metaphysics is carried out to its conclusion, the existence of an infinite incorporeal being and universal cause will be demonstrated. The metaphysician is concerned with the existence of all things and how they come into existence. Hence, the goal of metaphysical thinking is the knowledge of being that is universal in causation. The logician is concerned with being that is universal in predication. Thus, in spite of their superficial similarities, one can see that logic and metaphysics are radically different.

Metaphysics and the Philosophy of Nature

We shall now take up the question of how metaphysics is related to the philosophy of nature. This question concerns the differences in the formal subjects of these sciences, their method of inquiry, and the formal order of learning in philosophy.

It was pointed out earlier that it is necessary to know not only what the formal subject of a science is but also that there is such a subject. If metaphysics is independent of matter, then prior to the science of metaphysics one must establish the existence of beings that are separated or separable from matter. In accordance with this principle, St. Thomas advances several arguments to show that the metaphysician derives the knowledge of his formal subject by means of the philosophy of nature and therefore that metaphysics should follow the philosophy of nature in the formal order of learning.

First, the philosophy of nature should precede metaphysics because the subject of metaphysics is being under the formal aspect of its independence of matter in definition and existence. Unless the philosophy of nature comes before metaphysics, we should have to begin metaphysics without having proved that its proper subject matter really exists. Otherwise it would be hard to see why a first philosophy really distinct from the philosophy of nature is necessary. This is why St. Thomas points out that, if there were no immobile and spiritual beings, the philosophy of nature would be first philosophy. For example, in the *Commentary on the Metaphysics* he says:

> If there were no other substance beyond those in nature of which physics treats, physics would be first science. But if there is some other immobile

substance, that will be prior to natural substance, and consequently the philosophy treating of this kind of substance will be first philosophy. And because it is first, it will be universal and its function will be to investigate being as such.[15]

Consequently, the philosophy of nature must establish that there are beings that are independent of the laws of matter in their operation and existence. For example, the philosophy of inanimate nature shows that there must be an immobile mover to cause motion, and the philosophy of animate nature demonstrates the existence of a substantial, spiritual soul.

Once it is proved that there is an immobile being to account for movement in nature, it is evident that the principles intrinsic to nature itself cannot be considered coextensive with all being. Likewise the study of the soul in psychology proves the necessity of a metaphysics. In his *Commentary on the de Anima* of Aristotle, St. Thomas speaks of the utility of psychology, and he says that the knowledge of the spirituality of the soul is the medium by which we come to know the existence of separated substances. And the proper subject of metaphysics cannot be scientifically established until the existence of separated substances is established, that is, until beings whose definition and existence do not include matter are proved to exist.

> In the first philosophy, for example, we cannot reach a knowledge of the divine and highest causes except through those things which we know from the power of our possible intellect, for if the nature of the possible intellect were unknown to us we could not know the realm of separated substances — as the Commentator says when writing on Book XI of the *Metaphysics*.[16]

St. Thomas proposes the objection that a science on which others depend should be studied before the dependent sciences, because the principles of the latter sciences depend upon the former. But he answers his own objection by making a distinction between priority according to nature and priority according to time. Then he adds a psychological or pedagogical reason why the philosophy of nature should precede metaphysics. He says:

> Although divine science is by nature the first of all the sciences, with respect to us the other sciences come before it. For, as Avicenna says, the order of this science is that it be learned after the natural sciences, which explain many things used by metaphysics, such as generation, corruption, motion, and the like. It should be learned after mathematics, because to know the separate substances metaphysics has to know the number and disposition of the heavenly spheres, and this is impossible without astron-

---

[15] St. Thomas, *Commentary on the Metaphysics*, VI, lesson 1, no. 1170.
[16] St. Thomas, *Commentary on the de Anima*, I, lesson 1, no. 7.

omy, which presupposes the whole of mathematics; and other sciences, like music, ethics and the like, contribute to its fullness of perfection.

Moreover, that this science presupposes some things as proved in the other sciences while it itself proves the principles of those other sciences, does not necessarily involve a vicious circle. For the principles which another science (such as natural philosophy) takes from first philosophy do not prove what the same first philosopher takes from the natural philosopher. Rather they are proved through other self-evident principles. Similarly the first philosopher does not prove the principles he gives the natural philosopher by principles he receives from him, but by other self-evident principles. So there is no vicious circle in defining.

Moreover, in the beginning the sensible effects from which the demonstrations of natural science proceed are more evident to us. But when through them we come to know the first causes, from these latter there will become evident to us the reason for the effects on which the proof of the demonstrations of fact (*quia*) rest. In this way natural science contributes something to divine science and nevertheless it is divine science which explains its principles. That is why Boethius places divine science last, because it is the last relatively to us.[17]

The dependence of metaphysics on the philosophy of nature is in accord with the natural progression of human knowledge. A metaphysics deprived of its natural development and established prematurely, if it survives at all, will always be weak. Unable to sustain itself, because the existence of spiritual reality is not yet known or is held on faith, it cannot sustain the attacks of a materialistic philosophy. A metaphysics built without concern for the order of learning will be like a house whose foundations were laid without foresight — the owner will continually have to make adjustments for parts of a building that do not fit. Thus it is through the study of the general principles of nature in the *Physics* and in the *de Anima* that we come to the conclusion that being cannot be adequately explained within the framework of the philosophy of nature but needs a metaphysics.

Apart from the demands of the order of the subject matter, there is an important pedagogical reason for delaying the study of metaphysics until some familiarity is had with other parts of philosophy. Metaphysics is too difficult for a beginner, because it is too far removed from the kind of thinking that a young person is accustomed to. The natural order of the mind is to go from concrete sense experience to more abstract thinking. Like all natural capacities, the intellect moves slowly from potency to act. Therefore, metaphysics, which treats of beings furthest removed from matter, should come last in the chronological order of natural learning even though it is first in the order of dignity. This view is held by St. Thomas both in his *Commentary on the Physics* and in his *Commentary on the Metaphysics* of Aristotle:

---

[17] St. Thomas, *Exposition of the Trinity of Boethius*, q. 5, art. 1, ad 9.

Our knowledge has its origin in sensory realities that are material and intelligible in potency; therefore they are known by us before we know separated substances which are objects more intellectual by nature.[18]

The first intellectual knowledge that we have is a realization of being that remains connected with sense experience. This is called by Cajetan: *Ens concretum quidditati sensibili* (Being experienced in the concrete order of a sensory essence). The human mind's first contact with being is with corporeal essences embodied in matter. Regarding the dependence of the metaphysician on the initial grasp of these embodied essences in the objects of sense, St. Thomas says:

> Because it is joined to the body, the human intellect has as its proper object the essence or nature that exists in corporeal matter; and from the natures of visible things one can rise to some knowledge of invisible things.[19]

The philosopher of nature works with the essences of corporeal substances as they are presented to him through sense experience. The formal aspect under which he views corporeal substances is motion and the principles of motion. As yet, the existence of an immaterial or immobile substance is not known. At this point, the philosopher could argue dialectically, that is, hypothetically, that the philosophy of nature is first philosophy since it seems to include all real being within its scope — all knowledge of reality originates in sense experience. But when the philosopher of nature carries the study of the cosmos and of the soul to its logical conclusions, he will see that the scope of philosophy must be extended. The phenomena of natural motion in the physical universe and the phenomena of immanent activity in man cannot be rationally explained except by concluding to the existence of an immobile first cause. Whether the unmoved mover is one or many cannot yet be determined, since only the metaphysician can prove that the unmoved mover is pure act and must, therefore, be unique. And from the study of the human soul the philosopher of nature concludes that he is dealing with a distinct category of substance, since the soul acts in a way essentially superior to the laws of matter. But as a philosopher of nature he studies the soul as the form of the body and the principle of its operation and not specifically as a spiritual substance.

From the knowledge that he derives from the philosophy of nature, the philosopher must now rethink the meaning of being. There are real beings which are the principles of motion that do not depend on matter for their definition or existence. Therefore, there will be a new kind of inquiry which is called *metaphysics*, that is, a *transphysics*, because it transcends the principles and causes that are proper to mobile beings as

---

[18] St. Thomas, *Commentary on the Physics*, I, lesson 1, no. 7.
[19] St. Thomas, *Summa Theologiae*, I, q. 84, art. 7. c.

such. Thus the philosopher realizes that the limited notion of being with which his inquiry began is not broad enough. If there were no incorporeal beings the philosophy of nature would be first philosophy. Hence it is understandable that ancient cosmologists, thinking that there was no reality other than material substance and its accidents, assigned the role of first philosophy to the philosophy of nature. However, in the philosophy of nature St. Thomas proved that natural substances are not the primary substances and that they are not the first causes of all being. Consequently the philosophy of nature is not first philosophy.

The Proper Subject of Metaphysics

Having shown on the one hand that the formal subject of metaphysics differs from logic because it treats of extramental reality whereas logic does not, and from the philosophy of nature because reason can prove that there is another kind of reality essentially different from that which makes up the formal subject of the study of nature, we shall try to give a more positive explanation of what the formal subject of metaphysics is.

In the prologue to his *Commentary on the Metaphysics* of Aristotle, St. Thomas says that metaphysical being is predicated of three classes of reality: those that really exist in matter but have no essential tie-up with matter either in definition or in the act of existence, such as substance, potency, act, etc.; those that are spiritual by nature but are not the most universal cause; and finally the first and most universal cause of all being, namely God. Thus not only God, the angels, and the human soul are considered in metaphysics but also all real things insofar as they are considered from a metaphysical point of view. There is a truth and an intelligibility about natural beings apart from the characteristics that they have as mobile beings. A man, for example, has substance, existence, potencies, and these can be studied from the point of view of their deepest significance, a significance which lies beyond the fact that they are beings found in the space-time world. St. Thomas sees in being as such or common being the subject matter of metaphysics:

> Although the subject of this science is common being, the latter is predicated of entities that are wholly separated from matter, existentially as well as logically (by definition). For among things said to be separated existentially and logically (by definition) are found not only those that never can exist in matter, as God and intellectual substances, but also those that can be without matter, as common being.[20]

And later in the same *Commentary* St. Thomas says:

----

[20] St. Thomas, *Commentary on the Metaphysics*, Preface.

Note that to first philosophy pertain not only those beings that are
separated from matter and motion according to existence and definition
but also sensible beings, in so far as they are beings.[21]

Because the subject of metaphysics, being separated from matter and
motion, includes not only God and intellectual substances who actually
exist independently of matter but also every being that *can be* without
matter, we may ask whether there could be a science of metaphysics if
one considers the mere possibility of being that can exist without matter
instead of first really proving the existence of such beings. Is St. Thomas
using the words *can exist* without matter to mean *possibility* as opposed
to *contradiction*, or does he mean *possibility* in the sense of real *potentiality?* The first meaning of possibility is a logical one and does not tell us
that such a being really does or can really exist without matter. If St.
Thomas means the first kind of possibility, then the subject of the
science of metaphysics is simply hypothetical being. Whatever conclusions
might follow logically from the first principles of such a subject would
be purely tentative or dialectical. They would not necessarily be true
in the real order.

Is it possible to have a philosophic knowledge of separated substance
at the outset of metaphysics without going through the proofs offered
by the philosophy of nature? Some philosophers have argued that it is
possible because the intellect can see immediately that existence is not
necessarily limited to corporeal substances. Existence considered in itself
is regarded as analogical. They think this preliminary grasp of the
act of existence is sufficient to constitute the subject of the science of
metaphysics.

One of the objections to this position is that existence as such,
apart from the essences which it actualizes, is not intelligible. It is necessary that the science of metaphysics treats of really existing things; but
reality, as we know it, consists in the diverse substances and properties
that come under sense experience. To know these is to know more
than the fact that they exist. Metaphysics treats of being as a whole, in
which essence and existence are combined. This is not to say that the
subject of metaphysics is being found only in material reality, for we
saw that a philosophy of nature does not suffice to explain reality. But
the mind does not grasp the existence of immaterial reality by an intuition; the existence of these beings must be proved by reason.

In view of what St. Thomas has to say in the *Contra Gentiles*, we
hold that one does not arrive quickly at the truth of the analogy of
being in the contingency of the act of existence, for this would mean
that at the very start of metaphysics one would treat of the existence of

---

[21] St. Thomas, *Commentary on the Metaphysics*, VI, lesson 1, no. 1165.

God. The fact is that we cannot know God as the primary existing reality except after long inquiry.

> In order to know the things that reason can investigate concerning God, a knowledge of many things must already be possessed. For almost all of philosophy is directed towards the knowledge of God, and that is why metaphysics, which deals with divine things, is the last part of philosophy to be learned. This means that we are able to arrive at the inquiry concerning the aforementioned truth only on the basis of a great deal of labor spent in study.[22]

In his *Commentary on the Metaphysics of Aristotle* St. Thomas explicitly affirms that the knowledge of being that exists or can exist without matter requires a philosophical conditioning of the human mind.

> Those beings that are completely separated from matter in their existence, like immaterial substances, are even more difficult for us to know than universals. Therefore that science which is called wisdom is first in dignity but last in the order of learning.[23]

It has been said that the metaphysics of St. Thomas is radically different from that of Aristotle precisely on the point of the role of existence in metaphysics. Some hold that for Aristotle metaphysics is fundamentally a doctrine of forms, while for St. Thomas it is a philosophy of existence. Granted for the sake of argument that the distinction between essence and the act of existence is fundamental to Thomistic metaphysics, and perhaps not to be found in Aristotle, it does not follow that this distinction can be understood at the very outset of metaphysics, at least not in the certain and analytical way that the foundation of the subject of a science demands. If Aristotle's failure to understand this distinction is conceded, this very weakness in his philosophy would be a corroboration of the reason why one should not start metaphysics with a principle as difficult as that of the real distinction between essence and existence. If the real distinction between essence and existence is immediately obvious, a man of the intellectual genius of Aristotle would have seen it.

In conclusion, then, we hold that the formal subject of metaphysics can be known scientifically only after proving the existence of immaterial substances as is done in the philosophy of nature. We do not agree that it is possible to grasp the immateriality of existence as such by an intuitive grasp of the analogy of being in the real distinction between essence and existence except after some progress has been made in the science of metaphysics.

---

[22] St. Thomas, *Summa Contra Gentiles*, I, chap. 4, par. 3. Translated by A. C. Pegis, *On the Truth of the Catholic Faith* (New York: Doubleday Image Book, 1955), I, p. 67.

[23] St. Thomas, *Commentary on the Metaphysics*, I, lesson 2, no. 46.

Metaphysics as Natural Theology

At the beginning of metaphysics one does not presuppose the existence of a supreme universal first cause. Rather, common being, as known in everyday experience, is the point of departure. Knowledge of the existence and of the nature of the universal first cause is the terminus of the science. Although this science does eventually treat of separated substances and of the first cause, it takes only common being as its subject.

> From what has been said it is apparent that although this science considers the three things just mentioned [common being, separated substance, and God], it does not take this one or that, indifferently, as its subject but only common being. The subject of a science is precisely that whose causes and properties we seek to know, not the causes themselves of any genus that is inquired into. It is the knowledge of the causes of a genus that is the end of scientific thought.[24]

The subject of any science, as we have seen, comes at the start of an investigation and must potentially contain the conclusions of the science within its framework. The mind seeks the causes and properties of a certain intelligible object. But God is not seen immediately as being, but it is demonstrated in metaphysics that He is the cause of being that we do know.

The first knowledge of the existence of God as the first cause depends upon a metaphysical inquiry. The mind is compelled to accept the existence of a first and necessary cause of the contingent world with which we are familiar. There is a difference between the kind of judgment we make about the existence of physical substances known by means of sensory experience and the kind of reasoned judgment of existence that we make about the first cause of physical substances.

Though knowledge of the existence of the first cause is not a presupposition of metaphysics, it is properly within the scope of this science. Indeed metaphysics would be incomplete unless it included a demonstration of a first cause. All the analyses of the general principles of common being lead eventually to the demonstration of this first cause. Therefore God is seen as the efficient cause of common being, and by the same kind of analysis one proves that God is the final cause of all imperfect being. Without a knowledge of the final cause, knowledge of any other cause would be incomplete, and the demonstration would be inconclusive. Metaphysics achieves its title of wisdom only when all imperfect being is seen to depend on a unique and absolute first cause both in the order of efficient and final causality. Thus, to demonstrate

---

[24] St. Thomas, *Commentary on the Metaphysics*, Preface.

the existence of God is, so to speak, "to put the cap on" this science.

In his *Exposition of the Trinity*, St. Thomas explains how and why metaphysics treats of God. He first of all differentiates natural theology and supernatural theology. Supernatural theology studies God in Himself, by means of revelation. In supernatural theology, God (as revealed) is the subject, and the theologian draws conclusions from the propositions that God has revealed about His own nature. But God is not the subject of natural theology; He is the principle of the subject of the science, which itself is common being. Since a science is complete only when the principle of its subject is known, it is necessary that metaphysics include a demonstration of the first cause of common being.

Metaphysics Is a Distinct Science

One might be led to think that because metaphysics has common being as its subject it is not really a distinct science. Some philosophers take this point of view and consider metaphysics as a preamble to science. In that case it would seem to be a part of every science and lose its autonomy. Because they conceive of metaphysics in this way, these philosophers hold that the order of learning calls for the study of metaphysics before the study of the other particular sciences. But this is to distort the nature of metaphysics and the universal scope of its object. Metaphysics is not a part of the other sciences for its whole intellectual approach is different. If it serves the other sciences it is in its role as wisdom — for metaphysics is autonomous knowledge and not instrumental knowledge. It is first philosophy in the sense of being first in dignity, in certitude, and in its intellectual penetration of reality. Though it is the science of common being, it does not cross over into the areas that are proper to the special sciences. Its approach to the knowledge of being is different from that of any other sciences; it has its own mode of illumination for the mind and therefore has its distinct formal character as a science.

Although the subjects of the other sciences are parts of being, which is the subject of metaphysics, the other sciences are not necessarily part of metaphysics. For each science treats of one part of being in a special way distinct from that in which metaphysics treats of being. So its subject is not, properly speaking, a part of the subject of metaphysics, for it is not a part of being according to that character (*ratio*) by which being is the subject of metaphysics. But from the point of view of this character it is a special science distinct from the others.[25]

Just as metaphysics is independent, so the particular sciences, too, are independent of metaphysics when operating within their own sphere.

[25] St. Thomas, *Exposition of the Trinity of Boethius*, q. 5, art. 1, ad 6.

There are truths of the particular sciences that can be known without an explicit knowledge of metaphysics. That is why it is possible to study them before metaphysics. It is only because the particular sciences cannot defend their own first principles that they must eventually depend on metaphysics which is prior to them not in time but in nature; the validity of natural philosophy as well as the general principles of ontology remain suspended until there has been a resolution in understanding by means of natural theology.

Now in its process of analysis the whole consideration of reason in all the sciences terminates in the consideration of divine science. For, as we have said, reason sometimes (1) advances from one thing to that which is other in reality, as when the demonstration is through external causes or effects: (a) by synthesis, indeed, when we go from causes to effects (for causes are simpler than effects and exist more unchangeably and uniformly); (b) by analysis when we proceed conversely. Consequently, the ultimate end of analysis in this life is when we arrive at the highest and most simple causes, which are the separate substances. Sometimes (2), however, reason advances from one concept to that which is other according to reason, as when we proceed according to intrinsic causes: (a) by synthesis, indeed, when we go from the most universal forms to more particular ones; (b) by analysis when we proceed conversely, because what is more universal is simpler. Now what is most universal is common to all beings; and so the ultimate end of analysis in this life is the consideration of being and the properties of being as being. And, as we said above, these are what divine science considers, namely the separate substances and what is common to all beings. It is clear, therefore, that its consideration is supremely intellectual.

It also follows from this that divine science gives all the other sciences their principles, inasmuch as intellectual consideration is the starting-point of rational consideration; and for this reason it is called *first philosophy*. Nevertheless, it is learned after physics and the other sciences inasmuch as intellectual consideration is the end of rational consideration. And for this reason it is called *metaphysics*, as being beyond physics, for in the order of analysis it comes after physics.[26]

We have seen so far that this science has the role of ruler with respect to the other sciences and is the defender of their principles; that its formal subject is common being considered under the condition of separation from matter and motion; and finally that the point of resolution is the demonstration of the existence of the first and most universal cause. From this threefold function we derive the three names that are applied to this science: it is called *first philosophy* insofar as it studies the common principles and causes of being and is the defender of the first principles of the particular sciences; it is called *metaphysics* insofar as it studies transphysical or immaterial being; and it is called *theology* or *divine science* insofar as it treats of God who is the first principle and cause of all being.

---

[26] St. Thomas, *Exposition of the Trinity of Boethius*, q. 6, art. 1, 3.

CHAPTER **III**

The Analogy of Being and the Unity of Metaphysics

The metaphysician investigates such diverse things as first principles, substance and accidents, act and potency, the transcendental properties of being, and even God Himself as the cause of finite being, "because it belongs to one and the same science to consider the proper causes of a genus and the genus itself."[1] We must be careful how we interpret the meaning of *genus* in this quotation. In various contexts St. Thomas uses the word *genus* in several different senses. For example, he sometimes uses it in the sense of a logical genus (one of the five predicables) in the order of second intentions.[2] As a logical genus the term *substance*, for example, has precisely the same signification when applied to corporeal and spiritual beings. A logical genus is a being of the mind, a classification of thought, a relationship of reason. Objects that are one according to this kind of genus have one mode of predication in which the signification always remains the same.

> Those things are one in genus that agree in the figure of predication, that is, they have one mode of predication.[3]

The term *genus* is also used by St. Thomas in the sense of a natural genus. This usage is pertinent for both the metaphysician and for the philosopher of nature, since each is concerned with things as they exist and not merely with the signification of a term.[4] For example, things in the natural genus of animated being or in the genus of substance have a unity that differs from the unity imposed by the mind in a logical genus. Thus the philosopher of nature sees a unity among various kinds of animated beings because they all have within them a principle of

---

[1] St. Thomas, *Commentary on the Metaphysics*, Preface.
[2] Cf. *On Being and Essence*, Ch. 3, *passim*.
[3] St. Thomas, *Commentary on the Metaphysics*, V, lesson 8, no. 878.
[4] Cf. St. Thomas, *Commentary on the Metaphysics*, X, lesson 12, no. 2142.

self-movement, though the unity is not absolute because the principle of animation is possessed in different modes by various members of the genus. The metaphysician sees a unity among the various things that can be called substances because they are all beings existing in such a way that they do not inhere in another and can be the subject's for the existence of other things, though the mode of existence differs in each case.

The term *genus* is also used by St. Thomas to designate the formal subject of the conclusions of a science. It is in this way that the term *genus* is applied to the science of metaphysics, in which various realities are conceived to be sufficiently one to constitute the formal subject of one science.[5] We have seen that the formal subject of a science gives unity to a particular kind of intellectual insight and makes it possible to demonstrate conclusions as from a principle. When St. Thomas says that it belongs to one science to consider the proper causes of a genus and the genus itself, he is using the term *genus* to designate the formal subject of the science. One must find in metaphysics a subject that is sufficiently unified to provide the framework within which the metaphysician can demonstrate properties that belong universally to all beings. As we shall see in a subsequent chapter, the unity of the formal subject of metaphysics is to be found in substance, which is the primary subject of investigation in this science. The unity of the science extends to other considerations of being because of their relationship to substance.

The kind of unity that is found in common being is brought out in the following text from St. Thomas:

> Whatever beings have a common mode of predication, even though not univocal but only analogical, belong to the consideration of one science. But *being* is predicated in this way of all things. Therefore, all beings belong to the consideration of this one science which considers being insofar as it is being.
>
> *Being* or *that which is* can be spoken of in various ways. Something can be predicated of different things in several ways. At times a term is predicated of things when the meaning is entirely the same, as *animal* is predicated of a horse and an ox, and this is called univocal predication. In other instances the same term is predicated of things when the meaning is completely different, as the term *dog* is applied to a star and to an animal. This is called equivocal predication. In still other cases the same term is predicated of things when the meaning is partly different and partly the same — different insofar as diverse relationships are implied, but the same in that these diverse relationships are all referred to one and the same thing. This is called analogical predication.[6]

Let us see what the analogical unity of being is.

---

[5] Cf. St. Thomas, *Commentary on the Posterior Analytics* I, lesson 41, no. 7.
[6] St. Thomas, *Commentary on the Metaphysics*, IV, lesson 1, nos. 534–535.

The Doctrine of Analogy

The use of analogy is fundamental to metaphysics, but we should not regard analogy as being uniquely or even primarily a metaphysical notion. A natural scientist employs analogy when he describes the nature of the invisible atomic world; the poet uses it when he describes a poetic experience in metaphors; Christ used analogy when He spoke to the common people of Judea in parables. No general discussion of analogy can prescind from its primary use as a logical instrument, inasmuch as logic deals with the signification of terms. But it is precisely on this point that the importance of the doctrine of analogy rests even for the metaphysician, for the purpose of all science and discourse is somehow linked to the signification of terms. It is true that no word, unless it is merely a sound of the voice, is completely without foundation in reality, so that unity and diversity in meaning are ultimately based on a unity and diversity in things outside the mind. Nevertheless, when St. Thomas defines analogous terms, he compares them to univocal and equivocal terms. Since these refer to signification in view of predication, the whole question of analogy belongs primarily to logic. When St. Thomas speaks of analogy in his doctrine on our manner of predicating terms of God and of creatures, it is evident that he first considers analogy from the viewpoint of the logician.[7] He is more explicit in his *Commentary on the Metaphysics* when he says:

He [Aristotle] sets down another division of unity, one that is primarily logical, when he says that some things are one numerically, others specifically, still others generically, and others by analogy.[8]

The word *analogy* comes from two Greek words: ἀνά which is a preposition meaning *back toward*, like the Latin word *retro*; and λόγος, which in the present context means *thought* or *idea*. Analogous terms are used in a discourse that entails a comparison, a reciprocal movement of thought. In analogy the human mind compares different things on the basis of some relationship that they have to each other, and thus it comes to understand them by seeing them in focus. Different things receive a common name because each bears a relationship to something that a common name principally signifies. By the use of a common name the mind attempts to reduce the diversity of objects to the unity of thought. In this sense analogous names always involve some form of equivocation, since what is merely related to a thing that is primarily signified cannot have precisely the same meaning as the other thing. Analogy is not, however, pure equivocation, which it would be if a

---

7 Cf. St. Thomas, *Summa Theologiae*, I, q. 13, art. 6.
8 St. Thomas, *Commentary on the Metaphysics*, V, lesson 8, no. 876.

common term were applied to things that are completely diverse and do not have any common bond between them except that of the sound of the voice or the appearance of the written word.

Since names at first usually designate some concrete experience, they have a limited application. But because language represents the vitality of the human mind that employs language, it has a natural growth and reproduction by which it achieves an ever widening extension of meaning. Sometimes this development may take it away from its original concrete signification, so that the relationship embodied in the analogous name moves from what is more concrete to what is more abstract and intangible. This extension of the meaning of terms is the source of the difficulty that comes from using analogous names in scientific demonstration.

The proper approach to the study of analogy will eliminate many of the difficulties of this very complex subject matter, for many difficulties arise from not realizing the connection between analogy and the way that the human mind arrives at knowledge. Since it is a potency that entails a kind of movement, the human intellect moves from one state of knowledge to another by using previous knowledge as a kind of stepping stone to the next. We move from what is more familiar to us and easier to grasp to what is more difficult by nature. The movement in understanding is achieved both in a synthetic and in an analytic manner in which relationships between one object and another become more obvious. Knowledge by analogy holds a very important place in this learning process, since there must be some bond by which various relationships are to be seen. Analogy is concerned with concepts that bridge the intelligible diversity between one thing and another. But concepts must be clothed in names. And it is with names as signs of common concepts that we must begin.

In all relationships that underlie analogical language there is a priority of one thing over another and a dependence of one thing on another. It is by reason of this priority and posteriority that the comparison is made between one thing and another, a comparison that necessarily implies a common term by which some kind of judgment of identity can be made. However, the priority of one analogue over another may refer either to the order of human knowledge or it may refer to the ontological order that does not depend upon the human mode of knowing and learning but is what we try to make human knowledge reflect objectively. Therefore, it is important in a discussion of analogy to be aware of the twofold kind of priority: one refers to the human mind and reflects the movement of thought; the other exists independently of the particular mode of human knowledge and refers to things.

The Mode of Signification and What Is Signified

In the understanding of analogy we must keep in mind an important distinction between what is signified by the common name and the mode of signification. An instance of this distinction is found, for example, in St. Thomas when he asks whether the name person is used in the proper sense when it is applied to the three persons of the Holy Trinity.[9] There St. Thomas observes that the name person, considered etymologically, was first given to men who held some high dignity. Later the name was applied to God. Although the mode of signification of the name is primarily realized in man, the reality it signifies belongs primarily to God and by participation to human beings. By transferring the name person from human beings to God, we are led from what is better known to us to what objectively has a greater depth of meaning. Thus by means of analogy we can rise from the knowledge of what is inferior to some kind of understanding of what is above us. Consequently, there is a twofold kind of priority in analogy: first, the priority with respect to the imposition of the analogous term; and second, the priority with respect to the nature of the thing signified by the common name.

> We give names to things according to the manner in which we receive our knowledge from things. Hence, since those things which come after others in the order of nature are usually the ones that we know first, it frequently happens that in applying names to things, we first use a name of one of two things when the reality it signifies primarily exists in the second. We have a clear example of this in the names that are used of both God and creatures. Being, good, and words of this sort are first applied to creatures, and then transferred from creatures to God, even though the act of existence and good are found primarily in God.[10]

Knowledge of the analogy of names is presupposed in a formal study of metaphysics. In Book IV of the Metaphysics both Aristotle and St. Thomas presuppose this use of analogy before the more strictly metaphysical use of analogy is considered, for it is the kind that people generally employ without being aware of a deeper metaphysical meaning. When, for example, people use the term healthy with reference to the condition of an organism and to the things that relate to a healthy organism such as food or climate, they realize that they are using the term in a somewhat equivocal sense though it retains some unity in its various applications. The same can be said of a term like being. People without any philosophical training can understand this term in an analogical sense, as for example when they use an expression like "That is

---

9 Cf. St. Thomas, Commentary on the Sentences, I, d. 25, q. 1, art. 2; and the Summa Theologiae, I, q. 29, art. 3, ad 2.

10 St. Thomas, Truth, q. 4, art. 1. Translated by Robert Mulligan, S.J. (Chicago: Henry Regnery, 1952), Vol. I, p. 171.

being rude"; or when they hear the line from Hamlet, "To be or not to be, that is the question."

But for the metaphysician analogous concepts consisting only in a unity of signification do not satisfy the needs of his science, for he is concerned not only with the signification of terms, but much more precisely with knowing reality as it is. This does not mean that the signification of names is not important for the metaphysician. On the contrary, the most metaphysical use of analogy presupposes the signification of names as when transcendental notions like truth and goodness are applied to God and to creatures. For the metaphysician analogy includes both the signification of terms and the various modes in which what is signified exists in different things. Thus the analogy of names is an instrument of metaphysics, just as logic generally is an instrument of metaphysics and of the other sciences.

We can apply the distinction about the priority of names and the priority in being to the problem of analogy — for analogy is itself analogical, and the primary though not most important meaning of analogy is that used by the logician. Just as the meaning of person, for example, is derived from our own experience yet can be extended to divine persons, giving us some vague insight into what is really above us, so analogy can be transformed from a logical device to a mode of knowing necessary to the science of metaphysics.

For the logician analogy is based on the mode of signification of concepts and refers to the manner in which our mind attains its concepts. For the metaphysician analogy is a question of both the mode of signification and the modes of existence outside the mind and consequently refers more precisely to the thing signified. It is true that logical entities have a basis in reality, but having a basis in reality and being really what the mind conceives are two very different things. The logical use of analogy refers primarily to the mode of signification of names; the metaphysical use of analogy is directed primarily to the unity and diversity that is radically found in existing things. Analogous names which may properly refer to the realm of logic do not necessarily reflect the diversity in being that is found in the real order of existence. For this reason, the mode of signification of the analogous name and the ontological reality signified by the name may or may not correspond as to priority. The prime analogate in the logical order of analogy (which reflects the order of our coming to know) may actually be only of secondary importance when compared to the secondary analogate in the metaphysical order. Thus the primacy in the mode of signification of the name quality, when comparing physical qualities like heat and color with spiritual qualities like virtue and knowledge, is found in the former, although the latter are superior in being. The same can be said of corporeal substance and of spiritual substance. Or to use another example in the order of metaphysics, we may say that the mode of signification of causality is found first in efficient causality and then in final causality, since we know efficient cause before we know final cause; but in the order of causality itself, the final cause is prior to the efficient cause.

There is a passage in St. Thomas in which he brings out this relationship of the logical and the metaphysical use of analogy:

> In this second mode of analogical predication the order according to the name and according to reality is sometimes found to be the same and sometimes not. For the order of the name follows the order of knowledge, because it is the sign of an intelligible conception. When, therefore, that which is prior in reality is found likewise to be prior in knowledge, the same thing is found to be prior both according to the meaning of the name and according to the nature of the thing. Thus, substance is prior to accident both in nature, insofar as substance is the cause of accident, and in knowledge, insofar as substance is included in the definition of accident. Hence, *being* is said of substance by priority over accident both according to the nature of the thing and according to the meaning of the name. But when that which is prior in nature is subsequent in our knowledge, then there is not the same order in analogicals according to reality and according to the meaning of the name. Thus, the power to heal, which is found in all health-giving things, is by nature prior to the health that is in the animal, as a cause is prior to an effect; but because we know this healing power through an effect, we likewise name it from its effect. Hence it is that *health-giving* is prior in reality, but animal is by priority called *healthy* according to the meaning of the name.[11]

The importance of this distinction between the logical mode of analogy and the metaphysical needs to be emphasized, otherwise it will be difficult to show how metaphysics is not merely a logic of being. In metaphysics, analogy is not based solely upon our manner of conceiving reality but upon the objective unity and diversity found in existing things.

Thus a comparison of analogy used in logic and in metaphysics shows us that analogy is itself analogical. The logician's and the metaphysician's views are not precisely the same thing. There is more than a quantitative or qualitative difference between them; it is more than a specific difference belonging to a common genus of analogy. It is a difference in mode, that is, a difference between conceptual and real being.

Divisions of Analogy According to Signification and Existence

In the following passage St. Thomas distinguishes various kinds of analogy according to the mode of being of the analogates. This is the

---

11 St. Thomas, *Summa Contra Gentiles*, I, 34. Translated by Anton C. Pegis in *On the Truth of the Catholic Faith* (New York: Doubleday Image Books, 1955), Vol. I, p. 148.

context of the passage. He had asked himself the question whether *truth* is analogical when applied to the divine and human intellect in the same way that *health* is analogical when applied to animal and to medicine. It is evident that the reality signified by the name *health* exists only in the animal, and that medicine is called healthy because it is effective of the animal's health. Is all truth one in the sense that there is only divine truth to which our minds are related by an extrinsic relationship, as medicine is related to the health of the animal? Let us see how St. Thomas solves this difficulty.

> Something is predicated analogously in three ways. First, there is *analogy according to signification only and not according to existence.* This takes place when one meaning is related to several things according to priority and posteriority, though the existence of such a thing is found in only one of them. For example, the word *health* refers to an animal, to urine, and to diet in different ways, according to priority and posteriority, but not according to different acts of existence, because health is actually found only in an animal.
>
> Second, there is *analogy according to existence but not according to signification.* This takes place when several things are alike as regards the signification of some common reality, but that common reality does not exist in the same way in all of them. Thus all bodies are alike in the notion of body. The logician, who is concerned with signification only, says that the name *body* is predicated univocally of all bodies, even though the existence of this natural being is not the same in corruptible and in incorruptible bodies. Therefore, as far as the metaphysician and the philosopher of nature are concerned — since they consider things according to their existence — the name *body* and any other thing like it is not predicated univocally of corruptible and of incorruptible things, as is clear in *Metaphysics* X, according to the Philosopher and the Commentator.
>
> Third, there is *analogy according to signification and according to existence.* This takes place when there is no identity either in a common signification or in existence, as in the case of *being* predicated of substance and accident. What is common in them has existence in each one of the things of which it is predicated, but this differs according to a greater or lesser perfection. In the same way we say that truth and goodness and all things of this kind are predicated analogously of God and of creatures.[12]

In this text St. Thomas gives a threefold division of analogy:

1. *Analogy according to signification only.* Here there is no analogy from the point of view of actual existence but only in the signification of a common name applied to several things. The logician, for example, employs an analogous name like health, not because health itself has diverse modes of existence, but because the name *health* has a kind of unity together with diversity when it is applied to various things that

---

[12] St. Thomas, *Commentary on the Sentences*, I, d. 19, q. 5, art. 2, ad 1.

are related to health: to the animal (subject of health); to urine (sign of health); to a diet or medicine (cause of health). Thus health is predicated of urine, of a diet, and of one's color because they are related to something else which is *actually healthy* and from which they receive their names, namely the health that a man may have.

This first use of analogy is based on the mode of signification only and not on the actual existence of the thing signified. The analogous unity comes from the relationship of the diverse subjects of predication to a common predicate. Of the diverse subjects there is one to which the name is applied by prior right. It is applied to the others according to their proximity to the subject to which it is first applied. The degree of proximity is based on a relationship to the subject of the original signification and not on the basis of actual existence. Among the members of the analogy there is only one basic signification and that is the one which is first in the series. For example, *healthy* signifies basically only the health of an animal. In the other members of the analogy the name is attributed for extrinsic reasons and not because the name refers to something really present in them.

2. *Analogy in existence but not in signification.* This kind of analogy occurs when several different things have one and the same signification but differ in the degree of perfection in which they possess the reality signified. The example of *body* used by St. Thomas may be confusing for us, but he used it because he thought of the matter of heavenly bodies as being of a different nature from that of terrestrial bodies. In order to avoid confusion, let us use a different example, that of *soul* as it is applied to man, to irrational animals, and to plants. The logician would consider the term *soul* as univocal because he is concerned only with the signification of the term, and as applied to all living beings. But the philosopher of nature is directly concerned with the reality of what is signified, and for him the term *soul* does not have a univocal mode of existence. He sees that the mere name is univocal when it is applied to a man and to a dog, but at the same time he realizes that what is signified exists in each in a different way. Hence, for him soul is predicated analogically of plants, of irrational animals, and of man.

3. *Analogy in existence and signification.* Third, there is an analogy both with respect to signification and to the existence of what is signified. In this case there is absolute identity neither in signification nor in the mode of existence, but there is a similarity. Thus the name *being* is predicated of both substance and accident, but substance and accident do not have absolutely the same signification with respect to the name *being* nor do they have the same mode of existence. However, the name is not purely equivocal because there is a basis of comparison both in the signification and in the existence of what is signified. The

metaphysician is especially interested in this kind of analogy because of its relevance to the transcendent order of being.

The Foundations of Analogous Terms

Much of the difficulty with the subject of analogy comes from not differentiating the relationships that are the foundations for the analogous terms from the analogous terms themselves. The analogical terms are formed as the result of seeing certain relationships between things. The metaphysician is concerned with both the foundations and the nature of the analogous concepts, and he must be aware of the modes of analogical unity that are suitable for metaphysical discourse and he must understand the kind of relationships upon which these modes are founded.

All analogy entails some kind of relationship between two things. Relationships can be established upon different bases. On the one hand, the relationships may be in the order of being that exists independently of the human mind. Thus the three bases for real relationships are the quantity that is found in natural bodies, the fact that one thing can act upon another or be acted upon, and the fact that one thing may be the standard or measure of another thing even apart from quantitative considerations. On the other hand, relationships may be established solely in the order of thought, even though there may be some remote basis in reality for the relationship that the mind imposes on beings that are only conceptually distinct.

In its original usage the relationship between analogues referred to a quantitative comparison of one thing to another and was designated as a *proportion*. But as this term took on a more generic meaning it was used in reference to all forms of relationships that could underlie analogical language. It is in its extended meaning that St. Thomas speaks of it in reference to a metaphysical use of analogy.

> Proportion is twofold. In one sense it means a certain relation of one quantity to another, according to which double, treble, and equal are species of proportion. In another sense, every relation of one thing to another is called proportion. And in this sense there can be a proportion of the creature to God, inasmuch as it is related to Him as the effect to its cause, and as potentiality to act; and in this way a created intellect can be proportioned to know God.[13]

The proportion upon which analogy is based may consist, first, in a relationship between two things that is definite and measurable. This kind of proportion is found, for example, between two bodies, one of which is half the size of the other. It is also found in the case of act-

---

[13] St. Thomas, *Summa Theologiae*, I, q. 12, art. 1, ad 4.

ting and being acted upon, when the movement of one body may be in direct ratio to the impulse that started the motion. Finally, it is found in the measure of likeness that exists between an object and its image, as in the case of an object that is photographed or reflected in a mirror. Second, the proportion may not be susceptible of strict measurement because the relationship between one thing and another is indeterminate. This could happen, for example, in the order of causal relationship as when a melody is proportioned to the composer but the relationship is not susceptible of a definite measure since an effect is not always a definite index of the perfection of the agent. There is a third kind of proportion that consists in a relationship of two proportions to each other, and this is called a *proportionality*. It consists in a similarity of proportions to each other rather than in a simple relationship of one thing to another. In a text from his work *Truth*, St. Thomas speaks of this third kind of proportion.

> A thing is said to be proportionate to another in two ways. In one way, a proportion is noted between two things. For example, we say that four is proportioned to two since its proportion to two is double. In the second way, they are proportioned as by a proportionality. For example, we say that six and eight are proportionate because, just as six is the double of three, so eight is the double of four; for proportionality is a similarity of proportions. Now since in every proportion a relation is noted between those things that are said to be proportioned because of some definite excess of one over the other, it is impossible for any infinite to be proportionate to a finite by way of proportion. When, however, things are said to be proportionate by way of proportionality, their relation to each other is not considered. All that is considered is the similarity of the relation of two things to two other things. Thus nothing prevents an infinite from being proportionate to an infinite; for just as a particular finite is equal to a certain finite, so an infinite is equal to another infinite.[14]

One of the most difficult points about St. Thomas' doctrine on analogy is that certain texts that speak of proportion and proportionality seem to contradict each other. Thus, in one place St. Thomas will say that analogy based on proportion is not applicable in metaphysics to things that belong to the finite and infinite order of being. Taken without qualification this would mean that an analogy based on proportion would not be used in the highest and most important area of metaphysical knowledge, namely that which deals with knowledge about God. Thus, in a passage from the disputed questions on *Truth*, St. Thomas says that no common term can be predicated of God and creatures if it is based on a *proportion*, but only if it is based on a similarity of proportions or a proportionality.

---

[14] St. Thomas, *Truth*, q. 2, art. 3, ad 4. Mulligan translation, Vol. I, p. 25.

Since an agreement according to proportion can happen in two ways, two kinds of community can be noted in analogy. There is a certain agreement between things having a proportion to each other from the fact that they have a determinate distance between each other or some other relation to each other, like the proportion which the number two has to unity in as far as it is the double of unity. Again, the agreement is occasionally noted not between two things which have a proportion between them, but rather between two related proportions, for example, six has something in common with four because six is two times three, just as four is two times two. The first type of agreement is one of proportion; the second, of proportionality.

We find something predicated analogously of two realities according to the first type of agreement when one of them has a relation to the other, as when *being* is predicated of substance and accident because of the relation which accident has to substance, or as when *healthy* is predicated of urine and animal because urine has some relation to the health of an animal. Sometimes, however, a thing is predicated analogously according to the second type of agreement, as when *sight* is predicated of bodily sight and of the intellect because understanding is in the mind as sight is in the eye.

In those terms predicated according to the first type of analogy, there must be some definite relation between the things having something in common analogously. Consequently, nothing can be predicated analogously of God and creature according to this type of analogy; for no creature has such a relation to God that it could determine the divine perfection. But in the other type of analogy, no definite relation is involved between the things which have something in common analogously, so there is no reason why some name cannot be predicated analogously of God and creature in this manner.

But this can happen in two ways. Sometimes the name implies something belonging to the thing primarily designated which cannot be common to God and creature even in the manner described above. This would be true, for example, of anything predicated of God metaphorically, as when God is called *lion*, which cannot be attributed to God. At other times, however, a term predicated of God and creature implies nothing in its principal meaning which would prevent our finding between a creature and God an agreement of the type described above. To this kind belong all attributes which include no defect nor depend on matter for their act of existence, for example, *being*, *the good*, and similar things.[15]

But in a text from the *Summa Theologiae*, his most mature work, and in a context of great significance regarding the knowledge of God through human reason, St. Thomas says that we can name God from creatures because there is a proportion between God and creatures, since creatures are the effects of God's causality. Admittedly all analogical knowledge is a kind of equivocation, but it is not pure equivocation, for what we know about God through analogy is true knowledge.

Names are thus [analogously] used in two ways: either according as many

15 St. Thomas, *Truth*, q. 2, art. 11, c. Mulligan translation, Vol. I, p. 36.

things are proportionate to one, thus, for example, *healthy* is predicated of medicine and urine in relation and in proportion to the health of the body, of which the former is the cause and the latter the sign: or according as one thing is proportionate to another, thus *healthy* is said of medicine and animal, since medicine is the cause of health in the animal body. And in this way some things are said of God and creatures analogically, and not in a purely equivocal nor in a purely univocal sense. For we can name God only from creatures. Thus, whatever is said of God and creatures is said according to the relation of a creature to God as its principle and cause, wherein all perfections of things pre-exist excellently.[16]

In this text St. Thomas makes a distinction between the kind of relationship that exists between things that are related to each other by some kind of extrinsic bond, namely, by reason of a third thing to which the signification of a particular term belongs primarily, and the kind of relationship that exists between one thing and another in a one to one association. When two things are related to each other by reason of a third, the common name that is attributed to them does not necessarily imply a real relationship between the first two members of the analogy. St. Thomas excludes the use of this kind of analogy from discourse about God because of two defects: first, the relationship is not based upon something *intrinsic* to the beings that are related and consequently cannot be the basis of any "true" predication about God; and second, there can be nothing prior to God by reason of which some perfection can be attributed to Him. St. Thomas does admit, however, that one may predicate certain common names such as true, being, one, good, and the like, on the basis of a one to one relationship between God and creatures, that is, by reason of the creature's dependence on God for whatever perfection of being he has.

The apparent contradiction between the text from the *Summa Theologiae* and that from *Truth* can be resolved, perhaps, if we recall that St. Thomas sometimes uses the words *proportionate* and *proportion* in a generic sense to mean any kind of relationship between two things, whether there is a determinate distance or measure between them or not. What St. Thomas wants to exclude from a metaphysical science about God is any kind of anthropomorphic thinking about God, such as would obtain in predication that would put God and the creature in the same category and set up a definite measure of distance between them. On the other hand, St. Thomas does not go to the extreme position of agnosticism and say that we cannot achieve any kind of true knowledge at all about God, even that tenuous kind that derives from the application of the principle that effects in some way truly represent their causes.

Now the proportion of the created intellect to the understanding of God

16 St. Thomas, *Summa Theologiae*, I, q. 13, art. 5.

is not, in fact, based on a commensuration in an existing proportion, but on the fact that proportion means any relation of one thing to another, as of matter to form, or of cause to effect. In this sense, then, nothing prevents there being a proportion of creature to God on the basis of a relation of one who understands to the thing understood, just as on the basis of the relation of effect to cause.[17]

St. Thomas excludes the kind of proportion between God and creatures that would posit a real relationship in God as well as in the creature. The relationship between God and the creature is not reciprocal from the aspect of the foundation in causality. From the viewpoint of the creature, the relationship is real; from the viewpoint of God, the relationship is not real. It is characteristic of the human mind to regard all relationships involving causality as reciprocal. But this does not necessarily follow. Not only in the relationship between creature and creator, but also in other relationships, the bond may be unilateral. Such, for example, is the relationship between the knower and the object known, to which St. Thomas refers in a passage from *Truth*.

A relation is merely conceptual, according to the Philosopher, when by it something is said to be related which is not dependent upon that to which it is referred, but vice versa; for a relation is a sort of dependence. An example is had in intellectual knowledge and its object, as also in sense and the sensible object. Knowledge depends on its object, but not the other way about. The relation by which knowledge is referred to its object is accordingly real, but the relation by which the object is referred to the knowledge is only conceptual. According to the Philosopher, the object of knowledge is said to be related, not because it is itself referred, but because something is referred to it. The same holds true of all other things which stand to one another as measure and thing measured or as perfective and perfectible.[18]

The analogy that is used in metaphysical knowledge about God is based neither upon a reciprocal relationship between God and creatures nor upon a definite measure of perfection between them, but only upon a similitude. That is why, as we shall see, it is more fitting that we speak of a *proportionality* between the Creator and the creature than a *proportion*, since a proportion seems to connote a definite measure. Since the distinction between God and the creature regards not only the mode of existence but even what is signified by the common name, the goodness that is found in a morally good man has only a similitude to the goodness of God.

Goodness, truth, and being in God are not to be measured by the analogous goodness, truth, and being found in creatures. It is true

---

[17] St. Thomas, *Summa Contra Gentiles*, III, ch. 54. Translated by Vernon Bourke in *On the Truth of the Catholic Faith* (New York: Doubleday Image, 1956), Vol. III, p. 186.
[18] St. Thomas, *Truth*, q. 21, art. 1, c.

that in one sense God is called good because He is the cause of goodness in creatures. But this is, in technical language, to be taken in a denominative sense. That is, in the order of learning we first name a thing from what we are familiar with. We name the divine attributes and think about them according to the ways that we understand. But this does not mean that the divine attributes are dependent on those of creatures. Being, truth, and goodness in God cannot be measured by what is found in creatures because "it is not necessary that the capacity of the passive potency be commensurate with the active power of the agent."[19] The kind of proportion between God and creatures is a relationship of order and does not imply that the effect is commensurate with the cause. Between the finite and the infinite there is only a similitude of proportions.

Comparison of Analogy Based on Simple Proportion and That Based on Proportionality

In an analogy based on a simple proportion between two things the analogues are on a single plane of reference, like a line in relation to a point from which it originates. But in an analogy based on a similarity of proportions it is possible to move on a second level of thought, because the analogy does not consist in a direct comparison of one thing with another but in a comparison of the proportions themselves. The two kinds of relationships might be illustrated in the following way. A simple proportion is constructed like a single wheel. The hub of the wheel is like the primary term of the relationship and the spokes radiate from the center as from their point of origin. In this way the term *healthy* is predicated of medicine, of climate, or a diet inasmuch as these things are related to health in an animal as spokes are related to the hub of the wheel. Likewise the analogy of the term *being* that is predicated of substance and accident is based on a similar relationship, for predicamental substance is like a hub from which radiate the nine predicamental accidents. Accidents exist by means of substance, and they implicitly contain substance in their definition. Substance is primarily named being, but accidents are named beings because of their relationship to substance. A proportionality, on the other hand, is like two wheels. Any two wheels are related to each other because within each wheel there is a proportion of one part to another. The wheel of a toy automobile is like the wheel of a locomotive.The two wheels have a relationship to each other because their parts are proportionately distributed. The knowledge of one kind of wheel will give knowledge of the second kind, not because the second is an exact copy of the first, but simply because it can be called a wheel if it has a proportional distribution of parts.

19 St. Thomas, *Commentary on the Sentences,* III, d. 1, q. 1, art. 1, ad 3.

Because it involves a duality of proportions, a proportional relationship can be a more effective basis of analogical terms that are to be applied to transcendental perfections that are found in both the finite and infinite orders. There is no continuity between the one order and the other; the unity between them is one of similarity. Thus the diversified meaning of *truth* is an analogy based upon a proportionality. Truth for the human mind consists in an identity in the intentional order between the knower and the known in an act of judgment; truth for the divine intellect consists in an identity between the substance of God and the divine knowledge inasmuch as the divine essence is the source of all intelligibility. Although the human and the divine are essentially separate spheres, the truth in one order tells us something of truth in the other order because they are proportionately alike.

Divisions of Proportionality

Proportionality can be of two kinds, metaphorical and proper, as St. Thomas pointed out in a passage from *Truth* that we have already seen:

> Sometimes the name implies something belonging to the thing primarily designated which cannot be common to God and creatures even in the manner described above. This would be true, for example, of anything predicated of God metaphorically, as when God is called *lion*, which cannot be attributed to God. At other times, however, a term predicated of God and creatures implies nothing in its principal meaning which would prevent our finding between a creature and God an agreement of the type described above. To this kind belong all attributes which include no defect nor depend on matter for their act of existence, for example, *being*, the *good*, and similar things.[20]

Metaphorical Proportionality

In the analogy based on proportionality, the term of comparison in some instances cannot directly apply to both the members that are compared. For example, the term *anger* cannot be directly applied to God; its meaning must first be purified in order to get at what is signified. Analogy based on metaphorical proportionality is very common in Sacred Scripture. For example, the doctrine of our union with Christ in the order of grace is brought out in this kind of analogy:

> I am the true vine, and my Father is the vine-dresser. Every branch in me that bears no fruit he will take away; and every branch that bears fruit he will cleanse, that it may bear more fruit. You are already clean because of the word that I have spoken to you. Abide in me, and I in you. As the branch cannot bear fruit of itself unless it remain on the vine, so neither

---

20 St. Thomas, *Truth*, q. 2, art. 11, c. Mulligan translation, Vol. I, p. 113.

can you unless you abide in me. I am the vine, you are the branches. He who abides in me, and I in him, he bears much fruit; for without me you can do nothing. If anyone does not abide in me, he shall be cast out as the branch and wither; and they shall gather them up and cast them into the fire and they shall burn.[21]

There is a correspondence between the life in the main stock of the vine and life in the branches as there is between the life of supernatural grace in the main stock which is Christ and the members who are His followers. Since being a vine is properly predicated only of a plant, it is evident that we are dealing here with a primary signification that is applied to God only metaphorically. But what is signified by the vine, namely the vital process, the unity and harmony among the members, does apply to Christ and to His members as it does to the vine and its branches.

Analogy based on metaphorical proportionality is used to convey ideas that cannot be expressed in literal language as forcefully or as clearly as in figurative concepts. Therefore, when a writer employs figurative language to communicate knowledge that cannot be communicated directly through exact words, his purpose is to transfer the mind of the reader from a familiar to a nonfamiliar order of being. As in the analogy based on proper proportionality, *there can be* a transition to an order that transcends previous experience or temporal and spatial limitations.

Metaphorical proportionality does not have a simple common concept even of the analogous kind found in proper proportionality, since the analogates are compared on the basis of an extrinsic relation to a form that exists properly in only one member. Anger, for example, is found only in beings that have passions, yet it is predicated metaphorically of God. Therefore no strictly scientific demonstration is possible in metaphorical proportionality. At best, the use of metaphor gives the kind of knowledge derived from dialectical argumentation. When the mind does range from one order of being to another, the movement from one level to the other is tentative. Though metaphor is applicable to transcendent beings, it does not belong properly to the science of metaphysics because concepts of the existential order cannot be properly predicated of both the analogates. Nevertheless, the use of metaphor is not a falsification, for the purpose of the one using metaphor is not to give a scientific demonstration but an impression or an illustration.

To speak metaphorically is not to speak falsely; for by such speech one does not intend to express the natures of things signified by the words one

---

[21] Jn. 15:1–7, in the *New Testament*, Confraternity of Christian Doctrine edition (Paterson, N. J.: St. Anthony Guild Press, 1947).

uses, but rather those characteristics that have a certain likeness to those things.[22]

Therefore, metaphor may be superior to the analogy based on simple proportion because through it one can indirectly enter into a different order of reality, and that is why the writers of Sacred Scripture often use the analogy of metaphor.

Analogy Based on Proper Proportionality

In the analogy based on a proportionality both the common term that is predicated and the reality signified are truly found in the analogues. This is the most useful kind of analogy from the viewpoint of the metaphysician. In a passage from his *Commentary on the Ethics* St. Thomas tells us why Aristotle regarded this kind of analogy as most metaphysical. One reason is that the perfection spoken of exists formally and intrinsically in both members of the analogy, while this is not found in analogy according to signification only. Since the metaphysician treats of existence as well as of meaning, analogy based on proportionality both according to signification and existence is most properly used to convey a true judgment about the transcendental properties of being.

> Thus, he [Aristotle] says that goodness is predicated of many things, not according to a meaning that is entirely different, as happens in those things that are equivocal by chance, but rather according to analogy, that is, they are proportionately the same insofar as all good things depend on one principle of goodness, or insofar as they are all ordered to one end. Or also all good things are analogously good, that is, according to a similar proportion, as vision in the eye is a good of the body and vision of the intellect is a good of the soul. Therefore he [Aristotle] prefers this kind of analogy, because it is taken to refer to goodness that is really inhering in things.[23]

The Causal Relationship in Analogy Based on Proper Proportionality

The analogous names that we can apply to God are arrived at by way of causality, since we can know transcendent being only as the cause of imperfect being. Hence a causal relationship is the basis of our knowing God. As Gilson puts it:

> To avoid complete equivocation, then, it becomes necessary to rely upon the relation binding each effect to its cause, the only link enabling us to make an accurate ascent from creature to creator.[24]

---

[22] St. Thomas, *Commentary on the Sentences*, I, d. 16, q. 1, art. 3, ad 3.
[23] St. Thomas, *Commentary on the Ethics*, I, lesson 7, no. 96.
[24] Gilson, *The Christian Philosophy of St. Thomas Aquinas*, p. 106.

St. Thomas says that creatures can be designated as good, because they carry within themselves a likeness of their cause insofar as they are the effects of an agent that is good.

> Every agent is found to effect something like itself. If, therefore, the first goodness is the effective cause of all goods, it must imprint its likeness upon the things produced; and so each thing will be called good by reason of an inherent form because of the highest good implanted in it, and also because of the first goodness taken as the exemplar and effective cause of all created goodness.[25]

Nevertheless the likeness of God in creatures is not similar to the likeness of a man's face in a mirror, in which there is a definite measure between the object and its image. Again in a theological context St. Thomas explains why the analogy based on simple proportion consisting in a definite measure of cause by the effect cannot be applied to God, whereas the analogy based on a proportionality which stresses only the similarity in the modes of being that belong to two distinct orders of reality, can. St. Thomas asked whether the human soul of Christ could know in the Word of God all that the Word knows. We can transfer his answer to the problem of analogous names as they apply to God and to creatures.

> We must remember that a thing can be seen in something only in the way in which it exists in that thing. However, there are two ways in which a number of things can come to exist in one thing. In one way, they exist there in separation and multiplicity, as for instance, with many forms, each is reflected separately in a mirror, and as many men are in one house. In the other way, they are there according to one simple form, as many effects exist virtually in a cause, as conclusions in a principle, and as bodily members in seed.
>
> Accordingly, whoever sees anything must, as a consequence, also see those things which exist in it in multiplicity and divison. For each one of them presents itself to him in the same way as that single thing in which they are contained presents itself. To this extent, one who sees a mirror sees the forms reflected by the mirror. But one who sees some one thing does not have to see all the things which exist in it as united in one form, except when he comprehends the total power of that one thing. Thus, one who sees some principle does not have to see all the conclusions which exist virtually in it, unless he comprehends the principle.
>
> But created things are not in God in multiplicity, but in unity, as Dionysius says. Hence when we say that a thing is in God, this is more like the manner in which effects are in a cause and conclusions in a principle, than like the manner in which forms are in a mirror.[26]

The primary signification of transcendent names comes from our own experience, and these names are applied to God secondarily insofar as a cause can be known through it effects. However, any attempt to apply a precise measure to the attributes of God by reason of their

[25] St. Thomas, *Truth*, q. 21, art. 4.   [26] St. Thomas, *Truth*, q. 20, art. 4.

dependence on divine causality is to make a false transition from the finite to the infinite.

From examples used by St. Thomas it is sometimes difficult to know whether he is speaking of the analogy based on simple proportion or on a relationship of proportions. In one text, for example, he says that the analogy of being as applied to substance and accident is based on a simple proportion, and he thereby seems to exclude the analogy of proper proportionality. But in another text he puts the division of being into substance and accident under the relationship of proper proportionality. However, this does not mean that St. Thomas is contradicting himself, because the analogy of being found in substance and accident can be based upon both kinds of relationships, depending upon how the intellect regards these two modes of being. Going back to the simile of a wheel, if one looks at substance as the hub of the wheel and accidents as the spokes, he will see an order of direct dependence of accident on substance. This would be a simple proportion because the being of accident would be measured directly by substance. But if we look at substance and accidents as constituting two wheels, we have a ratio in which substance is related to its existence as accident is related to its existence. This is a relationship of proportionality. The fact that St. Thomas uses the example of substance and accident under both headings seems to make it plausible that several kinds of analogy can apply to the same analogues.

Is all analogy based on proper proportionality necessarily an analogy according to signification and existence? Some authors have identified the two. But various kinds of proportion and proportionality are found in both the logical and the ontological order in the order of conception and in the order of existing realities. For example, there is a proportionality between the category *substance* and its subdivisions in the Porphyrian tree like that between the category *quality* and its subdivisions. But the analogy "according to signification and existence" transcends logical categories and refers to actualities outside the mind. Therefore analogy based on proper proportionality is not synonymous with analogy according to signification and existence. However every analogy according to signification and existence is an analogy according to a proper proportionality, because it involves a dual relationship in which the mind compares the signification and existence of one analogue with those of another. The signification and the existence of each analogue are integral parts of a proportion and they are to be considered as constituting a unit, just as in the order of being essence and existence constitute one substance. Since any discourse about God and creatures necessarily involves such a dual proportion, St. Thomas can say in the passage from *Truth* that only the analogy according to a proportionality is applicable to God and creatures. In both orders what is signified really exists. In each order the signification of the term and the existence of what is signified are considered to constitute a unity that is comparable to the unity of essence and existence in the order of substance. Thus in God what is signified by *true* is proportioned to the divine mode of existence in a way that is similar to what is signified by *true* as it is proportioned to the existence of truth in the human mind. Since any discourse that combines the finite and the infinite must take into account the diversity both as to the signification of the common term used and the manner in which what is signified exists, it follows that when a common term is predicated as belonging properly to God and creatures there cannot be more than a similarity of proportions, as St. Thomas says in *Truth* (q. 2, art. 11).

Application of Analogy to the Subject of Metaphysics

We are now in a position to apply the doctrine of analogy to common being, the formal subject of metaphysics. Everything that is is being: substance and accident, potency and act, the finite and the infinite, the good, the true, the one, and the beautiful. Being is not a logical genus — it is an analogical genus both with respect to the mode of signification and to what is signified. The analogy of being is the bond of unity in the science of metaphysics. It does not have an identity in signification or being for it includes the diversity both in the mode of signification and in the mode of existence of each thing. The common being of metaphysics, as the subject of the science, is the analogical bond that brings together all created being; although it does not give direct knowledge of infinite being, it opens the way to the possibility of a science about God based on human reason.

However, the philosopher and the student of philosophy must not think that the human mind can examine the *concept* of being and have the science of metaphysics unfold before him. It is not a magician's hat from which a skillful metaphysician can draw out anything that the audience names. St. Thomas sees the human mind as essentially dependent upon the experience of the senses, the source from which the knowledge of the transfinite must eventually come. By examining the formality of being in the sensory world man can rise through his power of reason to a knowledge of the transfinite world that is the efficient and final cause of the finite world. Thus the metaphysical analogy of being makes the unity of the science of metaphysics possible. Metaphysics exists first as the analogously common science of all finite being, and then moves in its final resolution through the efficient and final cause to a science of the infinite and divine.

Just as there is a natural progression in the intellect from ignorance to knowledge, so in the science of metaphysics and the use of analogy there is a progression. The imperfect kinds of analogy are more readily grasped, and consequently the notion of metaphysics as first philosophy and as ontology is more readily grasped than the knowledge of metaphysics as a theology. The analogy based on proper proportionality in signification and existence, which is most properly metaphysical, is necessary for the final achievement of the science of metaphysics as natural theology. However, it must be present, even though vaguely understood, from the very first moment that the science of metaphysics begins, when the object of metaphysics as common being is grasped as analogous by an act of judgment, for it is precisely the existence of each thing that cannot be put into a univocal concept.

Summary

For man the natural path to knowledge is through the experience of sensible reality. Yet reason shows that in the background of reality there lies another world hidden to the senses, whose existence is as certain as the world of sensory phenomena, because the phenomena of the sensible world depend on the causality of this hidden world. The principles and criteria of the sensible world are not directly applicable to this other world. Consequently, a common bond between the two must be found if we are to know something of the existence and nature of this transcendent world. The common bond of being, which at the beginning appears so vague, latently contains the principles and causes of a science that rightfully lays claim to the name *wisdom*. The analogy of being, seen vaguely at first in the diverse categories of things in the physical universe, is extended as our philosophical experience grows to a deeper realization of a bond existing on a higher level in unity, truth, goodness, and beauty, and finally in the knowledge of the bond that unites contingent being to a first transcendent cause, in which we live and move. This is wisdom, the goal of metaphysical thinking. It is the gradual unfolding of what was first known only as a fact without understanding the significance of the fact, namely, that a real world of immaterial beings exists and that in some way we are joined to them, and that eventually our happiness will consist in the knowledge of the transcendent first and total cause of all participated being.

CHAPTER IV

Substance and Accidents

Aristotle and St. Thomas begin their study of metaphysical being with the analogy of being as found in substance. The natural order of learning begins with a study of the analogy of being as found in substance rather than with the analogy of being in potency and act, essence and existence, in the transcendental properties of being, or in the causes of being, because these other notions presuppose the study of substance as the primary subject of metaphysics.

Though both the logician and metaphysician may study the categories of being, inasmuch as logic has the same extension as metaphysics, they study them from two different points of view. The metaphysician is primarily concerned with the categories as they relate to real beings existing independently of the mind. The logician is primarily concerned with the categories as correctly ordering the operations of the mind. Even in logic, however, we cannot consider the categories as though they were completely independent of reality, for the purpose of logic ultimately is to reach truth, and the logical rules governing predication depend in last analysis on the objective truth of things. As St. Thomas notes:

> Being is divided into different genera according to the different modes of predication that follow the different modes of being because there are as many different modes of predicating being as there are kinds of existence to be signified. Therefore the primary divisions of being are called *predicaments* because they are differentiated according to different modes of predication. Among the things predicated, some signify a something, that is, a substance; some signify a quality or a quantity and so on. To each mode of predication there must be an existing something signifying the same thing.

> The second mode [that of predication or of being in the mind] is compared to the first [that of real being] as effect to cause. From the fact that there is something in reality, the truth or falsity of a proposition follows. This is what the intellect signifies by the word *is*, a verbal copula. But

61

the intellect can conceive of something that is not really a being as though it were a being, as negation and things of this kind. Being is predicated sometimes in the first way and sometimes in the second. Blindness, for example, is predicated in the second way because of a true proposition relating to something that is without sight, but it is not predicated in the first way, for blindness is not something actually in things, but is a privation of being.[1]

Thus in judgments involving the categories the copula *is* can belong to two different orders: it can refer to the composition of the mind in which the intellect affirms the union of subject and predicate in the order of thought; or it can refer to a composition in reality outside the mind. Hence we can have a proposition that is true but does not have an exact counterpart in the order of existence, as when I say: "Helen Keller is blind." At other times the copula refers directly to reality, as when I say: "I am a person."

> *To be* can mean either of two things. It may mean the act of being, or it may mean the composition of a proposition effected by the mind in joining a predicate to a subject.[2]

In grasping reality with the intellect, one sees that there are various kinds of beings. If all possible relationships to real existence are examined, it will be seen that there are ten categories of judgment that refer to ten actual modes of existence. Some beings have existence in themselves while others exist only in other beings as in a subject. The first are called *substances*; the others, *accidents*. An example of substance is a human person who has self-contained existence, for no man can be part of the existence of another man. Examples of accidents are shapes, colors, and positions. These do not have self-contained existence, but exist only in that which has shape, color, and position.

Metaphysics Deals Primarily With Substance

A science studies primarily only what properly belongs to its subject, for incidental manifestations of the subject cannot be resolved into general propositions and formulated within the necessary laws of the science. Only those properties that belong directly (*per se*) to the subject or necessarily follow from it as properties lie immediately within the scope of science. The primary subject of metaphysics is substance, since it alone is being that has existence in itself (*in se*). However, in order to avoid confusion on this point, we should state immediately that the

---

[1] St. Thomas, *Commentary on the Metaphysics*, V, lesson 9, nos. 890, 896.
[2] St. Thomas, *Summa Theologiae*, I, q. 3, art. 4, ad 2.

division of real being of the categories into substance and accident is not the equivalent of the division into *being per se* and *being per accidens* of predication. The division into substance and accident is an absolute consideration; that is, it refers to the thing in itself. Each of the categories, substance and the nine accidents, refers to a special mode of existence and in this respect can be called a *being per se*. But the division into *being per se* and *being per accidens* may be based upon predication in which the predicate is related to the subject of a proposition; this is more properly a logical consideration. If the predicate refers intrinsically to the subject either as belonging to its essence or as a property following directly from its essence, it is called a *being per se* of predication. But if the predicate is extrinsic and incidental to the essence, it is called *being per accidens* of predication. This is called *predicable accident*, and it must be distinguished from *predicamental accident*.[3] For example, in the proposition: *Man is white*, the form *whiteness* does not belong to the subject essentially; but in the proposition *man is rational*, the form *rationality* belongs essentially to the subject. In the first instance *white* is a predicable accident; in the second, *rational* is an essential predicate. But when speaking of substance and accident we refer to the modes of real existence in nature. Thus substance is *being per se* from the viewpoint of existence and the nine (predicamental) accidents are *being per accidens* because they are added to the substance and they exist only by means of the substance.

Metaphysics treats all categories of beings whether substances or accidents. Primarily, however, it is concerned with substance because the prime analogate of being is substance. Nevertheless, it does not pass over accidents because analogically they, too, are beings.

> Whatever beings have a common mode of predication, even though not univocal but only analogical, belong to the consideration of one science. But being is predicated in this way of all things. Therefore, all beings belong to the consideration of this one science, which considers being insofar as it is being. Consequently, it treats of both substances and accidents.[4]

Yet we must hold that metaphysics treats primarily of substance and only secondarily of accidents, because metaphysics, as the science of being, will, first of all, consider that which primarily is, namely, substance. Accidents, since they have being only in substance, are a secondary consideration of metaphysics.

> The fourth way [of speaking of being] is that which is most perfect. This is the kind that has real existence without an admixture of privation. It has being solidly rooted, existing in itself: and substance is of this kind.

---

3 Cf. p. 76.
4 St. Thomas, *Commentary on the Metaphysics*, IV, lesson 1, no. 534.

And all other beings are related to this kind as to the first and most necessary kind of being. For quantities and qualities are called beings insofar as they are present in substances; motion and generation are called beings insofar as they tend to substance or to the aforesaid quantities or qualities; privations and negations are called beings insofar as they indicate the absence of the aforementioned beings.[5]

Every science which treats of diverse things related to one primary being treats most properly and primarily of that first being. It is upon this being that the others depend for their existence and through it they are designated. This is true in all cases. But substance is the first among all beings. Therefore a metaphysician, who considers all beings, primarily and principally should consider the principles and causes of substances; consequently he treats principally and primarily of substances.[6]

Various Notions of Substance

To show what substance means, we shall begin with a text in which St. Thomas gives the various notions of substance and shows which one the metaphysician treats of.

There are at least four ways, if not more, of speaking of substance . . . Of these ways, the first is according to "what a thing was to be"; that is, the quiddity or essence or nature of the thing is called its substance.

The second mode is that in which a universal is said to be a substance according to the opinion of those who say that the ideal forms are the universals that are predicated of singulars and are, therefore, the substances of these singulars.

The third mode is according to the view that the "primary genus of each thing is its substance." And according to this mode the one and being are said to be the substances of all things insofar as they are the primary genera of all things.

The fourth mode refers to the subject, that is, to the particular substance. . . . It is clear, however, that the subject referred to here is called in the work On the Categories "first substance," because the same definition applies to both.

Therefore, he [Aristotle] concludes that we should investigate this kind of being, that is, the subject or first substance, because such a subject is seen above all to be substance. Therefore, in the work On the Categories it is said that that meaning of substance is the most proper and principal one. This kind, by virtue of its own being, underlies all others, namely, species, genera, and accidents. Second substances, on the contrary, that is, genera and species, only underlie accidents. But they do even this only by reason of first substances. Man [as a species] is white only because this individual man is white.[7]

Let us examine the four ways in which philosophers have spoken of substance:

---

[5] St. Thomas, Commentary on the Metaphysics, IV, lesson 1, no. 543.
[6] St. Thomas, Commentary on the Metaphysics, IV, lesson 1, no. 546.
[7] St. Thomas, Commentary on the Metaphysics, VII, lesson 2, nos. 1270–1274.

First, one man consider substance as an essence. Some philosophers with an idealistic point of view, such as the Kantian, Platonic, or Hegelian notion of being, held that essence or form is identical with substance and that the act of existence adds nothing significant from the point of view of philosophy. Their argument is that existence apart from essence cannot be grasped by the intellect and therefore cannot add anything to our knowledge of reality. On the contrary, St. Thomas holds that essence is not substance in its full sense because it is not a complete being — it is a principle of being. But only complete beings belong in the categories, for it is only of complete beings that we can properly say "they exist." As we shall see, the act of existence is the supreme perfection of being to which all other aspects of being are subordinate since they are related to existence as potency to act. Nature or essence is not fully substance in the metaphysical sense. St. Thomas tells the difference between the fully metaphysical and the essentialistic conceptions of substance:

> Substance may be taken in two ways. In one sense it is the ultimate subject which is not predicated of another, and this is the individual in the genus of substance; in another sense it is the form or nature of a subject. The reason for this distinction is that several subjects may have a common nature; thus several men have in common the nature of man. Hence the need of distinguishing that which is one from that which is multiple: for the common nature is signified by the definition which indicates what a thing is: so that this common nature is called the essence or quiddity. Wherefore whatsoever a thing contains pertaining to the common nature is included in the signification of the essence, whereas this cannot be said of all that is contained in the individual substance. For if whatsoever is in the individual substance were to belong to the common nature, there would be no possible distinction between individual substances of the same nature. Now that which is in the individual substance besides the common nature is individual matter which is the principle of individuation and consequently individual accidents which determine this same matter. Accordingly, the essence is compared to the individual substance as a formal part thereof, for instance, human nature in Socrates. Hence in things composed of matter and form, the essence is not quite the same as the subject, and consequently it is not predicated of the subject: for we do not say that Socrates is his human nature.[8]

Essence in this context is related to first substance, that is, to the particular, existent subject, as its formal part. In this sense it is in the genus of substance, since it makes the individual substance to be of a specific kind. Nevertheless, essence is not a subject, because of itself it is not an existing thing — rather it is that *by which* an individual thing is what it is. We know that among corporeal substances there can be many individuals that have the same essence, as many individual men have the same human

---

[8] St. Thomas, *On the Power of God*, q. 9, art. 1.

nature. Nature, essence, or form taken by itself is neither one nor many, and it is neutral with respect to the mode of existence, whether it be in the mind as a universal or concretely in the individual. But substances, as we take them in metaphysics, are existing realities, and only individuals have real, extramental existence. Therefore, essence is not a substance in the full sense and cannot be the subject of an existential predication. We should not say, for example, that *Rational animality is white*, though we may say that this *Man is white*. However, whatever belongs to a substance by reason of a common nature, or more simply whatever is implied by the essence, can be predicated of the essence. We can say, for example, that *Humanity is composed of animality and rationality*. But this is a formal predication and not one in the order of first substance — it belongs only in the abstract order.

The second meaning of substance that St. Thomas takes up is that of the *abstract universal*. Like essence, this is not the primary meaning of substance. The Platonists, it is true, supposed that being consists primarily in abstract universal forms. These were thought to be the primary prototypes of reality. Aristotle and St. Thomas, however, show in their psychology that the Platonic doctrine of abstract universal forms is both contrary to the evidence of natural philosophy and unnecessary to solve the problem of the origin of scientific knowledge. In reality, this view is hardly different from that which considers essence alone as substance.

Substance may, in the third place, be understood in the sense of the *primary genus* of all things. Reference is here made to the view that so-called substantial differences in all things, between living and non-living beings, between men and plants and irrational animals, are really only variations in a fundamental constitutive element, a common substratum, in which all things participate in different degrees. This would amount to saying that all things are one substance. This view is summarily dismissed as being evidently false.

The fourth way of considering a substance is that which is most properly metaphysical. According to this view substance is primarily predicated of *first substance*. This is the individual substance as it exists in nature. The other analogous uses of the word *substance* are derived from this. First substance is that which is recognized by the intellect as being a subject of which other things are predicated either in the essential or in the accidental order. The intellect, in its act of judging, recognizes that first substance holds the primacy in the order of existing things and that all other reality is dependent on first substance. This substance, as it exists outside the mind and is grasped through the mediation of the senses, is the proper subject of metaphysics.

What differentiates this mode of being from all others is that it cannot be predicated of anything else, while every other mode of substance must eventually be predicated of this primary kind. Thus all the various meanings of substance suggest a primary reality upon which others depend. Hence we can formulate a working definition of substance: "Substance is that which primarily exists."

A Descriptive Definition of Substance

In the absence of a strict definition of substance, the philosopher tries to reach some kind of descriptive definition. We have selected the following texts as epitomizing what might be said about substance in a summary description.

> The name *substance* signifies not only what is being of itself — for being cannot of itself be a genus — but it also signifies an essence to which it belongs in this way, namely, of itself, which being (i.e., existence) however is not its essence.[9]

> A substance is that which does not exist in a subject.[10]

> This is the meaning of substance insofar as it is a category according to Avicenna, namely, that it is something having an essence to which belongs existence in itself and not in another.[11]

> The nature of substance, therefore, must be understood as follows. A substance is *a thing to which it belongs to be not in a subject.* The name *thing* takes its origin from the *quiddity,* just as the name *being* comes from *to be.* In this way, the definition of substance is understood as *that which has a quiddity to which it belongs to be not in another.* Now, this is not appropriate to God, for He has no quiddity save His being. In no way, then, is God in the genus of substance. Thus He is in no genus, since we have shown that He is not in the genus of accident.[12]

> According to Avicenna (*Metaph.* III, 8), substance is not rightly defined as a self-subsistent being; for being cannot be the genus of a thing, as the Philosopher says (*Metaph.* II, 3), because nothing can be added to being that has not a share of being, and a difference should not be a part of the genus. If, however, substance can be defined notwithstanding that it is the most universal of genera, its definition will be a thing whose quiddity is competent to have being not in a subject (Cf. also *Summa Theologiae,* I, q. 3, art. 5, ad 1 and 3; q. 77, art. 1, ad 2). Hence the definition of substance cannot be applied to God, whose quiddity is not different from His being. Wherefore God is not contained in the genus of substance, but is above all substance.[13]

As we gather from the descriptive definitions of substance as a category of being, the definition applies properly only to imperfect substances in which the essence is in potency to the act of existence. It

---

[9] St. Thomas, *Summa Theologiae,* I, q. 3, art. 5, ad 1.
[10] St. Thomas, *Commentary on the Sentences,* I, d. 8, q. 4, a. 2, ad 2.
[11] St. Thomas, *Commentary on the Sentences,* II, d. 3, q. 1, art. 5, *corpus.*
[12] St. Thomas, *Summa Contra Gentiles,* I, 25, 10. Pegis translation, I, p. 128.
[13] St. Thomas, *On the Power of God,* q. 7, art. 3, ad 4.

does not apply immediately to God. This leads to another question related to the definition of substance: What does it mean to say that substance is that "to which is due existence *per se*"? Because of the differences in interpreting the meaning of *per se*, philosophers draw vastly different conclusions about the application of the term to finite and infinite being.

The *per se* can mean that substance has no dependence on any other being for its act of existence. If this is taken in an absolute sense, it means that only one substance exists, namely, divine substance. If other beings are called substance it is because divinity is indistinguishable from the substances of human experience. Thus we have a pantheistic conception of reality. Or, divinity alone is substance and other things are illusions of substance. We are back to Parmenides' question about being: Is it one or many? This kind of question supposes a univocal understanding of the meaning of substance.

The *per se* in the definition of substance can be taken in opposition to *in alio*. The opposition is between *being a subject* and *being in a subject*. As we defined substance, the *per se* is the equivalent of *in se*: substance exists *in itself* and is the subject and does not exist in another. Substance is that of which other things are predicated and which itself is predicated of nothing else.

Per se, as St. Thomas points out in his *Commentary on the Physics of Aristotle*,[14] can be taken in two senses: in opposition to accident, that is, what exists *in* another, or in opposition to what exists *through* another. The occasion for this distinction was an objection that a certain philosopher Galenus made to the Aristotelian view that "whatever moves is moved by another." Even living beings that are said to have a principle of movement within themselves are said to be moved by another. Galenus objected that the movement of living beings could be called movement *per se*. His objection, according to St. Thomas, was due to an equivocal use of the phrase *per se*: In the one case the *per se* is compatible with what is a secondary cause; in the other case it is not.

Hence, to say that imperfect substance is being *per se* is not to say that its existence is not caused. It means that imperfect substances have natures that call for a primary kind of existence that constitutes them as subjects in their own right. It does not mean that they are so constituted that they do not depend upon extrinsic causes to bring about this kind of existence.

The Reality of Substance

Can we prove that substances exist? We cannot demonstrate their existence syllogistically. *Demonstration* refers to the act by which the

---

[14] Book VII, lesson 1.

mind scientifically proves a conclusion from certain premises by means of syllogistic reasoning. Demonstration of substance is impossible because there are no premises prior to and more certain than the conclusion. A substance is the subject about which properties and accidents are predicated. That a subject or substance exists is presupposed in any demonstration. Nevertheless a philosopher can offer various dialectical arguments that would make one more apt to see the significance of substance and realize that substance is a primary reality.[15]

One can argue dialectically that, if what we know as substance is not substance, then we must go back to the existence of some kind of being that is substance, for not every being can be a "non-autonomous" being or a modification of being, that is, an accident. Somewhere in the chain of reality there is a being that has existence in itself. Those who deny substance must substitute another name for this primary reality and without actually calling it *substance* attribute to it the autonomy in being that St. Thomas attributes to substance.

Though substance can be known through changes in nature, the strongest evidence is in self-consciousness which gives evidence of the reality at least of our own substance. We are aware of the presence of a primary existing subject in which a sequence of changing emotions, thoughts, decisions, and movements exist. We do not identify these passing states with the permanent substratum. We give evidence of this by using the word *have* rather than *is* to indicate that we do not consider changing states such as those of being happy or unhappy, of knowledge or ignorance, the same as being our substance. We say: *I have a cold* or *I have an idea* but never *I am a cold* or *I am an idea*. Thus we implicitly make a distinction between our substance and the accidental states that we pass through.

We cannot doubt that such states as sorrow, pain, happiness, and knowledge really exist. Yet it is unthinkable that they simply exist as isolated states or abstractions. It is equally unthinkable that these passing states are the same as our own person because they are transitory, are acquired and lost, while our person remains one and the same. There is an underlying continuity that persists through all our changes of mood. Even William James was not satisfied with his "stream of consciousness" theory but felt that on a different basis of reasoning one should posit the existence of a soul.

The reality of substance is partially made evident simply by the

---

[15] A dialectical argument in this context is based not on intrinsic knowledge of the causes such as is had in true demonstration but is more negative, namely, the argument shows that one who denies the starting point must eventually contradict himself. In this sense the arguments of Zeno against motion and change in being are called dialectical.

etymology of the word, for words are often implicit evidence of the reality behind them. *Substance* comes from *sub stare*, which means literally to "stand under" and, by extension of meaning, "to be a support or foundation." Substance is like the foundation of a building: it is the first part of the building to be made and must be strong enough to support the weight put upon it. The shape, mass, and size of the building appear above the surface and they are the properties by which a building is judged. But they do not sustain themselves, for their quality and shape and size are predetermined by the foundation that is under them. A substance, then, is the foundation upon which other things rest; it is the foundation of reality because it is that which primarily exists.

The Phenomenalist Rejection of Substance

Substance is hidden from our senses as the foundation of a building is hidden from our eyes. That is why some philosophers deny or question the reality of substance while others hold that its existence cannot be known with certainty but only assumed as a convenient explanation of experience. Among those who deny or question the reality of substance are the *phenomenalists* — they admit what they see, namely phenomena, but they cannot see substance, and so deny it. Since they can see and measure movement and shapes, they will agree that these are real. Some will admit the reality of the so-called primary qualities, such as size, shape, and weight. Since substance does not appear in the senses, since it cannot be measured, the phenomenalist concludes that it is not real. If one could remove the size, weight, and shape of bread, they ask, where would be its substance?

Some empiricists admit the reality of substance but say that we cannot prove its existence or nature. Such is John Locke, the English empiricist who is sometimes cited as one who denied the reality of substance. But what he actually said is that substances exist but cannot be known as they are.

> I have always affirmed that man is a substance. Sensation convinces us that there are solid and extended substances. And reflection convinces us that there are thinking substances.[16]

However, he thought that there could not be a science about substance, because knowledge of it is not accessible to the human mind. Another English empiricist, Hume, took the more skeptical position that substance cannot be known to exist at all. His view seems to have been based on a mechanistic conception of the process of understanding, for

---

[16] John Locke, *An Essay on Human Understanding*, II, ch. 23, par. 29, Britannica, Great Books Edition.

he thought that ideas are formed from streams of physical impressions or images. Composite ideas are associations of such images. And since he thought that there is no need of positing the existence of a soul to explain the origin of ideas through association, he denied the validity of the argument from consciousness.

But the major difficulty in this position is that it opposes common sense. The mind implicitly admits the existence of substances when it thinks of sensory impressions arising from external bodies and affecting us as subjects. What is a body if not a material substance? And even if one denies the spiritual nature of man, one still has to think of himself as a subject of varied psychological experiences. In the final analysis, what Hume really denies is the distinction between substance and accidents. In other words, he does not question the reality of substance, but the reality of accidents. In Hume's understanding of the term, everything is a substance, even the fleeting sensory impressions.

> Every perception is a substance and every distinct part of a perception is a distinct substance.[17]

Phenomenalism as a philosophy admits the reality of nothing except what is proved or evident through sense experience. Since sense experience as such cannot attain the substance of things, phenomenalists conclude that substances in the Thomistic sense are not real. Hence there is an essential philosophical conflict between the Thomistic view and that of the phenomenalists. This conflict has to be resolved on the plane of epistemology and psychology. By showing that the Aristotelian view of sensory and intellectual knowledge is correct, one is on the way to prove the reality of both spiritual and corporeal substances and to show the essential difference between substance and accident. If we can prove that sensory phenomena have a type of existence different from that of the knowing subject, and if we can show that the basic constitution of bodies in the external world cannot be identified with the quantitative and qualitative differences such bodies manifest, we can prove that phenomenalism is false. This is primarily the work of philosophical psychology, because in it we have the most effective arguments for the existence of a substance distinct from the passing modes of consciousness. The knowledge of self as a constant and of our sensations as variables gives evidence that we are substances and that our sensations are accidents.

One source of difficulty in admitting a real distinction between substances and accident is the failure to see that *distinction* is not the same as *separation* and that realities which are distinct are not necessarily separable. All created substances have accidental characteristics by which their inner nature manifests itself. Created substances are never found

---

[17] David Hume, *Treatise on Human Nature*, I, part 4, sect. 5.

without some accidents. But inseparability by no means implies that there is no real distinction. One never has, for example, a quality like whiteness in the paper of this book without having extension or quantity. But the extension of the page and the whiteness of the page are not the same. They are distinct, but in the present case the whiteness could not exist without the quantity; and the quantity could not exist without some quality.

The basic source of difficulty regarding substance, however, is the denial of a real distinction between sensory and intellectual knowledge. The intellect perceives substances but the senses do not. The intellect sees the necessity of a permanent substratum for sensory appearances both within ourselves and within the bodies from which sensory impressions originate. But sense knowledge does not convey this necessity and therefore it cannot manifest substance. In other words, if the senses are taken as the only criterion of truth, one will not admit the reality of substance.

It is true that the human intellect does not work independently of the senses, for all knowledge comes to us through the senses. But the intellect alone is able to understand what the senses are in contact with. A child may have found some pretty pebbles, but it may take a jeweler to identify them as precious stones. Each sees the object in his own way. Resistance of another body means hardness, pain, roughness to the hand and the sense of touch; but to the intellect it means a corporeal substance that contains or produces the qualities we experience with our senses. The existence of accidents proves that substances *must* exist. No one has ever perceived an odor or a color or a sound or a shape or size that did not have its origin in a body. *Things* are colored, sweet or bitter, three-sided or square. The quantity or quality cannot exist in or by itself but only in some material body. The body is not the same as those particular qualities because it can remain fundamentally the same kind of body while these other qualifications are changing. Nor is our physical self the same as our thoughts and impressions. We think thoughts and we feel pain. The distinction between ourselves as subjects and our experiences as modifications of the subject is evident from the fact that we try to get rid of painful sensations and to acquire other experiences which are pleasant. Evidently, then, these experiences are different from ourselves. They are not substances in themselves for they have reality only when they are attached to us.

If a person admits the reality of accidents, he should have no difficulty in admitting the reality of substance, for accidents are the modifications of substance and necessarily imply substance. It is not necessary, however, from an analysis of substance, to conclude that if there is a substance accidents must also be present. Substances are beings that exist in themselves and not in another as in a subject. They are capable of supporting accidents but it is not essential that they actually do support them. But, on the contrary, if there are accidents, there must be substance because, as we have already said, accidents are modifications of substance. Nothing can be modification purely and simply. Common sense tells us the truth of this: We can never make judgments that leave aside the substance. We do not say, for example: "I see a white ——. I am touching a hard ——." These are incomplete statements because they do not include a substance as an object. We are indirectly aware of the reality of substance in every judgment involving accidental qualities. The human mind will not do without substance.

Perhaps a legitimate excuse for the empiricist's denial of substance is that too many realist philosophers are so vague in their definition and description of it. But in a sense these philosophers too may be excused, because substance cannot strictly be defined, as we have already seen. We are strangely myopic when confronted with such basic realities, as if we were trying to see the point of a pencil that is touching our nose. A distortion of the true meaning of substance leads to its denial. Some deny substance because they conceive of it as a kind of stuff from which reality is fashioned; others because they conceive of it as an abstraction, with no essential relationship to matter. They do not realize that substance is to be judged primarily from the act of existence rather than from a concept that refers more to the essence. They do not realize that substance is something dynamic and not like a set of building blocks.

Analogical Character of Substance

Many of the ancient philosophers of nature did not rise above a materialistic conception of substance. Therefore, their conception of substance was more related to matter than to form, more to potency than to act. Substance to them seemed to be like the basic element to which something else could be added much in the way that wood can be given a form by an artist. Because they considered the material element the essential element of substance, they could not rise to a metaphysical understanding of it. They had a univocal conception of substance, because basically all substance seemed to them to be matter. They did not see that it is through form and its perfection, the act of existence, that substance exists and that it is, as a result, analogical. Real differences among substances seemed to them rather in the category of what we call accidental differences.

The ignorance of the meaning of substantial form led the ancient philosophers into error in the following way: they had not yet arrived at the point where their intellects were sufficiently raised above sensible reality.

Consequently, they investigated only those forms that we call *proper* or *common* sensibles. These are evidently accidents, for example, white and black, great and small, and so on. Substantial form, however, is perceptible by the senses only indirectly. They [the ancient philosophers] had not sufficient knowledge to realize that it is distinct from matter. The total subject that we say is composed of matter and form they said was prime matter, either air or water or something of this kind. But they said that those things are forms that we call accidents such as quantities and qualities whose proper subject is not prime matter but composite substance which is substance in act.[18]

The source of the difficulty of the ancient philosophers of nature, St. Thomas points out, was that they had not yet reached that point in philosophy where they understood substance to be independent from a materially existing reality. Restricted as they were in their thinking, it was inconceivable that there could be a primary existence apart from matter. But it is impossible that matter alone be substance. As St. Thomas shows:

It is impossible that matter alone be substance or that it be substance in any primary sense. For there are two things that are especially characteristic of substance, the first of which is that it is *separable*. Accident is not separable from substance but substance can be separated from accident. The second thing is that substance can be designated as a *particular thing*. But other classes of beings do not signify a particular thing.

But these two characteristics, namely, that something be separable and a particular thing, do not apply to matter. For matter cannot exist by itself without form by which it is constituted a being in act, since of itself it is only in potency. Nor is it a particular thing except by reason of the form through which it is actualized.[19]

The analogical character of substance is brought out primarily by the fact that substance connotes a relation to existence which can be realized in various modes and is not limited to the mode proper to natural bodies. The metaphysician investigates natural beings precisely insofar as they are beings and this is what differentiates his science from the philosophy of nature. It is a metaphysics (a *transphysics*) precisely because being as such transcends the material order. The metaphysician uses material substances as the point of departure of his science.

In this science [metaphysics] we try to analyze sensible substances. "for the sake of this," that is, for the sake of immaterial substances, because speculation about sensible and material substances belongs in some way to the philosophy of nature which is not first philosophy but second philosophy, as was stated in Book IV. For first philosophy treats of primary substances which are immaterial substances, and one speculates about them not only insofar as they are substances but insofar as they are of

---

[18] St. Thomas, *Commentary on the Metaphysics*, VII, lesson 2, no. 1284.
[19] St. Thomas, *Commentary on the Metaphysics*, VII, lesson 2, nos. 1291–1292.

this kind, namely, immaterial. The metaphysician does not investigate sensible substances precisely because they are sensible but rather because they are substances or because they are beings, or finally, because through them we are led to the knowledge of immaterial substances. But the philosopher of nature treats of material substances not precisely insofar as they are substances but insofar as they are material and have in themselves a principle of motion.[20]

Since the metaphysician considers natural substances precisely from the point of view of being (that is, as primary existing realities), it is interesting to see St. Thomas' comment on the opinion of Avicenna that the existence of imperfect beings is so different from their essence or substance that existence is thought to be purely extrinsic to and, as it were, inconsequential for substance. St. Thomas says:

> Although the existence of a being is distinct from its essence, one should not understand this in the sense that it is something superadded after the manner of an accident, but rather that it is constituted by the principles of the essence. Therefore, the name *being* that is derived from the act of existence signifies the same thing as that which is designated by the essence.[21]

The Being of Accidents

Since metaphysics is the science of all being, nothing that exists is to be excluded from this science. Thus metaphysics investigates not only substance, its primary subject, but also the accidents that are found in the subject (see St. Thomas, *Commentary on the Metaphysics,* IV, lesson 1, no. 529). It is not our purpose to attempt a defense of the view that accidents really exist. This is a question that can be decided without much subtle investigation; to attempt a proof would simply be belaboring what is obvious to common sense. We do not mean that it is immediately obvious that all the predicamental accidents are really distinct from each other, for example, that a clear-cut distinction is easily seen between position and place. But that some accidents do exist is obvious from the experience that each one has of the permanence of his substance and of his changing thoughts, moods, and bodily dispositions.

Nor shall we undertake an analysis of each of the nine categories of the predicamental accidents. Nowhere does St. Thomas himself give an *ex professo* exposition of each of the accidents. What we know of his doctrine on the various kinds of accidents comes to us indirectly, for example, when he discusses the nature of quantity with reference to the principle of individuation and multiplication of corporeal beings, or tells us what predica-

---

[20] St. Thomas, *Commentary on the Metaphysics,* VII, lesson 11, no. 1526.
[21] St. Thomas, *Commentary on the Metaphysics,* IV, lesson 2, no. 558.

mental relation is while treating of the transcendental relationships in the Trinity.

The metaphysician treats of accidents insofar as they are real beings and are directly related to the kind of substance that is considered by the philosopher. Though accidents are forms distinct from substance, they are caused by the principles of the substance. It is true that a science treats only what belongs *per se* to its subject. The science of human anatomy, for instance, does not treat *per se* of a man's nationality or religion, because these do not contribute anything to a biological science, though they are pertinent to a sociological study of man.

Predicable and Predicamental Accident

The term *accident* can be taken in two ways. First it can mean what is incidental to a subject of inquiry, in the way that sociological characteristics are incidental to a biological study of man. Second, it can signify what is opposed to the *being per se* of *substance*.

> If we take accident as meaning what is divided against substance, then there can be no medium between substance and accident; for they are divided by affirmation and negation, that is, according to being in a subject, and not being in a subject. But if we take accident as one of the five predicables, in this sense there is a medium between substance and accident. For the substance is all that belongs to the essence of a thing. But whatever is beyond the essence of a thing cannot be called accident in this sense; but only what is not caused by the essential principles of the species. For *property* does not belong to the essence of a thing, but is caused by the essential principles of the species; and hence it is a medium between the essence and accident thus understood.[22]

The first of these is called *predicamental accident* and the second is called *predicable accident*. Among the modes of connecting a predicate to a subject, four are connected with the essence of the subject or follow necessarily from it as properties, but the fifth is one in which the predicate is only incidentally connected with the subject as when we say *John is sitting*. This notion of predicable accident belongs to logic and not to metaphysics.

The predicamental accidents are not incidental to the subject of metaphysics, since every imperfect substance necessarily has accidents. That is why the metaphysician must consider both substance and accidents, but *as it were simultaneously*, since accidents exist naturally only when substance exists and because substance exists. Thus when Aristotle and St. Thomas ask whether the consideration of accidents belongs to the science of metaphysics, they say that it does:

---

[22] St. Thomas, *Summa Theologiae*, I, q. 77, art. 1, ad 5.

Whatever things receive the predication of one common term, even though not univocal but only analogical, belong to the consideration of one science. But *being* is predicated in this way of all things. Therefore, all beings belong to the consideration of this one science which considers being insofar as it is being. Consequently, it treats of both substance and accidents.[23]

Accident cannot be defined without substance because accident is not a complete being. Therefore there cannot be a science of accidents as such. Just as we cannot conceive of a hand or of an eye except as integral parts of a living substance, neither can we speak of the being of accidents without implicitly referring to the being of substance. We do not want to affirm that accidents are essential to substance, or deny that accidents have an existence of their own. But as far as the science of metaphysics is concerned, accidents can be understood only as modifications of substance.

Predicamental accidents are like modifiers in a sentence. A modifier presupposes a subject and a verb. Being per se implies a subject and also the verb *to be*. Thus only substance qualifies *per se* as the subject and predicate of a proposition. Adjectives and adverbs in a real sentence modify the subject and predicate but have no real existence apart from what they modify. However, they can be understood in an abstract way and then serve as the subject of a sentence, as for example when we say, *White is a color* or *Quickly is an adverb*. But this kind of existence is abstract and belongs only in the order of thought. The predicamental accidents really exist only by reason of substance in which they inhere or by which they are sustained. They do not have a real definition when we consider them in the concrete order of existence, because they are incomplete beings and they cannot be subjects of being in the order of existence.

The Analogy of Being in the Relationship of Substance to Accident

The name *being*, applied analogically to substance and to accidents, is applied primarily to substance and only secondarily to accidents, because they have being only through their relationship to substance.

What is predicated of some things according to priority and posteriority is certainly not predicated univocally. For the prior is included in the definition of the posterior, as *substance* is included in the definition of accident according as an accident is a being. If, then, *being* were said univocally of substance and accident, substance would have to be included in the definition of being insofar as being is predicated of substance. But this is clearly impossible.[24]

---

[23] St. Thomas, *Commentary on the Metaphysics*, IV, lesson 1, no. 534.
[24] St. Thomas, *Summa Contra Gentiles*, I, 32, 7. Pegis translation, I, p. 145.

Metaphysics treats of both substance and accident under the common aspect of being, although primarily and principally the science of metaphysics is concerned with substance.[25]

All being is predicated by reference to one primary being but this primary being, as is clear from the examples given, is not the final or efficient cause but the subject. Some things are called beings or are said to have existence because they have existence in themselves as substances which principally and first of all are called beings. Other things [are called beings] because they are the properties or the modifications of substance, such as the *per se* accidents of each and every substance.[26]

It might be argued that accidents do not have their own act of existence because they have existence only by reason of the subject in which they are found. The following are texts in which St. Thomas seems to hold this view and to maintain that the analogy between substance and accidents is one according to signification only.

Accidents, however, do not have existence except by being in a subject, and therefore their essence depends on the subject. For this reason, it is necessary that the subject be placed in the definition of the accident.[27]

For being taken absolutely is said to be that which has existence in itself, namely, substance. Other things are called beings because they belong to that which is *per se*, either as a property or permanent disposition [*habitus*] or something of this kind. For a quality is not called a being because it has existence, but rather because through it substance is modified. This is true of all the other accidents.[28]

The first type of agreement is one of proportion; the second, of proportionality. We find something predicated analogously of two realities according to the first type of agreement when one of them has a relation to the other, as when *being* is predicated of substance and accident because of the relation which accident has to substance . . .[29]

But in other passages St. Thomas does admit a distinctive mode of existence for accidents. However, the accidents are not to be conceived of as inferior types of substances. The mode of existence of substance is unlike that of accidents, and that is why accidents are not simply said *to exist* as substances are; rather, accidents *exist in* a substance; they modify the being of substance and are said to be *beings of a being*. Nevertheless, in a properly analogical way the accidents have a mode of existence comparable to their mode of essence and in this respect their existence differs from that of substance. In his treatise, *On Being and*

---

[25] See St. Thomas, *Commentary on the Metaphysics*, IV, lesson 1, no. 546.
[26] St. Thomas, *Commentary on the Metaphysics*, IV, lesson 1, no. 539.
[27] St. Thomas, *Commentary on the Metaphysics*, VII, lesson 4, no. 1352.
[28] St. Thomas, *Commentary on the Metaphysics*, XI, lesson 3, no. 2197.
[29] St. Thomas, *Truth*, q. 2, art. 11, c. Mulligan translation, I, p. 113.

Essence, St. Thomas says that through accidents a secondary kind of existence is attributed to substance:

> Hence the supervening accident, by union with its subject, does not cause the act of existing in which the thing subsists, rendering the thing a substantial being. Rather, it causes a certain *secondary act of existing,* without which the subsistent thing can be understood, as what is first can be understood without what is second.[30]

In the *Contra Gentiles,* St. Thomas says more explicitly that the existence of accidents is not that of substance, though the point he makes is brought out only incidentally in a theological context where he says that relationships in God are not accidents and do not have their own act of existence, whereas in creatures the contrary is true:

> Although, of course, one holds that there is a relation in God, it does not, for all that, follow that there is in God something which has a dependent being, for in us the relations have a dependent being because their being is other than the being of the substance. Hence, they have a proper mode of being in their proper essence, just as happens in the case of the other accidents. In view of the fact that all accidents are forms of a sort superadded to the substance and caused by the principles of the substance, it must be that their being is superadded to the being of the substance and dependent on that being.[31]

St. Thomas speaks of the being of substance and accident as differing both as to the mode of existence and of signification:

> [Some things are analogous] both according to signification and existence. This takes place when there is not complete identity either in meaning or in existence, as when *being* is predicated of substance and accident. With regard to these, the common nature must have some kind of existence in each of the members of which it is predicated though they differ according to greater or lesser perfection.[32]

Even to hold an opinion on whether or not accidents have their own act of existence, we must determine in what sense the word *properly* is to be used. In one sense "properly" is opposed to "secondarily" and in this sense we can say that God alone is *properly* called good, although we will also admit that goodness really exists in created reality. But "properly" can also be used in opposition to what is "not really so." In this way we can say that health is not really in a climate, although health can be predicated of a climate inasmuch as climate has an effect on human beings, in whom health really does exist. Although accidents cannot be said to exist "properly," if the term is used in opposition to "secondarily," they can be said to exist in this way if the term is used in opposition to what is "not really so."

---

[30] St. Thomas, *On Being and Essence,* Ch. 6, para. 3.

[31] St. Thomas, *Summa Contra Gentes,* IV, ch. 14, 12. O'Neil translation, Vol. IV, p. 102.

[32] St. Thomas, *Commentary on the Sentences,* I, d. 19, q. 5, art. 2, ad 1.

It seems that accidents have an existence peculiar to themselves. When bodies acquire qualities like color, heat, size, or when a man is educated, substances acquire perfections they did not have by the very reason that they are substances. Something new is added over and above the original perfection of the subject. Does this mean that accidents have an existence of their own? St. Thomas admits that all the categories of being have an existence that is different from the *is* that serves as the copula in propositions. But he also makes a distinction between the existence of substance and that of accidents. He says that existence properly and truly is said to belong only to substance.[33] According to St. Thomas, existence is properly predicated of the subject, which is first substance.[34] Substance is the proper subject of existence. On the other hand, accidents cannot be the underlying subjects of their own existence. Unlike substance, the essence and existence of an accident do not make up a true composite of which we can predicate existence in the real order of things. This would be the same as saying that accidents are really substances, though of an inferior kind.

But a twofold mode of existence can be predicated of the subject when an accidental perfection is added to the substance. St. Thomas says that accidents have their own proper mode of existence distinct from that of substance.[35] The accident is not the subject of accidental existence, for there is only one subject, namely, the subsistent being. But two really distinct modes of existence can be predicated of the same subject, namely substantial and accidental. Nor can these two modes really be identified. To identify them would lead to an untenable conclusion, namely, that the accidents are already contained in the original existence of the substance, and that substances are in act by reason of their own nature. It is true that there is no *essential* change in the existence of a substance when it acquires accidental perfections. But if the existence of accidents is not really different from that of substance, then accidents *do not really add a perfection* to a substance.

Furthermore, if accidents do not have their own mode of existence, it would follow that there is no real distinction in being between the essence of accident and its existence (cf. Chapter VIII, p. 187 ff.). However, the doctrine of the real distinction of essence and existence in creatures (which is really the distinction between potency and act) is applicable both to accidents and substance. If not, a capacity for an accidental perfection is really the same as its actuality.

Finally, if accidents do not really have a distinct kind of existence, then their existence must be that of the subject. It seems incongruous

---

[33] See *Summa Theologiae*, I, q. 90, art. 2, c.

[34] Though existence is not of the essence of any creature, this does not mean that the existence of the substance is a predicamental accident.

[35] See *Summa Contra Gentiles*, IV, 14.

that two orders of being could thus unite in one act of existence. Existence is the ultimate perfection of a being. Hence the view that denies the proper being of accidents would end in the conclusion that accidents are the same as substance. Existence is the ultimate perfection of a being; it is the actuality to which essence is in potency. The existence of acquired accidents cannot, then, be the existence of the original substance. There would be only one existence but two essences (one of which is taken in the analogical sense).

On this point we feel that the denial of a special mode of existence to accidents comes from a univocal conception of existence. We hold that there is a proper proportionality between substance and accident as to signification and existence, just as there is, for example, between the truth in the mind of God and that of man.

The Relationship of Substance to Its Accidents

The metaphysical notion of being is an analogical, intensive notion. The relationship of substance to its accidents is not to be calculated according to a quantitative or numerical scale but according to an intensive, analogical, perfective conception of substance. Thus it would be incorrect to view substance and its accidents as a multiplicity of beings, numerically distinct, as though accidents were miniature types of substance, or species of some common genus. Only material things that have some common genus are subject to strict numerical description.

Accidents are specifications of substance. There is only one subject of being, namely, substance. But substance can be more or less perfect either in its entitative or in its operational character, for it is correctly said that a substance manifests itself through its accidents. This is not to deny that there is a real distinction between substance considered in itself and its accidental modes of being. Every created substance is a potency with respect to its accidental modes for a reason that will be developed later, namely, that potency and act in every imperfect being are really distinct. This distinction holds even in the state of possession of the accidental form by the substance. However it would be a mistake to think of the nine categories of accidents as constituting *nine beings* distinct from substance. If accidents are beings at all it is only because of a relationship to what is primarily signified as being, namely, substance.

The substance may be considered in itself, and in this case it is seen to be other than the accidental forms to which it is "joined" in the composite. The accidents may be considered in themselves but they cannot be defined without reference to their subject. Finally, one can consider the substance as specified by its accidents; this is what we designate as the *thing* or the *composite*. Is the *thing* an *unum per se*? In one sense it is not and in another sense it is. It is not an *unum per se* in the sense that the essence of the substance is to be identified with the accidental modes of being, for the states of potency and act, as characteristic of contingent beings, are really distinct. But the *thing* is an *unum per se* in the sense that a substance and its accidents make up one being, since no imperfect being can be without some form or other of accidental specification. This is precisely the point — only pure act is without the accidental specifications that are implied by contingent being. The *perfection* (in an analogical sense) of contingent beings is brought about by their accidents. That is why we think it is more correct to speak of an intensive, analogical union of substance and its accidents rather than a quantitative or numerical unity that would constitute, as it were, an aggregate in which heterogeneous parts having some kind of common genus in matter come together.

The intensive, analogical kind of unity is to be found, for example, in living beings. In his consideration of the soul and its powers, St. Thomas refers to the powers as proper accidents and says that they are distinct from the essence of the soul. He goes on to say that the operations of the powers are distinct both from the substance of the soul and from its powers inasmuch as no created being is in act by reason of itself. The substantial unity of living beings as manifested in the vital operations is a unity of intensity and not one of extension. It is only by an indirect process that one can enumerate the various activities of the living being, namely, by referring them to the measurable corporeal aspects of the organs of the various powers. For example, the activity of understanding is the act of the intellect, exercised through the medium of an organ, the brain, which has measurable corporeal aspects.

CHAPTER V

Potency and Act; Essence and Existence

The knowledge of being in substance and accidents is one view of the analogy of being; there is a second view that is much more important for the metaphysician. In his *Commentary on the Metaphysics*, St. Thomas points out this development in the doctrine of being when he says that after the first division into the categories the philosopher takes up a second division of being into potency and act.[1] After investigating the analogous character of being as discerned in the various objects of sense experience — primarily in sensible substances and then in the accidents that are proportionate to them — one enters upon a path of metaphysical analogy that leads upward to a new understanding of being. Here one can see that imperfect being is directed toward the perfect, that the substances and the accidents of the predicamental world constitute a state of imperfection with respect to a higher world of being. This movement will eventually lead us to the knowledge of a First Cause that is pure actuality. However, we are still engaged at this point in the critical examination of finite beings, for it is from an examination of the principles of finite things that reason leads us to accept the existence of the infinite.

One of the most profound observations that philosophers have made about the world of sense experience is that it is composed of contrary elements, not in the sense of elements in conflict, but in the sense of correlative but imperfect principles like those found in moving and growing substances. Ours is a world tending toward perfection, not one of achievement. The inner construction of this world reveals itself as a

---

[1] See St. Thomas, *Commentary on the Metaphysics*, IX, lesson 1, nos. 1768–1769.

composite of potential and actual being, as one of partially attained goodness with an ever present capacity for greater good.

The Meaning of Potency

What is the point of departure for a general discussion of act and potency? Since our knowledge of act and potency is a reflection of the world of beings in motion, we shall begin our investigation with an analysis of potency in its broadest meaning. It is not a question whether potency is chronologically prior to act or whether act is before potency, because all potencies trace their origin to being in act. Here we are concerned with the order of learning.

Although the starting point will be a description of potency as discovered in beings of the sensible order, it is not the intention of the metaphysician to limit himself to potency of this kind. He wants to know potency insofar as it can be applied to his proper subject, namely common being, which includes *all* beings, even those that can exist and be defined without matter. Yet it is from our knowledge of this type of potency that we are led to grasp the meaning of a higher potency, the kind that is found in spiritual beings.

The universal notion of potency in the metaphysical sense is taken from an active principle really existing in things. This is active potency or the ability to effect change in others. There is also a *potency in the passive sense*, but its meaning is to be gathered from our knowledge of active potency, since the change that takes place in a subject with passive potency is due to an active potency. All potencies are, in fact, reducible to the kind of potency that is the original principle of change in another insofar as it is other. It can happen that both active and passive potency will exist in the same subject, as when a living being moves itself, but even there the active principle cannot be identical with the passive. The passive potency is a capacity to receive something from something else. Therefore the very definition of passive potency presupposes an active potency.

All other kinds of potency in animate and inanimate, rational and irrational, spiritual and corporeal things are related by analogy with the primary notion of active potency found in the changeable things of nature. Just as the nature of life differs in various animated beings, so does the nature of potency differ in a proportional manner among all the potencies except those that are equivocally so named.

The etymology of the word *potency* will help us understand the general metaphysical meaning of potency and show how the name is predicated analogically.

The name *potency* was first used to signify the power of man, as when we say that some men are powerful . . . Then the name was transferred to things in nature. Among men he is recognized as potent who can do what he wants with other things and is not impeded; to the extent that he can be impeded, his power is diminished. The potency of someone, or of a natural agent, is impeded (even in the case of a being with volition) insofar as it can be impeded by another. Therefore, as regards the meaning of potency in its first use as a name, the reference is to the not-being-affected by another. Hence what cannot be acted upon, even though it cannot act, is called *potent*, as in the case of something hard which does not have the potency to be cut. . . .

In answer to the first objection we say that the notion of primary potency does not signify matter according to its more proper signification, because, as we said, the name *potency* was first used to signify a principle of action. Later it was transferred to mean that whatever receives the action of an agent is said to have a potency. This is passive potency. Just as the operation or action in which an active potency is completed corresponds to active potency, so what corresponds to passive potency as its perfection and complement is called act.[2]

The Reality of Potency as a Mode of Being

The denial of the reality of potency as something distinct from actuality is not an antiquated view held only by some early Greek philosophers against whom Aristotle argued. In our day the reality of potency is implicitly denied by most pragmatic philosophers and explicitly by contemporary atheistic existentialists. The denial of potency is a fundamental position of contemporary existentialism, for this deterministic philosophy of being recognizes nothing except what is — potency, tendency, essence, purpose mean nothing apart from the actuality, the inexorable law of fact. In the statements of the Greek determinists the error appeared more obvious because it was not hidden behind esoteric vocabulary. They simply said that everything happens by necessity; what does not take place is impossible; what takes place is possible only because it is. For example, the carpenter who is not actually building does not have the potency to build; if he is actually building, he can build.

The denial of potency seems so contrary to common sense that we might wonder how anyone could propose it as a philosophical point of view. But it does not sound so strange to one who accepts the position that *whatever is has to be just as it is.* Given the accumulation of elements and conditions at any given moment, then nothing other than what actually is could possibly be. This position does not deny that something comes to be, in an incidental sense, but it does deny that

---

[2] St. Thomas, *Commentary on the Sentences*, I, d. 42, q. 1, art. 1, c, and ad 1.

there can be a real potentiality to something that will never be realized and it does deny substantial becoming. What *will be will be*, because it has already been absolutely predetermined in the elements that already exist. To speak of a state of potency apart from what already is implies that there is real contingency in nature. This is not acceptable to determinist or existentialist philosophers. They will admit that there can be ignorance of what is and, therefore, they admit the idea of potentiality in the mind of the observer, but they will not admit objective contingency that implies a state of indeterminism in reality itself.

How is one to argue against this point of view? There are several possible ways. One is to show by a dialectical argument what the logical conclusion of this position is — a conclusion that should be untenable even for its proponents. Another way is to show that this position takes only the logical interpretation of the meaning of possible[3] and does not take into account a real tendency in being toward what is more perfect.

The dialectical argument could take the following form. If one holds that there is potency in a being only when it has been actualized, these conclusions would follow: (1) a person would have an art or a skill only when he is using it, so that he would have it and lose it many times each day; (2) the sensible and intelligible qualities of things are real only when they are being known (This was the view of Protagoras in ancient times.); (3) a person would be blind and deaf many times a day, because frequently he would not be using his powers of sensation; (4) if a person is not acting he cannot act, hence he never could begin to act.

All of these conclusions are evidently false. Hence the argument puts the one who denies potency in a dilemma: Either he must admit that potency is real and distinct from activity; or he must admit that the conclusions stated above are correct.

The contrary of the position that denies real potency holds that all things are possible and that nothing is impossible. But what makes a thing impossible? It is not necessary that what is possible or potential actually come to be; nevertheless, it seems unreasonable to hold that all things are possible, even though some of them will never come to be. To be impossible is not the same as to be false. For example, if I say that you are standing when you are sitting, the statement is false, but it is not impossible that you stand. Some things, however, are both false and impossible. In determining what makes a thing possible or impossible we must first make a distinction regarding the meaning of *potency* and *possibility*.

The name *potency* or possible has a twofold meaning, one of which

---

[3] See below, p. 87 ff.

refers to a *positive capacity with respect to coming-to-be* and another which refers to *noncontradiction*.[4] Used by the metaphysician the first meaning of potency or possibility means something that is not actual but is capable of being or becoming actual or acting in a certain way. The first meaning of potency implies a radical contingency in being, because its actualization cannot be realized through its own capacity. The actuality is something over and above the potency and must be brought about by an agent already in act and really distinct from the potency. For example, an artist has a potency or capacity to paint. The actual painting is something quite different, for it may be done or not done. A walnut log has a potency to be made into a statue or it has a potency to produce heat. It may never become the one or do the other, and the reason is that the agent required to actualize the potency never acted upon what was only a potency in a subject.

Possibility is judged not only by the necessity of the formal cause. One must include the efficient and final causes (especially the idea of a free efficient cause), if he is to speak of possible in the sense of contingency.

The notion of possibility in the sense of *noncontradiction*, as used by the logician for example, is identical with the notion of essence. The possibility of a being in this sense is the same as its necessity. Whatever is, in this view, cannot be other than it actually is, because it is precisely what its causes made it to be and it cannot be anything else without denying its own being.

Hence it is logical for those who admit only this meaning of possible to deny its reality in the sense of contingency. If, with the determinist, one says that the possible is the necessary, then it would be absurd to say that anything is *possible*. Furthermore, such a statement would imply that some nonpredetermined cause exists. Hence for a determinist to say that "nothing is possible" is the same as saying "everything is possible." It would mean the same thing because *everything* means the same as *what actually exists* — the rest would merely be a being of the mind. *Thus whatever is is possible, and whatever is not is unthinkable*, for to say what is possible is to say all that is. One is back in the Parminedean view that all being is eternal and that nothing comes to be.

What could one who does not believe in a transcendent intelligence give as a criterion of what is possible and what is impossible? He would have to agree with those whose only criterion is: *What is is possible; what is not is impossible*. There would be no other way of judging whether something is possible than the fact that a thing exists. This is the point of view of the atheistic existentialists whose only criterion is

---

[4] St. Thomas, *Commentary on the Metaphysics*, IX, lesson 3, nos. 1811–1812.

existence. Essences are subsequent to existence, for they are only the thought which one has about what he sees to exist. Unlike Descartes who believed in God but posited the will of God as the ultimate criterion of what is possible, these philosophers can have no objective basis either in knowledge or volition for judging what is possible or impossible, what is right or wrong, what is good or bad. If some basis is to be designated it will be the will of man who is confronted with the actual state of affairs. It is his to give some kind of meaning or essence to existence that defies any kind of objective intellectual classification.

Atheistic existentialists are absolute determinists because they do not think that anything is possible in the sense of being contingent. Therefore, they must hold that nothing really new comes into existence. Whatever will be, already is — for if something is not at a given time, it never will be. To say that something can come to be is to admit contingency; and to admit contingency in the world is to admit (at least it can be demonstrated) that there is an absolute cause somewhere. When the existentialists speak of possible, they can only mean possible in the sense of noncontradictory. But this can be shown to be an untenable position, even from the viewpoint of an atheistic existentialist. For unless there is a Mind that is the prototype of the reality that is, the words *possible* or *noncontradictory* as opposed to *contradictory* cannot really mean anything. To speak of something being contradictory or impossible presupposes the validity of the intellect which can grasp the essences of things. But to grasp the essences of things is to admit eventually that the truth of things depends upon some first Intellect. If one were to deny the existence of such an objective norm for truth, one would have to concede that there is no objective difference between what is possible and what is impossible, or between what is not-contradictory and what is contradictory. The words would all have the same meaning, since none of them would have an objective basis for differentiation. Thus, for an existentialist to say that nothing is possible is the same as saying that everything is possible. This does not mean that an existentialist would expressly accept this position; but many self-contradictory positions in philosophy are unwittingly accepted.

Thus in contemporary existentialism we have a concrete example of how metaphysical problems and metaphysical principles transcend a particular period in history, for this philosophy is at root a revival of a position that Aristotle had confronted over 2000 years ago.

The Meaning of Act

We can further clarify the general meaning of potency by investigating its correlative principle of being, act. As with potency, the definition of act is derived by way of analysis from examples. Since the best examples for learning are those closest to experience, the philosopher uses examples from things of sense experience and from either the practical or fine arts. Although the examples do not rise above the material universe, they are like a branch from which a bird takes flight: once the metaphysician is aware of the basic analogical meaning of act, he can rise to the immaterial world of activity and leave for the moment his point of departure.

The first notion of act is that of *perfection* that comes to things that are in a state of potency. Examples are the form that can be put into matter, the movement of which a body in a state of rest is capable, the knowledge that a person can master, the art or skill that a person can use, seeing in one who has the power of sight. Thus act is known as a correlative of potency — not a correlative on the same plane of existence, like a biological correlative, male and female, but on the plane of the more perfect related to the imperfect, the achievement related to the capacity, for act and potency are two states of being within the same genus.

There are several distinct but not altogether unlike meanings of act: First, act can refer to a *form that is present in a subject*, as the form of Napoleon is present, for example, in bronze. This matter-form relationship is found in either the substantial or accidental order, as when it is said that the soul of man is his form or that the shape of his fingers is the form of his fingers. Second, act can refer to *activity*. This presupposes the existence of a subject with natural or acquired powers. This notion of act is more obvious to us than the first, because what first strikes the senses is movement, from which the presence of a form or nature that is its principle can be deduced. This is the way that Aristotle, for example, goes about proving the nature of the soul. Third, act can refer to things that are in the *state of becoming*, midway between act and potency. Biological growth is an example of this: it is not mere potency because the organism has already begun to exercise its vital power but it has not achieved the goal toward which that power is directed. A fourth meaning of act, one that St. Thomas stressed above all, is what he called the "greatest of all perfections," or the "actuality of all things," namely the *act of existence* that is proper to every substance.[5] This is act in its fullest meaning because here act is related most fully to the meaning of potency as essence. We shall subsequently develop more fully this relationship of essence and existence as the more mature expression of the doctrine of potency and act.

Analogous Notion of Act

Among the kinds of acts just mentioned, there are some that are

[5] See *De Potentia*, q. 7, art. 2, ad 9; *Summa Theologiae*, I, q. 4, art. 1, ad 3.

essentially related directly to movement and others that are not. This distinction is useful as an insight into the analogous character of act and will be of great importance in studying the transcendentals and the analogical perfection of the First Cause of being. Aristotle said that there is no end in the kind of act that entails movement *per se*.[6] Let us take, for example, the process of learning. One could say that there is an end *per accidens* of learning, but the end does not belong to the movement as such. But there is connected with learning another kind of act, and in connection with this we can speak of an end in the strict sense. This end is the purpose or perfection to be achieved, namely knowledge or truth.

Knowledge, which is the end of learning, is a perfection of the intellect. It does not by its nature involve movement or any imperfection. It is an end in the fullest sense. But learning itself necessarily implies imperfection. This is important for a correct notion of education. Is it the learning process or the effect of learning that is the goal of education? Learning is not of itself an imperfect state of knowing. The two are on different planes of being. That is why knowledge can be attributed to God but learning cannot. Even in man *learning*, which entails a kind of movement, is not identical with the possession of knowledge. For example, the term *learning* would be used improperly with reference to divinely revealed faith, for there is no learning process that will lead directly to faith. One does not learn the virtue of faith. Knowledge is an act specifically different from learning and requires a distinct act of illumination of the intellect. Knowledge is an immanent act, a vision, that consists in an identity between the knower and the known. The word *vision* does not apply properly to the learning process itself except insofar as we are using the word in its broadest sense to include not only the process but the truth which comes about partially through its instrumentality.

Thus we set up a distinction between act which is movement in the proper sense and act which is perfection. In the first case the movement in the strict sense always includes a continuity from the starting point, through the medium, to the conclusion. Movement in this sense is found, according to St. Thomas: (1) in local motion; (2) in quantitative increase and decrease; (3) in alteration between two contraries. Therefore in the viewpoint expressed by Aristotle and approved by St. Thomas, we see that there are two kinds of act:

1) one whose definition has no essential connection with imperfection in any order (whether in the infinite or finite);

2) another whose very definition necessarily implies imperfection. Acts of this kind are called movements.

---

[6] See *Metaphysics*, IX, ch. 6, 1048b 14 ff.

Many other subdivisions of potency and act might be exemplified and defined, but we are concerned at this time only with the general definition of potency and act insofar as they show the intrinsic analogical character of the subject of metaphysics, common being, as found in the categories of common experience.

A Comparison of Potency and Act

The next point St. Thomas covers in his *Commentary on the Metaphysics* is a comparison of the two principles of act and potency.

The priority of act in definition. Act is said to be prior to potency from the viewpoint of definition. The primary meaning of potency in general, as we say, comes from active potency, which seems to presuppose some knowledge of act. But, if we define potency through act, and if we come to realize what act is by comparison with potency, are we not in a vicious circle in defining terms?

It is true that what we first know is act in the sense of *actual being*. But all our knowledge originates through beings in motion. We do not know act in itself, for we cannot have a *proper* conception of act apart from its correlative potency. We come to know what act is by examples ("analogies," as Aristotle says). These examples are part of a dynamic process of learning. In themselves they express the actuality of things without giving a clear understanding of act or potency as such. The knowledge of act gained through examples is prescientific knowledge presupposed in a metaphysical analysis of potency. Nevertheless, from examples the intellect can derive a metaphysical understanding of act. Therefore, the knowledge of potency presupposes at least a prescientific knowledge of actuality. Act itself can be defined only through examples, for in the origin of knowledge we cannot presuppose something prior to actuality, since all knowledge is caused by being in act.

The priority of act in time. The being in act is of the same species as the being in potency. Aristotle argues that act must precede potency in any given species. The man in act precedes semen which is man in potency. The *individual* potency, however, precedes the *individual* actuality to which it tends, just as the semen which is potentially a man precedes in time the human being that is generated from it. In any given order act precedes potency if we consider the relationship from the order of universal causes. Absolutely speaking, and in a context that includes analogical causes, it is contradictory to suppose that potency precedes actuality, for this would be the equivalent of saying that being comes from nonbeing. But here a difficulty arises. If it is true, as Aristotle says, that "from the potentially existing the actually existing is always produced by an actually existing thing, e.g., man from man, and musician by musician,"[7] doesn't this mean that there is an infinite series of acts in each category? Would it not mean, for example, that there could be no real coming-to-be of a musician unless there were a musician to produce the new musician? Would there not be an infinite number of musicians? Or is God the first musician?

This difficulty can be solved if we admit that whatever comes to be can participate analogously in what already has the perfection. All coming-to-be is a participation by an imperfect subject in actual being. If we attempt to answer this difficulty from a univocal consideration of priority and posteriority, or of cause and effect, we shall be entangled in a contradiction. There must be "*something of the actual*" already existing, but this something need not be unconditionally the same as that which comes to be. Otherwise nothing new would ever come to be. Thus the artist already "contains" the form that he will introduce into the wood or stone. The cause need not contain the effect in a univocal way, but can contain it in an analogous or eminent way.

The priority of act in substance.   Although the essence of natural substances is not form alone, but matter and form, it is principally to the form that we owe our knowledge of the material substances with which we are most familiar. This form is sometimes called the essence of substance because this form, the specific element of composite being, renders natural beings intelligible, rather than matter which all natural beings have in common. Matter itself can be known only through form since by definition it is a capacity for form and is nothing determinate in itself. But matter is part of the essence. Matter is related to form as the potential principle of the essence to the actual principle of the essence. Though matter and form in a composite substance are not related to each other in exactly the same way that the power of sight and actual sight are related, the likeness is analogous according to proper proportionality.

What is true of the relationship of potency and act in natural beings is true in its own way of the entire relationship of natural beings to incorruptible spiritual beings. For with respect to both the existence and the activity of natural beings, immaterial substances are like act compared to potency. For corruptible beings are caused by and are orientated toward a spiritual world. This point will be brought out in the last part of metaphysics that treats of the relationship of natural substances to a transcendent First Cause.

The priority of act in goodness and truth.   Let us begin with a question: Is the good toward which a potency naturally tends prior to the potency? There are two aspects of this question. First, is the final cause

---

[7] *Metaphysics*, IX, ch. 8, 1049 b 24.

superior to the good to be attained by the potency? To this question we answer that the goal of any natural tendency must be superior to the potency, because it is the state of perfection as compared to the state of imperfection. If there is any tendency at all, it is because something better can be had; a tendency to what is worse is completely irrational. If there is order and intelligence in nature, the act toward which a potency tends has to be superior to the state of the unfulfilled capacity. This does not mean that there cannot be a corruption of what is good. But we do not speak of potency to a privation of what is had but to the possession of what is not had. Second, need the object of a potency already have existence? It is evident that the particular good which fulfills the particular potency is posterior in time to the potency. But the good which fulfills the potency must already have an intentional existence either in the mind of the proximate agent or in the intelligence of the Author of nature. The tendency can be present only to the extent that this idea is a tendency toward the real form. Potency decreases in proportion to the distance from the possibility of actual realization. But there is something even more than the conceptional (though possible) existence of the good that explains a tendency. The good attracts or pulls the efficient cause. And in order to pull, the good must exist in some real way. However, the good that is the fulfillment of a potency does not exist as this particular good, otherwise there would be no true becoming or production. But since this is a contingent good and not an absolute one, the goodness of this object of striving depends eventually on the existence of a transcendent self-contained good, for the reality of a contingent good is dependent upon the existence of a transcendent good. The same kind of reasoning applies to truth. Consequently, in an absolute sense act is prior to potency in goodness and in truth.

Limitation of Act by Potency

One of the most important and far-reaching principles of the metaphysics of St. Thomas is that concerning the limitation of act by potency. The meaning of this principle can be manifested by taking a concrete example of the limitation of act by potency. When an artist, let us say a sculptor, has hit upon an idea that he would like to work with, his thoughts may be well defined as to shape, color, character, position of the figures. But his total idea still retains a kind of indeterminateness until the medium in which the artist wants to express his idea is selected. In selecting a certain medium, he finds restrictions put upon his idea by the type of material he is working with. Thus the medium of stone may not restrict him as much as the medium of clay, and a medium of wood may not limit him as much as a medium of stone. Furthermore, one kind of wood will limit him more than another. And even in the same kind of wood one sample will be more difficult to work with than another.

The doctrine of the limitation of act by potency in terms of limitation of forms by matter is clearly contained in Aristotle's Metaphysics. However, one will notice that in the examples Aristotle employs the doctrine of the limitation of act by potency is found only in those subjects that undergo change. Did Aristotle see the broader implications of this metaphysical principle? For example, did he see that this principle is not only applicable to the changes that take place in the physical world but also universally applicable to the order of predicamental substance? And did he see that the principle was applicable to an even deeper metaphysical area, namely, that of the limitation of existence by essence? In the ninth book of the Metaphysics, Aristotle does make a distinction between those acts which are ends in themselves, such as the act of understanding, and those acts which are essentially a process of becoming, analogous to the process of walking or reducing. Often Aristotle uses examples from art to make his point, but in his examples it is not clear that the principle of limitation of act by potency is a principle that applies to perfections such as knowledge, love, life and the like (perfections that we call simple perfections in contrast with such things as the movement of the sense appetites, reasoning, etc.). Nor is it clear that Aristotle saw that the principle of the limitation of act by potency is universally applicable to the order of imperfect substance through a composition in substance of essence and existence. We shall not try to answer this historical and textual problem,[8] but shall limit ourselves to what St. Thomas taught on this point, insofar as this can be gathered from various passages in his philosophical and theological writings. We shall merely comment briefly on several statements from the writings of St. Thomas in which he speaks of the limitation of act by potency. In a later part of this book we shall return to the more profoundly metaphysical question of the limitation of existence by essence as the basis of the real distinction between essence and existence.

The first text that we shall employ to manifest the teaching of St. Thomas on the limitation of act by potency is taken from the Summa Theologiae, in which he is speaking of the diversity in the perfection of understanding among men:

> One may understand the same thing better than someone else, through having a greater power of understanding; just as a man may see a thing better with his bodily sight, whose power is greater and whose sight is more perfect. This same thing applies to the intellect in two ways. First,

8 "The Limitation of Act by Potency," by W. Norris Clarke, S.J., in the New Scholasticism, Vol. XXVI, No. 2, April, 1952, pp. 167–194.

as regards the intellect itself, which is more perfect. For it is plain that the better the disposition of a body, the better is the soul allotted to it; which clearly appears in things of different species. The reason for this is that act and form are received into matter according to the capacity of matter; and thus because some men have bodies of better disposition, their souls have a greater power of understanding.[9]

In other texts, St. Thomas makes the general statement that act is limited by reason of the potency into which it is received. For example, in the *Compendium Theologiae*, he says:

> No act is found to be limited except through the potency which receives it; thus we find forms limited according to the potency of matter.[10]

And in the *Contra Gentiles*, he says:

> Every act inhering in another is terminated by that in which it inheres, since what is in another is in it according to the mode of the receiver. Hence an act that exists in nothing is terminated by nothing.[11]

St. Thomas' view is based on the fact that perfections such as existence, life, and goodness are not limited by themselves, for in their definition there is no evidence of a principle of limitation. If such perfections are found limited and multiplied in various individuals, the limitation must come from something outside the perfection itself.

One might think that in his position on the limitation of act by potency, St. Thomas has involved himself in a circular form of argumentation. Cannot one ask that if act is limited by potency, and potency also is limited, how potency can be limited except by act? For nothing can be the principle of its own limitation, just as nothing can be the efficient cause of its own existence. In answer to this difficulty we can say that potency and act are mutual causes and principles in different orders. Act limits potency insofar as act is the end toward which the potency tends. Thus potency is limited by act in the order of *final causality*, as every power is limited by the kind of object which makes it to be the kind of potency that it is. It is according to this principle of Thomistic metaphysics that we say that powers or potencies are specified by their formal objects.[12] On the other hand, in the order of coming-to-be, act is limited or specified by the potency into which it is received. In this respect, potency is a *material cause* with reference to act. This point is clearly contained in the texts cited from St. Thomas, for example, in the text where he says that understanding is limited by the individual capacity of the intellect, and that the individual capacity of the intellect is limited by the matter into which it is received.

---

[9] St. Thomas, *Summa Theologiae*, I, q. 85, art. 7, c.

[10] St. Thomas, *Compendium Theologiae*, ch. 18, par. 35.

[11] St. Thomas, *Contra Gentiles*, Bk. I, ch. 43. For parallel texts, see *On Spiritual Creatures*, art. 1; *Commentary on the Sentences*, Bk. 2, dist. 3, q. 2, art. 1, ad 5.

[12] See St. Thomas, *Summa Theologiae*, Part I, q. 77, art. 3, c.

Much of the difficulty regarding the principle of the limitation of act by potency comes from looking upon the two principles of act and potency as complete and independently existing realities, rather than as the mutual causes that they are. Act and potency do not exist in any isolated fashion. Even in the stage of potency prior to actualization, as realized in the intellect prior to a particular act of understanding, one can speak of intellectual potency only because of an existing actuality, namely, a power existing in the soul. Potency should not be identified with mere possibility. At no point can real potency prescind completely from the act of existence, for potency, in the sense of a component principle of real being, is more than mere possibility; it is already related in a positive way to existence. The subject in which potency exists is an existing subject. And the good toward which potency is directed must already exist at least according to the species or kind of actuality that is to be attained, if not in numerically the same way that it will exist when the potency is actualized. In other words, unless there is a real good toward which the potency tends, there will not be any tendency or potency. The reality of this good, however, is not to be understood in a univocal sense but rather in the analogical sense that is proper to the science of metaphysics. This point will be developed more fully in the chapter which deals with the principle of final causality.

Essence and Existence

One source for St. Thomas' teaching on essence and existence is a small work, *On Being and Essence*, written during the first years of his teaching at the University of Paris, probably about the year 1254. The purpose of the treatise was to clarify some fundamental notions on being and essence, first by explaining how logical terms differ from metaphysical ones, and then, after showing what essence means for the metaphysician, by concluding that in all creatures there is a real distinction between essence and existence. This distinction was not unknown before St. Thomas, but he explained it much more fully and used it as one of the fundamental principles upon which his natural theology was to be built.

The meaning of essence. St. Thomas says that the knowledge of essence comes after the knowledge of being. By this he means that we know being, taken as the existing reality (a composite of essence and the act of existing), before we come to a knowledge of the essence taken by itself. This knowledge of being belongs to the mode of prescientific or common-sense knowing that naturally comes before a strict philosophical analysis. The meaning of essence is discovered in those beings that belong in the categories, primarily in substance and by analogy in accidents.[13] Beings of the mind do not have an essence in the strict sense because they do not have a real relation to the act of existence. For example, there is no essence of blindness, but only a description, by negation, namely, the absence of a power that should exist in higher animals.

The word *essence* signifies that by which things are placed in different categories of being. There are various names that are used as synonyms for essence, such as *definition* (the Latin *quidditas* or *quod quid erat esse*), *form*, and *nature*. The definition gives an answer to the question that one might ask when he sees something new: "What is it?" This word also expresses the direction that nature takes, the effect that it intends, thus giving a response to the question: "What was it meant to be?" The word *form*, taken from the act by which a thing is formed, as clay is formed by the potter, tells how a being impresses itself upon our senses or upon our intellect. Form[14] is that which is specific in being in contradistinction to matter, the underlying common substratum, as wood, for example, which can be made into the figure of a man or into a table, is common to various artificial forms. The word *nature* is taken in the sense of the intrinsic principle of operation by which a being acts in a way proper to its kind. In other words, it is essence from the viewpoint of its proper activity. It expresses the dynamic character of being.

Essence has a meaning over and above that contained in its synonyms. It tells more than what a thing is, how it appears to us, or how it acts — it directs one's attention to the reality that constitutes the world and about which we have knowledge. "Essence means that through which and in which a being has its act of existing (*esse*)."[15]

The essence of natural substances. Essence, as a principle of being, is not a univocal term applying in exactly the same way to substance and accidents in the natural order or to natural and to transphysical substance and accidents. The essence of natural beings is not form alone but form and matter. Proof of this in the case of man is given in Thomistic psychology where the essential union of matter and form is shown to hold not only in the union of soul and body as substantial principles but also in the subsequent operations of the powers of the soul. Not only the activities of the vegetative and sensory powers but

---

[13] Since being is predicated absolutely and primarily of substances and in a qualified sense of accidents, essence is found truly and properly in substances. In accidents it is present only in a qualified sense. See *On Being and Essence*, ch. 1.

[14] In this context the form implicitly includes the matter, because the essence of natural substances is the total determining principle that is actualized by the act of existence. Cf. *On Being and Essence*, ch. 1.

[15] *On Being and Essence*, ch. 1, translated by Armand Maurer (Toronto: Pontifical Institute of Mediaeval Studies, 1949).

also the powers of reason and will manifest this essential unity, a view-point confirmed by more and more evidence from experimental psychology.

A clear statement of the composition of matter and form in natural beings is found at the beginning of Chapter 2 of the treatise *On Being and Essence:*

> Form and matter are found in composite substances, for example, soul and body in man. It cannot be said, however, that either one of these alone is called the essence. That matter alone is not the essence of a thing is evident, for through its essence a thing is knowable and fixed in its species and genus. But matter is not a principle of knowledge, nor does it determine anything in a genus or species. Only that which is actually something does this. Neither can the form alone of a composite substance be called its essence, although some would endeavor to assert it. For it is evident from what has been said that *essence is what the definition of a thing signifies*. Now, the definition of physical substances includes not only form but matter; otherwise there would be no difference between physical and mathematical definitions. Neither can it be said that the definition of a physical substance includes matter as something added to its essence, or as a being outside of its essence, because this manner of definition is proper to accidents, which do not have a perfect essence. That is the reason why the definition of accidents must include their sub-ject which is outside their genus. . . .
>
> Reason likewise is in agreement with this, because the act of existing of a composite substance belongs neither to the form alone nor to the matter alone, but the composite itself. Now, essence is that according to which a thing is said to be. On this account, the essence by which a thing is called a being, cannot be either form alone or matter alone, but is the two together, even though the form alone in its own way is the cause of such an act of existing.[16]

The matter which is a co-principle of a natural essence is called by St. Thomas *common matter* to distinguish it from *designated matter* which is the principle of individuation. The metaphysical essence as such is neither an abstracted or logical universal nor is it a particularized being, for it is something apart from both these modes of existence — the one exists only as a being of reason, the other only in the individual. If the matter that belongs to the essence of man were only a logical abstraction, it could not be predicated of a real man; and if it were only individual, it could not be a common predicate of all men. St. Thomas is quite clear in explaining what he means by the common matter that belongs to the essence of man:

> However, since matter is the principle of individuation, it might perhaps seem to follow that the essence which includes within itself both matter and form is only particular and not universal. If this were so, it would follow that, the essence being what the definition signifies, universals would have no definition. Hence we must realize that the matter which is

---

[16] St. Thomas, *On Being and Essence*, ch. 2, par. 1 and 3 (Maurer trans.), pp. 30–31.

the principle of individuation is not any matter whatsoever, but only designated matter. By designated matter I mean matter considered under determined dimensions. Now, we do not include matter of this sort in the definition of man as man, but we would include it in Socrates' definition if Socrates had a definition. The definition of man, however, does include undesignated matter. For we do not include in the definition of man this particular bone and this particular flesh, but only bone and flesh, which are the undesignated matter of man.[17]

Logical and real composition in essence. As in the time of Aristotle, so in the time of St. Thomas certain philosophers, confusing the order of logic and the order of reality, held that the mind could not possess truth unless the logical composition of essence corresponded in every detail to the order of being. Thus, for example, the essence of man, taken as a logical whole, is composed of the genus *animal* and the specific difference *rational*. According to them, man's essence must be really composed of the form *animal* and the form *rational* even in the order of extramental reality. By showing that essence can be considered in three ways, one of which is metaphysical, St. Thomas avoided the difficulty about the predication of essential forms. Essence can be taken: (a) in its concrete existence as individualized; (b) in itself as prescinding both from individual existence and from logical existence; (c) as a logical universal existing as a being of the mind. This distinction is the foundation of the moderate realism of St. Thomas, for it avoids the extremes of both nominalism and exaggerated realism.

The essence in its third sense as a formal abstraction cannot be predicated of the individual. For example, it is incorrect to say: *John is humanity*, because humanity is only a formal part of the reality that is John. In predication there must be an identity between the subject and predicate — the whole is not identical with a part. But it is correct to say: *John is man* because *man* is the whole essence and contains potentially, or implicitly, whatever belongs to the entire individual. Hence St. Thomas can say:

> The word *man* and the word *humanity*, then, clearly signify man's essence, but as we have said, they do so in different ways. The word *man* expresses it as a whole, inasmuch as it does not exclude the designation of matter, but it contains it implicitly and indistinctly. As we said previously, the genus contains the difference. For this reason the word *man* is predicated of individuals. The word *humanity*, on the other hand, signifies man's essence as a part, because it signifies only what belongs to man, excluding all designation of matter. Therefore it is not predicated of individual men. And this is why we sometimes find the word *essence* predicated of a thing (for we say that Socrates is a certain essence), and sometimes denied (as when we say that Socrates' essence is not Socrates).[18]

---

[17] St. Thomas, *On Being and Essence*, ch. 2 (Maurer trans.), p. 32.
[18] St. Thomas, *On Being and Essence*, ch. 3 (Maurer trans.), p. 38.

The essence which is predicated when one says *John is man* is the essence taken absolutely, that is, neither as individualized nor as a logical universal. This is called the metaphysical essence. If the name *man* is simply individual, it is impossible to predicate the term in any significant way of several individual men since it would mean something different for each one. At the same time, one should not identify the individual named John with a logical universal that can exist only as a product of thought. When we say *John is man* and *Joseph is man* we mean that the judgment corresponds in an objective way with what exists.

The act of existence.[19]   Because of its stress on the act of existence rather than upon substantial form, Thomistic metaphysics is said to rise above Aristotelian metaphysics. Though he did not neglect the aspect of existence, Aristotle is thought to have been unable to free himself from the doctrine of form, a position that doubtlessly can be explained partially from his proximity to Plato. Perhaps the human mind was not yet ready to take this decisive step in metaphysics — perhaps it would never have made it except through the help of revelation.

Existence is called by St. Thomas the perfection of all perfections. Like the final cause it is the source of all other intermediary perfections. It is the goal of all movement among changeable beings. It is the perfection of every potency, for it is *that which makes them to be* in the fullest sense of the expression. Nothing can be added to existence that will make it more perfect, since everything that is good and true and beautiful is so because of its existence.

Existence, as we understand it here, signifies the highest perfection of all: and the proof is that act is always more perfect than potentiality. Now no signate form is understood to be in act unless it be supposed to have being. Thus we may take human nature or fiery nature as existing potentially in matter, or as existing in the power of an agent, or even as in the mind: but when it has existence it becomes actually existent. Wherefore it is clear that existence as we understand it here is the actuality of all acts, and therefore the perfection of all perfections. Nor may we think that existence, in this sense, can have anything added to it that is more formal and determines it as act determines potentiality: because existence in this latter sense is essentially distinct from that to which it is added and whereby it is determined. But nothing that is outside the range of existence can be added to existence: for nothing is outside its range except non-being, which can be neither form nor matter. Hence existence is not determined by something else as potentiality by act but rather as act by potentiality, since in defining a form we include its proper matter instead of the difference: thus we define a soul as the act of an organic physical body. Accord-

19 The question of the real distinction between essence and existence will be taken up in the final chapter where the formal demonstration of the real distinction is given in connection with the third way of demonstrating God's existence from the contingency of the beings of experience.

ingly this existence is distinct from that existence inasmuch as it is the existence of this or that nature.[20]

The essence is a potency with respect to the act of existence, because only those things are fully designated as substantial beings that have received existence. In a true sense, then, the most formal, that is, most perfective element of substance is existence and not substantial form.

> Being (esse) itself is the most perfect of all things, for it is compared to all things as that which is act; for nothing has actuality except so far as it is. Hence being is the actuality of all things, even of forms themselves. There-fore it is not compared to other things as the receiver is to the received, but rather as the received to the receiver. When therefore I speak of the being of man, or of a horse, or of anything else, being is considered as a formal principle, and as something received, and not as that to which being belongs.[21]

Contemporary existentialist philosophy, however, should be a warn-ing to us that in the consideration of being the act of existence cannot be isolated from essence. This kind of existentialism is contrary to true philosophy; it neglects the intelligibility of essence and is a corruption of true metaphysics. It is futile to try to divorce existence from essence. If extreme idealism is a sickness in the body of philosophy, its cure does not consist in annihilating the body. Whether sick or healthy, we cannot dispense with the body. Saying that something is more important does not mean that nothing else is important. Essence and existence are one like husband and wife in marriage: they constitute one bond, one purpose in being.

Although there is little danger that twentieth-century philosophy will soon revert to an exaggerated essentialism, there is a grave peril that more and more philosophers will turn to an exaggerated and isolated existentialism. Existentialism is a philosophy of action, and people of today are more interested in action than they are in understanding. Contemporary existentialism is at heart a voluntarist philosophy, a philosophy of action and not one of contemplation. Despite its attraction for men who are considered intellectuals, it is anti-intellectual because it is anti-intelligible. Existence apart from essence is not intelligible, for the act of existence by itself is not reducible to concepts, a point that "essence-less" existentialists try to hammer home. It seems much more important to contemporary existentialist philosophers, as it did to Marx, that philosophers "change the world rather than try to interpret it."[22]

For man "to be" means to live as a rational being. The existence of man cannot be identified with the kind of existence a stone or plant

---

[20] St. Thomas, *De Potentia*, q. 7, art. 2, ad 9.
[21] St. Thomas, *Summa Theologiae*, I, q. 4, art. 1, ad 3.
[22] See Marx's XIth Thesis against Feuerbach.

might have, for if man ceases to be rational he simply ceases to be. His existence cannot be isolated from his essence. That is why man cannot, in his knowledge of existing things, isolate their existence from their essence. They would just as surely cease to be, if essence were taken away from them, as they would if existence were taken away.

The indeterminate act of existence is not enough to constitute a being as first substance. The act of existence is not the same for all substances. The perfection of substance consists not simply in existing but in existing after the manner and with the perfection that is due to a particular essence or nature. To be a human substance means more than to exist as stones and plants do. The perfection of existence is achieved through the full development of one's nature and one's individual capacities. To fall short of this goal is to fail to some extent in existence. The analogy of being includes both the essential and the existential orders. This is the existential being of which metaphysics treats. Thus the order of being as well as the order of knowing ceases entirely, unless the bond of essence and existence is maintained.

Existence and the Individual

Like all truly metaphysical terms, the name *individual* is analogous. There are various kinds of individuality. There is what we might call numerical individuality. Instances are the individuality of one leaf of a tree as it differs from every other, or that of one man differing from every other man. When we compare individuals in a class we are presupposing an underlying univocity, for it is evident that the difference between one being and another in this kind of comparison is not due to the kind of nature each possesses. Our first notion of individuality comes from the numerical individuality in things that are separate from each other in space, though alike in nature. One criterion for judging this kind of individuation is the physical location of one being with respect to others. This kind of individuation is more evident in the order of substance, but it is also found in the order of accident. For example, the whiteness in one sheet of paper is numerically distinct from the whiteness in another. There is the same essence of whiteness in each case but the existence of whiteness is multiplied. Basically, however, the whiteness in one piece of paper is distinct from another because the subjects themselves are distinct in space. Individuation in this case is said to be due proximately to the quantity of extension of the material from which the substance is made. In many passages St. Thomas says that the formal principle of individuation in corporeal beings is quantity, or more properly matter as extended. For example, in the *Summa Contra Gentiles* he says:

Forms that are not predicated of subsisting things, whether these be considered universally or each is taken singly, are forms that do not subsist through themselves as singulars individuated in themselves. We do not say that Socrates, or man, or animal is whiteness, because whiteness does not subsist as a singular through itself but is individuated through its subsisting subjects. In the same way, also, natural forms do not subsist as singulars through themselves but are individuated in their proper matters. This is why we do not say that this fire, or fire, is its own form. The very essences or quiddities of genera and species are individuated through the *designated matter* of this or that individual, even though the quiddity of the genus or the species should include common form and matter. That is why we do not say that Socrates or man is humanity.[23]

This kind of individuation is properly restricted to sensible or corporeal beings in which there are quantitative aspects in the strict sense. We say quantitative *in the strict sense* because there is something analogous to quantitative measure in spiritual activities, as when, for example, it is said one can measure a person's intelligence. However, because intelligence is spiritual and quantity does not apply to it in a strict sense, one cannot measure spiritual properties as he would measure distance or count the number of matches in a box.

Numerical individuation is only one kind of individuation. Or we might say that it is only one side of individuation, for it can be compared to a mask that covers the true individuality. Material substance has a twofold aspect of individuality: the first is quantitative and allows the individual to be compared with other individuals in a class, as exemplified by the individual men that make up a group of men; the second is a perfection of being by which one being cannot be separated into parts without altering its character and significance. This is inner individuation. In our acts of free choice, each of us is aware of this second kind of individuation. This self-containment transcends numerical individuation. It is because one recognizes in himself an independence in existence by reason of his thoughts and desires that he knows that he is distinct from every other human being.

It is sometimes said that substances are individualized through their accidents. Thus we can differentiate one tree from another in a forest because of the size, shape, color, texture of the bark, and so on. We can distinguish one person from another by his walk, the tilt of his head, and so on. It is true that we ordinarily distinguish one person from another through accidental differences. But it is not basically due to accidental differences that substances are really distinct from each other. Even if the accidents were changed, the substances would not necessarily be changed; but if the substances in which the accidents exist were destroyed, then the accidental differences, too, would vanish.

---

[23] St. Thomas, *Summa Contra Gentiles*, I, 21, 4. Pegis translation, I, p. 117.

What difference is there between the individuality of particular accidents such as colors, shapes, and the like, and the individuality of substances themselves? It is not enough to say that the individuality of substance is greater than that of accidents, for the difference is more than qualitative or quantitative. Individuality is not merely a difference of degree but an analogical difference in the strict sense. The mode of individuality of accidents is not the same as that of substance and the individuality of corporeal substances is not the same as that of spiritual substances.

In a passage from the *Quodlibetalia*, St. Thomas speaks of the analogous character of individuality.

> Of the names that signify individuality, some are found in all classes of being such as the names *singular*, *particular*, and *individual*. Thus a designated whiteness is singular, particular, and individual. . . . Other names signify the individual only in the genus of substance, such as the name *hypostasis* which signifies an individual substance of a rational nature, or the name *supposite*, or a "thing of nature," none of which can be predicated of the designated whiteness even though the whiteness is individual. The reason for this is that those names signify something subsistent but accidents do not subsist. Likewise with regard to the parts of substances, although they are of the nature of subsistent things, they do not subsist of themselves but are in something else. Therefore, the above-mentioned names are not predicated of the parts as substances, for we do not say that this hand is a *hypostasis*, a person, or supposite, or a "thing of nature" even though one can say that it is something *individual*, *particular*, or *singular*, names that can be applied to accidents.[24]

Hence the individuality of accidents presupposes the individuality of the substance upon which they depend.

> Although universal and particular exists in every genus [that is, in all the categories and even in things that do not fit into the categories such as motion, aggregates, or works or art] nevertheless, in a special way the individual belongs to the genus of substance. For substance is individuated through itself, whereas the accidents are individuated by the subject, which is the substance. For this particular whiteness is called *this* because it exists in this particular subject. And so it is reasonable that the individuals of the genus substance should have a special name of their own; for they are called *hypostases* or *first substances*.
>
> Further still, in a more special and perfect way, the particular and the individual are found in rational substances, which have dominion over their own actions, and which are not only made to act, as are others, but act of themselves; for actions belong to singulars. Therefore, individuals of a rational nature even have a special name among other substances; and this name is *person*.[25]

---

24 St. Thomas, *Quodlibetalia*, IX, q. 2, art. 2.
25 St. Thomas, *Summa Theologiae*, I, q. 29, art. 1, c.

Individuality and Subsistence

We have seen that the act of existence not only completes the essence or nature in the order of substance and makes it possible to be the subject of predication, but it also sets this essence apart from other substances so that it cannot be predicated of them. Hence individuality in the metaphysical sense has a special relation to the act of existence, the final perfection of substance. In both the substantial and accidental order existence brings about individuality because everything that actually exists is an individual. Thus an existing human nature is substantially distinct from every other existing human nature, though considered in the order of essence only it is one with all other human natures.

Within substance itself there is a twofold notion of individuality depending upon different relationships to existence. We can say that substantial parts exist and are individual, or we can say that complete substances exist and are individual. But neither body nor soul exists in the same sense that a person named John, for example, exists, nor are they individuals in the same sense. Existence in the broad sense, as it can apply to the integral part of a substance, means the act by which a being is no longer in the state of potency but has been actualized by its efficient and final causes. But the existence of John as a person is something more than that. The act of existence completes him in the order of being and sets him apart so that he cannot be in another or part of another. This special character of individual existence we call *subsistence*.

When St. Thomas speaks of substance in metaphysics as first substance, this is the kind of being he means. This being enjoys an autonomy in existence so that neither in whole nor in part does it exist in or through another; it has, because of its primacy in existence, the ability to sustain other beings in existence. Therefore it has a twofold aspect: one of these considers the act of existence as intrinsic to substance and it is in reference to this that we speak of *subsisting being*; the other considers the substantial act of existence with respect to other beings that depend on it for their existence, and it is here that we speak of *substance*. To illustrate this meaning of individual existence and to differentiate it from other notions, let us take an example. Since I, as particular person, exist as an individual man with full consciousness of my independence in my person and activity, my being has an independent existence that makes me different from all other men. If there are bonds of a common nature that make men alike, each one's act of existence is unique and like an impenetrable wall that keeps him from being absorbed into any other, and this is the most complete notion of substance.

The Act of Subsistence

The act of existence in its most general sense does not explain a subsisting being. It must be a special aspect of the act of existence by which a being becomes an individual in such a way that it has a unity within itself, is complete in the order of existence, is incapable of being assumed into the existence of another, though it can sustain the other beings in existence. This special function of the act of existence is called subsistence. Therefore, with Boethius, St. Thomas distinguishes between the act of existence and the act of subsistence, pointing out that the latter designates a determinate mode of being.

> It is clear that existence is something common and does not determine any particular mode of being. Subsistence, however, designates a determinate mode of being, namely, that something exists in itself and not in another as do accidents. . . . Therefore, it is clear that *to be* designates something common to all beings, while *to subsist* and to support others is proper to the first category of being.[26]

Whether or not Aristotle clearly saw that substance in the metaphysical sense is constituted not merely by the nature or essence but by the act of subsistence added to a nature is a historical question for the experts to decide. What St. Thomas' own philosophical position was is clear from a text in the *Summa Theologiae* where he differentiates nature or essence from the hypostasis or first substance. St. Thomas writes:

> According to the Philosopher, substance is twofold. In one sense, it means *the quiddity of a thing*, signified by the definition, and thus we say that the definition signifies the substance of a thing; in which sense substance is called by the Greeks *ousia*, which we may call *essence*. In another sense, substance means a *subject* or *suppositum*, which subsists in the genus of substance. To this, taken in a general sense, can be applied a name expressive of an intention; and thus it is called the *suppositum*. It is also called by three names signifying a reality — that is, *a thing of nature*, *subsistent being*, and *hypostasis*, according to a threefold consideration of the substance thus named. For, as it exists in itself and not in another, it is called *subsistent being*, for we say that those things subsist which exist in themselves and not in another. As it underlies some common nature, it is called *a thing of nature*. . . . As it underlies the accidents, it is called *hypostasis* or *substance*. What these three names signify in common in the whole genus of substances, this name person signifies in the genus of rational substances.[27]

The Person: The Highest Form of Subsistent Being

Substances differ among themselves in their acts of existence not

---

[26] St. Thomas, *Commentary on the Sentences*, I, d. 23, q. 1, art. 1.
[27] St. Thomas, *Summa Theologiae*, I, q. 29, art. 2, c.

only numerically but also according to mode, for existence is not something that is to be predicated univocally of all substances. Some substances enjoy a superior mode of being than others. This is especially true in those that have control over their own activities. In man's use of free will we have evidence that there is a more profound kind of substance than that realized in minerals, plants, and in irrational sensory beings. Therefore a special name is given to this kind of substance. Intellectual substances are called *persons*.

> In a more special and perfect way, the particular and the individual are found in rational substances, which have dominion over their own actions, and which are not only made to act, as are others, but act of themselves; for actions belong to singulars. Therefore, individuals of a rational nature even have a special name among other substances; and this name is *person*.[28]

What a person means to a sociologist or to an empirical psychologist is usually very different from what it means to a metaphysician. But even among philosophers, and medieval philosophers included, there has been disagreement as to the meaning of person. However, in his analysis of various definitions of person given by philosophers, St. Thomas optimistically concludes that all of the views are to some extent correct. Perhaps the same could be said of contemporary views on the person and personality, for even pragmatic notions, when based on experience, give some insight to the natures of things.

The name *person* is a term taken from the ancient theater. In ancient comedies and tragedies actors wore a mask which was called a *persona*, since their voices "sounded through" (*per-sonare*) the mask. In giving directions to the actors the playwrights felt that the natural features of the actors and actresses should not appear, for this would take away the dignity befitting the part they played. The name *person* was later transferred to men. We do not know why. Perhaps it lay in the fact that actors on the stage usually represented noble men, those of great dignity, and hence *person* refers to the dignity of men. Perhaps this term was applied to men because every human being is in his deepest being inscrutable, like one wearing a mask. Perhaps there is a mask over one's personality so that no one can see behind it even when he looks into the mirror of his own conscience. Whatever the correct historical explanation of the transfer of the name to men, it is true that each of us is a mystery behind a mask that reveals very little of our inner self.

It was Boethius (*De duabus naturis*) who gave us the definition of person traditionally used by scholastic philosophers and theologians: *a person is an individual substance of a rational nature*. In writing on the

---

[28] St. Thomas, *Summa Theologiae*, I, q. 29, art. 1, c.

general meaning of person before discussing the theological question of the three divine Persons in God, St. Thomas shows that the perfection of individuality is found in various modes — in accidents as well as in substances — but that it is found most perfectly in free intellectual beings who have dominion over these acts. This name would apply then to any spiritual substance — human, angelic, and divine — but not to any other kind of subsistent being. The dignity of a substance that overflows into acts so individual that they cannot belong to any other and cannot even be shared with any other — such as the use of free will — calls for a special name. If it were a question of only a qualitative or quantitative increase in the perfection of individuality, such as is had among plants and animals, no special name would be needed. The actual use of free will does not constitute the person but is rather a sign of it insofar as *activity is rooted in substance* and is assigned to the substance as its proper subject.

The dignity of a person underlies the use of his intellectual capacities and the power of free choice. It is something deep within him. Man is really a world unto himself, or an island that cannot become the possession of any other man. Though the exercise of his freedom as a person can be hindered, either because he does not have the maturity necessary for its operation, or because he is prevented from operating through violence, there remains deeper than the exercise of freedom an inner sanctuary of personality that consists in the act of subsistence joined to an intellectual nature. It is indestructible because the act of subsistence is spiritual and is beyond the power of physical forces to destroy it. It is so great that St. Thomas calls it "the most perfect thing in the whole of creation." Hence by analogy it can also be applied to God in a transcendent way.

> Person signifies what is most perfect in all nature — that is, a subsistent individual of a rational nature. Hence, since everything that is perfect must be attributed to God, inasmuch as His essence contains every perfection, this name *person* is fittingly applied to God; not, however, as it is applied to creatures, but in a more excellent way.[29]

---

[29] St. Thomas, *Summa Theologiae*, I, q. 29, art. 3, c.

CHAPTER VI

The Transcendentals

In our investigation of the analogy of being we saw first that the world with which we are familiar is divided into various categories of reality and that being is predicated of these categories in analogously similar modes. Then, through the experience that we have of ourselves and of things around us, we are able to recognize in things two correlative principles of potency and act, which again constitute an analogous division of being. We now investigate common being from the point of view of its transcendental properties. It is true that nothing can be added to being, as though it were really distinct from being, for being includes everything that exists or can exist; nevertheless, there are certain transcendental properties which belong to every being precisely because it is being. We come to know these properties by analyzing reality, not by analyzing a concept. For St. Thomas, as we have already said, metaphysics is a science of reality; and reality comes to us through experience. Consequently, the transcendental properties of being will not be made explicit by an apriori demonstration but become known through an examination of the realities that are first brought to our attention through sense experience. By working directly with experience we can avoid the danger of making our metaphysics a mere logic of being; we can safeguard the unique character of being that is found in each individual, finding in each something unique, good, and true that cannot be found in anything else in exactly the same way.

Logical Ordering of the Transcendentals

In a passage that displays the precise and orderly movement of his thought, St. Thomas shows how the metaphysician moves from a general consideration of being to the transcendental properties that are implicitly contained in the concrete experience of being. In his treatise on *Truth* he says:

When investigating the nature of anything, one should make the same kind of analysis as he makes when he reduces a proposition to certain self-evident principles. Otherwise, both types of knowledge will become involved in an infinite regress, and science and our knowledge of things will perish.

Now, as Avicenna says, that which the intellect first conceives as, in a way, the most evident, and to which it reduces all its concepts, is being. Consequently, all the other conceptions of the intellect are had by additions to being. But nothing can be added to being as though it were something not included in being — in the way that a difference is added to a genus or an accident to a subject — for every reality is essentially a being. The Philosopher has shown this by proving that being cannot be a genus. Yet, in this sense, some predicates may be said to add to being inasmuch as they express a mode of being not expressed by the term being. This happens in two ways.

First, the mode expressed is a certain *special* manner of being; for there are different grades of being according to which we speak when we speak of different levels of existence, and according to these grades different things are classified. Consequently, *substance* does not add a difference to being by signifying some reality added to it, but *substance* simply expresses a special manner of existing, namely, as a being in itself. The same is true of the other classes of existents (categories).

Second, some are said to add to being because the mode they express is one that is *common*, and consequent upon every being. This mode can be taken in two ways: first, in so far as it follows upon every being considered absolutely: second, in so far as it follows upon every being in relation to another. In the first the term is used in two ways, because it expresses something in the being either affirmatively or negatively. We can, however, find nothing that can be predicated of every being affirmatively and, at the same time, absolutely, with the exception of its essence by which the being is said to be. To express this the term *thing* is used; for, according to Avicenna, *thing* differs from *being* because *being* gets its name from to-be, but *thing* expresses the quiddity or essence of the being. There is however, a negation consequent upon every being considered absolutely: its undividedness, and this is expressed by *one*. For the *one* is simply undivided being.

If the mode of being is taken in the second way — according to the relation of one being to another — we find a twofold use. The first is based on the distinction of one being from another, and this distinctness is expressed by the word *something*, which implies, as it were, *some other thing*. For, just as a being is said to be *one* in so far as it is without division in itself, so it is said to be *something* in so far as it is divided from others. The second division is based on the correspondence one being has with another. This is possible only if there is something which is such that it agrees with every being. Such a being is the soul, which as is said in *The Soul*, "in some way is all things." The soul, however, has both knowing and appetitive powers. *Good* expresses correspondence of being to the appetitive power, for, and so we note in the *Ethics*, the good is "that which all desire." *True* expresses the correspondence of being to the knowing power, for all knowing is produced by an assimilation of the knower to the thing known, so that assimilation is said to be the cause of knowledge. Similarly, the sense of sight knows a color by being informed with a species of the color.[1]

Of these five properties brought out by an analysis of reality, only three of them call for further study at this time, namely, the one, the true, and the good. We have already seen being as essence, that is, being as an object of knowledge (res) and we shall take up the property by which being is expressed as something (aliquid), that is, insofar as it is divided from others, in a discussion of the principles of identity and contradiction.

The Transcendental One

The unity of being, says St. Thomas, adds nothing real to being but only the negation of division, for unity signifies only that being is undivided.[2] St. Thomas does not, however, say "absence of divisibility," just as he does not say "absence of composition in being." For all natural substances are divisible because they have matter, and all created substances are composite because they have potency.

The transcendental one is *like a privation*. It is not a real privation, which is the absence of something that ought to be, but it is known, as St. Thomas says, "after the manner of a privation." We conceive the unity of being negatively, just as we conceive of infinity. Implicitly it signifies something positive, namely the substance; directly and explicitly, however, it signifies something negative, the absence of division. Since being is capable of being divided — and therefore of being dispersed and destroyed — we come to know the unity of being or its absence of division as a kind of privation. Unity in being signifies that a being is without something of which it is capable, namely, of being divided.

The absence of division has a foundation in being, which is not the case in privations like blindness or ignorance. The absence of division is something which is rooted in a positive perfection of being. The positive perfection is only implied by the negative expression of unity as the absence of division, just as evil connotes or implies the good of which it is a privation. The transcendental one, more positively considered, implies a cohesiveness, an integrity, a self-sufficiency, a wholeness from within.

We can illustrate the unity of being by the unity of the parts of an automobile. The carburetor, the wheels, the steering column, and other parts, taken by themselves, do not make an automobile. As separated parts of the automobile they do not have a unity. Their being an automobile consists in their being unified. But a wheel, a carburetor,

---

[1] St. Thomas, *Truth*, q. 1, art. 1, Reply. Mulligan translation, I, pp. 5–6.
[2] See *Summa Theologiae*, I, q. 11, art. 1.

and a steering column do have a unity of their own insofar as they are things, that is, insofar as they exist in themselves. Less perfect beings have less perfect unity, are more contingent, closer to otherness, divisible, and more potential. From this we can see that substance has more unity than accidents, that higher substances have more unity than lower substances, and that necessary events have more unity than chance events. Evidently this kind of unity is based more on form than on matter, more on act than on potency.

Identity of Being With the Transcendental One

Everything is being insofar as it is what it is in itself and is removed from otherness, that is, distinct from every other being. No real being can be completely devoid of being something in itself; if it were, it would be absolutely nothing. The more perfect a being is, the more it is self-contained and the less it has of another and the less it depends on another. Substance is a greater being than accident because it has existence in itself; spiritual substance is a greater being than corporeal substance because it has less potency to change to something other; divine substance is most perfectly being because it is in no way dependent on another nor subject to becoming other. The more a being is in act, the less it is potential and the less it is liable to be other than itself. The conclusion is, then, that the transcendental unity of being comes from act.

Ultimately, the unity and perfection of being come from form and the act of existence that follows form. Since being and unity are convertible, and being and perfection are convertible, it follows that the highest perfection of unity comes from the form or act. The highest type of transcendental unity comes from the highest type of act, which is the act of existence. Matter, on the contrary, is the principle of non-unity. The more a form is immersed in matter the less perfect it is. The more material a being is the more it is divisible and lacking in unity and perfection. Thus the inferior things of nature, being more material, lose less by being divided than do more perfect beings.

Metaphysics, we saw, deals primarily with substances and secondarily with accidents. Likewise transcendental unity is found primarily in substance and only secondarily in accidental being. But we should not suppose that transcendental unity is found only in individual substances and that it does not exist in accidents, even though it is found in accidents only in an analogous sense. There is a complex unity in being that corresponds to the inner relationships found in the common good and to the concatenations of eternal and created truth. To consider but only one species of accident, let us see, for example, how unity is found in the category of relation. If the being of a family, nation, or church is something real over and above the reality of the individuals that compose these societies, there is a corresponding unity in being over and above that of the individuals. There is a bond of unity among the members of society, and this bond is such that the being of society arises from the unity. If the unity ceased to exist, the very being of society would cease to exit.

It was against an exaggerated isolationist conception of unity and reality that William James wrote *A Pluralistic Universe.* He says that being considered as isolated from other reality is a false conception of being, and he points out that both the view that beings are isolated and the view that being is all one and thoroughly indistinguishable are wrong because they are contrary to experience. Whether or not he found in his philosophy the source of unity and being in the universe is not of importance here, for we are concerned only with his observation. He has pointed out in our times a conception of reality that was remarkably like St. Thomas' view of the hierarchical nature of reality and the primacy of the universal conception of reality, or what he (James) calls the "manyness in oneness that indubitably characterizes the world we inhabit." He says:

> If the "each-form" be the eternal form of reality no less than it is the form of temporal appearance, we still have a coherent world, and not an incarnate incoherence, as is charged by so many absolutists. Our "multiverse" still makes a "universe"; for every part, though it may not be in actual or immediate connexion, is nevertheless in some possible or mediate connexion, with every other part however remote, through the fact that each part hangs together with its very next neighbors in inextricable interfusion. The type of union, it is true, is different here from the monistic type of *all-einheit.* It is not a universal so-implication, or integration of all things *durcheinander.* It is what I call the strung-along type, the type of continuity, contiguity, or concatenation. If you prefer Greek words, you may call it the *synechistic* type. At all events, you see that it forms a definitely conceivable alternative to the through-and-through unity of all things at once, which is the type opposed to it by monism. You see also that it stands or falls with the notion I have taken such pains to defend, of the through-and-through union of adjacent minima of experience, of the confluence of every passing moment of concretely felt experience with its immediately next neighbors. The recognition of this fact of coalescence of next with next is concrete experience, so that all the insulating cuts we make there are artificial products of the conceptualizing faculty, it is what distinguishes the empiricism which I call "radical" from the bugaboo empiricism of the traditional rationalist critics, which (rightly or wrongly) is accused of chopping up experience into atomistic sensations, incapable of union with one another until a purely intellectual principle has swooped down upon them from on high and folded them in its own conjunctive categories.[3]

---

[3] William James, *A Pluralistic Universe,* p. 325.

Transcendental and predicamental unity. When we think of unity we normally think first of the number one or of something that can be designated as one — for example, one man as opposed to many men. Transcendental unity is opposed to this kind of unity because the unity proper to number is univocal. Since it is based on quantity it is found only in those beings that require matter in their definition and existence. This fact excludes it from the formal subject of metaphysics, which is being that transcends matter both in definition and existence. The unity of number is a univocal unity based on quantity and it is opposed to the analogical unity of metaphysical being which is based on form and the act of existence.

Certain early Greek philosophers who had not attained a conception of being transcending the physical universe believed that the unity of number or predicamental unity constituted the essence of reality. St. Thomas refers to them when he compares predicamental and transcendental unity.

> Some, thinking that the *one* convertible with *being* is the same as the *one* which is the principle of number, were divided into contrary opinions. Pythagoras and Plato, seeing that the *one* convertible with *being* did not add reality to *being*, but signified the substance of *being* as undivided, thought that the same applied to the *one* which is the principle of number. And because number is composed of unities, they thought that numbers were the substances of things. Avicenna, however, on the contrary, considering that the *one* which is the principle of number added a reality to the substance of being (otherwise number made up of unities would not be a species of quantity), thought that the *one* convertible with *being* added a reality to the substance of beings; as *white* adds to *man*. This, however, is manifestly false, inasmuch as each thing is one by its substance. For if a thing were one by anything but by its substance, since this again would be one, supposing it were again one by another thing, we should be driven on to infinity. Hence we must adhere to the former statement; therefore we must say that the one which is convertible with being does not add a reality to being; but that the one which is the principle of number does add a reality to being belonging to the genus of quantity.[4]

The Pythagoreans and Platonists had substituted predicamental unity for transcendental unity. Consequently they thought that nature was constituted of numbers, which in turn are made up of predicamental unity. Hence mathematics was given such great importance in their philosophy. Their influence can be found in almost any period of the history of philosophy. St. Augustine, for example, was greatly influenced by his contact with neo-Platonists; and the ancient theories are not far removed from the attempts of modern logico-mathematicians who think that nature can only be interpreted by mathematics.

---

[4] St. Thomas, *Summa Theologiae*, I, q. 11, art. 1, ad 1.

We can realize the seriousness of the error of those who would substitute the unity of number or predicamental unity for transcendental unity, if we recall the analogy of being and the analogous character of transcendental unity. Substituting predicamental unity for transcendental unity entails a univocal conception of reality, reducing everything to the homogeneity of quantity and extension. Of all unities, predicamental unity is the least perfect, since it is based on matter, the principle of multiplicity and potentiality. Transcendental unity, as we have seen, is based on the form, on act, ultimately on the most perfect of all acts, the act of existence. By confusing the univocal unity of predicamental being with the analogous unity of metaphysical being, philosophers render metaphysics impossible, making of it a purely logical and mathematical manipulation of concepts.

The practical consequences of the difference between transcendental and predicamental unity can be seen, for example, when one analyzes the basic concept of unity as it applies to the ideal society founded upon the principles of Marxist philosophy and that based on truly democratic principles. In theory, at least, the Marxist society is striving for homogeneity, for it professes to move toward a classless society, whereas the unity of a true democracy is, theoretically, organic, that is to say, transcendental. Application might be also made to a philosophy of education. That theory which sets up as the ideal a system in which the same opportunities and subject-matter are given to all, without paying any heed to personal differences and preferences, is not realistic. This is in opposition to Cardinal Newman's view that "a few highly endowed men will rescue the world for centuries to come."[5] A strong educational system does not have a goal of equal education for all. Wherever it is found, in society, in the school, in the individual person, transcendental unity is not the unity of homogeneity, but rather the unity that is based upon the strength of the inner principles of being, a unity that is compatible with great diversity of parts, a unity that is consistent with a hierarchical dependence of members upon each other.

Transcendental Truth

The words of the English philosopher, Berkeley, *Esse est percepi,* are usually taken as the essence of idealistic philosophy. Did Berkeley mean that a thing exists as an "object" when it is known? If this were so, the statement is redundant. Or did he mean that the very being or actuality of anything consists in its being known? This would make the act of knowing the cause of being. This latter view seems to be the

---

[5] Cardinal Newman, *University Sermons.*

position that St. Thomas holds with respect to truth in the transcendental sense, inasmuch as the truth of things depends on God's act of knowing.

In the passage that follows, St. Thomas points out various ways in which one can speak of truth. We can consider truth (1) as the reality which is basis of truth because it is the basis of knowledge; (2) as the actual conformity between the act of understanding and what is real; (3) as the effect or consequence of true judgment, as when we speak of a "living truth."

> Truth or the true has been defined in three ways, First of all, it is defined according to that which precedes truth and is the basis of truth. This is why Augustine writes: "The true is that which is"; and Avicenna: "The truth of each thing is a property of the act of being which has been established for it." Still others say: "The true is the undividedness of the act of existence from that which is."
>
> Truth is also defined in another way according to that in which its intelligible determination is formally completed. Thus Isaac writes: "Truth is the conformity of thing and intellect"; and Anselm: "Truth is a rectitude perceptible only by the mind." This rectitude, of course, is said to be based on some conformity. The Philosopher says that in defining truth we say that truth is had when one affirms that "to be which is, and that not to be which is not."
>
> The third way of defining truth is according to the effect following upon it. Thus, Hilary says that the true is that which manifests and proclaims existence. And Augustine says: "Truth is that by which *that which is* is shown"; and also: "Truth is that according to which we judge about inferior things."[6]

Knowing has been defined as the immanent act in which the knower becomes one with what is known. Thus *knowing is being*, because there is no difference between the being of the thing in the mind and its being in reality except its mode of existence. This is true more obviously of practical knowledge that is the cause of reality than it is of speculative knowledge that is a conformity with reality. We can see how this is true, in a limited way, of the practical knowledge called *art*. The being of the work of art consists in a conformity with the artist acting as an artist. The mind of the artist is creative, for art is more a work of intelligence than it is a work of the hands. The hands are the tools that implant the artistic form into a subject capable of receiving it and holding it. Thus it is evident that the truth and the being of a work of art consist in the degree of conformity with the mind of the artist.

What is true on a limited plane of the human arts is true in a universal sense of all things that exist. A thing is a being insofar as it

---

[6] St. Thomas, *Truth*, q. 1, art. 1, Reply. Mulligan translation, I, pp. 6–7.

is the reflection of intelligence, that is, insofar as it conforms to some mind. Aristotle and St. Thomas speak of nature as an intelligence placed in things (*ratio indita rebus*). Each being has a nature, which in turn is the essence of the thing considered as the dynamic principle of activity. The essence, in turn, is based primarily on the form, and is one of the intrinsic principles that constitute a being in existence. This essence is also the principle of knowability. Those things that are most indeterminate in essence are closest to nonbeing, that is, they are most potential and contingent. In this sense we can interpret Berkeley's *Esse est percipi* as signifying that the being of a thing is the same as its intelligibility. But there is an even deeper meaning contained in the expression, and it is possibly the one which Berkeley had in mind, namely, that the very being of each thing is contingent upon its being known by some intellect and that its content as existing being is identical with its intellectual content.

In a Platonic conception, the essence of truth would consist in a conformity of the intellect with the abstract essence or form. But in the view of St. Thomas the being of anything is predicated more by reason of the existence than of the essence because existence is the perfection of essence. Hence for St. Thomas the truth of being is found more in the judgment of existence than in the essential judgment that joins or separates concepts. The composition of concepts in a judgment whose copula *is* does not go beyond the act of existence in the mind to reach existence as exercised by reality on the mind may be a true definition, but it is not a truth until what is in the mind is affirmed to correspond to reality outside the mind.

The Basis of Transcendental Truth

An analysis of the properties of common being brings us to the point where metaphysics emerges more definitely as a form of natural theology. However, as yet we have not seen a formal proof of the existence of a First Cause of composite being. The discussion of God belongs to the subject-matter of metaphysics only as an explanation of the reality that is the proper object of human knowledge. God is brought into metaphysics because the mind is forced to seek this explanation, or, as St. Thomas says in his preface to the *Commentary on the Metaphysics*, "by way of resolution."

With the study of the transcendental properties of unity and truth, reason cannot remain completely in the order of contingent reality. The analysis of potency and act, of essence and existence already points to the necessity of a transcendent being in which no distinction can be made between potency and act and essence and existence. The analysis of truth now compels the metaphysician to admit a foundation in reality for the certitude of any judgment. If things can be necessary objects of judgment it is only because they contain evidence of a reality that surpasses the contingency of their natural composition.

In his treatise *Truth*, St. Thomas asks the question whether truth is found primarily in the intellect or in things. In his answer he makes a distinction between the truth of the thing as compared with the human intellect and with the divine intellect. In comparison with the human intellect, which is measured by the truth of objects, the truth of being is prior to human truth in the way that act is prior to potency. But in comparison with the divine intellect the truth of things is subsequent to divine truth in the way that an effect comes after its cause. Even if there were no human intellects, things would still be true because of their relation to the divine intellect. But if there were no divine intellect, there would be no truth of things, as St. Thomas notes:

> It is clear, therefore, that, as is said in the *Metaphysics*, natural things from which our intellect gets its scientific knowledge measure our intellect. Yet these things are themselves measured by the divine intellect, in which are all created things — just as all works of art find their origin in the intellect of an artist. The divine intellect, therefore, measures and is not measured; a natural thing both measures and is measured; but our intellect is measured and measures only artifacts, not natural things.
>
> A natural thing, therefore, being placed between two intellects, is called *true* insofar as it conforms to either. It is said to be true with respect to its conformity with the divine intellect in so far as it fulfills the end to which it was ordained by the divine intellect. This is clear from the writings of Anselm and Augustine, as well as from the definition of Avicenna, previously cited: "The truth of anything is a property of the act of being which has been established for it." With respect to its conformity with a human intellect, a thing is said to be true in so far as it is such as to cause a true estimate about itself; and a thing is said to be false if, as Aristotle says, "by nature it is such that it seems to be what it is not, or seems to possess qualities which it does not possess."
>
> In a natural thing, truth is found especially in the first, rather than in the second, sense; for its reference to the divine intellect comes before its reference to a human intellect. Even if there were no human intellects, things could be said to be true because of their relation to the divine intellect. But if, by an impossible supposition, intellect did not exist and things did continue to exist, then the essentials of truth would in no way remain.[7]

When truth is predicated in an act of judgment, nothing real is added to the things themselves. The relationship of the object and knower is real only in the man who knows, but nothing new is present in the thing known. For example, the colors of a sky in the evening are not more beautiful nor less beautiful because they are seen, though a

---

[7] St. Thomas, *Truth*, q. 1, art. 2, Reply. Mulligan translation, I, p. 11.

man is better for having seen them. If the human race were to become extinct, the truth of other things would not change. Of course, the truth in things would change to the extent that the brightest of all natural beings would no longer exist as the point of mediation between the world and God. But this is considering man from the point of view of ontological truth, that is, insofar as he is a being, participating like other things in the light of divine intelligence. But from another point of view he is beyond comparison with the participated intelligence in corporeal things because theirs is not a direct reflection of the divine intelligence, whereas man is said to be made after God's "own image and likeness."

Therefore the meaning of truth cannot be applied univocally to these three kinds of being: (a) to the divine intellect that is the cause of things; (b) to things themselves; and (c) to the human intellect that consciously reflects the participation of the divine intelligence. Thus the name *truth* has a plurality of meanings recognized in human judgments but based on a primary meaning belonging to the divine intellect.

Truth, therefore, is properly and primarily in the divine intellect. In the human intellect, it exists properly but secondarily, for it exists there only because of a relation to either one of the two truths just mentioned.

In his gloss on these words of Psalm 11 (v. 2), "Truths are decayed from among the children of men," Augustine writes that the truth of the divine intellect is one, and from it are drawn the many truths that are in the human intellect — "just as from one man's face many likenesses are reflected in a mirror." Now, there are many truths in things, just as there there are many entities of things. But truth predicated of things because of their relation to the human intellect is, as it were, accidental to those things; for, supposing that the human intellect did not or could not exist, things would still remain essentially the same. But truth predicated of things because of their relation to the divine intellect is inseparably attendant on them, for they cannot exist except by reason of the divine intellect which keeps bringing them into being. Again, truth is primarily in a thing because of its relation to the divine intellect, not to the human intellect, because it is related to the divine intellect as to its cause, but to the human intellect as to its effect in the sense that the latter receives its knowledge from things. For this reason, a thing is said to be true principally because of its order to the truth of the divine intellect rather than because of its relation to the truth of a human intellect.

So, if truth in its proper sense be taken as that by which all things are primarily true, then all things are true by means of one truth, the truth of the divine intellect. This is the truth which Anselm writes about. But if truth in its proper sense be taken as that by which things are said to be true secondarily, then there are many truths about many true things, and even many truths in different minds about one true thing. Finally, if truth in its improper sense be taken as that by which all things are said to be true, then there are many truths for many true things, but only one truth for one true thing.[8]

---

[8] St. Thomas, *Truth*, q. 1, art. 4, Reply. Mulligan translation, I, pp. 17–18.

Transcendental Good

Because it is as universal as being itself, transcendental good cannot be defined, though it can be described in terms of function which is enough to give us a lead for our metaphysical analysis of being as good. Aristotle described good "as that which all things seek." Good cannot be separated from the notion of end — whatever has the character of end also has that of good. The two notes that are essential to a good are that it is something worth being sought or desired and that being possessed it gives satisfaction or pleasure to those that have it. It is clear that our first notion of good applies directly only to the imperfect goods and beings that strive for an end in order to achieve a perfection. But the second condition, namely, that a good is something that gives pleasure, can be predicated of all goodness, even of divine goodness with respect to the divine will, because the essential happiness of God consists in possessing the infinite perfection that belongs to Him by essence. The tendency toward the good and the enjoyment of it both belong to the same basic meaning of good, because together they constitute one complete act, just as the movement of the intellect to knowledge and the possession of truth constitute one and the same species of perfection.

The relationship of the good to existence. Though in one respect the notion of the good is more extensive than that of being,[9] it is in another respect less extensive than the notions of being and truth because only those things that have a direct relationship to existence can be called good in the strict sense. One can speak of beings of the mind, such as *genera* and *species*, or of privations without bringing in either actual existence or potency to real existence. But for the transcendental good one cannot prescind from real existence or at least from potency to real existence. However, in defining the good one should not insist on the state of accomplishment or perfection, because the potency, as we said, already shares in the goodness of the end. Whatever does not yet participate in the act of being can tend toward it by an act of the natural appetite. Once the good is reached, the appetite rests in it and enjoys it.

St. Thomas sees in the act of existence the very essence of goodness:

> Existence itself, therefore, has the essential note of goodness. Just as it is impossible, then, for anything to be a being which does not have existence, so too it is necessary that every being be good by the very fact of having existence, even though in many beings many other aspects of goodness are added over and above the act of existence by which they subsist.
>
> Since, moreover, good includes the note of being, as is clear from what has been said, it is impossible for anything to be good which is not a being.

---

[9] See *Summa Theologiae*, I, q. 5, art. 2, ad 1.

Thus we are left with the conclusion that good and being are interchangeable.[10]

Since the good and the actuality of being are one and the same, the transcendental note *good* adds nothing real to being. Because there is nothing real outside of being, no new perfection of any kind can be added by the notion of good. All that the notion of good can add to being is a further exposition and clarification of what being is. The notion of good makes explicit in being the status of final causality and the note of reality. Under the aspect of essence alone something would not be called good in the absolute sense, but only relatively inasmuch as essence is a real potency for existence. The notion of good brings out the existential character of being, since only what is real or can be real can be desired and loved. In the words of St. Thomas:

> A being is perfective of another not only according to its specific character but also according to the existence which it has in reality. In this fashion the good is perfective; for the good is in things, as the Philosopher says. Inasmuch as one being by reason of its act of existing is such as to perfect and complete another, it stands to that other as an end. And hence it is that all who rightly define good put in its notion something about its status as an end. The Philosopher accordingly says that they excellently defined good who said that it is "that which all things desire."[11]

The Kinds of Good

We saw that the meaning of good is first found in beings insofar as they strive for what is capable of perfecting them and giving satisfaction. Because man is composed of potency and act both in his substance and operations, he does not by essence have everything that is desirable for him. To attain what is desirable there is in man a kind of movement, similar to but not entirely like what takes place in the motion of bodies. As in local motion there is first a state of potency; second, the gradual attaining of the goal; and finally a state of rest after the goal has been reached. One can find in man three stages of good that correspond somehow to three stages of local motion and to the movement of natural appetite. In the stage of transition from potency to act we have the *useful good* (*bonum utile*); as the goal is reached we have the *autonomous good* (*bonum honestum*); and in the state of rest we have the pleasure of the *good possessed* (*bonum delectabile*).

In the most proper sense of the word, good applies only to the second stage, good sought as the terminus and perfection of appetite. This is good for its own sake. Hence good is not predicated univocally in this triple division.

---

[10] St. Thomas, *Truth*, q. 21, art. 2, Reply. Schmidt translation, III, p. 11.
[11] St. Thomas, *Truth*, q. 21, art. 1, Reply. Schmidt translation, III, p. 7.

Goodness is not divided into these three as something univocal which is predicated equally of them all, but as something analogical which is predicated of them according to priority and posteriority. For it is predicated by priority of the autonomous good, then of the pleasure of the good possessed, and lastly of the useful good.[12]

The useful good least of all can be called good since it does not by itself constitute the perfection which is the end of human life. Nor can the useful good cause happiness since it does not have in itself the kind of perfection capable of fulfilling a basic human need. To say that a useful good can satisfy is like saying that a knife, spoon, and fork can take away a man's hunger by being useful for eating.

To substitute a useful good for the autonomous good to which it is naturally ordered is contrary to right reason. Therefore, any use of a power to the exclusion of the natural good that follows its use is contrary to right reason. There are some goods that by nature should be sought for themselves and there are others that should be sought only because of something else. Knowledge and friendship belong to the former class; the use of food and sex belong to the latter.

The pleasure produced by an autonomous good is on the same plane as the good itself, whereas the natural pleasure produced by the useful good in on the plane of the useful good. In each case the pleasure is a property that follows necessarily from the nature of the good. A useful good participates in the goodness of the end as long as it is directed toward it, and the pleasure derived from it is good and befitting reason as long as it is not sought for itself. The pleasure attendant on the possession of autonomous good is always reasonable because it is of the same nature as the good itself. The pleasure is the fulfillment of nature. Hence Aristotle at one time said that happiness for man will consist in the pleasure that comes from the possession of the highest goods due to his nature, namely, the good of his intellect and of his will.

That no created good can be completely autonomous and therefore good in an unqualified sense comes from the fact that no good can be identical with the essence of a creature. Goodness, like existence, is a gift to nature. The goodness of creatures can only share in a supreme autonomous goodness. Created goods participate in divine goodness in the order of their perfection of existence. In the degree that the creature approximates in its nature the breath and height of divine goodness, it finds its place in the spiral of goods pointing to God. Thus the limitations of inanimate things are overcome by the perfections of intelligence and freedom.

In summing up the nature of good as a property of being, St. Thomas relates the goodness of things to the divine goodness and shows that no

---

12 St. Thomas, *Summa Theologiae*, I, q. 5, art. 6, ad 3.

creature can be called an autonomous good without qualification because goodness does not belong to the essence of creature.

We have pointed out in Book Two that no created substance is its own act of being. Hence, if anything is good by virtue of the fact that it exists, none of them is its own act of being; none of them is its own goodness. Rather each of them is good by participation in goodness, just as it is being by participation in existing being itself.

. . . Though God has His own perfect and complete goodness, in accord with His simple existing being, creatures do not attain the perfection of their goodness through their being alone, but through many things. Hence although any one of them is good in so far as it exists, it cannot be called good without qualification, if it lack any other things required for its goodness. Thus, a man who is destitute of virtue and host to vices is indeed called good, relatively speaking; that is, to the extent that he is a being and a man. However, in the absolute sense, he is not good, but evil. So, it is not the same thing for any creature to be and to be good without qualification, although each of them is good in so far as it exists. In God, however, to be and to be good are simply the same thing.

So, if each thing tends toward a likeness of divine goodness as its end, and if each thing becomes like the divine goodness in respect of all the things that belong to its proper goodness, then the goodness of the thing consists not only in its mere being, but in all the things needed for its perfection, as we have shown. It is obvious, then, that things are ordered to God as an end, not merely according to their substantial act of being, but also according to those items which are added as pertinent to perfection.[13]

The Common Good

The superiority of the common good follows from the fact that things which resemble the divine goodness more closely and are more of the nature of ends are superior goods. Since the divine goodness is universal in existence, and since it is the supreme end of all, the greatest created goods will be those that are most universal in their causation as ends. Therefore in each order the common good is superior to the particular good. This is St. Thomas' view:

A particular good is ordered to the common good as to an end; indeed, the being of a part depends on the being of the whole. So, also, the good of a nation is more godlike than the good of one man.[14]

St. Thomas goes on to say that the superiority of the common good lies in the fact that, being an end, it spreads its goodness to the beings that partake of it.

---

[13] St. Thomas, *Summa Contra Gentiles*, III, ch. 20, par. 2, 7, 8. Translated by Vernon J. Bourke (New York: Doubleday Image, 1956), Volume Three of *On the Truth of the Catholic Faith*, pp. 77, 80–81.

[14] St. Thomas, *Summa Contra Gentiles*, III, ch. 17, par. 6. Bourke translation, p. 72. Cf. also Aristotle, *Politics*, I, 2, 1254 a 9; *Nicomachean Ethics*, I, 2, 1094 b 8–9.

Everything is at its peak perfection when it is able to make another like itself; thus, a thing is a perfect source of light when it can enlighten other things. Now, everything tending to its own perfection tends toward the divine likeness. So, a thing tends to the divine likeness by tending to be the cause of other things.[15]

The notion of common good is sometimes taken to mean the sum total of all the individual goods of a given order. This, however, is not the common good but an aggregate of individual goods. If, for example, money belonging to many individuals is pooled in a common financial investment so that the individuals will in turn each receive more money than they invested, the investment is not a common good in the metaphysical sense of the term. The difference between common good spoken of as an aggregate of individual goods and common good as something superior by nature to the individual good lies in the order of causality. The "common good" which is made up of many individuals is common in the sense of predication. In this sense one predicates human nature of many individual men. But the common good to which individual goods are subordinate has the nature of a final cause that draws many different things to itself.

A thing is said to be common in two senses. First, it is said to be common through effect or predication; that is, it is found in many things according to one intelligible character. In this sense, what is common is not more noble but more imperfect, as animal is, which is more common than man. Second, a thing is said to be common after the manner of a cause; that is, it resembles a cause which, while remaining numerically one, extends to many effects. In this sense, what is more common is more noble. For example, the preservation of a city is more noble than the preservation of a family.[16]

An organization composed of individuals for the sake of individual gain is no better than the sum total of its individual parts. If the end is the good of individuals as individuals then the so-called "common good" is reduced to the status of a useful good, for it is subordinate to the good of the individuals. For example, if the purpose of organization in a society is to produce the greatest number of goods for the greatest number of individuals, the unity of such a society has no inner form or essence to give it strength. It has no being of its own apart from the individuals that constitute it. Therefore, there is no good apart from that of the individual members.

But in a common good there is a bond of unity which by nature is prior to the individuals in it, and the good of the individual members comes precisely because they belong to and participate in this society.

---

[15] St. Thomas, *Summa Contra Gentiles*, III, ch. 21, par. 6. Bourke translation, p. 82.
[16] St. Thomas, *Truth*, q. 7, art. 6, ad 7. Mulligan translation, I, p. 304.

This we have, for example, in the common good of the family, of the state, and of the Church. The individual members of a family, the man, the woman, and the children are subordinate to the good of the whole which perfects them as human beings. That is why the individual members may at times have to sacrifice their personal preferences for the good of the whole. The man, the woman, and the children do not in themselves constitute the common good of the family — rather, they participate in it. The man becomes a father, the woman a mother, and the children sons and daughters by working together within the framework of something that is greater than all of them as individuals. The same is true of citizens and the state, as it is true in the supernatural order of the members of the Church.

The good of the individual is perfected by belonging to a common good. A common good is good of itself but the particular good is good by participation in the common good.

> He who seeks the common good of the group seeks in consequence his own good for two reasons. First, because the individual good is impossible without the common good of the family, state, or kingdom. . . . Secondly, because man, being a part of the home and state, must consider what is good for him by being prudent about the good of the group. For the good disposition of the parts depends on their relation to the whole.[17]

The common good is superior to the individual good in the particular genus in which it is found, but the common good of any order is not superior to all individual goods. The reason for this is obvious, since every common good is called so relatively to the nature of the good that is participated in. No created good is a common good in an absolute sense, because it cannot be final cause of all reality. There is a hierarchy of created goods reflecting, in varying degrees, the universal actuality of God who is the separate common good toward which all other common goods of the universe are orientated and from whom they receive their character of common good (cf. *Summa Theologiae*, I, q. 60, art. 5). Individual goods of the spiritual order are superior to the common good of the temporal order, because goods of a spiritual order have more the nature of end than do the greatest goods of a temporal order. Thus the common good is superior to a personal good if it is of the same genus, but a personal good can be better according to its own genus.[18]

Transcendental Beauty

The beautiful has been defined as "that which when seen gives pleasure."[19] The beauty of being is not a transcendental property distinct

---

[17] St. Thomas, *Summa Theologiae*, II–II, q. 47, art. 10, ad 2.
[18] *Summa Theologiae*, II–II, q. 152, art. 4, ad 3.
[19] *Summa Theologiae*, I, q. 5, art. 4, ad 1.

from those we have already considered because it does not add anything that is not at least implicitly expressed by the properties of unity, truth, and goodness. Being as beautiful is something accumulative. It is being considered with all its properties. It is *being* because it is something real; it is *one* because it can be recognized as something distinct from other things; it is *true* because it is an object of knowledge; it is *good* because it gives pleasure. Therefore it does not really differ from being or the transcendental properties of being.

But what does one mean when he says that something is beautiful? The word is not used indifferently for all things.

In the divisions of good, the good that gives pleasure corresponds most closely to this aspect of beauty. It is of the nature of autonomous goods to satisfy the appetite and cause pleasure. Since only autonomous goods satisfy the appetite, beauty belongs only to that category of good. A useful thing can be called beautiful not for reason of its utility, but only because it is the kind of good that is sought for itself. Therefore, to the extent that an object of the will tends toward utility only and away from knowledge or love of something for its own sake, the less beautiful it is.

The words "that which gives pleasure when seen" (*id quod visum placet*) are not a definition of the beautiful but a statement of fact. In other words, the beautiful is something objective to be seen and enjoyed. What is beautiful differs from the appreciation of beauty, which is a subjective element that can vary with each human being. The appreciation of something beautiful depends on sensitivity, education, habit, or the like. But a being is one, true, good, and beautiful according to the reality that it has. Beauty as a transcendental is coextensive with being because every being is beautiful to the degree that it has form and existence. Beauty is as varied as being itself.

The vision of the beautiful is more intellectual than sensory. The appreciation and the pleasure derived from the beautiful come when the mind at least implicitly recognizes the fundamental characteristics of beauty: integrity, harmony, and clarity. Since these are primarily intellectual, they need an intellect to appreciate them. But the vision also refers to ocular vision, and, in our present state of existence, sense knowledge of some kind is a prerequisite condition for intellectual pleasure in the beauty of natural form. Our knowledge of beauty comes through the senses. We have no innate sense for spiritual beauty. It is something known by analogy with corporeal beauty.

Most writers on the subject include the senses of sight and hearing among the faculties for appreciating beauty, but not taste, touch, and smell. Their reasoning is based on the fact that these two faculties are the most objective and the most disinterested sense faculties, since the pleasure in the object is hardly for the well-being of the faculty itself. With the other external senses the object offers pleasure, that is, physical satisfaction, to the sense organ itself. Food gives pleasure to the taste, smooth and soft things to the sense of touch, perfume to the sense of smell. Through hearing man takes pleasure in sounds but in addition there is an intellectual appreciation involved. Sight is most disinterested of all and closest to the intellect. However it seems that the exclusion of taste, touch, and smell is made arbitrarily. It is the intellect finally that must always enter into the experience of beauty, using the external senses as instruments.

The external senses that are generally thought to be related to beautiful things are the eyes and the ears. These are so regarded because they prescind most from mere utility and most approximate the activity of the understanding. The other senses — taste, touch, and smell — are associated more with the contingent practical affairs of life. Here we have a hint of the special note that something beautiful contains over and above that conveyed by the good. The beautiful is the good that gives pleasure *when it is seen.* The pleasure given by a beautiful thing comes from its being seen by the eyes, but most of all by the intellect.

St. Thomas says:

> The beautiful is the same as the good, different only in point of view. Since good is what all seek, the good is what calms the desire, while the beautiful is what calms the desire by being seen or known. Consequently those senses chiefly regard the beautiful which are the most cognitive, namely, sight and hearing in their role of instruments to reason, for we speak of beautiful sights and sounds. But as regards the objects of the other senses, we do not use the expression *beautiful,* for we do not speak of beautiful tastes and beautiful odors. Thus, it is evident that beauty adds to goodness a relation to the cognitive faculty, so that *good* means that which simply pleases the appetite, while the *beautiful* is something pleasant to apprehend.[20]

Notes of the beautiful. These are *integrity, harmony,* and *clarity.* St. Thomas, with many other philosophers, sets down three notes of beauty:

> Beauty includes three conditions: *Integrity* or *perfection,* since those things which are impaired are by that very fact ugly; *due proportion,* or *harmony;* and lastly, *brightness* or *clarity.*[21]

These three notes of beauty are rooted in three transcendental attributes of being, namely, unity, truth, and goodness. The beautiful is a combination of all three. At times we recognize these characteristics singly, but in the beautiful we see them simultaneously and in the concrete order of existence. The pleasure given by the beautiful comes

---

20 St. Thomas, *Summa Theologiae,* I–II, q. 27, art. 1, ad 3.
21 St. Thomas, *Summa Theologiae,* I, q. 39, art. 8, c.

from the fact that we perceive the object in its fullness. That is why the experience of beauty is more satisfying than abstract speculation, analytical reasoning, or scientific investigation. In abstract knowledge we leave behind something of the real. When we form universals we leave the concrete reality. Consequently, purely scientific investigation and mathematical reasoning do not ordinarily give as full a satisfaction as comes from an experience of what is beautiful.

Integrity. Integrity, the first characteristic of the beautiful, is not to be understood in the moral sense but in its primary ontological meaning. Integrity follows from transcendental unity which makes a being complete and undivided in itself and divided from others. The more divided a being is the less beauty it has. For example, dividing a work of art like a picture or statue into parts will cause its beauty to disappear. Likewise a beautiful thing must not lose its identity. Something that is immersed in surrounding objects to such an extent that it has no individuality is lacking in beauty. This is not to deny composition in a thing of beauty. A composite can have beauty because it has unity of form; but a conglomeration of individuals side by side, without unity, has no beauty.

Harmony. Harmony corresponds to the goodness of being and implies that it fulfills the purpose of its nature. Harmony is achieved when a being attains its proper perfection and fulfills its function in nature. This is as true of art as it is of nature. Since there are many degrees of perfection and many modes of finality, there will be many types of beautiful things and many levels in the hierarchy of beauty. But each will be beautiful insofar as it fulfills its own finality. It is evident, then, that harmony is not simply geometrical symmetry and balance, qualities that can be found only in corporeal beings.

At times in works of art the artist will include an irrational note to make the harmony appear more strikingly. Hence we more easily recognize goodness by contrast with evil, truth by contrast with irrational elements, the spontaneous characteristics by contrast with the necessary characteristics. Even God highlights beauty by making a universe that contains chance events, irrational elements, physical and moral evil. These are the discords that highlight the harmony of a symphony, the shadows on a canvas that make the lighting more brilliant and effective.

Clarity. Clarity follows from transcendental truth. It is the appearance of the form, the effulgence of the object through the maze of matter that surrounds it and permeates it. It is an intelligible radiance rooted in being, but recognized by our minds. Clarity is related to knowledge, both sensory and intellectual. It is always a concrete and intuitive experience, an illumination that is not separated from the object in its real existence.

The clarity in a thing of beauty is not simply for the sake of knowledge, but it is knowledge that gives pleasure. It satisfies not only the potentialities of the intellect but also the appetite for the good. The beautiful makes us happy. It is a complete object, satisfying the cognitive and the appetitive faculties of men.

Clarity presupposes honesty in the artist and in the work he creates. Therefore the beautiful should not deceive; it should not create an illusion. The beautiful should be and appear what it is supposed to be, because each beautiful thing has a nature of its own and it is beautiful to the extent that it attains that purpose. Eric Gill applies the criterion of truth to beauty in art and shows how the work can be beautiful only if the artist is honest with his subject matter and with the materials he uses.

"What I ask of a painting," said the French painter, Maurice Denis, "is that it should look like paint." But several centuries of insistence upon verisimilitude as being the highest quality of good painting have obfuscated our minds and filled us with the quite silly notion that everything reminiscent of natural appearance should be a faithful facsimile. We suppose that a portrait of a man of flesh and blood should produce the illusion that that man is standing before us. On the contrary it is better to say that things should look like what they are — that a stone carving should look like stone, a painting like paint, instrumental music like the music of flutes or bassoons or whatever it is, the tower bridge like the work of iron engineering and not a medieval castle, and a work of the imagination like a work of the imagination.[22]

Clarity is achieved by being truthful. It cannot be superadded to a work that is fundamentally false. Therefore, wherever beautiful things can be found, in all the various orders of being, if one looks after the truth of being beauty will look after herself.

The Contraries of Transcendental Unity, Truth, and Goodness

Metaphysics treats of the contraries of the transcendental properties of being because it belongs to one science to consider everything that affects its own proper subject matter. Since contraries are of the same genus, it belongs to metaphysics to treat of unity and multiplicity, of truth and falsehood, of good and evil. The metaphysician in this respect is like the medical student who studies not only the nature and causes of health but also the nature and causes of sickness. Just as the physician cannot effectively apply a remedy without knowing the causes of sickness, neither can the metaphysician adequately understand unity, truth, and goodness without knowing their opposites. For it is a property of human mind to reach truth through contrast.

---

[22] Eric Gill, *Beauty Looks After Herself*, p. 128.

Unity and multiplicity. Though transcendental unity is defined as the absence or privation of division, it does not imply a privation of the many (*multitudo*). It cannot imply this because we can only come to know the privation by first knowing that of which the being is deprived. Hence it would follow that unity, if it were simply a privation, would be known after the many, and the many would necessarily be a part of the definition of unity, since a privation is always defined by way of its opposite. Thus blindness is defined by sight. But multiplicity is not put into the definition of transcendental unity. Consequently we must conclude that the "privation" in unity is a privation of division and not of multitude.

Privation taken generally implies the absence of a form in an apt subject, for example, the privation of hearing in a man. Contraries are positive and call for a particular disposition of the subject in which they can be found. The subject with one contrary is in potency to the contrary form in the same genus. Unity and multiplicity are opposed in this way.

Among the four modes of opposition — contradiction, relation, privation, contrariety — the opposition between the one and the many or between unity and multiplicity is one of contrariety. It cannot be one of contradiction since *nonbeing* (the contradiction of being) is neither one nor many. Nor are they opposed by a relative opposition, since both the one and the many are predicated absolutely. Nor are they opposed as privation and possession in the strict sense. Though contraries do imply a privation, since the existence of one contrary in a subject entails the absence of the other, in the case of unity what is primarily signified is not the absence of multiplicity but the indivision of being within itself.

The priority of unity over multiplicity. It would seem that unity is posterior to multiplicity because in the definition of unity we refer to the absence of division. It is also a fact of experience that multiplicity is known before unity. In answering this difficulty, we have an analogy with other topics in metaphysics that relate to the order of learning and the order of being.

Unity is prior to multiplicity in existence and perfection. In the order of efficient and final causality the manifold of existent things is produced by and is directed toward a supreme unity. A consideration of formal causality also shows us that multiplicity is posterior to unity. Only when one realizes the unity in the individuals of a multitude, can one speak about a multitude of beings. There would be no multitude if each member of the aggregate did not have a transcendental unity, that is, the basis upon which a plurality can be predicated.[23]

Multiplicity in number and in being. There is, in the view of St.

---

[23] See *Commentary on the Metaphysics*, X, lesson 4, no. 1998.

Thomas, an essential difference between the unity and multiplicity of mathematics and the unity and multiplicity of metaphysics. The unity of quantity that is measured according to number is not opposed to plurality by an opposition of contrariety. They are opposed rather by a relative opposition. As St. Thomas points out:

> The unity which is the principle of number and is the principle of measure, and number which is a species of quantity and the multitude measured by unity are opposed to each other as one and many. They are not, however, contraries as is true of the unity which is opposed to plurality in the order of being. Rather they are opposed as related things are opposed.[24]

Thus one and two are not contraries but are relationships of comparison. But the existence of one being and the existence of many beings are contraries in the strict sense. It is with this kind of unity and plurality that the metaphysician deals.

Metaphysical multiplicity, which is opposed to transcendental unity, is not number in the strict sense because it is not based upon the divisibility of quantity but on the act of existence. Though there are some beings that have matter in their nature, and can be predicated numerically as we predicate one man and two men or one stone and two stones, there is a more basic unity and multiplicity, the kind that applies to all created beings, whether they are immaterial or material. When many men are looked upon as a multitude based upon the divisions of quantity, they must be considered in a univocal sense. Under this aspect they do not have the dignity that belongs to them as human beings. But underlying the numerical multitude is a unity and multiplicity that comes from the nature of man with the act of existence. Although many men exist, they are independent of each other because each one has a nature and an existence peculiar to himself and this constitutes his personality. Individuals composing a multiplicity in the transcendental sense can, however, be enumerated "as though they were divisions of quantity." Since the notion of number comes to us first from the sensible experience of divided quantity, the priority of multiplicity is in the sensory order. But from this one can rise to an analogical notion of number.[25]

Truth and falsehood. Since truth consists in the conformity of the intellect and reality, its contrary will consist in a nonconformity. But falsehood is more than a nonconformity of the intellect with reality. It is a distortion of the relation of the intellect and reality. Truth and falsehood are not contradictories but contraries. Falsehood is not simply a privation of the conformity between reality and an intellect that should have a correct relationship with reality. Neither absence of knowledge nor

---

[24] St. Thomas, *Commentary on the Metaphysics*, X, lesson 8, no. 2093.
[25] St. Thomas, *Commentary on the Metaphysics*, X, lesson 8, nos. 2090, 2092, *passim*.

ignorance is falsehood. Falsehood is a positive condition of the intellect in which the correct relationship with reality has been distorted. Just as moral evil is more than the absence of moral goodness in the will, so falsehood is the corruption of a true judgment of the intellect. To use an analogy, let us suppose that the parts of a watch are lying on a table but are not assembled — the hands, the wheels, the spring, the balance staff and other parts are not assembled. The parts are not a true time-piece because they are not a watch until they are assembled in correct order. This corresponds to ignorance in the order of knowing and to amoral acts in the order of human actions. But if the watch that is as-sembled is smashed with a hammer, the result is a chaos among the parts — wheels are bent, the hands broken, the balance staff smashed. The watch is not in the same condition that it was before the parts were assembled. Falsehood in the intellect and moral evil in the will are like a broken watch. This is the view held by St. Thomas, as is clear from the following passage.

> True and false are opposed as contraries, and not, as some have said, as affirmation and negation. In proof of which it must be considered that negation neither asserts anything nor determines for itself any subject. It can therefore be said of being as of non-being, for instance, *not-seeing* or *not-sitting*. But though privation asserts nothing, it determines a subject, for it is negation in a subject, as is stated in *Metaphysics IV*; for blindness is not said except of one whose nature it is to see. Contraries, however, both assert something and determine a subject, for blackness is a species of color. Now falsity asserts something, for a thing is false, as the Phi-losopher says, inasmuch as something is said or seems to be something that it is not, or not to be what it really is. For as truth implies an adequate apprehension of a thing, so falsity implies the contrary.[26]

The relationship between reality and the intellect can be said to be distorted in the relationship of a created intellect and reality, but not in the relationship of the divine intellect and reality. A thing is conformed to the divine intellect in whatever way it exists, since the reality of a thing and its truth are one and the same thing as regards the intellect of God. There is conformity between the divine intellect and reality even when it is a question of privation or a defect. Hence nothing can be false in this relationship.

> In regard to everything that is positively predicated of things or found in them, it [a thing] is related to the divine in one way as the measured to its measure; for all such things come from the divine intellect's art. A thing is related in another way to the divine intellect: as a thing known is related to the knower. In this way even negations and defects are equated to the divine intellect, since God knows all these even though He does not cause them. It is clear, then, that a thing is conformed to the divine intellect

---

[26] St. Thomas, *Summa Theologiae*, I, q. 17, art. 4, c.

in whatever way it exists, under any form whatsoever or even under a privation or a defect. Consequently, it is clear that everything is true in its relation to the divine intellect.[27]

The relationship between the human intellect and reality can be distorted, and consequently there can be falsehood. The cause of distortion can be considered either from the point of view of the object or from that of the intellect. There are, consequently, two conceptions of falsehood. Something outside the intellect is said to be false if it gives a false impression of itself. Thus a thing is called false if it is likely to deceive. The object, however, that deceives, must have some likeness to what would normally cause a true judgment. The cause of the defective judgment, then, lies in the fact that the object only partially corresponds to what it ought to be.

Hence, the philosopher says that those things that are called false, "which are such as to seem to be what they are not, or a kind which they are not." For example, that is called "false" gold which has in its external appearance the color and other accidents of genuine gold, whereas the nature of gold does not interiorly underlie them.[28]

But the primary meaning of falsehood is not in things but in the intellect whose act has been corrupted. Truth and falsity exist in things as health, in the analogy of proportion, exists in medicine, but they exist properly in the intellect as health exists in an animal. Nothing can be so false that it necessarily causes a false judgment. For the intellect is an active power with a capacity to penetrate an object and is not simply acted upon by things.

A thing is not said to be the cause of falsity in the soul in the sense that it necessarily causes falsity; for truth and falsity exist principally in the soul's judgment; and the soul, inasmuch as it judges about things, is not acted upon by things, but rather, in a sense, acts upon them. Hence, a thing is not said to be false because it always of itself causes a false apprehension, but rather because its natural appearance is likely to cause a false impression.[29]

Truth and falsity are found primarily and principally in the intellect as it judges the relationship of its own act with reality outside the mind. Since there is no judgment in sense cognition, there is neither truth nor falsity in sense knowledge except in an analogical sense.

The act of the intellect can be false in several ways. The first takes place in simple apprehension, in which the intellect apprehends the essence of a thing without affirming or denying anything about it. It can happen that error will enter at this stage, if the intellect in grasping

[27] St. Thomas, *Truth*, q. 1, art. 10. Mulligan translation, Vol. I, p. 44.
[28] St. Thomas, *Truth*, q. 1, art. 10. Mulligan translation, I, p. 44.
[29] St. Thomas, *Truth*, q. 1, art. 10. Mulligan translation, I, pp. 44–45.

essences falsely joins or separates parts that do not correspond with reality. Thus the intellect can attribute the definition of one thing to another, as would happen if it were to conceive the human soul as if it were a pure spirit, or if it were to join parts of a definition that cannot be joined, or separate parts of a definition that cannot be separated. For example, to associate the notion of spirituality with the soul of a cat, or to separate animality from the nature of man, would constitute a falsehood in the first operation of the mind.

The act of the intellect is most properly said to be false with respect to the other two operations of the mind, namely, judgment and reasoning, when the relationship between the form of the intellect and the form of reality is distorted. The prime analogate of truth and of falsehood is found in the act of judgment to which simple apprehension and reasoning are related as means to an end. Falsehood, in the strict sense of the term, is a distortion of the correct relationship between the intellect and reality in the act of judgment, while falsity in any of the other acts of the intellect is called such by analogy with the primary meaning of the term. It is only in judgment that the act of understanding is completed; it is only there that an identification takes place between the knowing subject and the object as it exists independently of the mind.

Good and evil. Philosophers have always held widely divergent views on the nature of evil. The Pythagoreans, for example, taught that evil is just as real as the good. Other philosophers have regarded evil, particularly what is called moral evil, as something that cannot be measured by an objective standard because it is relative to a given situation in the history and culture of man. St. Thomas, taking a middle course between these opinions, taught that evil is not something real in the way that goodness is real in the natural and in the moral order; nor is it something purely relative to a given situation or judged by a pragmatic standard.

Evil, he says, is the absence of what is good. But not every absence of good is an evil. For if the mere absence of a good were the same as evil, the very fact that every creature is limited to the perfection of its own being would mean that it is evil. Therefore a man would be evil because he is not as swift as a deer, as acute in vision as an eagle, as large or as strong as an elephant. But just as good is defined by what is proportionate to the nature and operations of each thing, so evil is defined by the absence of perfection in nature or operation due a being.

Evil in its broadest conception is not a contrary in the strict sense but a privation of what ought to be in a subject. Evil does not have an essence or a proper cause. Evil cannot be intended as the goal of intelligent activity or as the object of intellectual appetite. Hence it cannot be a real being. But unless it is a real being it cannot be called a contrary, since contraries belong to the same genus as the reality that is the point of comparison. This seems to be the view of St. Thomas in the *Contra Gentiles* where he says:

> Evil is simply a privation of something which a subject is entitled by its origin to possess and which it ought to have, as we have said. Such is the meaning of the word "evil" among all men. Now, privation is not an essence; it is, rather a negation in a substance.[30]

St. Thomas in this passage seems to make evil a being of the mind, for he says that evil is to be classified under being not as belonging to the ten categories of reality but under the being consisting in the truth of a proposition, as when privation is called a being. To say that a person is blind does not mean that blindness exists as a real form.

> Not everything which is a being in the second way [as the truth of a proposition] is a being in the first way [as a reality]. As regards a privation like blindness, one forms an affirmative proposition such as "there is blindness," but blindness is not something that exists in reality; it is rather the denial of something. Therefore, privations and negations are called beings in the second way.[31]

Whether evil should be considered as a reality or not depends on what kind of evil one has in mind. Moral evil, for example, is not a mere privation; it is a distortion. Moreover, evil can be considered in the abstract or in the concrete. When it is defined abstractly it is said to be the privation of a perfection in a subject, like the loss of sight in the eye. This is called evil *per se*, inasmuch as this describes in a semiformal way what evil is in itself. Since a privation, like blindness, is a being of the mind, the definition is not essential in the real order but in the order of propositions. Evil can also be considered from the point of view of the *subject which evil affects* or from the point of view of the *object that is said to cause evil*. These two concrete aspects of evil are called evil *per accidens*, because they are related to evil in a formal sense. Considered as a privation and abstractly, evil is not something real. It is only when one considers the cause or the effect of evil that one can call evil real.

The subject of evil. The subject of evil is that in which there is privation of a proper good. The term *subject*, if taken in an analogous way, can also refer to accidents. Anything that can be defective is the subject of evil. Thus an action is defective and evil if it does not produce the good that it should naturally produce, as when the digestive organs do not prepare food for proper assimilation by the body. This kind of evil

---

[30] St. Thomas, *Summa Contra Gentiles*, III, ch. 7, par. 2. Bourke translation, III, p. 48.

[31] St. Thomas, *Commentary on the Sentences*, II, d. 34, q. 1, art. 1.

is called a fault (*malum culpae*), and is found most properly in the will but by analogy the meaning is extended to any active power. The habit that is generated from repeated faulty acts is also called evil. This again is found properly in habits of the intellectual nature and by extension of the term in other powers. The powers of the soul are the subject of evil insofar as they can be injured by what acts upon them, as when the sense of hearing is injured by too loud a noise. But the subject of evil is above all the substance itself in which various powers, capacities, and habits reside.

The cause of evil. The cause of evil is sometimes found on the side of the matter that is improperly disposed to receive the action of the agent. For example, in the reproductive process, a defective sexual organ could prevent conception from taking place or might cause a defect in the offspring. At other times the cause of evil is found on the side of the agent, as for example, in the power of the will in the case of moral evil. Or the cause may be on the part of the object of the will, insofar as it could act upon the will and be an indirect cause of an evil choice. In either case there is no proper cause of evil because every agent acts in virtue of its own power in view of a good, and every capacity to receive the influence of an outside agency is a potency for what is good. Nothing can be a proper cause of evil by the very fact that evil considered formally is a privation. Evil is positive only with respect to a real subject that suffers a privation, or with respect to the good that is indirectly the cause of evil.

Evil does not have a proper cause. This is evident from the fact that what is caused *per se* (properly) is intended and whatever happens beyond the intention or natural direction of an agent is accidental. Since evil is the privation of good, it is not desirable and cannot be intended. Consequently whenever any agent causes evil it does so because it is attracted by a good, as in the case of one who lies, steals, or commits adultery. Every agent acts in virtue of the being that it is — but every being is good insofar as it is in act.

Though it does not have a proper cause, evil does have a cause, otherwise evil would not be in a subject. Everything that is not naturally present in a subject must have a cause of some kind. But not everything that is has a proper cause, for there are many things that are chance events, that is, effects beyond the intention or natural capacity of an agent. A very different meaning of causality applies to a proper and an accidental cause. Causality is not a genus that is divided univocally into proper and accidental causes. As being itself does not comprise a univocal genus of beings *per se* and beings *per accidens*, neither do the causes constitute one genus. As each thing is a being so is it a cause. Just as there are accidental beings, so there are accidental causes. (See Chap. VII.)

Accidental causes are based in last analysis on some proper cause. Accidental causes, even if their series were infinite, are not capable of producing anything by themselves. It would be like saying that the color or shape of the watch is the cause of its keeping time or of its not keeping time. Therefore, in any action in which evil results, at the source is some proper cause that initiates the movement that turns out to be evil, for without a proper cause there would be no movement or effect at all, either good or bad. It is because a person decides to walk across the street, for example, that he steps into a hole and breaks his leg; it is because a person wants the satisfaction of having money that he turns out to be a robber.

Moral evil. In voluntary actions, the cause of evil is not identical with the kind of cause that produces evil in nonintellectual beings. The difference is caused by the fact that the will is not acted upon by the good in the way that a potency in the irrational world is acted upon by an outside cause. It is within the power of the will to receive or not to receive the influence of an outside agent. Hence it is more the will than the extrinsic agent that is the cause of evil that takes place. The will is an accidental cause insofar as it inclines actively to something that is good or appears good but which has joined with it what is disordered and evil. For example, the will as a universal appetite is drawn to all goods, but insofar as it is an intellectual appetite it is drawn naturally to what is reasonable and according to order. If the will consents to the desire for money and accepts the disordered consequence of violated justice, it is both an accidental cause and, in a manner of speaking, a proper cause of evil; it is an accidental cause in that it did not directly desire the irrational consequence of its act; it is a proper cause in that it did not make a good choice when it was capable of doing so. In not acting as it should have done, it became a kind of cause of evil in a negative way — by not doing what it should have done. It causes evil not as an effect but as a defect; it is not an efficient cause in the strict sense, but rather a deficient cause. St. Thomas compares the will to a carpenter who makes a mistake in cutting a board because he neglects to use a measure when he knows he should have used it. The further question, "Why didn't he use the measure?" has no other answer than the fact that the will is free.

In all those things in which one is the rule and measure of another the good of that which is ruled and measured consists precisely in its being ruled and conformed to a rule and a measure; and evil consists in not being ruled or measured. If there were some artisan who should cut a piece of wood according to a certain pattern but does not cut it correctly but badly, the bad cut is caused by the fact that the artisan did not use a rule and a measure. Likewise, sensible pleasure and anything of this kind found in human life is to be measured and regulated by the rule of right reason and divine law. Therefore, not using the rule of reason and divine law is presupposed in the will before any inordinate choice takes place.

One should not try to find out the reason for not using the afore-mentioned rule. The freedom of will suffices to explain this, for it is through the will that one can act or not act. Not to pay attention to such a rule, if considered in itself, is neither an evil of fault nor of penalty, because the mind is not obliged nor can it always be aware of such a rule in every act. The first notion of guilt arises from the fact that without explicit attention to the rule the person goes ahead and makes a choice. Thus the artisan is not at fault by the fact that he does not always have a rule in his hand, but rather by proceeding to cut without using a rule. Likewise the fault of the will does not consist in not attending to the rule of reason or of divine law, but rather in proceeding to make a choice without using the rule or measure.[32]

Moral evil is most properly called evil because it is a *contrary* of the good, but physical evil is simply a *privation* of the good that could be or ought to be in a subject. Physical evil is relative to a particular subject and not to a universal norm. Therefore it is compatible with the common good. But moral evil is evil absolutely; it can never be desired even indirectly for it is not compatible with the common good. A particular evil in nature, like the destruction of the branches of a tree by a violent wind, may be evil relative to the particular branches but good relative to the whole tree and to the species. But moral evil cannot participate in or contribute to the common good, for by its nature it is something irrational, something in which an intellectual appetite cannot find a sufficient reason for being. Hence moral evil is the prime analogate in evil.

In moral matters more than in material things is evil said to be a contrary of the good, because moral matters depend on the will, and the object of the will is good and evil. Every act is moved and receives its species from the object. Thus if an act of the will tends to what is evil, it is called evil and is evil. This kind of evil is most properly the contrary of good.[33]

In conclusion, then, the question whether or not evil is to be called a contrary of good depends upon whether one is speaking of moral evil or physical evil. The reason for the difference between moral and physical evil is that moral actions are specified by the end freely chosen by the will, but natural actions are specified by the form of the active principle. Things are called morally good or bad because they conform or do not conform to reason, which is the measure belonging to the nature of man.

Evil and good are assigned as specific differences in moral matters, as the first argument asserted, because moral matters depend on the will. For this

---

[32] St. Thomas, *On Evil*, q. 1, art. 3, body of the article.
[33] St. Thomas, *On Evil*, q. 1, art. 1, ad 4.

reason, anything that is voluntary belongs in the class of moral matters. Now, the object of the will is the end and the good. Hence, moral matters get their species from the end, just as natural actions are specified by the form of the active principle; for instance, the act of heating is specified by heat. Hence, because good and evil are so termed by virtue of a universal order, or privation of order, to the end, it is necessary in moral matters for the primary distinction to be between good and evil. Now, there must be but one primary standard in any one genus. The standard in moral matters is reason. Therefore, it must be from a rational end that things in the moral area are termed good or evil. So, in moral matters, that which is specified by an end that is in accord with reason is called good specifically; and that which is specified by an end contrary to the rational end is termed evil specifically. Yet that contrary end, even though it runs counter to the rational end, is nevertheless some sort of good: for instance, something that delights on the sense level, or anything like that. Thus, these are goods for certain animals and even for man, when they are moderated by reason. It also happens that what is evil for one being is good for another. So evil, as a specific difference in the genus of moral matters, does not imply something that is evil in its own essence, but something that is good in itself, though evil for man inasmuch as it takes away the order of reason which is the good for man.

From this it is also clear that evil and good are contraries according to the way they are understood in the area of moral matters, but they are not when taken without qualification.[34]

Good and evil, taken in the broadest sense of opposition between possession and privation, are compatible with the notion of an ordered universe. Good and evil coexist because the privation of what should be in a subject does not completely destroy the good present under some other aspect. Not only are good and evil compatible, but taken in view of the common good, evil is necessarily present in the world as it is. This view of St. Thomas seems at first to argue against the existence of a supremely intelligent and benevolent first cause. But the reasonableness of this view appears once a person stops thinking in the abstract and begins to think concretely and practically about the world in which we live. One can ask himself questions like these: Would it be better if plants and animals did not die? Would it be better if men and women did not grow old? Would it better if there were no weakness of mind and body among all men, no differences in talents, so that all men would be equal in all respects? St. Thomas answers that the world in which no evil takes place is not only a less perfect world but in its present make-up an impossible world. The perfection of the universe requires that there be inequality in things so that every grade of goodness be realized. As the perfection of the universe requires that there should be both incorruptible and corruptible things, so there should be some beings that can fail in

---

[34] St. Thomas, *Summa Contra Gentiles*, III, ch. 9, par. 1, 2. Bourke translation, III, pp. 51–52.

goodness and suffer evil. Everyone can find in his own experience the truth of this position. He knows of evils in his life that have been in fact great benefits. What is true of the individual good of a person is true in a higher way of the various orders of individual good related to the common good. That is the argument of St. Thomas:

> God and nature and any other agent make what is better in the whole, but not what is better in every single part, except in relation to the whole, as was said above. And the whole itself, which is the universe of creatures, is all the better and more perfect if there be some things in it which can fail in goodness, and which do sometimes fail, without God preventing it. This happens, firstly, because it belongs to Providence, not to destroy, but to save nature, as Dionysius says. But it belongs to nature that what may fail should sometimes fail. It happens, secondly, because, as Augustine says, God is so powerful that He can even make good out of evil. Hence many good things would be taken away if God permitted no evil to exist; for fire would not be generated if air was not corrupted, nor would the life of a lion be preserved unless the ass were killed. Neither would avenging justice nor the patience of a sufferer be praised if there were no injustice.[35]

---

[35] St. Thomas, *Summa Theologiae*, I, q. 48, art. 2, ad 3.

CHAPTER **VII**

The Metaphysical Principles of
Knowledge and the Causes of Being

The study of the first principles can be made before taking up that part of metaphysics called *ontology*, which is concerned with the ultimate structure and causes of existing reality. This Aristotle and St. Thomas do in the fourth book of the *Metaphysics* when they show through various dialectical arguments that one must accept the first principles of the knowledge of being. However, a study of the first principles is again taken up after ontology, in the eleventh book, when the validity of the first principles can be seen in the light of the properties of being. The first principles are the laws of thought which the mind discovers in its experience of being. The nonphilosopher has a common sense understanding of these laws. This is evident from the fact that he uses them without questioning their validity; but he does not know why they are valid.

Not all philosophers are in substantial agreement about the first principles, nor do all of them recognize the validity of these principles. For some, the principle of identity is considered mere tautology. For others, the principle of contradiction[1] is thought to apply only to the order of concepts. But others, like the Marxist philosophers who accepted the Hegelian law of dialectics, consider contradiction to be of the very essence of being.

Admitting that the first principles are primarily for us principles of thought, St. Thomas pointed out that man's thoughts do not exist independently of reality. Though our thoughts do not correspond in every detail to reality, they do have a foundation in reality. For example, the concept of man as a species does not exist outside the mind, for only individual men exist, but there is a real human nature existing in each human being upon which the logical notion of species depends. So, too,

---

[1] We use the more familiar designation *principle of contradiction*, although, as some authors point out, it may be more logical to speak of the *principle of noncontradiction*.

the first principles of thought are dependent upon the reality of being and its transcendental properties. The logical validity of the first principles is based immediately upon their ontological foundation. Logical necessity comes only from the objective ontological necessity which is independent of our minds. Because being is what it is and is different from nonbeing we can see the validity of the principles of identity and of contradiction.

All our judgments are ultimately reducible to the truth of the first principles of being. This does not mean that we discover the content of our judgments in an analysis of the first principles, for our knowledge does not come about in this magic way. The metaphysician, like any other human being, must keep his feet on the ground of experience. He does not fabricate truth out of his thoughts nor do judgments about reality come from analyzing first principles; but the validity of our judgments is seen in the light of the first principles.

The First Principles

The name *principle* comes from the Latin *principium*, meaning a starting point. St. Thomas makes the following observation:

> A principle is that which is first either in the *existence* of a thing, as the first of something is called its principle; or in the *coming-to-be* of something, as the first mover is called a principle; or it is first in the *knowledge* of something.[2]

A principle is broader than a cause, for *principle* is a kind of genus under which causes are species. Every cause is a principle, since it is a starting point, but not every principle is a cause. For example, a point is the principle of a line but it is not the cause of a line. Principle implies an order and relationship of persons or things, but cause implies in addition a real influence of one thing upon another in the order of existence or of coming-to-be.

Principle is an analogical term and is applied to different things in different ways: points, parents, potencies, plaster are all principles. In the science of metaphysics the notion of first principle has a special meaning: a first principle is a starting point for an analysis of all our thinking about metaphysical problems. In this respect the study of first principles belongs to that part of metaphysics we call *first philosophy* or *epistemology*, as it is called in more recent philosophical literature.

A first principle must be so evident that no one can be deceived regarding it; it must be absolute and independent of other principles; it must be known immediately, through an analysis of the terms in which it is expressed, and not mediately through the help of demonstration.

---

[2] St. Thomas, *Commentary on the Metaphysics*, V, lesson 1, no. 761.

Can we verify these conditions? The principle of contradiction, "one and the same thing cannot be and not be at the same time," is generally regarded as the first principle of reason, yet it has been denied by various philosophers at one time or another.

In answering this difficulty, St. Thomas admits that this principle can be verbally denied, but he asserts that it cannot be really denied by the human mind. He notes that there is a difference between making a statement and accepting it intellectually, and maintains that it is impossible to deny first principles if they are correctly understood. The denial of first principles may come from misunderstanding the terms employed and the rigid conditions that accompany the use of the principle. For example, if someone thought that the principle of contradiction applies equally to all forms of opposition, he would not understand its meaning. When Engels, for example, in his *Dialectics of Nature* spoke of the identity of opposites as one of the laws of dialectics upon which the Marxist philosophy of nature is built, he misunderstood the meaning of the terms. This is evident from the fact that his examples are presumed to refer always to contradictories whereas they sometimes refer to opposition of relation (as in the diversity of the sexes) or to opposition of contraries (as in the opposition between dying and healthy cells in the body).

Are the first principles demonstrable? To seek a demonstration for every kind of truth is to enter an endless series in which the mind could never prove anything. The conclusion of every demonstration becomes certain by a reduction to a principle of demonstration that eventually cannot be demonstrated and does not need demonstration. All demonstration proceeds from what is more clear to what is less clear, since the purpose of demonstration is to clarify what is obscure. Some propositions must in the end be clear by the very fact that they are stated and seen; these propositions do not need the medium of any evidence other than that of experience and an understanding of terms. The first principles are of this kind.

Experience is necessary for the knowledge of first principles, since by nature the intellect is a potency that is brought to act by something already possessing, in some way, that which it comes to be. In knowing, one becomes the thing known, not in a subjective but in an objective way. Man's intellect functions with a dependence on sensory impressions, analogously to the way that the soul exists and operates in conjunction with the body. No knowledge is completely innate, not even the understanding of first principles. We need some kind of radical experience, as, for example, the knowledge of our own existence and that of a world outside us, to recognize what is generally conceded to be the first principle of all: "One and the same thing cannot be and not be at the same time." My consciousness tells me that I am myself and that I am not whatever is apart from me. Hence my knowledge of being and otherness and of the principle that follows from this knowledge is made known to me in this experience.

The First Principle of Knowledge

After showing what the characteristics of the first principles are, we move on to the question of whether or not there is one first principle that is absolutely first. It is not a question whether or not there can be several first principles that are independent of each other or whether one comes chronologically before the others. Principles, like properties of being, are simultaneous. However there is for our mind a priority and posteriority in the recognition of the principles or laws of being. In this sense we can ask whether there is one principle upon which the others depend. The subsequent principles are not demonstrated by the first, for all are objectively primary laws of being, but the order of the origin of principles in the mind is such that some principles are defended by showing that their denial leads to a denial of some basic principle of reason that cannot be denied without self-contradiction.

St. Thomas holds that the very first principle of all is the one that is contained immediately in the first judgment that we make about being: "It is impossible for the same thing to be and not to be at the same time." The principle is so fundamental to thought that no proposition can make sense without it. Why? Because to deny this principle is to deny that our knowledge of being is real. Therefore, there can be no real deception about the validity of this principle.

> If therefore someone were of the opinion that two contradictions could be true at the same time, thinking that to be is the same as not to be, he would hold at one and the same time contrary points of view. But it is impossible that contraries be present simultaneously. Therefore one cannot be interiorly deceived on this point or think that to be is the same as not to be. Therefore all demonstrations reduce their propositions to this one, which is the universal and first basic thought for all thought.[3]

The Principle of Identity

This first principle can be looked at in two ways: as the positive expression of the first law of thought following an understanding of the unity of being, where it is called the principle of identity; or as the negative expression of the judgment that reveals the division of being from nonbeing, where it is called the principle of contradiction. Both the

---

[3] St. Thomas, *Commentary on the Metaphysics*, IV, lesson 6, no. 603.

principle of contradiction and the principle of identity are based upon the same analysis of being as discovered in experience. But in the principle of contradiction the mind compares being and nonbeing and asserts an opposition between them. Being is not nonbeing. Because it refers to the truth of a proposition in the principle of contradiction, the word *is* has a different meaning from the *is* belonging to a positive judgment about reality. In the principle of identity, on the other hand, the mind focuses attention upon the positive side of being and asserts in a judgment the reality of what is seen. This is a true judgment about the order of reality.

The principle of identity states that what is, is, and cannot not be. This simply means that every being is identified with itself. At first this sounds tautological because it seems that the predicate repeats exactly what is already in the subject, as when we say: *Man is man*, or *John is John*. If the statement is tautological, it does not add anything to knowledge. But if the predicate does not add anything to knowledge, then it is a useless proposition, and the principle that it is based on is useless. First let us see whether the principle of identity confers new meaning and whether a judgment based upon it does add to our knowledge.

In any affirmative proposition the subject is identified in some way with the predicate, as in the propositions: *Man is a substance; man is rational.* In order that the proposition be true there must be unity between the subject and the predicate. This identity can be in one of two orders, in the abstract order of essences or in the order of concrete existence. For example, the proposition: *Man is a rational animal* is an identification in the order of essence. But the proposition: *This man is my father* is an example of a concrete predication that includes extramental existence. In both of these examples the truth of the proposition is based upon the principle that the being in question is identical with itself, because what is predicated is found within the subject.

The principle of identity, upon which predication is based, is primarily a metaphysical principle because it deals with reality. Secondarily it is a logical principle, and it is such only because it applies primarily to the real, since our thoughts must conform with objective reality if they are to be true. As a metaphysical principle, the principle of identity states that in reality a thing is what it is made up of. *A being is what it is.* The identity here is not absolute because it is compatible with a composition of the various properties which constitute it. But it is an identity which gives unity to being, and keeps it from being something else. The principle of identity expresses the unity that is found in every real being, in every essence, and sets it apart from other things which also have their unity. The unity of being makes the truth of any proposition or judgment possible, since the mind is capable of seeing the unity that exists in different objects. If the metaphysical principle of identity were not valid, one could make contradictory statements about one and the same thing and the position of the Sophists would, *per impossibile*, be a "true" one.

Identity is not tautology. Judgment implies a plurality, and plurality implies distinction. First principles, then, must imply judgments that are not mere tautologies, but which, by their combination or disjunction, really express something to our minds. If the statement: *A triangle is a triangle*, is a tautology, as much is contained for the mind in the first use of the word as in the whole phrase. It would not be a true judgment since the purpose of a judgment is to move the mind forward from a simple apprehension. A tautology is simply a repetition of an essential concept without even a hint of anything more than what is already present in the first concept. As tautology, it is not a judgment. Judgment always implies a composition, at least in the conceptual order, and requires at least two conceptually distinct objects. Truth is not contained in simple apprehension but in the composition and division made by the mind. It is contained imperfectly in propositions whose copula is only of the essential order and most properly in propositions of the existential order. Even when a statement of identity does not reach actual existence and remains only in the essential order, a truth is stated and the proposition is at least related to an existential judgment.

There are two stages in the application of the principle of identity, both necessary for its complete understanding. The principle is first employed in our primary intellectual experience of being as found in the objects of sense. In this stage the relationship between essence and existence is not yet clearly defined. Second, it is employed in a judgment in which the full significance of the principle is brought out. The principle of identity is based upon the transcendental note of unity in the act of existence. The identity in the order of essence in the mind ultimately depends upon a composition of essence and existence outside the mind. This is why the principle of identity is not in last analysis a mere tautology, which it would be if the identity it expresses did not pass beyond the conceptual order.

A judgment based on the principle of identity shows that the beings of our experience are contingent, because it implies that their essence is distinct from their existence. The very fact that there is a self-identity in each being gives it an individuality and separates it from other realities, thus giving evidence of their imperfection and contingency. For if a being is not identical with another, it lacks the perfection of that other. Consequently, it is clear that this being is not pure act and perfection in an unqualified sense. It is only in a being whose essence is pure act, whose unity is so great that it lacks no perfection, that one can fully understand the significance of the principle of identity.

The Principle of Contradiction

In its negative form the first principle is called the "principle of contradiction." The positive consideration of being, in which its transcendental unity is recognized, necessarily brings to mind a contrast, an opposition with being, and this we call *nonbeing*. Whatever is not "this being" is something else. In this act, whereby we recognize that reality is a manifold, we see the limitation of being. When we know being as it is found in ourselves, for example, we know that we have substantial existence and certain accidental forms that set us apart from other imperfect things. Above all, the recognition of the contingency of our being prepares our intellect for a judgment of opposition between the perfection of being that we have and the nothingness or emptiness that might have always been.

As for the principle of identity, so for the principle of contradiction the immediate foundation is the transcendental unity of being. This is the view of St. Thomas as expressed in the passage in which he lists the various judgments that follow the knowledge of being.

> Unity that is convertible with being implies the privation of actual division that takes place among opposites, the basic kind of which is affirmation and negation. For those are mutually divided that are such that one is not the other. First, then, one understands being itself, then non-being, then division, then unity as the privation of division, and finally multiplicity, in which there is real division, as in unity there is undividedness.[4]

What is expressed in the first judgment of being is something positive; but a negation immediately follows, because that is the way that the human intellect operates. When we know something, we know it by contrast with something else. We know heat by contrast with cold; we know one color by contrast with another; we know rest by contrast with movement or vice versa. The necessary connection between the positive judgment of what a thing is and the negative judgment of what it is not comes out not only in every act of learning, but also whenever we define something or explain something. In a way, the description of what something is consists in telling what it is not. We prove things through their contraries. That is why the defense of truth in first philosophy devolves immediately upon the principle of contradiction rather than upon its positive counterpart, the principle of identity.

Defense of the First Principle

At the end of that part of metaphysics which is called *first philosophy*, Aristotle (in Book IV of the *Metaphysics*) and St. Thomas

---

4 St. Thomas, *Commentary on the Metaphysics*, IV, lesson 3, no. 566.

defend the validity of the first principle of being and knowledge. They use only dialectical arguments because the nature, divisions, and properties of the subject have not yet been explained sufficiently to permit a more analytical defense of the principle. Against the view of Heraclitus and of the Sophists St. Thomas argues that to deny the validity of the first principle is not only to deny the possibility of science but to make useless any statement whatsoever, since, in the supposition given, there would be no difference between a true and a false statement. No statement could have any definite meaning. More fundamental still, in the order of being, all differences would be done away with, for potency would be the same as act, possible the same as impossible, being the same as nonbeing. Thus the validity of the first principle of metaphysics is defended by showing how its denial would lead to the denial of what should be obvious to anyone. The defense of the first principle is taken up again in a later part of the *Metaphysics* (Book X), after the metaphysician has developed the subject of his science to the point where a positive defense can be made. In the later defense, the *ad hominem* argument gives way to an argument based on the analysis of being itself.

In defending the validity of the first principle of knowledge against those who deny it, St. Thomas first proceeds in a dialectical fashion. First he points out that one must start out with a statement that is acceptable to those who would deny the principle, but which does not appear to be the same as the principle to be defended. On analysis this statement is shown to rest on the validity of the principle denied. This defense can be made in several ways. First, whenever two people are debating a point they must communicate their thoughts in such a way that each will understand what the other means. If one is to understand the point that the other makes, both must agree at least on the signification of the terms — hence there is a basic area of agreement, namely, one in which words have a meaning that is not equivocal. To deny the validity of the first principle in this case is the same as saying that words do not signify anything at all. Therefore *to be* is not the same as *not to be* in the order of signification.

If a name does signify something and is predicated of a subject, it must somehow be present in the subject if the proposition is true. If the proposition is false whatever is signified is not in the subject. Even if the proposition refers to a contingent state, it is necessary that it be true while it is. But *whatever is* at some time or other, *cannot not be* at that time. Therefore, what is affirmed about something cannot at the same time be denied, even though one is talking about something contingent. If this is not true, then words have no meaning.

If an affirmation is no more true than its negation, then absurd consequences will follow. For example, when a person says that *Socrates is a man*, he is saying something that is no more true than saying *Socrates is not a man*. And to say that *Man is not a horse* would be just as true as saying *Man is a horse*. It would follow that man is a man, or a horse, or any animal at all, if contradictions could be true at the same time.

Heraclitus is said[5] to have held that both an affirmative and a negative proposition about the same thing can be true simultaneously. But if and when he proposed this view, he himself made a statement that he wanted to be accepted, namely, that his view on contradiction is the correct one. In doing this, he would implicitly admit the validity of the principle. Therefore he would contradict his own position by making the statement about contradictories. Thus to deny the validity of the first principle is to take away all meaning from words and statements and to preclude all discussion. The only logical position for a person to take if he absolutely denies the principle is to say nothing at all.

Another argument given by St. Thomas against those who deny the first principle consists in finding the reasons why they denied the principle, and then in showing that their reasons are without foundation. Some individuals deny the first principle because they do not understand the analogical meaning of being and of the principles of potency and act by which coming-to-be can be explained. Parmenides, for example, apparently was caught in a dilemma of words when he attempted to explain how things come to be what they are. If he said that being comes from being, his statement would appear nonsensical, because something cannot come to be if it already is. If he said that being comes from nonbeing, his statement would violate the experience of common sense. Some of those who sought to escape this dilemma tried to join the two apparently contradictory positions by saying that being is the same as nonbeing. For example, they would say that lifeless matter, like the food we eat, must, if it is to become living substance, already be alive. It would, consequently, be both lifeless and alive at the same time. Since they did not understand that becoming is intelligible in terms of potency and act, which are not contradictories but contraries, they thought that one must either deny becoming or hold that being and nonbeing are the same. Since they gave an answer to this difficulty through their teaching on potency and act, Aristotle and St. Thomas can successfully argue against those who deny the validity of the first principle.

The denial of the first principle can also be traced to the opinion that, since everything in nature is in a state of flux, there is really no determinate nature in things. Although it is true that material substances are not absolutely stable because matter is mobile by its very essence, there

---

[5] Both Parmenides and Heraclitus have suffered at the hands of interpreters who see only the letter of the text and not the metaphysical thought behind it.

are, in nature, substances that have some element of stability, and the strongest evidence for this is in the experience we have of ourselves:

> If we ourselves are not completely changed, but remain as we were, there will be in some things something permanent, and consequently some determinate truth about which we can judge precisely. For we judge not only of other things, but also of our own human nature.[6]

Our practical judgment also gives evidence of the validity of the first principle of speculative reason. Anyone can find, even in the daily lives of those who deny this principle, many instances of judgments that show their implicit acceptance of it. The example given by St. Thomas is very simple and direct:

> If there is nothing determinate about things, either that they are or that they are not, why does someone bring the kind of food that the doctor ordered and not any other? According to the aforementioned opinion, one could ask, "Is bread something more than no bread at all?" as though affirmation is no more than negation. Thus it would make no difference whether one ate or not. But we know that those who bring the food that the physician ordered have a correct judgment about the food, and that it is the kind that the physician ordered. None of this would be necessary if there were no perduring nature among sensible things to cause certitude, but on the contrary everything were mobile and fluid.[7]

After offering arguments against those who deny the first principle, St. Thomas finally gives advice to those who have debated the question of the truth of the first principle and have been frustrated because of a completely negative attitude on the part of those who deny it. He says that there is no point in trying to continue a discussion with them:

> If those who have taken up the aforementioned position not on some reasonable ground but out of obstinacy concede nothing at all and do not even look for reasons for what they say and remain obstinate in their opinions, it is not easy to rid them of such an opinion. For every kind of reason and argument has this in common that conceding some point one goes on to examine the reason for what is said. But those who concede nothing cut off a discussion and argumentation at the roots. For then there can be no question of a reasoning process that will get rid of their error.[8]

The Principle of Sufficient Reason

This principle is a corollary of the transcendental truth of being. The expression "sufficient reason" is sometimes erroneously thought to be

---

[6] St. Thomas, *Commentary on the Metaphysics*, XI, lesson 6, no. 2240.
[7] St. Thomas, *Commentary on the Metaphysics*, XI, lesson 6, no. 2237.
[8] St. Thomas, *Commentary on the Metaphysics*, XI, lesson 6, no. 2241.

synonymous with per se "efficient causality," as though every being needs a cause outside itself to explain what it is and why it is. This conception of the principle is wrong, first of all because the principle refers to the intelligibility of each being and not to its efficient cause. It has, therefore, a much broader meaning than this principle of causality. We cannot, for example, apply the principle of causality to God, as we do to imperfect things, and say that there is a sufficient "cause" for God's being what He is. But taken to refer to the intelligibility and truth of being, this principle can be applied pre-eminently to God, for the truth of His being is completely autonomous. In imperfect things the truth of things is relative to divine truth.

This causal interpretation of the principle is also wrong because not all things have a proper efficient cause but all things have a sufficient reason for being what they are. Chance events do not have a proper efficient cause, but they are not beyond the scope of intelligibility with reference to divine intelligence.[9] Hence they too participate in being and in truth and have a sufficient reason for their being.

For us, this principle, like the principle of identity, is to be understood in the light of the judgment that follows the recognition of certain transcendental properties in being. As a principle of reason, it has meaning first of all for man in his pursuit of knowledge. The note of transcendental truth in being has an outward or objective counterpart in the principle of sufficient reason that consists in a judgment of intelligibility for the human mind. These two aspects — that of transcendental truth and that of the principle of sufficient reason — are found in the same being, but in the first case the emphasis is on being as conforming to a creative intelligence, while in the second case the emphasis is on being as related to the act of understanding. Thus the principle means that each thing has within itself some truth or intelligibility by which it is capable of being understood either by our human intellect or by some other intellect.

The necessity of the principle of sufficient reason is based upon formal causality, taken in the most universal sense of perfection and intelligibility found within being. When applied to imperfect beings, the principle of sufficient reason is indirectly related to efficient causality. Whenever our mind sees that the beings to which it is conformed by a true judgment are of an imperfect and incomplete nature, not completely intelligible in themselves, we realize that, being contingent, they depend on some extrinsic agent for their existence.

Although the principle of sufficient reason is subsequent in thought to the principle of identity and of contradiction, the dialectical arguments used by St. Thomas to prove the validity of the principle of identity generally begin with propositions related to the principle of

[9] Cf. p. 168 ff.

sufficient reason. When he says, for example, that words must have a meaning he refers to their intelligibility, that is, their sufficient reason for being what they are. To deny this is to undermine all discourse. When he says that to say *Man is man* is not the same as saying *Man is not man* or *Man is a horse* or any other kind of animal, he is pointing to the truth content of beings and saying that to deny this content is sheer nonsense, for it inevitably leads the one who argues against this principle to deny the very position he must maintain to argue against it.

The intelligibility of things, namely, their sufficient reason, is not always clear to man. Because being in all its intelligibility cannot be comprehended by a finite intelligence, the principle of sufficient reason is applicable in its fullest sense only to the divine intelligence. There is little need to insist on this point, once we realize that every individual thing in nature has a mystery about it that keeps it from becoming a truth fully possessed by man. The truth of individual existence is only partially within the natural potency of the human mind; it cannot be possessed as a thing, and it cannot be comprehended. Both natural beings and chance beings are intelligible because they exist and have sufficient reason for being what they are. But they are beyond man, being, in a sense, infinite, insofar as they are related to the infinite possibilities of divine intelligence and free choice.

Causes in General

A nominal definition of cause. The term *cause* does not have a strict definition, because it is one of the primary concepts that follow immediately from the understanding of being. No proximate genus and specific difference can be assigned to it. It can, however, be described in a roundabout way by using words that tell in an abstract way what is present in the concrete order of existence. For example, we can speak of the relationship between potency and act and the coming-to-be or passing away of something. But it is in the concrete experience of the many modes of being that we first know what a cause is.

In trying to give a nominal definition, some consider the definition of cause from the part of the cause and others from the effect. Viewing the problem from the side of the cause itself, they emphasize the influence which gives rise to the thing caused. Viewing the matter from the aspect of the effect, they emphasize the note of dependence in imperfect beings. Thus, some authors say: "A cause is that which by itself (*per se*) brings about being in another." Others change this definition slightly and say: "A cause is that which an effect follows." Some authors define it as: "A cause is that from which another depends essentially (*per se*)." Others say that a "cause is that from which something else follows."

Others, like Avicenna, say that a "cause is that which gives being to a thing." But all these definitions seem to be begging the question, since they assume that the very thing we are seeking to define is already clear.

A suitable nominal definition of cause will bring in all of those conditions by which it is explained and by which it is differentiated from other things. The notion of cause implies first of all the idea of *principle*, as a kind of genus. Hence, it requires a sequence in being on the part of the thing caused. In addition it demands the influence of one thing on another or the derivation of one from another, a dependence on another. Hence it follows that there is a difference between the cause and the thing caused.

In various texts St. Thomas notes what features characterize a cause. In his *Commentary on the Physics* he says that those are called causes upon which things depend either for their being (*esse*) or for their coming into existence (*fieri*).[10] Thus he defines cause through the condition of dependence. In the *Summa Theologiae* he says that the name *cause* implies a diversity of substance and a dependence of one on the other, something that is not contained in the notion of *principle*.[11] In his *Commentary on the Metaphysics* he says that "*principle* implies some kind of order, while the word *cause* means some kind of influence (*influxum*) upon the thing caused."[12] Thus he defines cause through the influence it has on other things. Finally, he defines cause through the notion of sequence in the thing caused, saying that a cause is that after which something else follows. These different notions of cause are not contrary to each other, but help to explain each other. From these various statements we can make up a tentative definition made up of these various aspects: A *cause is that from which something proceeds* (*principle*) *with dependence*.

The word *principle* is used as a kind of generic term to indicate a source or origin of something. The word *dependence* is put in to show how it differs from the generic meaning of principle, which does not necessarily imply dependency, but only points out the order between the principle and that which proceeds from it. Dependence is not the same as a *conditio sine qua non*, since this latter expression does not connote influence but something merely concomitant or simply requisite for the real cause.

The Four Species of Causes

The complete definition of anything is a kind of demonstration

---

[10] St. Thomas, *Commentary on the Physics*, I, lesson 1, no. 5.
[11] St. Thomas, *Summa Theologiae*, I, q. 33, art. 1, ad 1.
[12] St. Thomas, *Commentary on the Metaphysics*, V, lesson 1, no. 751.

because it contains all four causes that make a being intelligible. Two causes relate to the intrinsic structure of the being, and two other causes refer to its origin and end. This division of causes into four primary species in the natural order is given in various passages in St. Thomas.[13] In the *Commentary on the Metaphysics* he gives descriptions of each of the four causes, which we shall paraphrase.

Material cause. First there is the cause out of which something is made. It is the material that is made into something or the subject that receives a new form and mode of existence, as the bronze is made into a statue. The material can receive the new form on condition that it does not already have it, and in this sense something can be said to come into existence from a state of nonbeing. It does not, however, come from nonbeing in an absolute sense, because the matter, such as bronze, has a reality of its own even before it becomes the subject of a new form and a new act of existence. This is called the material cause of being, and is found only in things pertaining to nature where generation and corruption take place, and in artifacts. Since it does not belong to all beings, the metaphysician does not directly place the study of material causality in the subject of his science.

Formal cause. Second there is the *formal cause*. A formal cause may be intrinsic to a being or extrinsic. If intrinsic, it is the principal part of the definition of something, for it, more than the material cause, tells what a thing is. The material is what is common to several distinct forms, as, for example, wood that is the subject of such varied forms as a house, a statue, a salad bowl, and the like. The material cause has a potency to new being; the formal cause actualizes this potency. Form completes the essence and is therefore put directly into the definition of something, whereas the matter is presupposed as a subject and is put into the definition obliquely, as when one defines a statue by telling whose figure is in it but mentions incidentally that it is made out of wood or marble.

The intrinsic formal cause pertains to the subject of metaphysics because it is through the form in conjunction with the act of existence that something is constituted in being. An extrinsic formal cause is related to being only indirectly, as the photograph is related to a real man. Signs are extrinsic formal causes, and may be natural or artificial. Thus there are natural signs like smoke which is a representation of fire, or crying which is a sign of an emotion. There are artificial signs, like a handshake which is a sign of friendship, or a flag which represents a nation. The extrinsic formal sign belongs in metaphysics only by analogy of signification with intrinsic formal cause.

Efficient cause. Third there is the *efficient cause*. This term has a narrower meaning than *agent cause* for it is applied only to the produc-

[13] See *Commentary on the Metaphysics*, V, lesson 2, *passim*.

tion of something outside the agent through what is called transitive activity. Agent cause, a more universally metaphysical concept, applies to activity of any kind, whether immanent or transient, and can be predicated of God, the highest form of life, existence, knowledge, and love, in whom the entire perfection of activity remains essentially within the individual that acts. Efficient causality in the narrower sense is found only among beings of the categories; it is of the essence of this kind of cause that it refers to imperfect being in which change takes place. An efficient cause is correlative to an effect: it, thus, implies a multiplicity in substance, dependency of one thing upon another, a priority and posteriority in the order of being, and a movement from potency to act.

Efficient cause is not predicated univocally of all things to which it can be applied in a proper sense. For example, the movement of bodies in space is due to efficient causality in a sense quite different from the movement of the intellect in the process of making a work of art. The category of action and its reciprocal category of passion follow from the one mode of efficient causality; but the category of quality follows from a second mode of efficient causality. Though the intellect and the will do produce things outside themselves, as works of art are produced by the intellect or habits are caused by the will, transitive activity is secondary to the essential activity which is immanent and remains totally within the agent. That is why we say that the term *agent cause* is more aptly applied to immanent activity and efficient causality to transitive activity.

The efficient cause can be subdivided into species that participate more or less in its primary meaning. Thus there are *dispositive causes, co-operative causes, instrumental causes,* and *accidental causes.* How these subdivisions operate in conjunction with a primary efficient cause will be seen in the final chapter on the proofs for the existence of God.

Final cause. The fourth species of cause is the *final cause.* It is that for the sake of which something takes place. Because the final cause is the last in the order of coming-to-be and seems to be nothing other than a *fait accompli,* some philosophers (in particular, materialistic determinists) hold that this should not really be classified as a proper cause. However, to deny the reality of final cause is to deny the distinction between potency and act and all real coming-to-be, for final causality is the foundation of all other causes. It is first among all the causes since all causes depend on it to exert their own causality. For example, the materials, the workers, and the form of the house have meaning only in relation to the end that is conceived before any other causes come into play.

Although the end is last in existence in some things, it is always first in causality. Hence it is called the cause of causes, for it is the cause of the causality in all other causes. As has been said, it is the cause of efficient causality. But an efficient cause is the cause of matter and form, for by its activity it causes matter to receive a form and causes form to exist in matter. Consequently the end is also the cause of the causality of matter and form.[14]

The final cause is found not only in the end that is absolutely the last, but also in any intermediate goal on the way. Any movement has stages which are sought because they are desirable in view of the final end. For example, a person eats to maintain his health, so that he can work to get money for study that will make him an educated man or woman. Thus one goal points to another. The intellect is compelled by the laws of being to find an absolute end through which all intermediary ends are established. This we shall see in the final chapter on the existence of a supreme good, the absolute end of all.

The Modes of the Causes

The division of causes into species is based upon the various ways in which something can properly be called a cause. The division of causes into modes depends on the relationship between cause and effect. Thus in each species of causality there is an order based on the way the cause exerts its influence: primarily or secondarily, principally or instrumentally, necessarily or accidentally, in a series or individually. All these modes of causality are found in the various species of cause. Let us examine briefly several of the modes as listed by St. Thomas in his *Commentary on the Metaphysics*.[15]

Principal cause and instrumental cause. A principal cause is directly productive of the substance or nature of the effect in any of the four species of causes; an instrumental cause is the medium through which the influence of the principal cause is transferred to the effect. For example, in building, workers transform their intelligence and energy into the form of a house through the medium of tools applied to suitable materials. The workers are principal causes of the house; the tools are instrumental. Without the principal cause the instrumental cause would have no activity of its own in the actual production of anything; however, the latter is a true cause since it makes the application of the efficient cause to the material cause possible. Moreover, something of the instrumental cause enters into the effect, as when the marks of the chisel, its bluntness or sharpness, are seen in the sculptured work, and it is because of this

---

[14] St. Thomas, *Commentary on the Metaphysics*, V, lesson 3, no. 782.
[15] St. Thomas, *Commentary on the Metaphysics*, V, lesson 3, nos. 783–794. Cf. Reading 5 for this chapter, "On the Four Classes of Causes."

that the instrumental cause is distinguished from a *conditio sine qua non*. The quality of the chisel marks belongs to the essence of the piece of art conceived by the artist.

Proper cause and accidental cause. A proper cause is one which influences the effect according to its nature and in proportion to its perfection. The axiom, "Every agent acts according to its nature" refers to proper causality. Proper causality is found not only in the four species of causes but also in some of the modes of the causes. For example, the chisel that is an instrumental cause with respect to the principal cause is a proper cause with respect to the effect, since some aspects of the thing produced are the immediate effect of the instrument used. An accidental cause, however, is one that is not by nature positively ordered toward the effect that is produced. It is a cause that is joined to the principal or proper cause without the direction of a free agent or beyond the intention of nature. For example, there would be no natural connection between the color of the pencil and the kind of writing that is produced by it, unless the color did actually influence the emotions or the thinking of the person writing. Nor would there be any natural connection between a woman's preference for red dresses and her giving birth to a red-headed baby. In the mode of *accidental cause* the term *accidental* does not refer to those categories of being that are added to a substance and are naturally representative of substance, such as shape, size, position, but to those things which, without positive purpose or direction, incidentally accompany the proper causes in the act of causing. Accidental cause can be divided into subspecies that are defined according to the distance (analogically speaking) that separates them from proper causality. First, there is the cause that takes away the obstacles in the path of the proper causes (*removens prohibens*), for example, the removal of a mosquito netting would be the accidental cause of malaria; second, there is the contingency that is always found in the operations of nature so that it does not always produce its natural effect but only in most cases; third, there is sheer coincidence that has no connection with nature at all, but which is thought to be a cause because of the sequence in which something occurs, such as the earthquake that takes place when someone blows a trumpet.

Universal causes and particular cause. As the names indicate, these modes of causality are defined according to the extent of the influence they have with respect to other things. According to one axiom on causality, the cause must be proportionate in power to the effect: universal causes produce universal effects, and particular causes produce particular effects. For example, in the process of reproduction the individual characteristics of the parents produce the particular qualities of children that make them resemble their parents. But in the parents there is a more universal cause, a human nature that is not peculiar to them as individuals, and it is this that is the cause of the reproduction of a human being, an effect more universal than the parental characteristics. A universal cause is one that produces effects that are not limited to an individual effect, or a series of effects that are specifically the same, or effects that belong to a particular genus, and so on — the universality of the cause is relative to the category of the effect in question. Hence, an absolutely universal cause is one that has within itself the whole perfection of being, for a thing can cause only in proportion to its nature. The proper effect of an absolutely universal cause is being without qualification. Hence it implies the power of total production of something — in other words, the power of creation in the strict sense.

Primary and secondary causes. This division of the modes of causality refers to the order of priority of perfection in the act of causing. It has nothing to do, per se, with a sequence in time but only with the dependence that causes arranged in a series have upon each other. Several things can be necessary causes, proper causes, per se causes, and yet in a series one of them is subordinate to another. For example, when a person turns a corner in his automobile, his muscles are per se necessary and proper causes, but they are subordinate to the intelligence and will of the man behind the steering wheel. All takes place simultaneously, but it is evident that the turning of the corner is due first to the intellect, then to the will, and then to the muscles that carry out the command. No member of the series can be dispensed with — the car will not turn simply because of knowledge, nor because of decision, but only when all three are lined up in proper sequence of dependence.

The Principle of Efficient Causality

When we speak of the causes as principles we are not using the term *principle* in the same sense as when we spoke of the first principles of knowledge. Causes are *principles of being* insofar as they positively influence the being of things. The causes are *principles of knowledge* insofar as they are seen in the light of the principles of identity, of contradiction, and of sufficient reason, which are the first principles of the science of metaphysics.

The principle of efficient causality can be stated as follows: "Whatever comes to be in any way whatever is caused by something other." We do not restrict the principle to beings in motion, for it is applicable universally to all contingent beings. However, the principle of efficient causality is first discovered in our experience of potency and act in the changes that take place in the sense world. For example, the movement of an automobile requires a motive force consisting of fuel turned into energy that moves the vehicle from one position in space to another.

The motive force is given to the vehicle by a cause already existing, which is so related to the effect to be produced that it can in some way be said to possess the effect already. It is evident that changes similar to local motion, for example, seeing, growing, reproduction, the creating of works of art, take place, and that these changes are always brought about by a being already in act and similar in some way or other to the effect produced. These are among those self-evident truths that require nothing more than common sense for evidence of their truth. But knowing the fact of change and realizing the necessity of an extrinsic cause in act is not enough for scientific knowledge. One must know the reason why the necessity is there.

Although the principle of efficient causality cannot be demonstrated, its validity can be defended. This is accomplished, first, by direct experiential knowledge that forces us to recognize the fact of change, and then by an analysis of the proposition that every changing being requires an extrinsic cause already in act. This is the kind of proposition that can be understood and accepted only when one understands the meaning of the terms used. However a dialectical argument, one based on suppositions, can be set up in syllogistic form to convince someone who denies this principle. By reducing this principle to the more fundamental ones of identity and of contradiction, one can make a reasonable defense of it. The dialectical argument supposes first of all that there are real changes in nature, that there are different states of being, and that these changes and diverse states necessarily require the intrinsic principles of potency and act. If someone were to deny all differences in states of being and the real generation and corruption of things, no discussion could continue. The argument presupposes secondly that the principles of identity and of contradiction are valid. It presupposes, finally, that the state of potency is really different from the state of actuality. To deny this principle of efficient causality is also to deny the principles of identity and of contradiction and, consequently, to deny being itself. What is predicated of a being without belonging to it by nature is not caused by that being itself but by another.[16] This means that when the perfection which is predicated of any being is seen to be different from it, one must conclude that the subject has received the perfection from a being already having that perfection. This is most obvious, for example, in the presence of such sensible phenomena as heat and cold, movement and rest. A body without heat becomes hot when it is in contact with another body that is hot or can produce heat. And blood does not move unless it is pumped by the heart. But the principle of efficient causality is found in all the categories and applies wherever there is a distinction between potency and act, whether this

---

[16] See St. Thomas, *Summa Contra Gentiles*, I, ch. 22.

is on the substantial plane as in the distinction between essence and existence, or on the plane of accidental perfection in any of the categories, or finally in both corporeal and spiritual beings.

The contingency of a composite being shows that it is dependent on and caused by an external agent. Something that can be received or lost is not identical with the subject and cannot have its origin solely in the subject. Hence the validity of this principle is based on the real distinction between potency and act. If a being is by nature a perfection, it cannot be said to be the cause of its own perfection. In it, the perfection is uncaused. Nor can it be the cause of this perfection in another if it does not have the perfection or its equivalent, for by definition a cause is that which by virtue of its form is capable of causing something like itself in another. This supposes a real distinction between the cause and the caused, or what is equivalent, between act and potency.

To be the cause of itself a being would have to be at one and the same time cause and effect, potency and act, perfection and absence of perfection. The truth of the principle of efficient causality is seen once the terms of the statement are understood, for it is nothing other than the principle of identity applied to the world of contingent being. To deny the principle is to be caught in a dilemma: Either we are deceived when we think that things really change or we must admit that whatever comes to be comes from nothing. If the first alternative is true, then everything is always what it was and what it will be; hence there is no coming to be and no such activity as efficient causality. If the second alternative is true, there is again no causality, for an efficient cause acts only in virtue of its existing form. What is not cannot act. We have seen that a thing cannot bring itself into existence if it already is existent, since *is* and *come-to-be* are two contrary aspects of being. The one, *is*, refers to act; the other, *come-to-be*, refers to potency. And it is clear that a non-existent cannot be a cause. Therefore the principle of efficient causality is seen to be valid by the analysis of its terms.

St. Thomas gives this kind of analytical proof to show that no being can be the cause of itself. He says that it is evident that a thing can be a cause only to the extent that it has existence, for "each thing stands in the same relation to the fact that it is a cause, as it does to the fact that it is a being."[17] Therefore nothing could be its own cause, because it would be prior to itself.[18] It would have to be and not be at the same time, and this is impossible.

Next St. Thomas shows that no being can be the cause of any perfection in other things unless it already possesses that perfection in

[17] St. Thomas, *Summa Contra Gentiles*, III, ch. 74. Translated by Vernon Bourke (New York: Doubleday Image, 1956), III, p. 247.

[18] St. Thomas, *Summa Contra Gentiles*, I, ch. 18.

its capacity as a cause. To be without the perfection in question is the same, relatively, as not to be. Each thing exists and can cause perfection in another only by virtue of the form that it has. The form is a principle of efficient causality. Hence a form would be purposeless unless it served as a principle of operation. All things created would seem, in a way, purposeless, if they lacked an operation proper to them since the purpose of everything is its operation.

> The operative powers which are seen to exist in things would be bestowed on things to no purpose, if things produced nothing through them. Indeed, all things created would seem, in a way, to be purposeless, if they lacked an operation proper to them; since the purpose of everything is its operation. For the less perfect is always for the sake of the more perfect. Consequently, just as the matter is for the sake of the form, so the form which is the first act is for the sake of its operation, which is the second act.[19]

Causality in living beings. Living beings are sometimes defined as those that can move themselves. This seems to exclude the activity of self-movement from the principle of efficient causality. It appears as though something can be the cause of its own perfection, as is the case, for example, in knowledge that is gained through one's own effort, or in a movement like walking which comes from an intrinsic principle.

But the principle of efficient causality still applies. Imperfect immanent activity requires an agent really distinct from the effect produced. In the case of living beings, there is a diversity of parts, of which one is active and the other passive, so that the principle of efficient causality is verified within the composite. True, living beings also possess immanent activity, or activity which remains totally within and whereby the very being itself is perfected. In activity of this kind the "distance" between the cause and effect is reduced as far as possible. Nevertheless, there remains a radical contingency even in the most perfect created living beings, a real distinction between their potency and act, between their being and their operation.

Every agent causes something like itself. Among the axioms that are contained in the principle of causality is the one that states that "every being must produce an effect like itself." It is not difficult to see that it is necessary for something to exist before it can cause, or that a thing causes by virtue of its form, but that a being must produce effects like itself appears to contradict common sense. For it seems possible that a virtuous man can sin, that a good artist can make a poor painting, that a substance with one essence can produce an effect with a different essence.

The difficulty can be answered when one realizes that there are both

---

[19] St. Thomas, *Summa Theologiae*, I, q. 105, art. 5.

univocal and analogical causes. There are some beings which naturally produce univocal effects, that is, effects that are of the same nature. For example, a lighted candle that falls upon combustible material will cause a fire in the material, and the local motion of one body can cause motion in another body. Among causes of this kind, there is the possibility of producing effects that are fundamentally the same, but which differ according to the nature of the subject in which the effect is produced. Thus moving water can produce electricity; electricity can cause light; and light can cause heat. Here is a series of different kinds of motion coming from a univocal source. The underlying cause, however, is a body in motion.

But there are other causes capable of producing analogical effects. The greater the power of the cause, the more varied will be the effects produced. In this way God causes the being of creatures; the artist is the analogical cause of a work of art. In every effect traces of the cause can be found. Even in defective things there is an image of the cause: a poor piece of art is evidence of a defective habit of art; an immoral act is evidence of a man of imperfect virtue. Each thing can cause according to the perfection of its being: univocal causes produce univocal effects; analogical causes produce analogical effects; universal causes produce universal effects.

A limited being is not able to cause a universal effect. That is why no creature can be more than an instrumental cause in the production of the total being of something. In the process of generation the parents are not the total cause of their children's being, but instruments of their coming-to-be. The particular native qualifications of the children are attributed to the particular qualifications of the parents, but their essence and existence must be attributed to universal causes. This is equivalently the teaching of St. Thomas.

> Every effect depends on its cause, so far as it is its cause. But we must observe that an agent may be the cause of the *becoming* of its effect, but not of its *being*. This may be seen both in artificial and in natural things. For the builder causes the house in its becoming, but he is not the direct cause of its being. For it is clear that the being of the house is a result of its form, which consists in the putting together and arrangement of the materials, and which results from the natural qualities of certain things. Thus the cook prepared the food by applying the natural activity of fire; and in the same way a builder constructs a house, by making use of cement, stones, and wood, which are able to be put together in a certain order and to conserve it. Therefore the being of the house depends on the nature of these materials, just as its becoming depends on the action of the builder. The same principle applies to natural things. For if an agent is not the cause of a form, as such, neither will it directly be the cause of the being which results from that form; but it will be the cause of the effect only in its becoming.

Now it is clear that of two things in the same species one cannot be essentially the cause of the other's form as such, since it would then be the cause of its own form, since both forms have the same nature; but it can be the cause of this form inasmuch as it is in matter — in other words, it may be the cause that *this* matter receives *this* form. And this is to be the cause of becoming, as when man begets man, and fire causes fire. Thus whenever a natural effect is such that it has an aptitude to receive from its active cause an impression specifically the same as that in the active cause, then the becoming of the effect depends on the agent, but not its being.[20]

Causality through a series. One of the questions connected with the principle of efficient causality is that of the effect of a series of causes. An effect may be produced by an arrangement of primary and secondary causes in what is called a *per se* subordinate series of proper causes. Their series has the following characteristics: the secondary causes cannot act except as members of the series, even though they have a nature that is properly a principle of movement; each member of the series affects the total effect; each cause in the series has a mode of causation proper to its nature; there must be a limited number of these causes, a first in the series, and this is not dependent upon other causes but the others are dependent upon it.

In accord with the principle of causality, if there were no first cause to which the effect can ultimately be traced, there would be no effect at all. The other members of the series cannot by themselves produce the effect, since intermediate causes operate not only in virtue of their own nature but require in addition the influence of a superior cause. If all causes were intermediate causes, even if there were an infinite series of such causes, there would not be in the series a sufficient explanation for the effect that takes place. Only the presence in the series of a cause that is universally the source of the total line of causality will explain the effect.

An accidental series exercises causality in a way essentially different from a *per se* subordinate series of causes. Its causality is necessarily univocal in the series and in its effects; there is no hierarchy of being among the causes; there is no proper causality in any or all members of the sequence with respect to the total effect produced; hence, any one member of the series can be dropped without affecting the result as long as the members of the series are conjoined; finally, there need not be a first within the series. Theoretically the series can be infinite. A series of such causes is not an adequate explanation of the actual effect. For example, a network of pipes from which water is flowing does not explain the flow of water from the last one. Even if pipe were laid to pipe *ad infinitum* the flow of water would not be explained. It can be explained only

---

[20] St. Thomas, *Summa Theologiae*, I, q. 104, art. 1, c.

by causes that relate naturally to water and to movement. Therefore, whenever something is produced by an accidental series of causes, one must look outside the series for the explanation. The same reason that excludes the possibility of an infinite series of *per se* subordinate causes proves that the *per accidens* series of causes will not explain a given effect, even though one admits the possibility of an infinite series of accidental causes.

This is the argument of St. Thomas, who admits that reason cannot prove that the world had to have a beginning in time (i.e., a first within an accidental series of moving bodies by which the intellect measures time), but denies that an infinite series can explain an effect that takes place here and now.

> In efficient causes it is impossible to proceed to infiinity *per se*. Thus, there cannot be an infinite number of causes that are *per se* required for a certain effect; for instance, that a stone be moved by a stick, the stick by the hand, and so on, to infinity. But it is not impossible to proceed to infinity *accidentally* as regards efficient causes; for instance, if all the causes thus infinitely multiplied should have the order of only one cause, while their multiplication is accidental; e.g., as an artificer acts by means of many hammers accidentally, because one after the other is broken. It is accidental, therefore, that one particular hammer should act after the action of another, and it is likewise accidental to this particular man as generator to be generated by another man; for he generates as a man, and not as the son of another man. For all men generating hold one grade in the order of efficient causes, viz., the grade of a particular generator. Hence it is not impossible for man to be generated by man to infinity; but this would be impossible if the generation of this man depended on this man, and on an elementary body, and on the sun, and so on to infinity.[21]

The Principle of Final Causality

The principle is stated as follows: "Every agent acts for an end." The principle of efficient causality cannot be separated from the principle of final causality because the form of a being, which is the principle of its efficient causality, also tends to the good that befits the being. Efficient causes act only to attain a good. There cannot be a tendency without a real good, a possible good, or a falsely represented good at the end of the activity. This is shown by the following argument. If there were no specific good as the end of the activity, either the movement of the agent would be completely unintelligible, because it would be contrary to the perfection of the agent to tend to something not worth attaining, or the movement could not take place at all, since there is no such thing as real movement in general. Every real movement and activity is a par-

---

[21] St. Thomas, *Summa Theologiae*, I, q. 46, art. 2, ad 7.

ticular movement toward a particular goal. Unless the end of the activity is specified there cannot be any activity at all. There can be tendencies in several directions, but the several directions must be distinctly specified. The movement of the appetites cannot be like the movements of the character who "leaped on his horse and rode off in all directions."

> If an agent did not incline toward some definite effect, all results would be a matter of indifference for him. Now, he who looks upon a manifold number of things with indifference no more succeeds in doing one of them than another. Hence, from an agent contingently indifferent to alternatives no effect follows, unless he be determined to one effect by something. So, it would be impossible for him to act. Therefore, every agent tends toward some determinate effect, and this is called his end.[22]

The end of activity is a good. Every action or movement is ordered toward being either as substance or as the accidental perfections that accompany substance or which it acquires later. By the very fact that something exists at all, it is good; it would not have come into being were it not the fulfillment of some potency. That toward which an agent tends in a definite way must be in accord with it, otherwise one would have to say that nature tends to harm rather than perfect itself. What is appropriate to any nature is called the good of that nature — though what is appropriate and good for one nature or one individual may not be so for another. For one cannot make generalizations about what is good or bad without taking into consideration both the universal nature and the individual substance that has that nature.

The fact that the action occasionally terminates in something other than what was intended does not alter the fact that there was originally a goal toward which the action was directed. This original purpose must be something that is possible or at least it must be regarded as possible, otherwise the movement could not start, for what is impossible cannot be a good, and what is not a good cannot affect the appetite of an agent either rational or irrational. For in every agent the principle of activity is an appetite that is either natural or elicited, that is, dependent on knowledge either sensory or intellectual. If agents occasionally seem to act at random and not intend the particular effect that is produced, they have some definite purpose that occasionally turns to an unexpected end. St. Thomas' argument is given in the following passage from the *Summa Contra Gentiles:*

> There are some actions that do not seem to be for an end. Examples are playful and contemplative actions, and those that are done without attention, like rubbing one's beard and the like. These examples could make a person think that there are some cases of acting without an end.

---

[22] St. Thomas, *Summa Contra Gentiles*, III, ch. 2, par. 8. Bourke translation, III, p. 37.

However, we must understand that contemplative actions are not for another end, but are themselves an end. On the other hand, acts of play are sometimes ends, as in the case of a man who plays solely for the pleasure attaching to play; at other times they are for an end, for instance, when we play so that we can study better afterward. Actions that are done without attention do not stem from the intellect but from some sudden act of imagination or from a natural source. Thus, a disorder of the humors produces an itch and is the cause of rubbing the beard, and this is done without intellectual attention. So these actions do tend to some end, though quite apart from the order of the intellect.[23]

In the order of coming-to-be, a qualified good presupposes the ideas of efficient, formal, and material causes. Such a good is said to be first in the order of intention but last in the order of execution. But in the transcendental order, the good in an unqualified sense is prior to the formal, efficient, and material causes, for all are for the sake of the real good that already exists.

From the twofold notion of good in the order of becoming and the order of being, Professor Maritain lists two formulations of the principle of finality.[24] The first formulation of the principle is: *Potency is determined by act* (*Potentia dicitur ad actum*); his second is: *Every agent acts for an end* (*omne agens agit propter finem*). The first formulation of the principle, with which we are most familiar, is based on our experience of the movement from potency to act in human activity. But the movement entails activity toward good in a qualified sense: a good that comes to be as the result of the activity of an efficient cause upon a subject in particular order. The second formulation is a more profound expression of the principle, for it prescinds from movement and coming-to-be, from efficient causality in the limited sense of the term. The term *agent*, as Maritain points out, is more universal than the term *efficient cause*. An agent is a principle of activity in the broad sense of a principle of perfection. It refers more properly to immanent activity in which the agent and the good are found identified in the one power, whereas an efficient cause is a principle of activity for the production of something outside the agent. Therefore it has the aspect of instrument for the good that is to be. Immanent activity does not imply imperfection as does efficient causality, because it is not directed toward something else. The activity of an agent in immanent activity does not necessarily entail a transition from potency to act and a sequence of priority and posteriority, whereas the notion of efficient cause implies a transition and sequence, at least in the recipient. Therefore the

---

[23] St. Thomas, *Summa Contra Gentiles*, III, ch. 2, par. 9. Bourke translation, III, pp. 37–38.

[24] See *Preface to Metaphysics* (New York: Sheed and Ward, 1948), Sixth Lecture, p. 110 ff.

transcendental formulation of the principle of final causality applies universally to all being in an analogical way.

Good diffuses itself. This axiom is implicitly contained in the principle of final causality. It is sometimes interpreted in the limited context of efficient causality, as though the principle meant that what is good must bring other things into existence. But this would subordinate the good to the act of production. On the contrary, nothing that comes to be imposes necessity on a universal good except in the sense of hypothetical necessity: If something comes to be, it must come from an agent that is good. But the hypothetical character of the proposition shows that it treats of contingent being. There is no necessity that compels the highest good to create, for creation is a free choice of a most perfect being. But in the hypothesis that God has chosen to make a particular being, what He makes is necessarily good. In this sense good is correctly said to diffuse itself. God's goodness is such that when it radiates outside itself everything touched by divine causality is good.

A more proper meaning of the axiom is that whatever is good is the measure and perfection of everything that is directed to it. Whatever is or comes to be is called good to the extent that it is ordered to that good. Good in the primary and unqualified sense is that which is self-contained and not directed to anything else. Secondarily, something is called good by analogy when it leads to the good, as useful things are called good; or when it naturally follows upon the end and is measured by it, as pleasure is measured by good that is for its own sake. This is the interpretation St. Thomas gives to the axiom that good diffuses itself.

> Though, according to the proper use of the word, to pour out seems to imply the operation of an efficient cause, yet taken broadly it can imply the status of any cause, as do to influence, to make, etc. When good is said to be of its very notion diffusive, however, diffusion is not to be understood as implying the operation of an efficient cause but rather the status of final cause. Nor is such diffusion brought about through the mediation of any added power. Good expresses the diffusion of a final cause and not that of an agent, both because the latter, as efficient, is not the measure and perfection of the thing caused but rather its beginning, and also because the effect participates in the efficient cause only in an assimilation of its form, whereas a thing is dependent upon its end in its whole existence.[25]

The capacity to diffuse goodness is the quality possessed by those things that are ends in themselves. It is like a source of light and warmth that attracts other things to itself. Other things share in the light and warmth to the degree that they are related to the source. The light and

---

[25] St. Thomas, *Truth*, q. 21, art. 1, ad 4. Translated by Robert W. Schmidt, S.J. (Chicago: Henry Regnery, 1953), Vol. III, p. 8.

warmth that represent the good in each thing are the result of a move-ment of love rather than a transitive action, as love is immanent activity. Love calls for a union with what is loved. What is secondarily good must tend toward its source.

The problem of chance. A difficult question connected with the principle of final causality is that relating to chance events. Not all philoso-phers are agreed that chance events are objective. Even among scholastic philosophers some are of the opinion that a chance event is real relative only to the knower, and that in last analysis there is no chance event but only ignorance of what is due to *per se* causality. Some hold that something is not to be called a "chance event" if we consider the interaction of all the physical parts of the universe and prescind from the interference of a free agent. Suarez, for example, says that what is contingent with respect to a proximate cause operating through a natural principle is not contingent but necessary if one relates this to the whole order and series of causes in the universe, provided that no free agent interferes with natural causes by applying other causes or by removing natural hindrances. Those who deny that anything can happen by chance say that chance is nothing other than ignorance on our part and that things are predetermined in their causes but that we, the observers, do not know what the causes are. They say that ignorance can be of two kinds: First, there is ignorance relative to a given observer but not to any and all observers. Thus what would appear to be chance for the person involved may actually be due to *per se* causes that are obvious to someone else. For example, if a person sent on an errand were to meet unexpectedly someone he had not seen for many years, he would call it chance. But if the person who met him foresaw the meeting, it would not be chance for him. Second, there is ignorance that is relative to any observer, so that it is impossible by the very nature of the object to predict what would happen because it is im-possible for any finite mind to know all the circumstances that enter into what would be an explanation of a chance event. In this conception a nature which acts for a given end is prevented from attaining that end because it is interfered with by another nature acting for a different end. It is impossible for a finite mind to grasp all the possibilities involved in the two natures. Even in this conception of chance, how-ever, the definition of chance would refer to ignorance on the part of the observer rather than to an objective indeterminism on the part of the natures involved. St. Thomas, however, relates chance events not primarily to the question of knowledge but to that of causality. He says:

> An effect follows in the line of its proximate cause. Therefore some-thing is said to *happen by chance* if it happens outside the direction of

nature at work, or *by fortune* if it happens outside the intention of a free agent, even though the thing is under divine providence.[26]

Thus if an agent acts for an end and does not attain it, even though proper causes are employed, or if the agent using proper means to attain one goal actually attains another, what takes place is called a chance event.

Though it may be difficult to point out a chance event among natural happenings, one can argue from analogy that the same basic contingency that is at the bottom of chance events in our lives can be found in other substances in nature. If intellectual beings are not so perfectly directed to their ends that they do not necessarily attain them, either because of a mishap within the agent or because of the defectibility of the thing acted upon, it seems reasonable to hold that beings less perfectly in act may be defective as efficient causes or as subjects that receive the influence of the agent. This conception of chance, founded on the imperfection of being, would make all creatures the subjects of chance happenings. This is an objective notion of chance, far different from that of the calculus of probabilities. When calculus is applied to the study of nature, a definite ratio of probability can be set up. But what can be calculated is not to be called chance, for chance is what is beyond the direction of the proximate causes in nature. Such would be the probability of calculating the movement of a particular electron in a mass.

Chance is to be defined first of all through the final cause insofar as it can be known, then in terms of the formal cause, then in terms of the efficient cause, and finally in terms of the material cause. The final cause is of primary importance because chance events take place only in those beings that knowingly act for an end. Formal, efficient, and material causes are brought in because the principle of contingency resides in them. No natural cause is so constituted that it can infallibly achieve the end to which it is directed. It would require a complete identity of cause and effect to lie beyond contingency and chance. The objective conception of chance takes it out of the order of knowing and places it in the order of being. This is the view held by Aristotle:

> Mistakes come to pass even in the operations of art: the grammarian makes a mistake in writing and the doctor pours out the wrong dose. Hence, clearly mistakes are possible in the operations of nature also. If then in art there are cases in which what is rightly produced serves a purpose, and if where mistakes occur there was a purpose in what was attempted, only it was not attained, so must it be also in natural products, and monstrosities will be failures in the purposive effort.[27]

The radical basis of a chance cause and of a chance event is a deep

---

[26] St. Thomas, *Commentary on the Sentences*, I, d. 39, q. 2, art. 2, ad 2.

[27] Aristotle, *Physics*, II, 199 a 34–199 b 5. In *The Basic Works of Aristotle*, edited by Richard McKeon (New York: Random House, 1941).

contingency in every created thing that permits defects to take place. No created being is absolutely perfect either in existence or operation. Only God is beyond defect. Angels, men, animals, plants, and inorganic substances are subject to their essential contingence, for they are not pure act. A chance event is possible in nature as sin is possible in man and in the angels.

Though one cannot give an explanation of a particular chance event (this would be to deny its character as chance), it is possible to explain, in general, how it is possible for chance events to occur both in the free actions of man and in the actions of nature. Chance is not to be defined with reference to the universal cause under whose direction all things, necessary and contingent, take place infallibly, but with reference to proximate causes that do not infallibly attain the end. The nature of anything is the primary *per se* principle of motion and rest and attains its natural goal in the *majority of cases.* That nature does not always attain its end is clear from examples in many areas of biology as well as in human affairs. Missing the goal can be attributed to a defect in the agent as a form, to a defect in its operation, or to a defect in the material with which it works, for the condition of contingency applies to all three kinds of causes: *they achieve their end ordinarily but not always.* This is what St. Thomas teaches when he explains what kind of necessity is to be found in nature. He says:

> It is therefore clear from what we have said that the necessity which arises from an efficient cause in some cases depends on the disposition of the agent alone; but in others, on the disposition of both agent and patient. Consequently, if this disposition, according to which the effect follows of necessity, be absolutely necessary both in the agent and in the patient, then there will be absolute necessity in the efficient cause, as with things that act necessarily and always. On the other hand, if this disposition be not absolutely necessary, but removable, then from the efficient cause no necessity will result, except on the supposition that both agent and patient possess the disposition necessary for acting. Thus we find no absolute necessity in those things that are sometimes impeded in their activity either through lack of power or the violent action of a contrary; such things, then, do not act always and necessarily, but in the majority of cases.[28]

If we can attribute chance to any one cause more than to others it is to the material cause, for the defectibility in the form and in its operation can in the final analysis be due only to the subject which has received the form. In the subject is to be found the basic contingency that is to be found wherever there is a distinction between matter and form, or potency and act, as St. Thomas holds:

> Chance is found only in things that are possibly otherwise; and the

---

[28] St. Thomas, *Summa Contra Gentiles,* II, ch. 30. Anderson translation, II, p. 90.

source of this possibility is matter, and not the form, which indeed determines the matter, which is a reservoir of multiple possibilities.[29]

Thus in St. Thomas' view all creatures are subject to chance.

[29] St. Thomas, *Summa Contra Gentiles*, II, ch. 39, par. 3. Anderson translation, II, p. 115.

CHAPTER **VIII**

The Origin and End of All

We have now come to that part of metaphysics where, after seeing the transcendental characteristics of imperfect beings and having examined the principles that make metaphysics a first philosophy, the philosopher rises through analogy to a consideration of the first cause of all contingent being.

The method and spirit with which one should approach the study of God is told us by Aristotle when he speaks of the traces of divinity that the penetrating mind can find in the knowledge of nature.

> We proceed to treat of animals, without omitting, to the best of our ability any member of the Kingdom, however ignoble. For if some have no graces to charm the sense, yet even these, by disclosing to intellectual perception the artistic spirit that designed them, give immense pleasure to all who can trace links of causation, and are inclined to philosophy.[1]

In natural theology we study God through the traces that He has left of Himself in His works. In this respect natural theology differs from sacred theology which studies God in what He has revealed of His inner life. The scanty illumination of mind that is given from imperfect beings should not discourage us, for anything that adds to the knowledge of the Supreme Being is worthwhile, since the worth of knowledge is to be judged by the nature of the object rather than by the amount of detail that is grasped by the mind. In view of man's end, namely the perfect happiness that will come from a union in intellect and will with the Supreme Truth and Good, even an imperfect knowledge of God will give him a foretaste of what is to come and will serve as a directive for the attainment of this final end. Thus the knowledge of God, more than any other part of metaphysics, is wisdom.

The possibility of knowing God by the light of reason is not limited

---

[1] Aristotle, *Parts of Animals*, Bk. I, ch. 5, 645 a 5. *Basic Works of Aristotle*, edited by Richard McKeon (New York: Random House, 1941), pp. 656–657.

to the genius of a few philosophers or theologians. The quality of knowledge, its clarity and subjective certitude, may differ greatly, but the existence of God is not completely hidden from anyone who can exercise his reason. Sacred Scripture itself testifies that the possibility of knowing the existence of a Supreme Cause is within the capacity of all men. What is said in the Book of Wisdom was not meant only as a revelation to the Jewish people who already know the existence of God on faith, but it was said for the gentiles as well.

> What folly it argues in man's nature, this ignorance of God! So much good seen, and he, who is existent Good, not known! Should they not learn to recognize the Artificer by the contemplation of his works? Instead, they have pointed us to fire, or wind, or to the invisible air, wheeling star, or tempestuous waves, or sun and moon, and made gods of them to rule the world! Perhaps the beauty of such things bewitched them into mistaking it for divinity? Ay, but what of him who is Master of them all; what excellence must be his, the Author of all beauty, that could make them! Or was it power, and power's exercises, that awoke their wonderment? Why, then, how many times greater must he be, who contrived it! Such great beauty even creatures have, reason is well able to contemplate the Source from which these perfections came.[2]

It has been said that no one with the use of reason can be an atheist. Atheism is often traced to personal, practical reasons rather than to speculative ones. However, it seems that someone could conceivably question the existence of God on speculative grounds. The presence of God in His works is not so obvious that the truth will always and everywhere break through obstacles that can obscure a person's vision. A person's environment, his education, his moral and intellectual habits, a deep sensitivity about evil, a disquiet over false optimism about the providence of God — these are some of the things that can prevent one from seeing God in His creatures. It is true that no argument based on these difficulties can be a proof that God does not exist, since any argument of this kind ultimately denies the first principles of reason and of being which are necessary for any valid demonstration. What could happen is that a person caught between the positive evidence of first principles and the negative reasons just mentioned would suspend judgment about the existence of God.

St. Thomas pointed out in the beginning of his *Summa Theologiae* that proof of the existence and nature of God is something quite different from faith in the existence and nature of God, and that God chose to reveal Himself to mankind in order to prevent the many difficulties that could hinder or falsify man's knowledge of Him.

> It was necessary for man's salvation that there should be a doctrine revealed by God, besides the philosophical disciplines investigated by human reason. First, because man is directed to God as to an end that

---

[2] Wisd. 13:6–19. Translated by Ronald A. Knox.

surpasses the grasp of his reason: "The eye hath not seen, O God, besides Thee, what things Thou hast prepared for them that wait for Thee" (Isa. 64:4). But the end must first be known by men who are to direct their intentions and actions to the end. Hence it was necessary for the salvation of man that certain truths which exceed human reason should be made known to him by divine revelation. Even as regards those truths about God which human reason can investigate, it was necessary that man be taught by a divine revelation. For the truth about God, such as reason can know it, would be known only by a few, and that after a long time, and with the admixture of many errors; whereas man's whole salvation, which is in God, depends upon the knowledge of this truth. Therefore, in order that the salvation of men might be brought about more fitly and more surely, it was necessary that they be taught divine truths by divine revelation. It was necessary, therefore, that besides the philosophical disciplines investigated by reason, there should be a sacred doctrine by way of revelation.[3]

Two extreme attitudes about the ability of the mind to prove the existence of God are found among people who ask whether a demonstration is possible. The first attitude, based upon an exaggerated intellectualism, accepts the Cartesian notion that as a thinking spirit man can find within his own intellect the truth of the existence of God. The second attitude regards speculative reason as incapable of proving the existence of God conclusively. A proof from speculative reason only is thought to have no more force than a merely logical reason. It is necessary, it is said, that the whole man enter into the proof, since the existence of God means more than the fulfilling of an intellectual capacity. The capacities of one's total being are involved: man's fears, his hopes, his ethical conduct, his artistic conceptions — in short, the total composite experience of living is involved in proving the existence of God. The extremely pessimistic deny that speculative reason or any other reason is capable of demonstrating beyond doubt the existence of God.

A complete answer cannot be given to the many difficulties entailed in demonstrating the existence of God without going far afield from metaphysics. Moreover, it is not the function of the metaphysician to convert someone to belief in God. The metaphysician presents arguments for scrutiny and does not attempt to enter into the field of conscience.

The Ontological Argument

One argument that philosophers have from time to time adduced to prove the existence of God is called the ontological argument. It runs as follows:

God is that being which must be considered most perfect — for that is the definition of God. But if God were to exist only as a concept and

---

[3] St. Thomas, *Summa Theologiae*, I, q. 1, art. 1.

not in reality, we could conceive of a being greater than God, namely an absolutely perfect being who exists in reality as well as in concept. Therefore the most perfect being must exist in reality as well as in thought.[4]

St. Thomas refutes this argument, first by showing that the major premise upon which the argument rests is not universally accepted by all men; second, he shows that the argument, though correct in logical form, does not go beyond the realm of logical reasoning, since the conclusion must be in the same order of being as the premises. If it were possible for man to understand directly what the essence of God is, the conclusion would follow. But since God's essence is not known in itself, the necessary connection with existence cannot be made. Unlike mathematics, in which the conclusions are deduced from prior principles, metaphysics argues to the existence of God through an inference made from experience. The reasoning is a *posteriori*, from effects to cause. St. Thomas' argument against the ontological argument proceeds as follows:

> To know that God exists in a general and confused way is implanted in us by nature, inasmuch as God is man's beatitude. For man naturally desires happiness, and what is naturally desired by man is naturally known by him. This, however, is not to know absolutely that God exists; just as to know that someone is approaching is not the same as to know that Peter is approaching, even though it is Peter who is approaching; for there are many who imagine that man's perfect good, which is happiness, consists in riches, and others in pleasures, and others in something else.
>
> Perhaps not everyone who hears this name *God* understands it to signify something than which nothing greater can be thought, seeing that some have believed God to be a body. Yet, granted that everyone understands that by this name *God* is signified something than which nothing greater can be thought, nevertheless, it does not therefore follow that he understands that what the name signifies exists actually, but only that it exists mentally. Nor can it be argued that it actually exists, unless it be admitted that there actually exists something than which nothing greater can be thought; and this precisely is not admitted by those who hold that God does not exist.[5]

It is true that the divine essence is identical with the divine existence and that, if we really understood the meaning of God's essence as a reality and not merely as a human conception, we would see that it is identical with existence. But we have only indirect knowledge of what the divine essence is. That is, we know it by relating it with the perfections of creatures. But as soon as we take our starting point from creatures, we are in some kind of a posteriori argument. Though all the steps are not expressed, the mind moves to the conclusion at least in a vague syllogistic form. Once we see that contingent things need a

---

[4] For various formulations of this argument, cf. Anselm, *Proslogium*, ch. 2; Descartes, *Meditations on First Philosophy*, Med. V; Leibniz, *Monadology*, No. 45.

[5] St. Thomas, *Summa Theologiae*, I, q. 2, art. 1, ad 1 and 2.

cause, we know that there is a being who is the contrary of contingent things, and this we call God.

It is not necessary to proceed by means of an explicit syllogism. Some would like to call it *intuition*. But it is really a posteriori reasoning. We experience the contingency of our universe, and by means of the first principles of reason understand that what is imperfect has a counterpart in perfect being. This judgment may remain vague because the truth gained through experience is not analyzed into its first principles, or the process can be so sudden that it seems to come from a light native to the intellect itself and not from the image of God found in things and transferred to the intellect.

Five Ways to Demonstrate the Existence of God

We do not call the arguments advanced by St. Thomas five proofs of the existence of God but five ways. There is only one proof from speculative reason, namely that which proceeds by means of the principle of causality. St. Thomas divides this proof into five ways that take up different aspects of this principle. The following presentation is based on the article concerning God's existence in the *Summa Theologiae*. We should note that this is a summary and not a full exposition of the argument such as is given in the *Contra Gentiles*.

The five ways are a form of demonstration that goes from an analysis of concrete facts and situations to the realization of their dependency; their dependency is a sign that they are not self-explanatory but are the effects of a prior cause; from this the mind can judge that behind the order of dependent things there is a first cause that cannot be dependent or caused. This is an a posteriori demonstration, going from effects to cause. In this kind of proof, the mind is drawn by evidence to admit the existence of a transcendent cause. This is known as a *quia* demonstration — a demonstration of a fact. But since the nature of the first cause is seen only as reflected in its effects, we do not have that direct knowledge of essence that will give the reason for the characteristics of the first cause that we find reflected in imperfect things. Hence, we do not have a *propter quid* demonstration of the existence of God. We know that God exists as the necessary cause of participated unity, truth, and goodness but we do not understand what God is in Himself. Our knowledge is, as Scripture says, like the knowledge gained from looking in a mirror — and, as we know, the image in the mirror is always inverted.

The ways of St. Thomas are, nevertheless, *scientific* in the sense in which the philosopher understands this term, for they give universal, certain, and necessary knowledge through an understanding of the metaphysical principles one employs. They are, however, only imperfectly scientific, since the absolute cause which renders perfect explanation possible is not known, while the proximate causes, though giving an explanation, do so incompletely and in a mode of understanding that is only analogous to the deepest explanation that could be given.

The ways of St. Thomas are strictly metaphysical, that is, they transcend the limited order of explanation that is proper to each of the particular sciences. When St. Thomas, for instance, argues from local motion that there is a first cause of motion, he does not reduce the argument to an explanation of physical motion. His argument applies to any order in which a transition from potency to act is found. Thus it applies to the kind of motion found among bodies, to the changes in nature that do not fall within the strict "genus" of motion, to certain qualitative changes in which there is no medium, and finally to changes found only in spiritual beings, such as growth in understanding or in virtue.

Each of the ways is complete in itself and explicitly independent of the others. Each way contains all the elements of the demonstration. But just as the mind can look at being from different angles it can also look at the Cause of being from several distinct starting points. Objectively, the sum total of the five ways is no stronger a demonstration than is given by any of them taken by itself. However, the convergence of demonstration from different sides may be more assuring, or one way may appeal more to one person than to another because he understands it better, inasmuch as each person's understanding of reality differs with the kind of experience he has. For example, someone who is not inclined to accept the way from motion may accept the way based on the order in the universe. Hence a subjective element in the probative value of the five ways is not to be overlooked.

A warning about the limitations of the five ways may prevent later difficulties. The saying that one who proves too much does not prove anything is particularly applicable here. A realization of the limits of a purely philosophical demonstration of the existence of God will obviate a number of difficulties that can arise. For example, we call each of the five arguments given by St. Thomas a way to prove the existence of God. The name God has for a Jew, a Christian, a Moslem, or a Hindu special connotations that have come through his environment and general religious background. These aspects are not known by a metaphysical demonstration. The Christian notion of a unique God with three distinct substantial relationships is not to be found in St. Thomas' argument. The fact that the prime mover or absolutely necessary being is really identical with the triune God is accidental, as far as the natural human judgment is concerned. When analyzing the a priori argument for the existence of God, St. Thomas said that when we see someone obscurely we can say with certainty that we see something, but not that we see Peter, even if the something we see is Peter. So here we argue that God exists, but not that we have proved the existence of the triune God of Christian revelation, even although the God of Christian revelation is the God proved to exist in philosophy.

There must be some general agreement on the meaning of God, otherwise the demonstration will mean nothing. Even an atheist could find in his experience some kind of being that he would like to identify with God. For the demonstration to have any permanent force, there must be some common understanding of what is meant by the name God. But what God means in a philosophical context cannot be decided a priori. For a Thomist God must be seen in relationship to reality. The name God is given to a certain member of the "genus" of existing things. What the name means depends on the analysis of being. If, as is shown, it is necessary to analyze being in its analogical modes, different names will be given to signify different modes, and consequently different meanings will be given to the name God. In other words, the name God is not assigned independently of the process of metaphysical analysis that brings out the necessity of the existence of God. This is why natural theology comes at the end of metaphysics, since the knowledge of God is the resolution of the analysis that has been made of the modes of finite being.

To join in discussion with a Thomist on the point of the existence of God there must already be some awareness of the stages of thought that are preliminary to the problem at hand. This does not mean that it is useless to present the five ways of St. Thomas to someone who has not made a formal study of metaphysics. For, as was pointed out in the first part of this work, everyone who is more than a child is equipped with enough experience to understand the principles upon which the proof of God's existence rests. The presentation of the proof will vary from person to person, from one cultural background to another. This is simply what St. Thomas has done in a general way when he presents the five different ways.

The First Way of Demonstration: From Motion in the Universe

In his *Summa Theologiae* St. Thomas gives the first way, from motion, in the following concise form:

> The first and more manifest way is the argument from motion. It is certain, and evident to our senses, that in the world some things are in motion. Now whatever is moved is moved by another, for nothing can be moved except it is in potentiality to that towards which it is moved; whereas a thing moves inasmuch as it is in act. For motion is nothing else than the reduction of something from potentiality to actuality. But

nothing can be reduced from potentiality to actuality, except by something in a state of actuality. Thus that which is actually hot, as fire, makes wood, which is potentially hot, to be actually hot, and thereby moves and changes it. Now it is not possible that the same thing should be at once in actuality and potentiality in the same respect, but only in different respects. For what is actually hot cannot simultaneously be potentially hot; but it is simultaneously potentially cold. It is therefore impossible that in the same respect and in the same way a thing should be both mover and moved, i.e., that it should move itself. Therefore, whatever is moved must be moved by another. If that by which it is moved be itself moved, then this also must needs be moved by another, and that by another again. But this cannot go on to infinity, because then there would be no first mover, and, consequently, no other mover, seeing that subsequent movers move only inasmuch as they are moved by the first mover; as the staff moves only because it is moved by the hand. Therefore it is necessary to arrive at a first mover, moved by no other; and this everyone understands to be God.[6]

In keeping with his pedagogical method, St. Thomas' first way is closer to sense experience and therefore easier to grasp, though it is not the most metaphysical of the five ways that he proposes. As we saw in our discussion of principles, the principle of efficient causality, which is the basis of the first three ways, is not as universal as the principles of formal and final causality that are the basis of the fourth and fifth ways. Though the demonstration begins most naturally with examples of local motion, St. Thomas does not limit it to this. His argument holds not only from all types of natural motion but for any kind of transition from potency to act.

To understand this argument it is most important, first, to see the validity of the metaphysical principle that there can be no passing from potency to act except through an efficient cause that is outside the immediate subject in which the change is to take place. Second, it is necessary to see the truth of the statement that a series of causes of motion, in which one being moves another, cannot be infinite but that there must be a first except in the case of an accidental series in which motion is not explained.

This first way is open to several objections. First, it is an obvious fact that some things in nature move themselves. If we consider movement in its widest sense, we can say that man certainly is able to move himself. Hence the argument seems to apply only to things that do not have a principle of self-motion. Another difficulty comes from what seems to be the relativity of motion. It is held by some that motion is not something real in things themselves but is relative to a point of view taken by an observer, so that looked at from different points of view, one and the same thing can be said to be in motion and at rest. A

---

[6] *Summa Theologiae*, I, q. 2, art. 3.

third difficulty comes from trying to prove that in every series of movers and things moved there must be a first — this seems to contradict a position accepted by Aristotle and St. Thomas, namely that an infinite series of motion is not *per se* impossible just as the eternity of the universe is not *per se* impossible.

St. Thomas answers the first difficulty by showing that living beings are self moving only with respect to the subject taken as a whole, some parts of which are in potency and can be moved to act by another part. But with respect to one and the same part nothing can be both mover and moved, since this would be contrary to the principle of identity. If it could be shown that in a living being there were a part that is always in act, there would be no transition from potency to act, and consequently no need to go further for an explanation. But as soon as one speaks of *motion* (not simply of a mover) he must admit a transition from potency to act — for that is in the very definition of motion. As far as man is concerned, everyone knows that his vital powers do undergo change from potency to act: they change from a state of rest to one of activity or from a state of activity to one of rest. Every change is necessarily contingent upon two distinct things, one, a subject which is without a particular form (a privation) but with a capacity for it; second, upon an agent already having in some way the perfection which it is to produce. Therefore, even in living beings the explanation of change and motion calls for a cause of movement distinct from what is moved.

While the concept of *motion* necessarily implies dependence, that of *mover* does not. *Mover* means the initiator of movement in something else. Therefore, it is applicable to a being in which there is no potency or coming-to-be. Causing motion in another does not imply a change for the agent itself.

It is said that the argument from motion takes for granted that the only true conception of the universe is that held by Aristotle. The Aristotelian conception of the universe, which is found in St. Thomas, is based upon common sense experience. According to Aristotle the universe is made up of a number of bodies — differing numerically and specifically, but all arranged within the universe in a definite order. There is a rest and movement characteristic of all of these bodies and a place of repose that is natural for them. If bodies are out of their natural place, they will tend to find again their natural place — falling or rising according to their nature. The universe itself is arranged in such a way that its motion is circular. Motion, as understood by Aristotle, is very difficult to define, because it is neither actuality nor pure potentiality. It is the state between potency and actuality. It is the least perfect form of actuality. Motion cannot be defined in static terms because motion is fluid.

The ordinary man using common sense as a guide sees the world as Aristotle did. But scientists have taken a new outlook on the universe and on motion, or if not new, at least one that is contrary to common sense experience. The scientists' key to the study of nature is mathematics. Aristotle used mathematics in some of the physical sciences — for example, in astronomy, optics, and acoustics, but he did not give mathematics anything more than a role of instrumental cause in the study of nature. In modern science mathematics assumes the role of an essential formal cause, a return in a more scientific way to the interpretation of the Pythagoreans who wished to reduce all essences to numbers. Among the more prominent men of the Renaissance period who employed mathematics to interpret nature were Pico di Mirondola, Nicholas of Cusa, and in modern times men like Meyerson, Planck, Poincaré, Eddington, Jeans, Einstein, and Le Broglie. They held that the book of nature is written in mathematical symbols and he who wants to understand nature must speak her language. Mere sense experience no longer has a dominant role. It is used only to check theories that are built upon principles of mathematics.

In this conception the universe is not a closed system. Natures and bodies are not absolutely distinct; they have no peculiar definite place in the universe; there is no need of a prime mover to explain the motion of bodies. For motion is not an objective absolute quality, as Aristotle viewed it, but something relative. Since motion is not an absolute, it has no need of an extrinsic efficient cause, i.e., a cause existing apart from the universe itself. Motion, when analyzed in terms of mathematics, is considered as made up of static points of reference between two bodies — the points of reference in space being correlated to points of time.

This view considers the universe as "essentially" one body whose parts are reducible to mathematical equations. Essential differences, as understood by Aristotle, are done away with. The energy that was in the universe at the beginning remains constant. It is merely transferred from one body to another. Motion and rest are regarded as different aspects of the same thing. Thus a body would be considered at rest and in movement at the same time. Ontologically, rest and movement would be the same, and no distinct ontological principle, such as the principle of causality, need be invoked to explain movement. Only when one views the universe as a closed system with its distinct and irreducible parts does one have to bring in the idea of efficient cause and Prime Mover to account for a transition from potency to act. If one chooses to accept Aristotle's system then he explains things as Aristotle did. If one chooses the other system he needs no explanation.

To retain a mathematical conception of the world one must sacrifice something of the world of common sense. It is true that for an observer the point of reference for judging motion is relative. But the principle of identity still applies, for something cannot be in motion and rest with respect to one point of reference. If a body has taken a position it will be necessary to apply an extrinsic force to one or other of the bodies. This expense of energy is the proximate cause of motion. Throughout the process of moving from one point of space to another the transferred energy must continue to exist in conjunction with the body in the state of motion. Movement adds something qualitatively new to a body. Therefore motion is not explained except by a being in act capable of causing a new state of being in a subject.

The possibility of an infinite series. As for the possibility of an infinite series of movers and moved beings, one must make the distinction, as St. Thomas does, between a series in which the members are *per se* subordinate and a series in which the members are *per accidens* subordinate to each other. St. Thomas[7] teaches that reason cannot prove that the physical universe is not eternal, and since the universe essentially embodies motion, reason cannot show that motion and the series of movers are not eternal. But the argument of St. Thomas takes this impossibility into account, for as was said earlier, a series of *per accidens* causes does not contain the explanation of motion. It no more explains the change from potency to act in any coming-to-be in nature than do many combinations of hammers and chisels explain the origin of a statue. An instrumental cause moves without a motion of its own. Therefore the possibility of an infinite series of accidental causes has nothing to do with explaining an effect. For even if one would grant that motion were eternal in the universe, because reason cannot discount the possibility of an endless series of accidental movers, the explanation of motion would still be necessary and it would have to be found outside the series. The addition of accidental movers does not add up to an explanation of motion any more than the addition of a series of zeros add up to one, for the mind does not solve the problem of motion by pushing it back into an endless series. If nothing in the series is an absolute cause of motion, but all have, as it were, borrowed movement, the source is still to be accounted for. In other words, to suppose that an infinite series of accidental movers can account for movement is to suppose that being *per accidens* is the same as being *per se*. This is the same as denying the principle of identity.

As a conclusion to this first way of demonstration, let us say that even if the difficulties from an analysis of local motion leave the demonstration obscure, the essence of the proof does not consist in an explanation of local motion only but in the explanation of any kind of real change in being, whether spiritual or corporeal. Hence it applies to any change analogous to motion. Every being in which changes take place

---

[7] See *Summa Theologiae*, I, q. 46, art. 2.

is subject eventually to a prime mover as understood in the transcendental sense. The only being that does not need the influence of the prime mover is one that is by essence pure act. But nothing in our experience is without potency. Therefore, the prime mover is outside the universe that we know.

The Second Way of Demonstration: From Efficient Causality

St. Thomas gives the following argument as the essence of the second way:

> The second way is from the nature of efficient cause. In the world of sensible things we find there is an order of efficient causes. There is no case known (neither is it, indeed, possible) in which a thing is found to be the efficient cause of itself; for so it would be prior to itself, which is impossible. Now in efficient causes it is not possible to go on to infinity, because in all efficient causes following in order, the first is the cause of the intermediate cause, and the intermediate is the cause of the ultimate cause, whether the intermediate cause be several, or one only. Now to take away the cause is to take away the effect. Therefore, if there be no first cause among efficient causes, there will be no ultimate, nor any intermediate cause. But if in efficient causes it is possible to go on to infinity, there will be no first efficient cause, neither will there be an ultimate effect, nor any intermediate efficient causes; all of which is plainly false. Therefore it is necessary to admit a first efficient cause, to which everyone gives the name of God.[8]

In the first way St. Thomas pointed out the necessity of a prime mover in a series of movers and things moved. This is one aspect of the relationship between an efficient cause and the subject upon which it acts. But in the second way St. Thomas looks more deeply into the nature of efficient causality and its relation to what comes into existence. In the second way the term *first efficient cause* has a more universal connotation than the term *prime mover* in the first way. Strictly speaking, the influence of a prime mover is only on these things that are in motion or are subject to change; but the influence of an efficient cause is extended to every kind of coming-to-be. Therefore, the second way takes up the whole question of the relationship between a primary efficient cause and the coming-to-be of anything in which existence is not identical with essence.

It is obvious that some things come into existence. It is sufficient for the purpose that St. Thomas had in mind to prove that there must be an uncaused efficient cause somewhere in the series of efficient causes that makes things come to be. Where or what that cause may be is not the point of issue. If someone insists that the primary efficient cause is within the physical universe, the burden of sustaining this position is up to him. As is clear from the total doctrine of St. Thomas, this position cannot be maintained because there are effects that surpass the perfection

---

[8] St. Thomas, *Summa Theologiae*, I, q. 2, art. 3.

of form of corporeal things. But everything is an efficient cause by reason of its form, as was shown in the discussion of the principle of efficient causality.

One of the antinomies of Immanuel Kant with respect to the proof of God's existence from efficient causality takes up the question of the necessity of priority of the efficient cause over the effect. As Kant saw it, this would mean that God *would have to be considered as existing in time* since He would exist before the effect which is in time. But God cannot exist in time, since by the very nature of His primacy in the order of causality He would have to transcend time and things in motion. Therefore, the argument from efficient causality seems to Kant to be self-contradictory.

This difficulty is based upon a univocal conception of efficient causality and of priority and posteriority in causation. If God were an efficient cause in the same way that natural bodies are efficient causes, He would be part of the series and would exist in time. His causality would presuppose a transition from potency to act, hence God would belong to what St. Thomas calls the *intermediary causes*. But causality is for God immanent activity in the most perfect sense: it does not cause the coming-to-be of things by means of physical energy. God causes through His intellect and will. That God's knowledge could be the cause of physical effects is not so strange if we consider that the same kind of causality is found even in the human order. The work of art, which is a beautiful form embodied in matter, is produced primarily by the intelligence of the artist and secondarily by the skill of his hands. St. Thomas makes this observation when he wants to show how the causality of God differs from that of natural forms:

> The knowledge of God is the cause of things. For the knowledge of God is to all creatures what the knowledge of the artificer is to things made by his art. Now the knowledge of the artificer is the cause of the things made by his art from the fact that the artificer works through his intellect. Hence the form in the intellect must be the principle of action, as heat is the principle of heating. Nevertheless, we must observe that a natural form, being a form that remains in that to which it gives being, denotes a principle of action according only as it has an inclination to an effect; and likewise, the intelligible form does not denote a principle of action insofar as it resides in the one who understands unless there is added to it the inclination to an effect, which inclination is through the will. For since the intelligible form has a relation to contraries (inasmuch as the same knowledge is related to contraries), it would not produce a determinate effect unless it were determined to one thing by the appetite, as the Philosopher says. Now it is manifest that God causes things by His intellect, since His being is His act of understanding; and hence His knowledge must be the cause of things, insofar as His will is joined to it.[9]

---

[9] St. Thomas, *Summa Theologiae*, I, q. 14, art. 8.

The Third Way of Demonstration: From the Contingency of the Universe

St. Thomas' third way of demonstrating the existence of God proceeds in this way:

> The third way is taken from possibility and necessity, and runs thus. We find in nature things that are possible to be and not to be, since they are found to be generated, and to be corrupted, and consequently, it is possible for them to be and not to be. But it is impossible for these always to exist, for that which can not-be at some time is not. Therefore, if everything can not-be, then at one time there was nothing in existence. Now if this were true, even now there would be nothing in existence, because that which does not exist begins to exist only through something already existing. Therefore, if at one time nothing was in existence, it would have been impossible for anything to have begun to exist; and thus even now nothing would be in existence — which is absurd. Therefore, not all beings are merely possible, but there must exist something the existence of which is necessary. But every necessary thing either has its necessity caused by another, or not. Now it is impossible to go to infinity in necessary things which have their necessity caused by another, as has already been proved in regard to efficient causes. Therefore we cannot but admit the existence of some being having of itself its own necessity, and not receiving it from another, but rather causing in others their necessity. This all men speak of as God.[10]

The exact wording of the text is important in trying to clarify St. Thomas' third way of demonstration. In most Latin texts, because of the placing of a comma in a certain position, the argument would read: "It is impossible for all things that are of that kind (contingent), always to exist" (*Impossible est autem omnia quae sunt talia, semper esse*). There are earlier manuscripts in which a comma is placed after *sunt*, so that the meaning of the text is changed from the impossibility of all contingent beings existing forever to the impossibility of all things being contingent. In the original text of St. Thomas there were no commas. The interpretation given to the text will have to be consistent with the rest of his philosophy. It may be possible to accept the reading that "It is impossible that all such things (contingent) always exist," but it is not the most obvious way to interpret the argument as consistent with what St. Thomas says about the impossibility of proving by reason alone that the universe had a beginning in time. Some commentators argue that every contingent being must have a beginning, if not in time, at least in the sense of a dependence in existence. But what follows in St. Thomas' argument would be more consistent with the other interpretation of the text, namely, that it is not possible for all things to be contingent. Reason demands that beings which are fundamentally con-

---

[10] St. Thomas, *Summa Theologiae*, I, q. 2, art. 3.

tingent with respect to their existence ultimately depend on an absolutely necessary being.

St. Thomas' third way of demonstration follows closely along the pattern of the second. But, there is this major difference. While the second way emphasized the necessity of a primary efficient cause to bring something into existence, the third way emphasizes the continued dependence of contingent beings an a necessary cause. The being that comes into existence remains a contingent being; therefore the influence of a noncontingent cause is needed to sustain the being in existence after the coming into existence.

The essential difference between the efficient causality of God and that of secondary causes is that He is not merely the cause of the coming-to-be of things but also of the continuation in being of things that are made. The dependence of the effect on secondary efficient causes, on the other hand, is only during the process of coming-to-be. After the statue is made, after the house is built the intermediary efficient causes can pass out of existence without effecting what had been produced. The power of God, however, is like the action of the sun. Every creature is related to God as light to the sun. If God were to suspend His power for an instant, the entire being of what was produced would cease to be, just as illumination would cease if the activity of the sun were suspended. Efficient causality in creatures is like reflected light that can illumine an object whose power is dependent on the source. Therefore creatures cannot cause except insofar as they are joined to God who is the primary efficient cause, and even then they do not cause the substance of what comes to be but act as intermediary causes in the coming-to-be of things.

> The being of every creature depends on God, so that not for a moment could it subsist, but would fall into nothingness, were it not kept in being by the operation of the divine power, as Gregory says. This is made clear as follows. Every effect depends on its cause, so far as it is its cause. But we must observe that an agent may be the cause of the *becoming* of its effect, but not directly of its *being*. This may be seen both in artificial and in natural things. For the builder causes the house in its *becoming*, but he is not the direct cause of its *being*.[11]

It is obvious that there are contingent beings in the world, because things come into existence and pass out of existence. Existence, then, is not of the very definition of such things. But it is not possible for all things to be contingent, since the fact of existence of contingent beings, like the fact of existence of beings in motion, is not explained by simply extending the contingent series. The total chain of contingent beings is sustained by a necessary being.

---

[11] St. Thomas, *Summa Theologiae*, I, q. 104, art. 1.

This argument is consistent with St. Thomas' view on the impossibility of proving by reason alone that the universe at one time did not exist. His reason presupposes the existence of an absolutely necessary being. If God is eternal, He can cause from eternity. He takes up various arguments that had been proposed by philosophers to prove that the world did not exist at one time. He sees no compelling argument in any of them, but he suggests a dialectical argument based on the fact that a temporal beginning would more clearly bring out the love of God and the freedom with which He created all things.

> A more effective approach toward proving the non-eternity of the world can be made from the point of view of the end of the divine will, as we have previously indicated (II, ch. 35). For in the production of things the end of God's will is His own goodness as it is manifested in His effects. Now, His power and goodness are made manifest above all by the fact that things other than Himself were not always in existence. For this fact shows clearly that these things owe their existence to Him, and also is proof that God does not act by a necessity of His nature, and that His power of acting is infinite. Respecting the divine goodness, therefore, it was entirely fitting that God should have given created things a temporal beginning.[12]

The Real Distinction Between Essence and Existence[13]

In his treatise *On Being and Essence*, Chap. IV, St. Thomas speaks of a real distinction between essence and existence in all creatures. In regard to this distinction we should keep in mind that, though distinct, essence and existence are not physically separable as though they were two real beings. They are mutually dependent principles of being. Together they do not make up a third being distinct from the integral parts, but only one being. There is no existence without an essence, and essence is not real apart from the act of existence. Other examples can be brought forward to show that real distinction does not necessarily imply separation. Thus quantity and quality, in the extension and whiteness of paper, are really distinct from each other but not separable in the piece of paper. Thus the quality of whiteness cannot be found apart from extension. If extension were removed the quality of whiteness itself would be reduced to a point without extension and would cease to exist.

St. Thomas argues for a real distinction between essence and existence in both corporeal and incorporeal created substances, for the same radical contingency is found in all imperfect beings.

---

[12] St. Thomas, *Summa Contra Gentiles*, II, ch. 38, par. 15. Anderson translation, II, p. 144.

[13] It seems that the logical place to bring up the question of the real distinction between essence and existence in all creatures is after one has demonstrated the existence of an absolutely necessary being. The truth of the real distinction follows from the truth of the contingency of imperfect beings by comparison with an absolutely necessary being where there is no such distinction.

Although substances of this kind (simple substances) are forms alone and immaterial, they are not in every way simple so as to be pure act. They do have an admixture of potency, which is evident from the following consideration. Whatever does not belong to the notion of an essence or quiddity comes from without and enters into composition with the essence, for no essence is intelligible without its parts. Now, every essence or quiddity can be understood without anything being known of its existing. I can know what a man or a phoenix is and still be ignorant whether it exists in reality. From this it is clear that the act of existing is other than essence or quiddity.

He goes on to say:

Whatever belongs to a being is either caused by the principles of its nature, as the capability of laughter in man, or it comes to it from some extrinsic principle, as light in the air from the sun's influence. But it is impossible that the act of existing be caused by a thing's form or its quiddity, (I say caused as by an efficient cause); for then something would be the cause of itself and would bring itself into existence — which is impossible. Everything, then, which is such that its act of existing is other than its nature must needs have its act of existing from something else. And since every being which exists through another is reduced, as to its first cause, to one existing in virtue of itself, there must be some being which is the cause of the existing of all things because it itself is the act of existing alone. If that were not so, we would proceed to infinity among causes, since, as we have said, every being which is not the act of existing alone has a cause of its existence. . . .

He concludes his argument by showing that essence is a potency:

Now, every being receiving something from another is potential with respect to what it receives, and what is received in it is its act. The quiddity itself, then, or the form which is the intelligence must be potential with respect to the existence which it receives from God, and that existence is received as an act.[14]

On first reading, this argument does not seem to go beyond a proof in the logical order. It reminds one of the proof of God's existence given by St. Anselm, of which St. Thomas said: "It does not follow, from the argument given, that what is signified by the name [God] actually exists, but exists only in the mind."[15] Does the fact that I can conceive of an essence without conceiving of its real existence actually prove that essence and existence are distinct? St. Thomas' argument, unlike St. Anselm's, is not based on an a priori reason. The gist of the argument is this: An examination of the real essences with which we are acquainted reveals to our judgment that they are such that existence is something that is not demanded by their very make-up. In other words, the contingency of the being appears on examination of its essence. This is not pure

---

[14] St. Thomas, *On Being and Essence*, ch. 4. Maurer translation, pp. 45–47.
[15] St. Thomas, *Summa Theologiae*, I, q. 2, art. 1, ad 2.

a priori reasoning that might fit into a discussion of logic or mathematics; on the contrary, it is reasoning based on observation of the contingent nature of the essences found in the world of human experience. The essences spoken of are real essences, for as a metaphysician St. Thomas is concerned not with the realm of abstractions but with reality as it confronts the human mind.

Why does he use the example of a phoenix which is evidently a being of reason, a fabrication of the human mind? Does not this seem to lead the argument out of the order of the real into the realm of fiction? St. Thomas is arguing here as a teacher, taking an example that can be understood by all. It is evident, he says, that real existence does not belong to a mental fabrication like a phoenix, an imaginary thing, described as being an animal that is half rational and half irrational. The very composition is contradictory and so cannot belong to the order of existing realities. But the phoenix does have a kind of existence in the order of imagination and thought. But even in this order existence is something that must be given to it — by the mind of man. Thus the essence of a phoenix is contingent — contingent upon the knower who has given it existence as a being of the mind and imagination.

Another source of difficulty in St. Thomas' thought comes from supposing that this argument lies only in the analysis of the first operation of the mind, simple apprehension. Like all analyses proper to metaphysics, the resolution of this argument is made in the *judgment* and not in the *concept* as such. We use concepts in making the judgment, but the conclusion reached is not an argument based solely on the analysis of concepts. Rather the force of the argument lies in understanding the relationship of essence to the act of real existence — whether the existence already be realized in the concrete order of things or whether it be potential existence (capacity for real existence). The potential existence is real from this point of view because the essence is looked at not as a logical entity but as a real capacity for real existence.

St. Thomas does not explicitly state in the work *On Being and Essence* the nature of the experience that gives him a basis for making the judgment that the essence of man, for example, is contingent with respect to existence. But evidence of contingency is found in common sense observation by which we see a man come into existence, maintain his existence precariously, and then die. Or the evidence is found in the kind of thinking that touches us more personally through a kind of natural contemplation, in which a man is given some realization that existence is a gift and that his own existence as a person presupposes a constant act of creation on the part of a higher being. In any event, the contingency of one's existence is realized by everyone in some way. Finally, if the philosopher has gone through the order of philosophy suggested by St. Thomas, he will discover in the philosophy of nature that the mobility of the universe calls for an unmoved mover; and in the study of the soul he will see the limitations and imperfections of man's nature; particularly through the contingency of one's acts in the moral order, he will understand the gulf between what man's nature calls for and what he is in fact through the act of existence.

The most perfect of all acts is existence. Of itself it is pure perfection, and if it is found to be limited in some beings the reason must be that there is in those beings a second principle that limits existence by receiving it into a limited capacity. Just as the cup which dips water from a spring limits the water received — though the actuality of water outside the cup far surpasses the limitations of the cup — so the essence of any contingent being limits the act of existence received from an unlimited source of existence. What limits another by receiving it must really be distinct from that which is received.

Thus, for St. Thomas, the doctrine of the real distinction between essence and existence is an application of the principle that act is limited by the potency into which it is received. But we should not suppose that there is an absolute parallel between potency and act on the one hand, and essence and existence on the other. These are not univocal correlatives. Rather, there is an analogy of proper proportionality between the relationship of potency to act and the relationship of essence to existence.

The problem of the real distinction between essence and existence can be summed up in the following question: When an essence is actualized by existence, is there present a real composite made up of potency and act, or, on the contrary, does the potency cease when the essence is made actual? If the potency ceases when things are real, it follows that only act remains and there is no true composite. This is an untenable position according to the metaphysical doctrine of St. Thomas. He holds that in every imperfect being, whether in the order of substance or accident, there is a true composition, in which there remain united in one subject a potency in the form of an essence and an act in the form of existence. That is why the total being is a composite and not simply an existing act or form. Essence is a capacity for existence, a capacity that remains real and distinct in the composite, even when it is actualized by its proper existence. This seems to be no different from what takes place when matter receives form. In a true sense, the capacity of a matter for form remains in the composite, for if the capacity did not remain, neither would the act remain since the form is dependent upon the capacity of the subject. Thus the capacity for an artistic form remains in the wood that is carved and the capacity for heat remains in the water that is heated. On the other hand, it is evident that a capacity to receive or become a certain form no longer exists once the subject contains or receives that particular form, for that would entail a contradiction: a being would at one and the same time be and not be. But it is true that the subject which receives the form retains a capacity to hold the form which it has received. It is obvious that St. Thomas taught that the relationship of essence to existence is an application of the broader principle of the relationship of potency to act. For instance, he writes:

> Every created substance is composed of potency and act. For it is clear that only God is His own existence, that is, existing by essence, insofar as His existence is His substance. This can be said of no other, for subsistent existence can only be one. It is necessary, therefore, that every other thing be being by participation so that in it the substance that participates in existence is one thing and the existence participated in is another. Every thing that participates is related to that which is participated in as potency is related to act. Thus every created substance is composed of potency and act, that is, it is made up of *that which is* and the *act of existence*, as Boethius says in the *Libro de Hebdomadibus*.[16]

Existence is limited by the essence which receives it, otherwise the act of existence would be unlimited and be pure act. But St. Thomas says that pure act or existence or a being whose essence is existence must be unique. From experience we know that there are many existing realities. Since there are many existing realities, and since those of which we have immediate experience are imperfect, the conclusion is that they do not have an unlimited act of existence.

How is the imperfection of existence made manifest? This is known by the fact that beings come into existence and pass out of existence. In other words, beings seem to be contingent. Therefore, their existence is imperfect because it is not without beginning and without end. Moreover, we can see that the beings of our experience are imperfect as regards their nature, which is the principle of their operation, for there are many things that these beings cannot do at all and many more that are done imperfectly. Therefore we know that we are in contact with imperfect essences or natures. In their own proper species, they are not imperfect, for each man is fully and perfectly a man as regards his essence. But human nature of itself is an imperfect kind of essence. This is the teaching of St. Thomas:

> For the existence of man is limited to the species of man because it is received into the nature of the human species; and this is true also of the existence of a horse or of any other creature. But the existence of God, since it is not received into something else but is pure existence, is not limited to a particular mode of perfection in being but has complete and perfect existence in itself.[17]

---

[16] St. Thomas, *Quaestiones Quodlibetales*, III, q. 8, art. 1.
[17] St. Thomas, *On the Power of God*, q. 1, art. 2.

Could we not say that the principle of limitation need not be distinct from the act of existence which is recognized as imperfect? On the supposition that there is a God, could it not be that God is the cause of imperfect beings without bringing into the picture the limitation of existence by a distinct potency? According to this point of view, the principle of limitation would not be in the essence but in the power or the will of God. This is a Cartesian point of view. Descartes held that the will of God is the primary divine attribute according to which all things are measured.

The point made by St. Thomas is that existence by itself is not diversified and even God cannot make it to be what it is not. Therefore, existence cannot be limited except by a second principle of being with which it forms a composite entity. In the *Contra Gentiles,* he says:

> Now being as being cannot be diverse, but it can be diversified by something beside itself. Thus the being of a stone is other than that of a man. Hence that which subsisting being can be one only.[18]

The act of existence cannot be simultaneously that which is common to all and that by which they are diverse. That would be the same as saying that existence is that which is unlimited and that which is the principle of limitation. The reason why God cannot arbitrarily set limits on the act of existence is that He acts according to wisdom which respects the natures of things, which means that He acts according to His own essence. For the natures of things are, in different ways, representations of the divine nature itself.

If existence is found to be distinct according to kind as well as numerically in various beings, it is because the act of existence can never be the common predicate in a univocal sense. It is for this reason that there cannot be a science of existence considered apart from essence. The science of metaphysics cannot be reduced to the univocity of a common genus precisely because the act of existence of each thing is limited and distinct. Science, which deals with universals, originates more precisely in the order of essences. Since, however, essences cannot prescind from the act by which they are made to exist, metaphysics includes as its proper subject matter both essence and existence. In a text from the *Commentary on the Sentences,* St. Thomas explains his position on the relationship of the act of existence to the essence:

> To exist by itself (per se) is not, strictly speaking, a definition of substance; because by this we do not manifest its essence, but its "to be." Its essence is not the same as its act of existence. Otherwise, substance could not be a genus because the act of existence cannot be com-

---

18 St. Thomas, *Contra Gentiles,* Bk. II, chap. 52. Anderson translation, II, p. 153.

mon after the manner of a genus, since each of the things contained under a genus differ in their own act of existence. But the definition or quasi definition of substance is a thing having an essence to which is added or due the act of existence as not in another. And likewise to be in a subject is not the definition of accident but rather an accident is something to which is due existence in another.[19]

Therefore, contrary to the opinion of Descartes, we hold with St. Thomas that essence is the principle of limitation of the act of existence in imperfect substances. God does not simply make an existing thing limited by an act of His power or of His will. The principle of limitation lies in the essence which is ultimately traceable to the divine intellect in its capacity as prototype of all created things. In no creature is the act of existence identical with its essence. Rather, every created thing is a composite of essence and existence which are distinct principles though united in the one being. St. Thomas argues that the act of existence does not mean, except in the case of God, *what a thing is* but only *that a thing is*. Therefore, in a creature existence is not the same as essence. Here St. Thomas presupposes a fundamental integrity about the human mind in its ability to judge when one thing is not another. Existence simply says that something is actual; of itself, existence is indeterminate. Existence does not tell what a thing is. When existing things are found to be of limited capacity and of a specific kind, this is to be accounted for by another principle joined to the act of existence.

That existence is not the same as a thing's essence is one of those primary truths of metaphysics that are so fundamental that they cannot be clearly described; they escape the kind of analysis that belongs to more detailed sciences such as mathematics. The truth of the real distinction of essence and existence enjoys the kind of evidence that is found in the principle of identity and not the kind that is found in the mathematical truth that two plus two equal four. Existence of itself does not express the essence, just as the essence does not express the act of existence. The understanding of what an essence is does not necessarily manifest the existence of such a thing; if it did, contingent beings would not have a finite essence. Just as the capacity for activity is not to be equated with activity itself because of the radical contingency of any created power, so in the substantial order no imperfect essence necessarily implies an act of extramental existence. Existence is a pure gift; existence is contingent. If existence were not contingent, all possible things would always exist. When we speak of essence and existence we are speaking of two distinct principles of being, one which is a limiting principle and the other which is the limited act of existence.

The essence of which St. Thomas speaks when he says that essence

---

[19] St. Thomas, *Commentary on the Sentences*, IV, dist. 12, q. 1, art. 1.

limits existence is to be taken in the sense of the total essence and not merely the form (*forma totius*). The essence includes both matter and form, because we are presumably dealing with the composite beings with which we are familiar. Thus human nature or the essence of man includes both form and matter and these together are the limiting principle with respect to man's existence. This essence is the limiting principle. First of all it limits the kind of existence that is received, for by it the existence of man differs, for example, from that of a cat. At the same time the total essence of man which includes matter and form is the principle of numerical limitation and distinction according to which one man differs from another man. Hence, the essence is in this respect also a principle of limitation. In each man, then, there is a composition of essence and existence. We do not say simply that the existence of one man differs from the existence of another, and that they have one and the same essence. Each man has his own individual nature or essence, for it is false to say that all individual men constitute one human nature. From the point of view of the philosophy of nature, essence is predicated univocally of several men. But from the point of view of metaphysics, which deals expressly with existing realities and not with abstractions, there is between one man and another a bond of analogy, since no two individuals can be identical in any true sense of the word.

The truth of the real distinction between essence and existence is the basis of the Thomistic doctrine of the analogy of being. Being is analogous because in each and every thing there is something that is distinctive and something that is similar to other beings. The act of existence creates the analogical bond among things, which apart from existence would be either totally univocal or purely equivocal. This holds not only in the order of substance. What is true of created substances is also true of all other compositions in the order of accidents. St. Thomas says:

> Since accidents have their own existence and essences, and their essence is not their existence, it follows that in them there is a difference between what they are and the fact that they are, and thus they have a composition.[20]

The metaphysical basis for the doctrine of the real distinction between essence and existence in any creature lies in the fact of the creature's radical contingency. The argument of St. Thomas is based on experience and not upon a logical analysis of concepts. It is the experience of every man that his own existence and that of things around him is imperfect and contingent. But if imperfect and contingent, the cause of the limitation is distinct from that which is caused. Existence as such contains no necessity of limitation, as can be seen from the existence of

---

20 St. Thomas, *Commentary on the Sentences*, IV, dist. 12, q. 1, art. 1, ad 5.

an absolutely necessary and perfect Being. Existence in creatures is limited by their capacity for existence, and this capacity is radically nothing other than the essence that receives the act of existence.

The Fourth Way of Demonstration: From the Grades of Perfection in Things

The argument of St. Thomas proceeds in this way:

> The fourth way is taken from the gradation to be found in things. Among beings there are some more and some less good, true, noble, and the like. But *more* and *less* are predicated of different things according as they resemble in their different ways something which is the maximum, as a thing is said to be hotter according as it more nearly resembles that which is hottest; so that there is something which is truest, something best, something noblest, and consequently, something which is most being, for those things that are greatest in truth are greatest in being, as it is written in *Metaph.* ii. Now the maximum in any genus is the cause of all in that genus, as fire, which is the maximum of heat, is the cause of all hot things, as is said in the same book. Therefore there must also be something which is to all beings the cause of their being, goodness, and every other perfection; and this we call God.[21]

This argument seems very much like a demonstration based upon a logical analysis of terms, rather than upon experience. Does not St. Thomas arbitrarily set up absolute standards for metaphysical properties as one would set up axioms in mathematics and measure things by means of these idealistic standards? Moreover, the example of heat used by St. Thomas seems to indicate that this is not a strict argument. Does he mean that there is an absolute heat, perfect in all respects, without potency of any kind? This would mean that God is fire. One could multiply ludicrous examples to show that the argument is not universally valid. For example, if some basketball players are better than others, is there an absolutely perfect basketball player? Or if some dogs are better than others, is there an absolutely perfect dog?

The argument of St. Thomas does not take its force from an idealistic conception of a standard. In fact, this argument, like the first three ways, is an a posteriori argument, from effects to cause. St. Thomas says that "we find" that there are gradations in perfection. They are present in things, to be discovered by the mind. It is possible that people disagree on what is more or less perfect, but everyone acknowledges that there is a gradation in values. In some areas of social and moral values, a person's education and cultural background enter into his judgment. But as long as a man is convinced that there are objects of different value, for example,

[21] St. Thomas, *Summa Theologiae*, I, q. 2, art. 3.

that human life is worth more than an inanimate thing like food, he must admit that there is an *objective standard* by which things are measured. A similar gradation will be evident in many other areas. The gradation is not due to our thinking about it. In other words, it is not we who primarily set up the differences in goodness, truth, nobility, and being. They are objectively different and it is our task to make our judgment correspond with what is objective.

How does one proceed from an objective judgment about a hierarchy of perfections in things to the conclusion that there is actually a perfect embodiment of that perfection, which is the standard by which other things in the class are measured? The principle of formal causality forms the link between the premise and the conclusion. However the argument from formal causality depends on the distinction between act and potency and the limitation of act by potency. The transcendental perfections that St. Thomas uses as examples of gradation are of themselves unlimited. Other perfections in things imply a limitation, such as the powers of vegetative growth, hearing, reasoning, and the like. These latter are intrinsically limited because they are found only in imperfect beings and imply a relationship to matter. Hearing, for example, is an external sensory power that depends on the operations of a physical organ; it can be injured, become diseased, or made less acute by noise. Hence perfections of this kind contain an essential limitation. But perfections like life, goodness, truth, and existence have no intrinsic principle of limitation. If they are found to be more or less perfect in various things, as life, for example, is found in a grain of wheat, in a flower, in a worm, in a horse, and in man, and some kind of order of value is assigned to them, one asks the question: Why is life less perfect in the wheat that man uses as food than in man himself? The potency of each thing determines the extent of the perfection that it can receive. For example, man has a capacity to become a musician, a scientist, a morally good person, but a grain of wheat evidently does not. A grain of wheat has a capacity to become something that a stone cannot become. Each thing, then, has its own capacities that define the kind and amount of perfection it is capable of receiving.

Since the potency that limits and the perfection of form that is limited are two distinct principles joined in a composition, and the potency itself is not the source of the perfection that comes into existence, there must be some source of goodness, truth, and life that is not composite and limited. For if all things were limited in these transcendental perfections there would be no satisfactory explanation of how they exist at all.

Hence this fourth way does not prescind entirely from the principle of efficient causality, since each thing is and acts through its form. Nor does it prescind from the principle of final causality, since what is good in an absolute sense is the *raison d'être* of participated good. The fourth way of demonstration, however, is distinctive in that the starting point is the realization that perfection is found in beings in different modes and stages of development.

The difficulty about St. Thomas' example of heat can be answered in two ways. The most obvious way is to say that St. Thomas used fire as an analogy and that he did not want this to be understood as proof of the existence of an absolute heat. The very notion is contradictory, if heat is taken as a physical quality, as a form of energy, belonging only in the corporeal world. Or one might give a more mystical interpretation of fire, as did some pre-Socratic philosophers like Heraclitus who identified fire and divinity. The second interpretation appears out of context with the precise manner in which St. Thomas proposes this and the other four ways of demonstrating the existence of God.

The fourth way is preferred by some who are inclined to a more Platonic approach to philosophy. The argument seems more intuitive, to possess greater warmth than the concise and impersonal arguments from motion and efficient causality. One can argue, however, that St. Thomas is no more intuitive or personal in this argument than in the others, and that here as elsewhere the connection must be made with the principle of limitation of act by potency, the basis upon which the entire proof rests. The danger in employing the fourth way of demonstration lies precisely in trying to dispense with the way of causality and substituting in its place some form of the ontological argument.

The Fifth Way of Demonstration: From the Ordering of Beings to Their End

St. Thomas argues as follows:

> The fifth way is taken from the governance of the world. We see that things which lack knowledge, such as natural bodies, act for an end, and this is evident from their acting always, or nearly always, in the same way, so as to obtain the best result. Hence it is plain that they achieve their end, not fortuitously, but designedly. Now whatever lacks knowledge cannot move towards an end, unless it be directed by some being endowed with knowledge and intelligence; as the arrow is directed by the archer. Therefore some intelligent being exists by whom all natural things are directed to their end; and this being we call God.[22]

St. Thomas has chosen for his examples things that do not have intelligence of their own. His intention is to show that direction toward an end is more evident in things that do not have any control over

---

[22] St. Thomas, *Summa Theologiae*, I, q. 2, art. 3.

their thoughts and actions. However, he does not exclude intelligent beings from the universal scope of the principle of finality, for all action is ultimately determined by a good that moves things by drawing to itself. It is not difficult to show that intellectual beings act for an end. Indeed, that is self-evident. But unless one understands the nature of freedom in man he may be halted at that point in the demonstration and suppose that since man chooses freely he is not directed in his actions by an absolute end. Thus the demonstration could not yet get beyond proving that there is intelligence in the universe. It would not demonstrate the existence of a transcendent and absolute intelligence by which all imperfect beings are directed to their end.

This proof is strictly metaphysical and is not limited to the examples given by St. Thomas. It is based upon the principle of final causality that is as universal in its application as the principle of identity. It is sometimes interpreted as the proof from order and design in the universe, taken in the physical sense in which the regularity of movement of the *parts of the universe* is emphasized. In this conception God's role is that of a giant watchmaker who has put things together in such a way that one must recognize it as the work of a superior intelligence.

The danger in such a simplification of the proof is that the examples used and the interpretation given them prevents the argument from rising to the metaphysical level where it belongs. To insist on examples from astronomy, biology, or any other physical science is grist for the mill of the mechanist. For him the natural causes hold enough of an explanation. Until the argument rises above the order of the physical universe, it cannot conclude to anything more than the existence of some kind of intelligence and power with which we have not yet become acquainted. Future investigation might conceivably reveal that there are powers of intelligence in the universe that we now have no evidence for.

The proof carries to its logical conclusion the analysis that we made earlier of the principle of final causality. It is evident that there are beings that have a source of activity within them — some of them have intelligence and some do not. The source of activity is the *form*, or more precisely the *nature*, which is the primary principle of movement and rest in a being. But nature never acts except to produce specific effects. Therefore, the activity of the nature is specified by the end which it tends to produce or to reach. This end is something good or at least it appears good. To act contrary to one's real or apparent good is to violate the law of one's own being.

The transition made in the demonstration from the presence of purposive action in natural things to the existence of an absolute end is made in the same way that one moved from bodies in motion to the existence of an unmoved mover, or from contingent beings to the existence of an absolutely necessary being. There must be an absolute end in which all striving will come to rest. The causality of the end is no less real than that found in someone who draws something to himself physically. Indeed the causality of the end is so much the greater the more it escapes the limitations of the physical order. While it is true that the final end affects each thing according to the disposition of the subject — for example, the aroma of a well-cooked dinner will not attract someone who is nauseated, though it will attract someone who is in good health and is hungry — it is more generally true that the more universal and spiritual the good in question, the more strongly it will draw things to itself. Therefore, the good that attracts all things of nature must be a universal and transcendent good. Such a good will necessarily be absolute perfection and pure actuality, for if it were imperfect or potential in any way it would be attracted by something more perfect and so on *ad infinitum*.

Conclusion

All things are good and are brought together in God who is the Origin and End of all. All creatures have unity in Him, to the extent that they tend to Him as to the ruler of the universe and the final good of everything. Since all reality comes to rest in Him, so metaphysics, which is the science of reality or being as such, comes to a conclusion in the knowledge of God. But the unity of all things is found in the love of God that is consequent upon knowledge. Whatever perfections man predicates of God — pure actuality, supreme intelligence, creativity, and whatever other attribute man can discover in God through analogy with creatures can be summed up in this: God is the absolute good who draws all things to Himself. It is on this note that St. Thomas ends his Commentary on the *Metaphysics*, namely, that God is the Ruler of the universe, the source of unity in all things, the good that all things seek.

> Therefore we conclude that the whole universe is like one people and one kingdom, in which there must be one ruler who directs all who are in it. This is the conclusion that he (Aristotle) comes to, that there is one Lord of the whole universe, namely the first Mover, the first Truth, and the first Good, whom we have called God. May He be blessed throughout all ages. Amen.[23]

---

[23] St. Thomas, *Commentary on the Metaphysics*, XII, 1, no. 2663.

READINGS FOR CHAPTER I.   THE NEED OF A
METAPHYSICS

1. What Is Metaphysics?

St. Thomas, *Commentary on the Metaphysics*, Prologue.*

When several things are ordained to one thing, one of them must rule or govern and the rest be ruled or governed, as the Philosopher[1] teaches in the *Politics*.[2] This is evident in the union of soul and body, for the soul naturally commands and the body obeys. The same thing is true of the soul's powers, for the concupiscible and irascible appetites are ruled in a natural order by reason. Now all the sciences and arts are ordained to one thing, namely, to man's perfection, which is happiness. Hence one of these sciences and arts must be the mistress of all the others, and this rightly lays claim to the name *wisdom;* for it is the office of the wise man to direct others.

We can discover which science this is and the sort of things with which it deals by carefully examining the qualities of a good ruler; for just as men of superior intelligence are naturally the rulers and masters of others, whereas those of great physical strength and little intelligence are naturally slaves, as the Philosopher says in the aforementioned book,[3] in a similar way that science which is intellectual in the highest degree should be naturally the ruler of the others. This science is the one which treats of the most intelligible objects.

Now the phrase "most intelligible objects" can be understood in three ways. First, from the viewpoint of the order of knowing; for those things from which the intellect derives certitude seem to be more intelligible. Therefore, since the certitude of science is acquired by the intellect knowing causes, a knowledge of causes seems to be intellectual in the highest degree. Hence that science which considers first causes also seems to be the ruler of the others in the highest degree.

Second, this phrase can be understood by comparing the intellect with the senses; for while sensory perception is a knowledge of particulars, the intellect seems to differ from sense by reason of the fact that it comprehends universals. Hence that science is pre-eminently intellectual which deals with the most

---

* All translations of St. Thomas' *Commentary on the Metaphysics*, as well as those from Aristotle's *Metaphysics* itself, are those of John P. Rowan, Ph.D., Duquesne University. Dr. Rowan's translation is to be published by the Henry Regnery Company and is used with permission.

[1] The title "Philosopher" was one which medieval thinkers reserved for Aristotle.
[2] *Politica*, I, 5 (1254a 20).
[3] *Ibid.*, I, 1 (1254a 31); 5 (1254b 29).

universal principles. These principles are *being* and those things which naturally accompany being, such as *unity* and *plurality*, *potency* and *act*. Now such principles should not remain entirely undetermined, since without them a complete knowledge of the principles which are proper to any genus or species cannot be had. Nor again should they be dealt with in any one particular science, for, since a knowledge of each class of beings stands in need of such principles, they would with equal reason be investigated in every particular science. It follows, then, that such principles should be treated by one common science, which, since it is intellectual in the highest degree, is the mistress of the others.

Third, this phrase can be understood from the viewpoint of the intellect's own knowledge. For since each thing has intellective power by virtue of being free from matter, those things must be intelligible in the highest degree which are altogether separate from matter. For the intellect and the intelligible object must be proportionate to each other and must belong to the same genus, since the intellect and the intelligible object are one in act. Now those things are separate from matter in the highest degree which abstract not only from signate matter (as the natural forms taken universally of which the philosophy of nature[4] treats) but from sensible matter altogether; and these are separate from matter not only in their intelligible constitution (*ratio*), as the objects of mathematics, but also in being (*esse*), as God and the intelligences. Therefore the science which considers such things seems to be the most intellectual and the ruler or mistress of the others.

Now this threefold consideration should be assigned to one and the same science and not to different sciences, because the aforementioned separate substances are the universal and first causes of being. Moreover, it pertains to one and the same science to consider both the proper causes of some genus and the genus itself; for example, the philosophy of nature considers the principles of a natural body. Therefore, it must be the office of one and the same science to consider the separate substances and being in general (*ens commune*), which is the genus[5] of which the aforementioned substances are the common and universal causes.

From this it is evident that, although this science (metaphysics or first philosophy) studies the three things mentioned above,[6] it does not investigate any one of them as its subject, but only being in general. For the subject of a science is the genus whose causes and properties we seek, and not the causes themselves of the particular genus studied; for a knowledge of the causes of

---

[4] In the works of Aristotle and St. Thomas the term *natural science* (*scientia naturalis*) is equivalent to the term *philosophy of nature* (*philosophia naturalis*). The ancients drew no distinction between a philosophic and what we call "scientific" study of nature.

[5] According to St. Thomas the term *being in general* is not a genus or generic term in the strict logical sense, for being is predicated of things analogically, or proportionally, and not univocally. See *Metaphysics*, III, lesson 8, no. 433.

[6] I.e., God, the intellectual substances, and being in general.

some genus is the goal to which the investigation of a science attains. Now although the subject of this science is being in general, the whole of it is predicated of those things which are separate from matter both in their intelligible constitution and in being. For it is not only those things which can never exist in matter that are said to be separate from matter in their intelligible constitution and being, such as God and the intellectual substances, but also those which can exist without matter, as being in general. This could not be the case, however, if their being depended on matter.

Therefore in accordance with the three things mentioned above from which this science derives its perfection, three names arise. It is called *divine science* or *theology* inasmuch as it considers the aforementioned substances. It is called *metaphysics* inasmuch as it considers being and the attributes which naturally accompany being (for things which transcend the physical order are discovered by the process of analysis, as the more common are discovered after the less common). And it is called *first philosophy* inasmuch as it considers the first causes of things. Therefore it is evident what the subject of this science is, and how it is related to the other sciences, and by what names it is designated.

2. Wisdom Considers Universal First Causes and First Principles

A.   Aristotle, *Metaphysics*, I, 2, 982a 4–982b 11.

But since we are in search of this science, it will therefore be necessary to consider with what kind of causes and what kind of principles wisdom or science deals. This will perhaps become evident if we take the opinions which we have about the wise man. First of all, then, we think that the wise man is one who knows all things in the highest degree, as becomes him,[1] without having a knowledge of them singly.

Next, we say that that man is wise who is capable of knowing things that are difficult and not easy for man to understand. For sensory perception is common to all and is therefore easy and not a matter of wisdom.

Again, we consider him wise who is more certain.

And in every branch of science we say that he is wiser who is more capable of teaching us about the causes of things.

Again, among the sciences we think that that science which exists for its own sake and is desirable for the sake of knowledge is wisdom to a greater degree than one which is desirable for the sake of contingent effects.

And we think that a superior science which is rather the more basic comes nearer to wisdom than a subordinate one. For a wise man must not be directed

---

[1] The Latin version reads *sicut decet.* The Greek text reads — "so far as possible."

but must direct, and he must not obey another but must be obeyed by one who is less wise. Such then and so many are the opinions which we have about the wise and about wisdom.

Now of these attributes, that of knowing all things necessarily belongs to him who has universal knowledge in the highest degree, because he knows in some respect all things which are subordinate.

But the things which are just about the most difficult for man to understand are also those which are most universal, for they are farthest removed from the senses.

Again, the most certain of the sciences are those which are most concerned with primary things. For sciences based on fewer principles are more certain than those having additional principles, as arithmetic is more certain than geometry.

Moreover, that science which speculates about the causes of things is more instructive; for those who instruct us are those who assign the causes of every single thing.

Again, understanding and knowledge for their own sake are found in the highest degree in the science which has as its object what is most knowable. For one who desires scientific knowledge for its own sake will desire in the highest degree the science which is most truly science, and such science has as its object what is most knowable. Now first principles and causes are most knowable; for it is by reason of these and from these that other things are known, and not these from things which are subordinate to them.

But that science is highest and is superior to subordinate sciences which knows the reason why every single thing must be done. And this is the good of every single thing, and viewed generally is the greatest good in the whole of nature.

In view of everything that has been said, then, it is evident that the term which we are investigating falls in the same science. For this science must speculate about first principles and causes, and the good, or that for the sake of which something is done, is also one of the causes.

B. St. Thomas, *Commentary on the Metaphysics,* I, lesson 2, nos. 36–51.

[36.] Having shown that wisdom is a knowledge of causes, the Philosopher's aim here is to establish with what kinds of causes and what kinds of principles it is concerned. Now he shows that it is concerned with the most universal and primary causes, and he argues this from the definition of wisdom.

In regard to this he does three things. First, he formulates a definition of wisdom from the different opinions which men hold about the wise man and about wisdom. Second, he shows that all these are proper to that universal science which considers first and universal causes, where he says, "Now of these." Third, he draws the conclusion at which he aims, where he says, "In view of."

In regard to the first he gives six common opinions which men have held about wisdom. He states the first where he says, "But since we are," and it is as follows: in general we consider all those to be wise who know all things in the highest degree (as becomes them) without having a knowledge of every single thing. For this is impossible, because singulars are infinite in number, and infinite things cannot be comprehended by the intellect.

[37.] "Next, we say."

Here he gives the second opinion, which runs thus: we hold that man to be wise who by reason of his intellect is capable of knowing difficult things and those which are not generally easy for men to understand; for sensory perception, i.e., the knowing of sensible things, is common to all, and is therefore easy and not a matter of wisdom; i.e., it is neither a part of wisdom nor pertains to wisdom. Thus it is clear that whatever pertains to wisdom is not easily known by all.

[38.] "Again, we consider."

Here he gives the third opinion, namely, that we consider him wise who, regarding what he knows, is more certain than other men generally are.

[39.] "And in every branch."

Here he gives the fourth opinion, namely, that in every branch of science that man is said to be wiser who can give the causes of anything that is investigated, and can teach by means of this.

[40.] "Again, among the sciences."

Here he gives the fifth opinion, namely, that among the many sciences, that science which is more desirable and willed for its own sake, i.e., chosen for the sake of knowledge and for knowledge alone, is wisdom to a greater degree than a science which is the cause of any of the other contingent effects which can be produced by knowledge, such as the necessities of life, pleasures, and so forth.

[41.] "And we think."

Here he gives the sixth opinion, namely, that this wisdom of which mention is made must be, or we say, is "rather the more basic," i.e., the nobler, science than "a subordinate one." This can be understood from the above. For in the field of the mechanical arts subordinate artisans are those who execute by manual operations the commands of superior artists, whom he referred to above as master artists and wise men.

[42.] That the notion of wisdom applies more appropriately to sciences which give orders than to those which carry them out, he proves in two ways.

First, on the grounds that subordinate sciences are directed to superior sciences. For subordinate arts are directed to the end of a superior art, as the art of horsemanship to the end of the military art. But according to every opinion it is not proper that a wise man should be directed by another, but rather that he should direct others. Second, on the grounds that subordinate artists are induced to act by superior ones inasmuch as they rely on the latter for the things which they must do or make. Thus the shipwright relies upon the instructions of the navigator for the kind of form which a ship ought to have. However, it is not proper that a wise man should be induced to act by someone else, but rather that he should use his knowledge to induce others to act.

[43.]   These, then, are such opinions which men have of wisdom and the wise man; and from all of these a definition of wisdom can be formulated, so that the wise man is described as one who knows all difficult matters with certitude and knows their cause, who seeks this knowledge for its own sake, and who directs others and induces them to act. And in this way the major premise of the syllogism becomes evident; for every wise man must be such, and, conversely, whosoever is such is wise.

[44.]   "Now of these."

Here he shows that all of the above attributes come together in the man who knows the first and universal causes of things; and he follows the same order which he did above. Hence he posited, first, that a knowledge of all things in the highest belongs to him who has universal knowledge. This was the first opinion, and it is made clear in this way. Whoever knows universals knows in some measure the things which are subordinate to universals, because he knows them in the universal. But all things are subordinate to those which are most universal. Therefore the one who knows the most universal things knows in some measure all other things.

[45.]   "But the things."

Then he proves that the second attribute belongs to the same science, by the following argument. Those things which are farthest removed from the senses are difficult for men to know; for sensory perception is common to all, since the whole of human knowledge originates with this. But things which are most universal are farthest removed from the sensible world, since the senses have to do with singulars. Hence universals are the most difficult for men to know. It is evident, then, that that science is the most difficult which deals chiefly with universals.

[46.]   But the statement which appears in Book I of the *Physics*[1] seems to contradict this; for it is said there that it is more universal things which are first known by us; and those things which are first known by us are those which are easier to know. But it must be said that it is those things which are more universal according to simple apprehension that are first known; for

---

[1] *Physica*, I, 1 (184a 24).

being is the first thing that comes into the intellect, as Avicenna says,[2] and *animal* comes into the intellect before *man* does. For just as in the order of nature, which proceeds from potentiality to actuality, *animal* is prior to *man*, so too in the genesis of knowledge the intellect conceives *animal* before it conceives *man*. But with respect to the investigation of natural properties, less universal things are known first, because we discover universal causes by means of the particular causes which belong to one genus or species. But those things which are universal in their causality are known by us later (notwithstanding the fact that they are things which are primarily knowable according to their nature), although things which are universal by predication are known to us in some degree before the less universal (notwithstanding the fact that they are prior to singular things). For in us sensory knowledge, which is cognitive of singular things, precedes intellective knowledge, which is cognitive of universals. Emphasis must also be placed on this, that he does not say that the most universal things are the most difficult absolutely, but "just about." For those things which are entirely separate from matter in being, as the immaterial substances, are more difficult for us to know than universals. Therefore, even though this science which is called wisdom is the first in dignity, it is still the last to be learned.

[47.] "Again, the most."

Here he shows that the third attribute belongs to the same science, by using this argument. The more prior any sciences are by nature, the more certain they are. This is clear from the fact that those sciences which are said to come about as a result of adding something to the other sciences are less certain than those which take fewer things into consideration. For example, arithmetic is more certain than geometry, because the objects considered in geometry are a result of adding to those considered in arithmetic. This becomes evident if we consider what these two sciences take as their first principles, namely, the unit and the point. For the point adds to the unit the notion of position. For undivided being constitutes the intelligible structure of the unit; and in so far as this has the function of a measure it becomes the principle of number. But the point adds to this the notion of position. However, particular sciences are subsequent in nature to universal sciences, because their subjects add something to the subjects of universal sciences. For example, it is evident that *mobile being*, with which the philosophy of nature deals, adds to *being* pure and simple, with which metaphysics deals, and to *quantified being*, with which mathematics is concerned. Hence that science which treats of being and the most universal things is the most certain. Moreover, the statement here that this science deals with fewer things is not opposed to the one made above that it knows all things; for the universal takes in fewer things actually but more potentially. And the more certain a science is, the fewer actual things it has to consider in investigating its subject-matter. Hence the practical sciences are the least certain, because they must consider the many circumstances attending singular effects.

---

[2] *Metaphysics*, I, 6 (72ab).

[48.] "Moreover, that science."

Here he shows that the fourth attribute belongs to the same science, by this argument: that science is more instructive, or better able to teach, which is more concerned with causes. For only those teach who assign the causes of every single thing, because knowledge comes about through some cause, and to teach is to cause knowledge in another. But that science which considers universals considers the first of all the causes. Therefore it is evidently the best fitted to teach.

[49.] "Again, understanding."

Here he shows that the fifth attribute belongs to the same science, by this argument. It is the business of those sciences which deal with things that are most knowable most properly to know and to understand for their own sake, i.e., for the sake of those sciences themselves and not for something else. But it is the sciences which deal with first causes that consider the things that are most knowable. Therefore those sciences are desired most for themselves. He proves the first premise in this way: one who most desires knowledge for the sake of knowledge most desires scientific knowledge. But the highest kind of knowledge is concerned with things that are most knowable. Therefore those sciences are desired most for themselves which have to do with things that are most knowable. He proves the second premise in this way: those things by reason of which and from which other things are known are more knowable than those which are known through them. But these other things are known through causes and principles, and not the reverse.

[50.] "But that science."

Here he shows that the sixth attribute belongs to the same science, by the following argument. That science which considers the final cause, or that for the sake of which particular things are done, is related to the other sciences as a chief or master science is to a subordinate or ancillary one, as is evident in the statements made above. For the navigator, to whom the use (i.e., end) of the ship belongs, is a kind of master artist in relation to the shipwright who serves him. But the aforesaid science is most concerned with the final cause of all things. This is clear from the fact that that for the sake of which every single thing is done "is the good of each," i.e., a particular good. Now in any class of things the end or goal is a good; and, as a matter of fact, that which is the end of all things, i.e., of the universe itself, is the greatest good in the whole of nature; and this pertains to the consideration of the aforesaid science. Therefore this science is the chief or architectonic science of all the others.

[51.] "In view of."

Then he draws his intended conclusion from the foregoing arguments, saying that it is clear from everything which has been said above that the name wisdom belongs to the same science for which we are searching, which is the theoretical, i.e., speculative, science of first principles and causes. This is evident from the six primary attributes which clearly belong to the science that considers universal causes. But since the sixth attribute touched on a consideration of the final cause, which was not clearly held to be a cause among the oldest philosophers, as will be said below, he therefore shows in a special way that this attribute belongs to the same science, namely, to the one which considers first causes; because the final cause itself, which is a good, and that for the sake of which other things are done, is one of the many causes. Hence the science which considers first and universal causes must also be the one which considers the universal end of all things, which is the greatest good in the whole of nature.

3. The Nature and Goal of Metaphysics

A. Aristotle, *Metaphysics*, I, 2, 982b 11–983a 23.

That this is not a practical science is evident from those who first philosophized. For it is because of wonder that men both now and formerly began to philosophize, wondering at first about less important problems, and then progressing little by little they raised questions about more important ones, such as the phases of the moon and the courses of the sun and of the stars and the generation of the universe. But one who raises questions and wonders seems to be ignorant. Hence the philosopher is also to some extent a lover of myth, for myths are composed of wonders. Therefore, if they philosophized in order to escape from ignorance, evidently they pursued their studies for the sake of knowledge and not for any utility.

And what has happened bears witness to this; for when nearly all the things necessary for life, leisure and learning were acquired, prudence of this sort began to be sought. It is clear, then, that we do not seek this knowledge for the sake of any other necessity.

But just as we say that that man is free who exists for himself and not for another, in a similar fashion only this science is free, because it alone exists for itself.

For this reason, too, it might rightly be thought that this science is not a human possession, since in many respects human nature is servile.

Hence, according to Simonides, "Only God has this honor,"[1] and it is unfitting[2] that a man should not seek a knowledge which befits him. Some poets accordingly say that the deity is naturally envious; and it is most likely that it should happen in this case, and that all those who are imperfect are unfortunate. But it is unfitting that the deity should be envious, for, as the proverb says, "The poets tell many lies."[3]

---

[1] Hiller, Frag. 3.
[2] Reading *indignum* for *dignum*.
[3] Hiller, Frag. 26 (Solon).

Nor must we think that any other science is more honorable than this. For what is most divine is most honorable. But then it alone will be such, and in two ways. For of all knowledge, that which God most properly has is divine; and if there is any such knowledge, it is concerned with divine matters. But this science alone has both of these characteristics; for according to all men God seems to be a cause and in some sense a principle; and such knowledge as this God either alone has, or has in the highest degree. Therefore all the other sciences are more necessary, but none is more excellent.

But it is necessary in a sense to bring to a halt the progression of this science at the contrary of our original questions. Indeed, as we have said, all men begin by wondering whether things are as strange as chance occurrences appear to those who do not yet know the cause of their motion; or by wondering about the changes in the course of the sun; or about the incommensurability of the diagonal of a square. For it would seem an object of wonder to all if something having the nature of number cannot be measured. But it is necessary to advance to the contrary view and, as the proverb says,[4] the worthier one, as also happens in these matters when men have learned them. For nothing would surprise a geometrician more than if the diagonal of a square should become commensurable with a side. It has been stated, then, what the nature is of the science we are seeking, and what its goal is for which our search and whole method must be undertaken.

B.   St. Thomas, *Commentary on the Metaphysics*, I, lesson 3, nos. 52–68.

[52.] Having shown with what things this science deals, Aristotle shows what kind of science it is; and in regard to this he does two things. First, he exposes the dignity of this science; and second, the object which it tries to reach, where he says, "But it is necessary."

In regard to the first he does four things. First, he shows that this science is not a practical science but a speculative one; second, that it is free in the highest degree, where he says, "But just as we say;" third, that it is not a human possession, where he says, "For this reason;" and fourth, that it is the most honorable science, where he says, "Nor must we."

He proves the first in two ways: first, by an argument, and second, by an example where he says, "And what has happened."

[53.] First, he gives this argument. No science in which knowledge itself is sought for its own sake is a practical science but a speculative one. But that science which is wisdom, or philosophy as it is called, exists for the sake of knowledge itself. Therefore it is speculative and not practical. He proves the minor premise in this way. Whoever seeks to escape from ignorance as an end tends towards knowledge itself for its own sake. But those who philosophize seek to escape from ignorance as an end. Therefore they tend towards knowledge itself for its own sake.

---

4 Leutsch & Schneidewin, *Paroemiographi Graeci*, I, 371.

[54.]   That they seek to escape from ignorance becomes clear from the fact
    that those who first philosophized and who now philosophize, began
to philosophize because of wonder about some cause, although they did this
at first in a different way than they did later on; for at first they wondered
about less difficult problems, which were more easily solved, in order that they
might come to know their causes; but later progressing little by little from a
knowledge of more evident things they raised questions about more important and obscure matters, such as the phases of the moon, i.e., of its eclipse,
and of its change in shape, which seems to vary according as its position
changes in relation to the sun. And similarly they raised questions about the
phenomena of the sun, as its eclipse, motion and size; and about the phenomena of the stars, such as their size, relationship, and so forth; and about
the origin of the whole universe, which some claimed to be produced by
chance, some by an intelligence, and some by love.

[55.]   Furthermore, he points out that doubt and wonder are a result of ignor-
    ance. For when we see certain obvious effects whose cause we do not
know, we then wonder about their cause. And since wonder was the cause
which led men to philosophy, it is clear that the philosopher is in a sense a
philo-myth, i.e., a lover of myth, which belongs properly to the poets. Hence
the first men to deal with the principles of things mythologically, such as
Perseus and certain others who comprise the seven sages, were called the the-
ologizing poets. The reason the philosopher is compared to the poet is that
both are concerned with wonders. For the myths with which the poets deal are
composed of certain wonders, and the philosophers themselves were moved to
philosophize because of wonder. And since wonder stems from ignorance, they
were obviously moved to philosophize in order to escape from ignorance. It
is evident from this, then, that "they pursued" knowledge, i.e., diligently
sought it, only for itself and not for any utility, or usefulness.

[56.]   Now it must be noted that, while this science was first designated by
    the name of wisdom, this was later changed to the name philosophy;
for they mean the same thing. For while the ancients who pursued the study
of wisdom were sophists, i.e., were called wise men, Pythagoras, when asked
what he professed himself to be, refused to call himself a wise man, as his
predecessors had done, because he thought this was presumptuous, but called
himself a philosopher, i.e., a lover of wisdom.[1] And from that time the name
wise man was changed to the name philosopher, and the name wisdom to
philosophy. This name also contributes something to the point under discussion, for that man seems to be a lover of wisdom who does not seek wisdom
for some other reason but for itself alone. For he who seeks one thing on
account of something else has greater love for that on whose account he
seeks than for that which he seeks.

[57.]   "And what has happened."

    Here he proves the same point by an example. The statement (he says)

[1] See St. Augustine, *De Civitate Dei*, Book VIII, 2 (PL 41:225).

that wisdom or philosophy is not sought for any utility but for knowledge itself is proved by "what has happened," i.e., by what occurred in the case of those who have pursued philosophy. For when nearly all those arts were discovered which are necessary for life, "leisure" (i.e., the sort of pleasure which consists in a life of ease), and also learning, such as the logical sciences, which are not sought for themselves but as introductions to the other arts, then man began for the first time to seek this kind of prudence, namely, wisdom. And from this it is clear that wisdom is not sought because of any necessity other than itself but for itself; for no one seeks something he already possesses. Hence, since wisdom was sought after all other knowledge had been discovered, it is evident that it was not sought for any reason other than itself but only for itself.

[58.] "But just as."

Then he proves that the second attribute belongs to wisdom, i.e., that it is free; and he uses the following argument. That man is properly said to be free who does not exist for the sake of another but for himself; for slaves exist for their masters, work for them, and acquire for them whatever they acquire, whereas free men exist for themselves inasmuch as they work for themselves and acquire things for themselves. But only this science exists for itself, and therefore among all the sciences only this science is free.

[59.] Now we must note that this can be understood in two ways. In one way, so that the expression "only this" may indicate every speculative science as a class; and then it is true that only this class of science is sought for itself. Hence only those arts which are directed to knowing are called free (or liberal) arts, whereas those which are directed to some useful end by controlling activity are called mechanical or servile arts. In another way, so that the expression may specifically indicate this philosophy, or wisdom, which deals with the highest causes; because the final cause is also among the highest causes, as he stated above (26:C 51). Therefore this science must consider the highest and universal end of all things; and thus all the other sciences are related to it as their end. Hence only this science exists in the highest degree for itself.

[60.] "For this reason."

Here he proves that the third attribute belongs to this science, i.e., that it is not a human possession; and in regard to this he does two things. First, he proves his thesis. Second, he rejects an error which some men made, where he says, "Hence, according to."

He proves his thesis by the following argument. A science which is free in the highest degree cannot be a possession of that nature which is servile and subservient in many respects. But human nature is servile "in many respects," i.e., in many ways. Therefore this science is not a human possession. Now human nature is said to be servile insofar as it stands in need of many things; and this is why it happens that man sometimes neglects what should be sought for its own sake because of the things necessary for life; as he says in Book III of the *Topics*,[2] it is better to philosophize than to become wealthy, although sometimes becoming wealthy is more desirable, i.e., to one lacking life's necessities. From this it is clear that that wisdom which is not properly possessed by man is sought only for its own sake. For man possesses what he can have at his command and what he can freely use. Now that science which is sought only for itself man cannot freely use, since he is often prevented from having it on account of the things necessary for life. And again it is not subject to man's command, because man cannot acquire it perfectly. Yet that very small part of it which he does have outweighs everything known by the other sciences.

[61.] "Hence, according to."

Here he rejects the error of a certain poet, Simonides, who said that it is proper to God alone to have the honor of deserving that knowledge which ought to be sought for itself and not for the sake of something else. But it is unfitting that man should not seek that knowledge which is in keeping with his condition, namely, one which is directed to the things necessary for life, of which man stands in need.

[62.] Now Simonides' error came from that of certain poets who said that the deity is envious, and that since He is envious He does not desire that the things pertaining to his honor should be shared by all. And if God is envious of man in other things, he is rightly more so in this case, i.e., with regard to that knowledge which is sought for itself, which is the most honorable of all. And according to the opinion of these men it follows that all who are imperfect are unfortunate; for they said that men are fortunate as a result of the providence of the gods, who communicate their goods to men. Hence, because of the envy of the gods, who are unwilling to communicate their goodness, it follows that men who remain outside the perfection of this science are unfortunate.

[63.] But the basis of this opinion is most false; because it is unfitting that anything divine should be envious. This is clear from the fact that envy is sadness at someone else's prosperity, and this can occur only because the one who is envious thinks that another's good diminishes his own. Now God cannot possibly be sad, because He is not subject to evil of any kind. Nor can His goodness be diminished by someone else's goodness, since every good flows from His goodness as from an unfailing spring. Hence Plato also said that there is no envy of any kind in God. But the poets have lied not only in this matter but in many others, as is stated in the common proverb.

[64.] "Nor must we."

Here he proves that the fourth attribute belongs to this science, i.e., that it is the most honorable science, and he uses the following argument. That

---

[2] *Topica*, III, 2 (118 a 10).

science which is most divine is most honorable, just as God Himself is also the most honorable of all things. But this science is the most divine, and is therefore the most honorable. The minor premise is proved in this way: a science is said to be divine in two ways, and only this science is said to be divine in both. In one way, the science which God has is said to be divine; and in another way, a science is said to be divine because it is about divine matters. Now it is clear that this science alone meets both of these requirements; for, since this science is about first causes and principles, it must be about God; because God is understood in this way by all inasmuch as He is one of the many causes and a certain principle of things. And such a science which is concerned with God and with first causes, either God alone has, or if He alone does not have it, He at least has it in the highest degree. Now He alone has such science in a perfectly comprehensive way. And He has it in the highest degree inasmuch as it is had by men in their own way, although it is not had by them as a human possession, but as something borrowed from Him.

[65.]   From these considerations he draws the further conclusion that all the other sciences are more necessary than this science for use in practical life; for these sciences are sought least of all for their own sake. But none of the other sciences can be more excellent than this science.

[66.]   "But it is necessary."

He now gives the goal toward which this science proceeds. He says that its progression comes to rest, or is terminated, in the contrary of what was previously found in those who first sought this science, as also happens in the case of natural generations and motions; for each motion is terminated in the contrary of that from which the motion begins. Hence, since investigation is a kind of motion towards knowledge, it must be terminated in the contrary of that from which it begins. But, as was stated above, the investigation of this science began with man's wonder about all things, because the first philosophers wondered about less important matters, and subsequent philosophers about more hidden ones. And the object of their wonder was whether something was like strange chance occurrences, i.e., things which seem to happen mysteriously by chance; for things which happen as if by themselves are called chance occurrences. For men wonder most when things happen by chance in this way, supposing that they were foreseen or determined by some cause. For chance occurrences are not determined by a cause, and wonder results from ignorance of a cause. Therefore, when men were not yet able to recognize the causes of things, they wondered about all things as if they were chance occurrences; just as they wondered about the changes in the course of the sun, of which there are two namely, the two solstices, that of winter and that of summer. For at the summer solstice the sun begins to decline toward the south, when formerly it declined toward the north. But at the winter solstice the opposite occurs. And they also wondered that the diagonal of a square should not be commensurable with a side. For since what is not measured seems to pertain only to what is indivisible, (as the unit alone is what is not measured by a number but itself measures all numbers), it seems a matter of wonder if something which is not indivisible cannot be measured; and again as a consequence of this that what is not a smallest part cannot be measured. But it is evident that the diagonal of a square and its side are not indivisible things or smallest parts, and therefore is seems a matter of wonder if they are not commensurable.

[67.]   Since philosophical investigation began with wonder, then it must end or terminate in the contrary of this, and this is to terminate in the worthier view, as the common proverb agrees, in which it is stated that one must always advance to this better view. For what this opposite and worthier view is in the case of the above wonders is evident, because when men have already learned the causes of these things, they do not wonder. Thus the geometrician does not wonder if the diagonal should not be commensurable with a side, because he knows the reason for this, namely, that the proportion of the diagonal squared to the square of a side is not as the proportion of the square of a number to the number squared, but as the proportion of two to one. Hence it follows that the proportion of a side to the diagonal is not like the proportion of one number to another. And from this it is evident that they cannot be made commensurable. For only those lines are commensurable which are proportioned to each other as one number to another. Therefore the goal toward which we should advance in this science will be this, that in knowing the causes we do not wonder about their effects.

[68.]   It is evident from the foregoing discussion, then, what the nature of this science is, because it is speculative and free, and is not a human possession but a divine one. And it is also evident what the object of this science is, that is, what the whole method and whole art of this science must investigate; for its object is the first and universal causes of things about which it also makes investigations and establishes the truth. And as a result of knowing these things it attains this object, so that evidently there is no wonder when the causes of things are known.

READINGS FOR CHAPTER II. THE FORMAL
SUBJECT OF METAPHYSICS

1. The Division of Speculative Science

St. Thomas, *Exposition of the Trinity of Boethius*, q. 5, art. 1.*

This is a two-fold question: first, the division of speculative science, which the text treats; secondly, the modes which it attributes to the parts of speculative science. Concerning the first of these, four questions must be asked; (1) Whether the division of speculative science into three parts, natural science, mathematics, and divine science, is a good one; (2) Whether natural science is concerned with those things which exist in matter and motion; (3) Whether the mathematical consideration is without matter and motion but concerned with things which exist in matter; (4) Whether divine science is concerned with things which exist without matter and motion.

Article One

Whether the division of speculative science into three
parts, natural science, mathematics, and divine science is a proper one?

We approach the first question thus: It seems that speculative science is improperly divided into these parts.

1. The parts of speculative science are those habits which perfect the contemplative part of the soul. But the Philosopher (in VI *Ethics*, chap. 1) says that the scientific part of the soul, which is its contemplative part, is perfected by three habits, namely, wisdom, science, and understanding. Therefore, these three are the parts of speculative science, and not those mentioned in the text.

2. Moreover, St. Augustine says in the Eighth Book of *The City of God*, chap. 4, that rational philosophy, which is logic, is included in speculative or contemplative philosophy. Since, therefore, it makes no mention of it, the division seems to be insufficient.

3. Moreover, philosophy is commonly divided into the seven liberal arts, among which neither natural nor divine science is numbered, but only rational and mathematical science. Therefore, natural and divine science ought not to be named as parts of the speculative science.

---

* All translations of the *Exposition of the Trinity of Boethius* are those of Ralph McInerny, Ph.D., University of Notre Dame, and are used with his permission.

4. Moreover, the science of medicine seems to be quite operative, and yet in it one part is speculative, another practical. For the same reason, there is a speculative part in every other operative science; thus mention ought to be made in this division of ethics or morals, although it is active, because of its speculative part.

5. Moreover, the science of medicine is a part of physics; so too are those other arts which are called mechanical, like agriculture, alchemy, etc. And, since these are operative, it seems that natural science should not be placed absolutely within speculative science.

6. Moreover, the whole should not be divided against the part. But divine science seems to be a whole with respect to mathematics and physics since their subjects are parts of its subject. For the subject of divine science, which is first philosophy, is being, a part of which is mobile substance which natural science considers; so too with quantity which the mathematician studies (cf. III *Metaphysics*, chap. 2). Therefore, divine science ought not to be divided against natural and mathematical science.

7. Moreover, sciences are divided as are things (III *On the Soul*, chap. 8). But philosophy is concerned with being; indeed it is knowledge of being, as Denys says in his letter to Polycarp. Since being is first divided by potency and act, and by the one and the many, and by substance and accident, it would seem that the parts of philosophy ought to be distinguished according to such things.

8. Moreover, there are many other divisions of being more essentially the concerns of science than mobile and immobile, abstract and not abstract, namely, coporeal and incorporeal, animate and inanimate, etc. Therefore, the division of the parts of philosophy ought to be based on differences of this kind rather than on the ones used here.

9. Moreover, that science which the others presuppose should be prior to them. But all the other sciences presuppose divine science, because it must prove the principles of the other sciences. Therefore, divine science should precede them.

10. Moreover, mathematics should be learned before natural science, since mathematics is easy for the young to learn whereas natural science is easy for the experienced (VI *Ethics*, chap. 9). Hence, among the ancients this order of learning the sciences was observed: men should first study logic, then mathematics before natural science, after that moral science, and finally divine science. Therefore, mathematics should precede natural science. Thus, this division is seen to be insufficient.

On the contrary: That this is the correct division is shown by the Philosopher in VI *Metaphysics*, chap. 1, where he says that "there will be three theoretical philosophical sciences, mathematics, physics, theology."

Moreover, in II *Physics*, chap. 2, three modes of science are given, which also seem to pertain to these three.
Moreover, Ptolemy, in the beginning of his *Almagest*, also uses this division.

Response: In reply it must be said that the theoretical or speculative intellect is properly distinguished from the operative or practical in that the speculative has for its end the truth that it considers, whereas the practical directs the truth known to operation as to an end. Aristotle says, (III *On the Soul*, chap. 10) therefore, that they differ from one another by their ends; in II *Metaphysics*, chap. 1, he says that, "the end of speculative science is truth, but the end of operative science is action." Therefore, since the matter should be proportioned to the end, the matter of practical sciences must be those things which can be products of our efforts if knowledge of them can be directed to operation as to an end. The matter of speculative sciences must be those things which cannot be made (or done) by us; hence the consideration of them cannot be directed to the goal of operation. It is according to the distinction of such things that the speculative sciences must be distinguished.

We should realize that when habits or potencies are distinguished by their objects, they are not distinguished by just any difference in their objects, but by those which belong to the objects precisely insofar as they are objects. For to be an animal or a plant is accidental to what is sensed insofar as it is sensible, and the distinction of the senses is not based on such difference, but rather on the differences of color and sound. Therefore, speculative sciences must be divided by the differences of speculable objects precisely as speculable. Two things belong to the speculable which is the object of the speculative potency: something from the side of the intellectual potency and something from the side of the habit of science by which the intellect is perfected. That it be immaterial belongs to it because of the intellect which is itself immaterial; that it be necessary belongs to it because science is of necessary things, as is proved in I *Posterior Analytics*, chap. 6. Every necessary thing, however, as such is immobile, for whatever is moved can to that degree be or not be either absolutely or in a certain respect (cf. IX *Metaphysics*, chap. 8). To the speculable, the object of speculative science, separation from matter and motion and from application to them belongs per se. Therefore, speculative sciences are distinguished by the degree of separation (*remotio*) from matter and motion.

Some speculables are such that they depend on matter for being, since they cannot be without matter; but these are distinguished, because some depend upon matter to be and to be known. These are such that sensible matter enters into their definition; therefore they cannot be understood without sensible matter; e.g., in the definition of man flesh and bones have to be included. Physics, or natural science, is concerned with such things. Other speculables are such that, although they depend upon matter in order to be, they do not so depend in order to be understood because sensible matter does not enter into their definition; e.g., line or number. Mathematics is concerned with these. There are some speculables, however, which do not depend upon matter in being, for they can be without matter; these are either never found in matter, like God and the angels, or sometimes are found in matter and sometimes are not, like substance, quality, being, potency and act, the one and many, etc. Theology is concerned with these things. It is called divine science because God is the chief thing known in it; it is also called by another name, metaphysics, that is beyond physics, because it happens that we must learn it after physics: it is necessary to go from sensible to insensible things. It is also called first philosophy because all the other sciences depend on it and take their principles from it.

It is impossible that there be anything which depends on matter to be known and not to be, because the intellect as such is immaterial. Therefore, there is not a fourth genus of philosophy to be added to those mentioned.

*   *   *

Ad 1: It should be said that the Philosopher in VI *Ethics*, chap. 3, is determining intellectual habits insofar as they are intellectual virtues. They are said to be virtues insofar as they perfect the intellect in its operation, for a virtue is that which makes the one having it good and renders his operation good. Therefore, insofar as the intellect is diversely perfected by these kinds of speculative habits, virtues are distinguished. It is in one way that the speculative part of the soul is perfected by understanding, which is the habit of principles whereby some things come to be known in themselves. From principles of this kind demonstrated conclusions are known, whether demonstration proceeds from inferior causes, as in the case of science, or from the highest causes, as in wisdom. When sciences are distinguished as habits, they are distinguished according to their objects, that is, according to the things with which the sciences are concerned. It is thus that the three parts of speculative philosophy are distinguished here and in VI *Metaphysics*, chap. 1.

Ad 2: It should be said that speculative sciences, as is plain from the beginning of the *Metaphysics* (I, 1), are concerned with things knowledge of which is sought for their own sake. One does not seek to know the things with which logic is concerned for their own sake, but as a kind of aid to the other sciences. Therefore, logic is not included in speculative philosophy as a principal part, but as something reducible to it insofar as it provides its instruments to speculative philosophy, e.g., syllogisms, definitions and the like which we need in the speculative sciences. Thus, according to Boethius in his commentary on Porphyry, it is not so much a science as the instrument of science.

Ad 3: It should be said that the seven liberal arts do not sufficiently divide theoretical philosophy, but as Hugh of St. Victor says in the third book of his *Didascalion*, chap. 3, certain others being dismissed, seven were enumerated because they were first learned by those who wanted to study philosophy. They are divided into the trivium and quadrivium "because by these as by so many ways the awakened mind could be introduced into the secrets of philosophy." This is in agreement with what the Philosopher says in II *Metaphysics*, chap. 3, namely that the mode of science should be sought before the sciences. The Commentator (Averroes) in the same place says that logic, which teaches the mode of all the sciences, should be learned before the other sciences. The trivium deals with this (i.e., logic). It is also said (VI *Ethics*, chap. 9) that mathematics can be learned by youths, but not physics which requires experience. Thus we are given to understand that mathematics should properly be studied after logic. The quadrivium takes care of this. Thus it is that by these "ways" the mind is prepared for the other philosophical disciplines.

Of the sciences, these are called arts because they not only have knowledge, but an *opus* as well which is immediately of reason, such as to form a construction, a syllogism or a speech, to number, measure, to form melodies or to compute the course of the heavens. Either the other sciences do not have an *opus*, but only knowledge, as, e.g., natural and divine science, and thus cannot receive the name art which is said to be productive reasoning (*ratio factiva*) in VI *Metaphysics*, chap. 1; or they have a corporeal *opus* as do medicine, alchemy and others like them, and thus cannot be called liberal arts, since actions of this kind are of that part of man whereby he is not free, namely his body. Moral science is directed to operation, but that operation is not an act of science, but rather of virtue, as is evident from the *Ethics*. Hence, it cannot be called an art, for in this type of operation virtue takes the place of art. That is why the ancients defined virtue as the art of living correctly and well, as St. Augustine does in IV *The City of God*, chap. 21.

Ad 4: It should be said that, as Avicenna points out in the beginning of his work *On Medicine*, the theoretical and practical mean one thing when philosophy is divided into theoretical and practical, another when the arts are divided into theoretical and practical, and yet another when medicine is so divided. For when philosophy, or even the arts, are distinguished into theoretical and practical, the distinction has to be taken from the end, so that the theoretical is said to be that which is ordered only to knowledge of truth and the practical what is ordered to operation. There is this difference, however, when the whole of philosophy and the arts are so divided, that in the division of philosophy the reference is to the end of happiness, to which the whole of human life is ordered. For, as Augustine says in XX *The City of God*, chap. 1, drawing on Varro, "man has no other reason for philosophizing than that he should be happy." And since a two-fold happiness is taught by philosophers, the one contemplative and the other active (X *Ethics*, chaps. 7, 8), it is according to these that they distinguished two parts of philosophy calling the practical moral, and natural and rational science theoretical. When, on the other hand, some arts are said to be speculative and others practical, the reference is to the special ends of those arts, as if we were to say that agriculture is a practical art and dialectics theoretical. When, however, medicine is divided into theoretical and practical, the division is not taken from the end, for thus the whole of medicine falls under the practical as ordered to operation. This division is taken from the remoteness or proximity to action of those things which are treated in medicine. For that part of medicine which teaches the manner of healing, e.g., what remedies should be prescribed for particular illnesses, is called practical; that part is called theoretical which teaches the principles by which the doctor is guided in acting, but not proximately, such as that the powers are three and that so many are the kinds of fever. Therefore, although a part of a practical science is called theoretical, it is not necessary that it should be included in speculative philosophy because of this part.

Ad 5: It should be said that one science is contained under another in two ways: in one way as a part of it, because its subject is a part of the subject of the other, as plant is a part of natural body. That is why the science of plants is included in natural science as a part. In another way, one science is contained by another as subalternated to it, namely, when in the superior science demonstrations of the reasoned fact (*propter quid*) are had of the things of which only the fact (*quia*) is demonstrated in the inferior science. In this way, music falls under arithmetic. Therefore, medicine is not put under physics as a part, for the subject of medicine is not a part of the subject of natural science under the same formality as it is the subject of medicine. For although curable body is a natural body, it is not the subject of medicine insofar as it is curable by nature, but insofar as it is curable by art. But because in artful healing, art is the minister of nature (since it is by dint of a natural power aided by art that health is restored) the (*propter quid*) demonstrated reason for the operation of art must depend upon the properties of natural things. For this reason, medicine is subalternated to physics, as are alchemy, the science of agriculture and the like. Physics in itself and in all its arts remains speculative then, although some operative sciences are subalternated to it.

Ad 6: It should be said that, although the subjects of the other sciences are parts of being which is the subject of metaphysics, it does not follow that the other sciences are parts of metaphysics. For each of the sciences takes one part of being under a special mode of consideration different from that whereby being is studied in metaphysics; therefore, properly speaking, the subject of the former is not a part of the subject of metaphysics. If we consider this formality, it (metaphysics) is a special science opposed to others. Something can be called a part of this science if it is concerned with potency, act, the one etc., because these have the same mode of consideration as being as it is treated in metaphysics.

Ad 7: It should be said that those parts of being require the same manner of treatment as being in common, because they too are independent of matter; therefore the science concerned with them is not distinguished from the science concerned with being in common.

Ad 8: It should be said that the other differences of things which the objection mentions are not *per se* differences of things insofar as they are knowable; therefore sciences are not distinguished according to them.

Ad 9: It should be said that although divine science is first among all the sciences, naturally, for us, the other sciences are prior. For, as Avicenna says in the beginning of his *Metaphysics*, the place of this science is that it should be learned after the natural sciences in which many things are determined which are used by this science, as generation, corruption, motion, etc.; similarly, too, after mathematics, for in order to know separate substances this science needs to know the number and order of the celestial bodies which is impossible without astronomy to which the whole of mathematics is ordered; the other sciences are necessary for its well-being, e.g., music, moral philosophy and the like. Nor need there be circularity due to the fact that first philosophy supposes things proved in other sciences whose principles it proves, for the principles which another science, say natural science, accepts from first philosophy do not prove those things which the first philosopher accepts from the natural philosopher; rather they are proved by other self-evident principles. Similarly, the first philosopher does not prove the principles he gives to the philosopher of nature through principles he receives from him, but through other self-evident principles.

Thus there is not a circle in definition. Moreover, the sensible effects from which physical demonstrations are drawn are more known to us in the beginning. But since from these we go on to arrive at knowledge of first causes which enable us to see the reason (*propter quid*) of the effects, although the fact (*quia*) of the causes is drawn from the effects, (we can say) that natural science contributes something to divine science by which, nevertheless, its principles are made known. That is why Boethius puts divine science last, because it is last for us.

Ad 10: It should be said that although natural science is learned after mathematics, since the universal notions of the former require experience and time, nonetheless, natural things, because they are sensible, are naturally more known than mathematical entities abstracted from sensible matter.

2. The Kinds of Abstraction

St. Thomas, *Exposition of the Trinity of Boethius*, q. 5, art. 3.

Whether the mathematical consideration
is without matter and motion but of
things which exist in matter?

We approach the third question in this way: It seems that the mathematical consideration is not an immaterial consideration of that which exists in matter.

1. For, since truth consists in the adequation of the thing to intellect, falsity must ensue whenever the thing is considered otherwise than as it is. If then, all things which are in matter are considered without matter in mathematics, its consideration will be false and there will be no science, for every science is of true things.

2. Moreover, according to the Philosopher in the 1st book of the *Posterior Analytics*, chap. 28, every science must consider its subject and the parts of its subject. But matter is a part of all material things according to their being. Therefore, it cannot be that any science would consider these things without considering their matter as well.

3. Moreover, every straight line is of the same species. But the mathematician considers straight lines by counting (*numerando*) them, otherwise he would not consider triangle and square. Therefore, he considers lines insofar as they differ in number and agree in species. But matter is the principle of difference of those things which agree in species, as is evident from the above. Therefore, matter is considered by the mathematician.

4. Moreover, no science which wholly abstracts from matter demonstrates through the material cause. But some of the demonstrations made in mathematics can be reduced only to the material cause, as when something is demonstrated of the whole from its parts. For parts are the matter of the whole, as is said in the 2nd book of the *Physics*, chap. 3. That is why, in the 2nd book of the *Posterior Analytics*, chap. 11, the demonstration which proves that the angle in the semicircle is a right angle, since both its parts are half a right angle, is reduced to the material cause. Therefore, mathematics does not wholly abstract from matter.

5. Moreover, motion is impossible without matter. But the mathematician has to consider motion, because when motion is measured by space, the same argument and science should consider the quantity of space, which falls to mathematics, and the quantity of motion. Therefore, the mathematician does not completely dispense with the consideration of matter.

6. Moreover, astronomy is a part of mathematics, as is the science of the moved spheres as well as that of weights and music. But in all these motion and mobile things are considered. Therefore, mathematics does not abstract completely from matter and motion.

7. Moreover, the whole of the natural consideration is of matter and motion. But some conclusions are demonstrated both by the mathematician and the philosopher of nature, e.g., whether the earth is round and whether it is in the center of the heavens. Therefore, it is impossible that mathematics abstract completely from matter. — Against the view that it abstracts from sensible matter alone, it can be said that sensible matter seems to be particular matter because the senses are concerned with particulars, from which every science abstracts. Therefore, the consideration of mathematics ought not to be called more abstract than that of the other sciences.

8. Moreover, the Philosopher, in the 2nd book of the *Physics*, chap. 7, enumerates three considerations, the first concerned with the mobile and corruptible, the second with the mobile and incorruptible, the third with the immobile and incorruptible. The first is natural, the second mathematical, and the third divine, as Ptolemy explains in the beginning of the *Almagest*. Therefore, mathematics deals with mobile beings.

On the contrary: what the Philosopher says in the 6th book of the *Metaphysics*, chap. 1, can be cited.

Moreover, there are some things which, although they exist in matter, nevertheless do not include matter in their definition, e.g., curve, which in this differs from snub. But if philosophy should consider all being, there should be a part of philosophy concerned with this kind. This part is mathematics, since it (this kind of being) belongs to no other.

Moreover, those things which are prior in understanding can be considered without what is posterior. But the mathematicals are prior to natural things which are in motion and matter, and which are had by an addition to mathematicals, as is said in the 3rd book of *On the Heavens*, chap. 1. Therefore, the consideration of mathematics can be without matter and motion.

Response: It should be said that an understanding of this question requires knowledge of how the intellect can abstract in virtue of its operation. Note, therefore, that according to the Philosopher in the 3rd book of *On the Soul*, chap. 6, there is a twofold operation of the intellect, one which is called the understanding of indivisibles by which the whatness of anything is known; the other that in which it composes and divides, namely, in forming affirmative and negative enunciations. These two operations answer to two things in reality. The first operation looks to the very nature of the thing according to which the thing understood has a certain rank among beings, whether it is something complete, like a whole, or incomplete, like a part or accident. The second operation looks to the very being of the thing, something which results from the conjunction of principles in composite things, and is concomitant with the simple nature of the thing in the case of simple substances.

Because the truth of the intellect is a result of its conformity with reality, it is obvious that the intellect cannot truly abstract by means of this second operation what is really conjoined, since by abstracting it would signify that there is a separation according to the being of the thing. For example, if I abstract man from whiteness, saying, "Man is not white," I signify that there is separation in reality. Hence, if man and whiteness are not separated in reality, my understanding will be false. Therefore, by means of this operation the intellect with truth abstracts only those things which are separate in reality, as when it is said, "Man is not an ass."

By means of the first operation it can abstract what is not separate in reality — not in every case, but in some. For since anything is intelligible to the degree that it is actual, as is said in the 9th book of *Metaphysics*, chap. 9, it is necessary that the nature or the quiddity of the thing be understood (1) either insofar as it is a certain act, as happens in the case of forms and simple substances; (2) or, by means of what is its act, as composed substances by means of their form; (3) or, by means of what is had in lieu of act, as prime matter by its relation to form, and· the vacuum by the privation of the located. From such as these the understanding of any nature is drawn.

Therefore, when that by which the notion of the nature is constituted and by means of which it is understood is ordered to and dependent upon something else, it is obvious that the nature cannot be understood without reference to the other thing, whether they are conjoined (1) by that conjunction which the part has to the whole (foot cannot be grasped without an understanding of the animal, because that by reason of which the foot has the notion of foot, depends on that by which an animal is an animal); (2) or conjoined in the way in which form is joined with matter, a part to another part, or accident to subject (snub cannot be understood without nose); (3) or even when they are separated in reality, as father cannot be understood unless child is, although these relations are found in diverse things.

If, however, one thing does not depend upon another with regard to that which constitutes the concept of its nature, then the one can be abstracted from the other by intellect and be understood without it, and not only if they are separate in reality, as man and rock, but even if they are found together in reality (1) related as part to whole, e.g., letter can be understood without syllable, but not vice versa, and animal without foot, but not conversely; (2) or even if they are joined as form is to matter and accident to subject, e.g., whiteness can be understood without man and vice versa.

The intellect, then, distinguishes one thing from another in diverse ways according to its diverse operations. By means of that operation whereby it composes and divides, it distinguishes one thing from another in this that it understands that the one is not in the other. In that operation whereby it understands the "what" of anything, it distinguishes one thing from another when it understands what this is and, with regard to the other, neither understands it to be with or separate from it. The latter kind of distinction is not properly called separation, but only the former. The latter is rightly called abstraction, but only when those things of which the one is understood without the other are actually united in reality. For we do not say that animal is abstracted from stone when animal is understood without understanding stone. It follows that there cannot be abstraction, properly speaking, except of things conjoined in reality. And according to the two modes mentioned above, namely as part and whole are united and as form and matter, there will be two kinds of abstraction; (1) the one by which form is abstracted from matter, (2) the second by which the whole is abstracted from its parts.

Form can be abstracted from a certain kind of matter, when an understanding of its essence does not depend on that kind of matter; form cannot be abstracted by the intellect from that matter on which an understanding of its essence depends. Therefore, since all accidents are compared to substance as form to matter and the notion of every accident depends upon substance, it is impossible that such forms be separated from substance. But accidents inhere in substance according to a definite order, for first quantity comes to it, then quality, then passions and motions. Thus, quantity can be understood in substance before the sensible qualities from which sensible matter is named are understood in it. Thus, according to the notion of its essence, quantity is independent of sensible matter but dependent on intelligible matter. For substance, apart from its accidents, is knowable by intellect alone, since the sensible powers do not attain to any knowledge of substance. Mathematics is concerned with abstract things of this sort, since it considers quantities and what is consequent on quantity, such as figure and the like.

The whole, too, cannot be abstracted from just any parts. For there are some parts on which the notion of the whole depends, namely, when to be such a whole is to be composed of such parts, as syllables of letters and a mixed body of elements. Such parts are called parts of the species or form, and without them the whole cannot be understood since they enter into its definition. There are some parts, however, which are accidental to the whole as such, e.g., semicircle of circle. It is accidental to circle that it be divided into two or more equal or unequal parts. However, it is not accidental to triangle that three lines are designated in it, because it is due to them that a triangle is a triangle. Similarly, too, it is essential to man that a rational soul and a body composed of four elements be found in him. Without these parts, man cannot be understood and they must enter into his definition since they are parts of species or form. Finger, foot, hand and other like parts are added to the simple understanding of what man is; hence the essential notion of man is independent of them and man can be understood without them. Whether or not he has feet, as long as there is a composition of rational soul and a body containing the proper elements, there will be a man. The second kind of parts mentioned are called parts of matter, because they are not posited in the definition of the whole, but rather conversely. It is thus that all signate parts relate to man, such as *this* soul, *this* body, *this* flesh, *this* bone, etc. For these are indeed essential to Socrates and Plato, but not to man as such. That is why man can be abstracted by the intellect from these parts. This abstraction is that of the universal from the particular.

There are, then, two abstractions of the intellect: (1) the one answering to the union of form and matter, or accident to subject, and this is the abstraction of form from sensible matter. (2) The second answers to the union of whole and part, namely the abstraction of the universal from the particular, which is the abstraction of the whole by which a nature is considered absolutely according to its essential notion, without all the parts which are accidental parts and not parts of the species.

There are no abstractions opposed to these whereby part would be abstracted from whole or matter from form, because (1) either the part cannot be abstracted by intellect from the whole, e.g., if it is one of the parts of matter, for the whole enters into the definition of such parts; or (2) it can also be without the whole, e.g., if it is one of the parts of the species, for line can be without triangle and letters without syllables and elements outside of mixed bodies. Those things which can exist apart are the concern of separation rather than abstraction.

When we say that form is abstracted from matter, it is not substantial form which should be understood, because substantial form and the matter answering to it depend upon one another in such a way that the one cannot be understood without the other, for the proper form is in its proper matter. What *is* meant is that accidental form which is quantity and figure. Sensible matter cannot be abstracted from these by the intellect, since sensible qualities cannot be grasped save by presupposing quantity, as is evident in surface and color; nor can something which is not quantified be taken as a subject of motion. Substance, however, which is the intelligible matter of quantity, can be without quantity. Therefore, to consider substance without quantity belongs to the genus of separation rather than that of abstraction.

A threefold distinction, therefore, can be discovered in the operation of the intellect: (1) one according to the operation of the intellect composing and dividing, which properly is called separation and which belongs to divine science or metaphysics; (2) another according to the operation by which the quiddities of things are formed, which is the abstraction of form from sensible matter, and this belongs to mathematics; (3) a third according to the same operation, that of the universal from the particular. This belongs to physics but is common to all the sciences, because in any science what is accidental is set aside and what is essential is sought. It is because some, e.g., the Pythagoreans and Platonists, did not understand the difference between the last two and the first that they fell into the error of positing mathematicals and the universals drawn from sensible things as separate.

*   *   *

Ad 1: It should be said that the mathematician, in abstracting, does not consider the thing otherwise than as it is. For he does not understand the line to be without sensible matter, but he considers the line and its properties without considering sensible matter. Thus there is no dissonance between what is understood and reality, since, even in reality, that which is of the nature of line does not depend on that which makes matter sensible, but rather the reverse. Thus it is clear that those who abstract do not lie, as is said in the 2nd book of the *Physics*, chap. 2.

Ad 2: It should be said that not only that of which matter is a part is said to be material, but also that which can have existence in matter, and in this way the sensible line can be called something material. This does not prevent a line's being understood without matter, for sensible matter is not related to the line as a part, but rather as a subject in which it has existence — so too with surface and body. For the mathematician does not consider the body which is in the genus of substance whose parts are matter and form, but according as it is in the genus of quantity perfected by three dimensions, which is related to body in the genus of substance of which physical matter is a part as accident to subject.

Ad 3: It should be said that matter is not the principle of numerical diversity except as divided into many parts and receiving in each of its parts a form of the same nature (*ratio*), thus constituting many individuals of the same species. However, matter cannot be divided unless quantity is presupposed, for if it is absent, every substance would be indivisible. That is why the first reason for the diversification of things of the same species is quantity, something proper to quantity insofar as position (*situs*), which is nothing else but the order of parts, is included in its notion as a constitutive difference. Thus, even when quantity is abstracted by the intellect from sensible matter, one can still imagine numerically diverse (individuals) of the same species, such as several equilateral triangles and many equal straight lines.

Ad 4: It should be said that mathematics does not abstract from all matter, but only from sensible matter. The parts of quantity, however, from which the demonstration seems to be drawn as from a material cause, are not sensible matter, but belong to intelligible matter, which does enter into mathematics, as is clear from the 7th book of the *Metaphysics*, chap. 10.

Ad 5: It should be said that motion does not of its nature belong to the genus of quantity, but it participates to some degree in something of the nature of quantity in that the division of motion is taken either from the division of space or from the division of the mobile. Therefore, it does not pertain to the mathematician to consider motion, although mathematical principles can be applied to motion. Therefore, when principles of quantity are applied to motion, it is the natural philosopher who considers the division and continuity of motion, as is clear from the 6th book of the *Physics*, chap. 4. And in the sciences which fall between (*scientiae mediae*) the mathematical and natural, the measures of motion are treated, as in the science of the moved sphere and astronomy.

Ad 6: It should be said that simple things as well as their properties are saved in composites, though in a different manner, as the proper qualities and motions of elements are found in the mixed body; what is proper to composites, however, is not found in simple things. So it is that to the degree that a science considers more abstract and simple things, its principles will be more applicable to other sciences. That is why the principles of mathematics are applicable to natural things, but not conversely, and because of this, physics presupposes mathematics, but not conversely, as is clear in the 3rd book *On the Heavens*, chap. 1. So it is that of natural and mathematical entities, there are three sciences: (1) Some are purely natural and consider the properties of natural things as such, such as physics, agriculture, and the like. (2) Some are purely mathematical, and consider quantities absolutely, as geometry magnitude and arithmetic number. (3) Some indeed are in between (*mediae*), and these apply mathematical principles to natural things, as music, astronomy, and the like. Nevertheless, they have more affinity with mathematics, since what is physical in their consideration is, as it were, material, whereas what is mathematical is formal. Music considers sounds, not as sounds, but as they are numerically proportional; so too with the others. On account of this they demonstrate conclusions of natural things, but by mathematical means (*media*); therefore, there is nothing to prevent their considering sensible things insofar as they have something in common with (pure) natural science. They are abstract insofar as they have something in common with mathematics.

Ad 7: It should be said that the middle sciences mentioned communicate with natural science according to that which is material in their consideration, but they differ according to that which is formal. Therefore, nothing prevents their sometimes arriving at the same conclusions as natural science. However, they do not demonstrate through the same (means) except as unmixed, and one science sometimes uses something of another, as the natural scientist proves the earth is round from gravity, and the astronomer from the consideration of lunar eclipses.

Ad 8: It should be said that, as the Commentator (Averroes) says in the same place, the Philosopher does not there intend to distinguish the speculative sciences, since the natural philosopher studies every mobile whether corruptible or incorruptible. The mathematician as such does not consider any mobile being. However, he does intend to distinguish the things which speculative sciences study and which ought first of all to be treated in orderly fashion; the three kinds of things, however, can be appropriated to three sciences. For incorruptible and immobile being belongs precisely to metaphysics. Mobile and incorruptible beings, due to their uniformity and regularity, can be studied as to their motion through mathematical principles, which cannot be said of corruptible, mobile being. The second genus of being, therefore, is attributed to mathematics by reason of astronomy. The third remains proper to the natural scientist alone, and it is thus that Ptolemy speaks.

3. Metaphysics as a Divine Science

Whether divine science is concerned with
things which exist without matter and motion?
St. Thomas, *Exposition of the Trinity of Boethius*, q. 5, art. 4.

We approach the fourth question in this way: It seems that divine science is not concerned with things separated from matter and motion:

1. For divine science seems to be especially concerned with God. But we are not able to arrive at knowledge of God save through visible effects which are constituted in matter and motion: *Epistle to the Romans*, 1, 20, "The invisible things of Him . . ." Therefore, divine science does not abstract from matter and motion.

2. Moreover, that to which motion in any way belongs is not wholly separate from matter and motion. But motion in some way belongs to God; hence it is said in Wisdom, 7, 22, of the Spirit of Wisdom that it is mobile and more mobile than all mobile things. And Augustine says in his *Literal Commentary on Genesis*, VIII, n. 20, that God moves Himself without time and place; and Plato holds that the first mover moves himself. Therefore, divine science, which studies God, is not wholly separate from motion.

3. Moreover, divine science does not only have to consider God, but the angels as well. But angels are moved, both according to choice, since from being good some became bad, and according to place, as is evident in those who are messengers. Therefore, those things considered by divine science are not wholly separate from motion.

4. Moreover, as the Commentator seems to say in the beginning of the *Physics*, whatever is is either pure matter, or pure form, or composed of matter and form. But an angel is not pure form, for then he would be pure act, which is proper to God alone; nor is the angel pure matter. Therefore, he is composed of matter and form. Thus, divine science does not abstract from matter.

5. Moreover, the divine science which is listed as the third part of speculative philosophy is the same as metaphysics whose subject is being and especially that being which is substance, as is clear from the 4th book of the *Metaphysics*, chap. 1. But being and substance do not abstract from matter, otherwise no being could be found which would have matter. Therefore, divine science does not abstract from matter.

6. Moreover, according to the Philosopher in the 1st book of the *Posterior Analytics*, chap. 28, a science must study not only its subject, but the parts and properties of its subject. But being is the subject of the divine science, as has been said. Therefore, divine science must consider all beings. But matter and motion are certain beings. Therefore, they belong to the consideration of metaphysics and divine science does not abstract from them.

7. Moreover, as the Commentator says in the 1st book of the *Physics*, divine science demonstrates through three causes, namely, the efficient, formal and final. But the efficient cause cannot be considered unless motion is, nor can the end — as is said in the 3rd book of the *Metaphysics*, chap. 2. That is why no demonstration through these causes is made of mathematical entities, for they are immobile. Therefore divine science does not abstract from motion.

8. Moreover, in theology the creation of heaven and earth, the actions of men and many other such things are studied, which contain matter and motion in themselves. Therefore, theology does not seem to abstract from matter and motion.

On the contrary: the Philosopher says in the 6th book of the *Metaphysics*, chap. 1, that first philosophy is of things separable from matter and immobile. First philosophy, however, is divine science, as is said in the same place. Therefore, divine science is abstracted from matter and motion.

Moreover, the most noble science is of the most noble things. But divine science is the most noble. Since therefore immaterial and immobile things are most noble, divine science will be of them.

Moreover, the Philosopher says in the beginning of the *Metaphysics* that divine science is of the first principles and causes; the same, however, are immaterial and immobile. Therefore, of such things is divine science.

Response: It should be said that the resolution of this question requires knowing which science ought to be called divine science. Note that whatever science considers a certain subject genus must consider the principles of that genus, since science is only perfected by knowledge of principles, as the Philosopher makes clear at the outset of the *Physics*. But there are two kinds of principles. (1) There are some which are both complete natures in themselves and are nonetheless principles of other things, as celestial bodies are principles of inferior bodies, and simple bodies of mixed bodies. Therefore, these are not considered in sciences solely as principles, but also insofar as they are in themselves certain things. Because of this they are not only studied in the science which studies the things of which they are the principles, but there is a separate science devoted to them. Just as a certain part of natural science is concerned with celestial bodies, apart from that in which mixed bodies are studied. (2) There are some principles, however, which are not in themselves complete natures, but are only the principles of natures, as unity of number, point of line, and matter and form of the physical body. Hence such principles are only studied in the science which deals with the things of which they are the principles.

Just as there are some common principles of any determinate genus which extend to all the principles of that genus, so too all beings to the degree that they communicate in being have some principles which are common to all beings. Such principles can be said to be common in two ways, according to Avicenna in his *Sufficientia*: in one way through predication, as I say form is common to all forms because it is predicated of each. In another way, through causality, as we say that a single sun is the principle of all generable things. There are common principles of all beings not only in the first manner, which the Philosopher mentions in the 11th book of the

Metaphysics, saying that all beings have the same principles according to analogy, but also in the second manner. There are certain things which remain numerically the same and are the principles of all things, insofar as the principles of accidents are reduced to the principles of substance, and the principles of corruptible substances are reduced to incorruptible substances, and thus by a certain gradation and order all beings are reduced to certain principles. And, because that which is the principle of all beings ought to be most perfectly being, as is said in the 2nd book of the *Metaphysics,* chap. 1, therefore principles of this kind ought to be the most complete. On account of this, they should be most actual, having little or nothing of potency, because act is prior to and more perfect than potency, as is said in the 9th book of the *Metaphysics,* chap. 8. Because of this, they should be without matter which is in potency, and without motion which is the act of what exists in potency. Such things are divine, or if the divine exists anywhere, it is in an immaterial and immobile nature especially, as is said in the 6th book of the *Metaphysics,* chap. 1.

Such divine things, because they are the principles of all beings and nevertheless complete natures in themselves, can be studied in two ways: in one way, insofar as they are common principles of all beings; in another way, insofar as they are in themselves certain things. But, because to first principles of this kind, though they are most knowable in themselves, our intellect is related as the owl's eye to the light of the sun, as is said in the 2nd book of the *Metaphysics,* chap. 1, we can arrive at them through the natural light of reason only insofar as we are led to them through effects. It is in this way that philosophers attain to them, as is evident in *Romans,* 1, 20: "The invisible things of God are seen through an understanding of what has been made." Hence such divine things are treated by philosophers only insofar as they are the principles of all things; therefore they are studied in that doctrine in which is posited what is common to all beings and which has as its subject being as being. This science is called divine science by the philosophers. There is, however, another way of knowing such things, not insofar as they are manifested through effects, but insofar as they manifest themselves. The Apostle speaks of this way in *I Corinthians,* II, 11: "Those things which are of God, no one knows but the spirit of God. We, however, do not accept the spirit of this world, but the spirit which is from God, in order that we may know." And in the same place: "To us however, God has revealed through his spirit" (II, 10). In this manner divine things are studied as they subsist in themselves, and not only as the principles of things.

Theology or divine science, therefore, is of two kinds. In one, divine things are considered not as the subject of the science, but as principles of the subject. Such is the theology philosophers seek, which is also named metaphysics. The other, however, considers divine things in themselves as subject of the science; this is the theology handed down in Sacred Scripture. Both, however, are concerned with things separate from matter and motion, but diversely, insofar as something can be separated from matter and motion according to existence in two ways. (1) In one way, such that matter and motion can in no wise be of the essence of the things which are said to be separate, as God and the angels are said to be separate from matter and motion. (2) In another way such that it is not of its essence to be in matter and motion; it can be without matter and motion although sometimes it is found in matter and motion. In this way being and substance and potency and act are separate from matter and motion, because they do not depend upon matter and motion to exist (as mathematicals do, for they can never exist except in matter although they can be understood without sensible matter). Philosophical theology, therefore, treats of things separate in the second way as belonging to its subject and of things separate in the first way as the principles of its subject. The theology of Sacred Scripture, however, treats of things separate in the first way as subjects, although sometimes things which are in matter and motion are treated in it insofar as the manifestation of divine things requires it.

Ad 1: It should be said that those things which are taken up in a science only in order to manifest something else do not belong as such to the science, but only accidentally. It is thus that certain mathematical truths are taken over by the natural sciences. There is nothing to prevent divine science from treating of some things in matter and motion in this way.

Ad 2: It should be said that to be moved is not properly attributed to God, but as it were metaphorically, and this in two ways. In one way insofar as the operation of intellect or will is improperly called motion, and in this way someone is said to move himself when he understands or loves himself. In this fashion, Plato's statement that the First Mover moves himself because he knows and loves himself can, as Averroes says (In VIII Phys., com. 40), be verified. In another way, insofar as the effluence of effects from their causes can be called a certain *processus* or motion of the cause to the caused: a certain likeness to the cause is produced in the effect and thus the cause, which was first in itself, afterwards comes to be in the effect through its likeness. In this manner, God, who has imparted His likeness to all creatures, in a certain respect is said to move through them or to proceed to all things. This is a manner of speaking frequently employed by Dionysius. It is in this way that those words of *Wisdom* should be understood, namely, that "wisdom is the most moving of moving things" and "it reaches from end to end mightily." This is not properly to move, however, and the argument therefore does not follow.

Ad 3: It should be said that divine science, which is received through divine inspiration, is not concerned with angels as with its subject, but only insofar as they are taken up to manifest the subject. Thus it is that Sacred Scripture deals with angels as with other creatures. In the divine science taught by philosophers, angels (called Intelligences) are considered for the same reason the first cause, God, is, for they are secondary principles of things, at least through the motions of the orbs, for they themselves can undergo no physical motion. The motion which is according to choice, however, is reduced to that mode by which the acts of intellect and will are called motion — improperly, that is, by identifying operation and motion. That motion as well whereby they are said to move from place to place is not due to any localization, but to the operation which they exercise in this place or in that, or through some other relation that they have to place which is purely equivocal with that relation that the located body has to place. Thus it is evident that motion does not belong to them in the way that natural things are said to be in motion.

Ad 4: It should be said that act and potency are more common than matter and form. Therefore, although no composition of matter and form is to be found in angels, there can be found composition of potency and act in them. Matter and form are parts of what is composed of matter and form; therefore, the composition of matter and form is found only in those things in which one part is related to the other as potency to act. However, what can be, can also not be; therefore one part can be found with and without the other. Therefore, as Averroes says (In I *de Coelo*, com. 20; In VIII *Phys.*, com. 4), a composition of matter and form is only found in things corruptible by nature. Nor does it matter that an accident can be preserved perpetually in a subject, as figure in the heavens: the celestial body cannot be without such a figure, for figure and all accidents follow on substance as on their cause, and the subject is therefore related to accidents not only as passive potency, but in somewise also as active potency. Therefore, some accidents are naturally perpetuated in their subjects. Matter, however, is not in this way the cause of form, and every matter which underlies any form, can also not underlie it, unless perhaps it is conserved by an extrinsic cause, just as we hold that some bodies, though composed of contraries, are by the divine power incorruptible, such as the bodies of those who have arisen from the dead. The essence of the angel, however, is by its very nature incorruptible. Therefore, in it there is no composition of matter and form. But, because the angel does not have existence from itself, it is in potency to the existence which it receives from God. Thus, the existence received from God is compared to its simple essence as act to potency. That is why they are said to be composed of *what* they are and that *by which* they are, so that existence is understood as *by which* and the nature of the angel is understood as *what*. However, if the angels were composed of matter and form, they would not have sensible matter from which mathematical entities must be abstracted and metaphysical entities separated.

Ad 5: It should be said that being and substance are said to be separated from matter and motion, not because the notion of them does not include matter and motion as the notion of ass does not include reason, but because it is not of their notion to be in matter and motion although sometimes they are, just as animal abstracts from reason although some animal is rational.

Ad 6: It should be said that the metaphysician also considers special beings,
not according to their proper notions by which they are this kind of
being or that, but insofar as they participate in the common notion of being.
Thus matter and form too come under his consideration.

Ad 7: It should be said that action and passion belong to things, not as
they are abstracted, but as they exist. The mathematician studies
abstract things according to abstraction alone, in which state they cannot
be a principle or end of motion; therefore the mathematician does not demonstrate through efficient and final cause. The things which the divine
(theologian, metaphysician) considers, however, in reality exist separately and
as such they can be the principle and end of motion. There is thus no impediment to his demonstrating through efficient and final cause.

Ad 8: It should be said that faith, which is as it were the habit of the first
principles of theology, has for its object the first truth itself, and yet
other things pertaining to creatures are also contained in the articles of faith
insofar as they touch in some way on the first truth. In the same way, theology
is principally of God as of its subject; however, it takes up many things concerning creatures as His effect or as having some kind of relation to Him.

READINGS FOR CHAPTER III. THE ANALOGY OF BEING

1. No Univocal Predication Between God and Things

St. Thomas, *Summa Contra Gentiles* I, Chapter 32.*

(1) It is thereby evident that nothing can be predicated univocally of God and other things.

(2) An effect that does not receive a form specifically the same as that through which the agent acts cannot receive according to a univocal predication the name arising from that form. Thus, the heat generated by the sun and the sun itself are not called univocally *hot*. Now, the forms of the things God has made do not measure up to a specific likeness of the divine power; for the things that God has made receive in a divided and particular way that which in Him is found in a simple and universal way. It is evident, then, that nothing can be said univocally of God and other things.

(3) If, furthermore, an effect should measure up to the species of its cause, it will not receive the univocal predication of the name unless it receives the same specific form according to the same mode of being. For the house that is in the art of the maker is not univocally the same house that is in matter, for the form of the house does not have the same being in the two locations. Now, even though the rest of things were to receive a form that is absolutely the same as it is in God, yet they do not receive it according to the same mode of being. For, as is clear from what we have said, there is nothing in God that is not the divine being itself, which is not the case with other things.[1] Nothing, therefore, can be predicated of God and other things univocally

(4) Moreover, whatever is predicated of many things univocally is either a genus, a species, a difference, an accident, or a property. But, as we have shown, nothing is predicated of God as a genus or a difference; and thus neither is anything predicated as a definition, nor likewise as a species, which is constituted of genus and difference. Nor, as we have shown, can there be any accident in God, and therefore nothing is predicated of Him either as an accident or a property, since property belongs to the genus of accidents.[2] It remains, then, that nothing is predicated univocally of God and other things.

---

* Translated by Anton C. Pegis, *On the Truth of the Catholic Faith*, Book One: God (New York: Doubleday Image, 1955).
[1] *Summa Contra Gentiles*, ch. 23.
[2] *Ibid.*, ch. 23–25.

(5)   Again, what is predicated of many things univocally is simpler than both of them, at least in concept. Now there can be nothing simpler than God either in reality or in concept. Nothing, therefore, is predicated univocally of God and other things.

(6)   Everything, likewise, that is predicated univocally of many things belongs through participation to each of the things of which it is predicated; for the species is said to participate in the genus and the individual in the species. But nothing is said of God by participation, since whatever is participated is determined to the mode of that which is participated and is thus possessed in a partial way and not according to every mode of perfection. Nothing, therefore, can be predicated univocally of God and other things.

(7)   Then, too, what is predicated of some things according to priority and posteriority is certainly not predicated univocally. For the prior is included in the definition of the posterior, as *substance* is included in the definition of accident according as an accident is a being. If, then, being were said univocally of substance and accident, substance would have to be included in the definition of being insofar as being is predicated of substance. But this is clearly impossible. Now nothing is predicated of God and creatures as though they were in the same order, but, rather, according to priority and posteriority. For all things are predicated of God essentially. For God is called being as being entity itself, and He is called good as being goodness itself. But in other beings predications are made by participation, as Socrates is said to be a man, not because he is humanity itself, but because he possesses humanity. It is impossible, therefore, that anything be predicated univocally of God and other things.

2. Not All Names Said of God and Creatures Are Equivocal

St. Thomas, *Summa Contra Gentiles* I, Chapter 33.*

(1)   From what we have said it likewise appears that not everything predicated of God and other things is said in a purely equivocal way, in the manner of equivocals by chance.

(2)   For in equivocals by chance there is no order of reference of one to another, but it is entirely accidental that one name is applied to diverse things: the application of the name to one of them does not signify that it has an order to the other. But this is not the situation with names said of God and creatures, since we note in the community of such names the order of cause and effect, as is clear from what we have said.[1] It is not, therefore, in the manner of pure equivocation that something is predicated of God and other things.

---

* Pegis, *op. cit.*
[1] *Summa Contra Gentiles*, ch. 32.

(3)   Furthermore, where there is pure equivocation, there is no likeness in things themselves; there is only the unity of a name. But, as is clear from what we have said, there is a certain mode of likeness of things to God.² It remains, then, that names are not said of God in a purely equivocal way.

(4)   Moreover, when one name is predicated of several things in a purely equivocal way, we cannot from one of them be led to the knowledge of another; for the knowledge of things does not depend on words, but on the meaning of names. Now, from what we find in other things, we do arrive at a knowledge of divine things, as is evident from what we have said. Such names, then, are not said of God and other things in a purely equivocal way.

(5)   Again, equivocation in a name impedes the process of reasoning. If then, nothing was said of God and creatures except in a purely equivocal way, no reasoning proceeding from creatures to God could take place. But, the contrary is evident from all those who have spoken about God.

(6)   It is also a fact that a name is predicated of some being uselessly unless through that name we understand something of the being. But, if names are said of God and creatures in a purely equivocal way, we understand nothing of God through those names; for the meanings of those names are known to us solely to the extent that they are said of creatures. In vain, therefore, would it be said or proved of God that He is a being, good, or the like.

(7)   Should it be replied that through such names we know only what God is not, namely, that God is called *living* because He does not belong to the genus of lifeless things, and so with the other names, it will at least have to be the case that *living* said of God and creatures agrees in the denial of the lifeless. Thus, it will not be said in a purely equivocal way.

------
² *Ibid.*, ch. 29.

3. Names Said of God and Creatures Are Analogical

St. Thomas, *Summa Contra Gentiles* I, Chapter 34.*

(1)   From what we have said, therefore, it remains that the names said of God and creatures are predicated neither univocally nor equivocally but analogically, that is, according to an order or reference to something one.

(2)   This can take place in two ways. In one way, according as many things have reference to something one. Thus, with reference to one *health* we say that an animal is healthy as the subject of health, medicine is healthy as its cause, food as its preserver, urine as its sign.

(3)   In another way, the analogy can obtain according as the order or reference of two things is not to something else but to one of them. Thus, *being* is said of substance and accident according as substance and accident are referred to a third thing.

------
* Pegis, *op. cit.*

(4) Now, the names said of God and things are not said analogically according to the first mode of analogy, since we should then have to posit something prior to God, but according to the second mode.

(5) In this second mode of analogical predication the order according to the name and according to reality is sometimes found to be the same and sometimes not. For the order of the name follows the order of knowledge, because it is the sign of an intelligible conception. When, therefore, that which is prior in reality is found likewise to be prior in knowledge, the same thing is found to be prior both according to the meaning of the name and according to the nature of the thing. Thus, substance is prior to accident both in nature, insofar as substance is the cause of accident, and in knowledge, insofar as substance is included in the definition of accident. Hence, *being* is said of substance by priority over accident both according to the nature of the thing and according to the meaning of the name. But when that which is prior in nature is subsequent in our knowledge, then there is not the same order in analogicals according to reality and according to the meaning of the name. Thus, the power to heal, which is found in all health-giving things, is by nature prior to the health that is in the animal, as a cause is prior to an effect; but because we know this healing power through an effect, we likewise name it from its effect. Hence it is that the *health-giving* is prior in reality, but animal is by priority called *healthy* according to the meaning of the name.

(6) Thus, therefore, because we come to a knowledge of God from other things, the reality in the names said of God and other things belongs by priority in God according to His mode of being, but the meaning of the name belongs to God by posteriority. And so He is said to be named from His effects.

4. No Univocation in Names Said of God and Creatures

St. Thomas, *Summa Theologiae* I, q. 13, art. 5.*

We proceed thus to the Fifth Article: —

Obj. 1. It seems that the things attributed to God and creatures are univocal. For every equivocal term is reduced to the univocal, as many are reduced to one: for if the name *dog* be said equivocally of the barking dog and of the dogfish, it must be said of some univocally — viz., of all barking dogs; otherwise we proceed to infinitude. Now there are some univocal agents which agree with their effects in name and definition, as man generates man; and there are some agents which are equivocal, as the sun which causes heat, although the sun is hot only in an equivocal sense. Therefore it seems that the first agent, to which all other agents are reduced, is a univocal agent: and thus what is said of God and creatures is predicated univocally.

* Translated by Anton C. Pegis, in *The Basic Writings of St. Thomas Aquinas* (New York: Random House, 1945), Vol. I.

Obj. 2. Further, no likeness is understood through equivocal names. There-fore, as creatures have a certain likeness to God, according to the text of Genesis (i. 26), *Let us make man to our image and likeness*, it seems that something can be said of God and creatures univocally.

Obj. 3. Further, measure is homogeneous with the thing measured, as is said in *Metaph.* x.[1] But God is the first measure of all beings. Therefore God is homogeneous with creatures; and thus a name may be applied univocally to God and to creatures.

On the contrary. Whatever is predicated of various things under the same name but not in the same sense is predicated equivocally. But no name belongs to God in the same sense that it belongs to creatures; for instance, wisdom in creatures is a quality, but not in God. Now a change in genus changes an essence since the genus is part of the definition; and the same applies to other things. Therefore whatever is said of God and of creatures is predicated equivocally.

Further, God is more distant from creatures than any creatures are from each other. But the distance of some creatuures makes any univocal predica-tion of them impossible, as in the case of those things which are not in the same genus. Therefore much less can anything be predicated univocally of God and creatures; and so only equivocal predication can be applied to them.

I answer that, Univocal predication is impossible between God and crea-tures. The reason of this is that every effect which is not a proportioned result of the power of the efficient cause receives the similitude of the agent not in its full degree, but in a measure that falls short; so that what is divided and multiplied in the effects resides in the agent simply, and in an unvaried manner. For example, the sun by the exercise of its one power produces manifold and various forms in these sublunary things. In the same way, as was said above, all perfections existing in creatures divided and multiplied pre-exist in God unitedly. Hence, when any name expressing perfection is applied to a creature, it signifies that perfection as distinct from the others according to the nature of its definition; as, for instance, by this term *wise* applied to a man, we signify some perfection distinct from a man's essence, and distinct from his power and his being, and from all similar things. But when we apply *wise* to God, we do not mean to signify anything distinct from His essence or power or being. And thus when this term *wise* is applied to man, in some degree it circumscribes and comprehends the thing signified; whereas this is not the case when it is applied to God, but it leaves the thing signified as uncomprehended and as exceeding the signification of the name. Hence it is evident that this term *wise* is not applied in the same way to God and to man. The same applies to other terms. Hence, no name is predicated univocally of God and of creatures.

Neither, on the other hand, are names applied to God and creatures in a

---

[1] Aristotle, *Metaph.*, X, 1 (1053a 24).

purely equivocal sense, as some have said.[2] Because if that were so, it follows that from creatures nothing at all could be known or demonstrated about God; for the reasoning would always be exposed to the fallacy of equivocation. Such a view is against the Philosopher, who proves many things about God, and also against what the Apostle says: *The invisible things of God are clearly seen being understood by the things that are made* (Rom. i. 20). Therefore it must be said that these names are said of God and creatures in an *analogous* sense, that is, according to proportion.

This can happen in two ways: either according as many things are proportioned to one (thus, for example, *healthy* is predicated of medicine and urine in relation and in proportion to health of body, of which the latter is the sign and the former the cause), or according as one thing is proportioned to another (thus, *healthy* is said of medicine and an animal, since medicine is the cause of health in the animal body). And in this way some things are said of God and creatures analogically, and not in a purely equivocal nor in a purely univocal sense. For we can name God only from creatures. Hence, whatever is said of God and creatures is said according as there is some relation of the creature to God as to its principle and cause, wherein all the perfections of things pre-exist excellently. Now this mode of community is a mean between pure equivocation and simple univocation. For in analogies the idea is not, as it is in univocals, one and the same; yet it is not totally diverse as in equivocals; but the name which is thus used in a multiple sense signifies various proportions to some one thing: e.g., *healthy*, applied to urine, signifies the sign of animal health; but applied to medicine, it signifies the cause of the same health.

Reply Obj. 1. Although in predications all equivocals must be reduced to univocals, still in actions the non-univocal agent must precede the univocal agent. For the non-univocal agent is the universal cause of the whole species, as the sun is the cause of the generation of all men. But the univocal agent is not the universal efficient cause of the whole species (otherwise it would be the cause of itself, since it is contained in the species), but is a particular cause of this individual which it places under the species by way of participation. Therefore the universal cause of the whole species is not a univocal agent: and the universal cause comes before the particular cause. But this universal agent, while not univocal, nevertheless is not altogether equivocal (otherwise it could not produce its own likeness); but it can be called an analogical agent, just as in predications all univocal names are reduced to one first non-univocal analogical name, which is *being.*

Reply Obj. 2. The likeness of the creature to God is imperfect, for it does not represent the same thing even generically, as we have said before.[3]

---

[2] Maimonides, *Guide*, I, 59 (p. 84); Averroes, *In Metaph.*, XII, comm. 51 (VIII, 158r).

[3] *Summa Theologiae*, I, q. 4, a. 3.

Reply Obj. 3. God is not a measure proportioned to the things measured; hence it is not necessary that God and creatures should be in the same genus.

The arguments adduced in the contrary sense prove indeed that these names are not predicated univocally of God and creatures; yet they do not prove that they are predicated equivocally.

5. The Primacy of Predication in Names Said of God and Creatures

St. Thomas, *Summa Theologiae* I, q. 13, art. 6.*

We proceed thus to the Sixth Article: —

Obj. 1. It seems that names are predicated primarily of creatures rather than of God. For we name anything accordingly as we know it, since *names, as the Philosopher says,*[1] *are signs of ideas.* But we know creatures before we know God. Therefore the names imposed by us are predicated primarily of creatures rather than of God.

Obj. 2. Further, Dionysius says that we name God from creatures.[2] But names transferred from creatures to God are said primarily of creatures rather than of God; as *lion, stone,* and the like. Therefore all names appplied to God and creatures are applied primarily to creatures rather than to God.

Obj. 3. Further, all names applied to God and creatures in common are *applied to God as the cause of all creatures,* as Dionysius says.[3] But what is applied to anything through its cause is applied to it secondarily; for *healthy* is primarily predicated of animal rather than of medicine, which is the cause of health. Therefore these names are said primarily of creatures rather than of God.

On the contrary. It is written, *I bow my knees to the Father of our Lord Jesus Christ, of Whom all paternity in heaven and earth is named* (Ephes. iii. 14, 15); and the same holds of the other names applied to God rather than to creatures.

I answer that, In names predicated of many in an analogical sense, all are predicated through a relation to some one thing; and this one thing must be placed in the definition of them all. And since *the essence expressed by the name is the definition,* as the Philosopher says,[4] such a name must be applied primarily to that which is put in the definition of the other things, and secondarily to these others according as they approach more or less to the first. Thus, for instance, *healthy* applied to animals comes into the definition of

---

* Pegis, *Basic Writings of St. Thomas.*
[1] *Perih.,* I (16a 3).
[2] *De Div. Nom.,* I, 6 (PG 3, 596).
[3] *De Myst. Theol.,* I, 2 (PG 3, 1000).
[4] Aristotle, *Metaph.,* III, 7 (1012 a 23).

healthy applied to medicine, which is called healthy as being the cause of health in the animal; and also into the definition of *healthy* which is applied to urine, which is called healthy insofar as it is the sign of the animal's health.

So it is that all names applied metaphorically to God are applied to creatures primarily rather than to God, because when said of God they mean only similitudes to such creatures. For as *smiling* applied to a field means only that the field in the beauty of its flowering is like to the beauty of the human smile by proportionate likeness, so the name of *lion* applied to God means only that God manifests strength in His works, as a lion in his. Thus it is clear that applied to God the signification of these names can be defined only from what is said of creatures.

But to other names not applied to God in a metaphorical sense, the same rule would apply if they were spoken of God as the cause only, as some have supposed.[5] For when it is said, *God is good*, it would then only mean, *God is the cause of the creature's goodness*; and thus the name *good* applied to God would include in its meaning the creature's goodness. Hence *good* would apply primarily to creatures rather than God. But, as was shown above, these names are applied to God not as the cause only, but also essentially. For the words, *God is good*, or *wise*, signify not only that He is the cause of wisdom or goodness, but that these exist in Him in a more excellent way. Hence as regards what the name signifies, these names are applied primarily to God rather than to creatures, because these perfections flow from God to creatures; but as regards the imposition of the names, they are primarily applied by us to creatures which we know first. Hence they have a mode of signification which belongs to creatures, as was said above.

Reply Obj. 1. This objection refers to the imposition of the name: to that extent it is true.

Reply Obj. 2. The same rule does not apply to metaphorical and to other names, as was said above.

Reply Obj. 3. This objection would be valid if these names were applied to God only as cause, and not also essentially, for instance, as *healthy* is applied to medicine.

6. How Names Are Predicated of God and Creatures

St. Thomas, *Commentary on the Sentences*, I, d. 35, q. 1, art. 4.

1. It seems that God's knowledge is univocally the same as ours, for an agent produces an effect univocally like itself by reason of its form, as fire by means of heat produces heat univocally the same as its own heat. This is

---

[5] Alain of Lille, *Theol. Reg.* XXI; XXVI (PL 210, 631; 633).

what Origen says in his *Commentary on the Romans*, Chap. 16, vs. 27, and Dionysius says in his work *On Divine Names*, Chap. 7, that God is called wise because He endows us with wisdom by means of His own wisdom. Therefore, it seems that His wisdom is univocally the same as ours.

2. Moreover, the measure and what is measured have one concept, so that for each there is a special measure, because a liquid and a solid, for example, are not measured in the same way, as it is said in *Meta*. III. But God's knowledge is the measure of our knowledge: the more truth we have, the more we approach more closely to Him. Therefore it seems that His knowledge is univocal with our knowledge.

3. If you were to say that it is not univocal with our knowledge because God's knowledge exceeds ours, one can answer to the contrary that more and less do not create diverse species. But greater knowledge comes from the fact that one knows more or less. Therefore it seems from this that univocity of knowledge is not taken away.

4. If one were to say, as does the Commentator in *Meta*. X, that God's knowledge is not univocal for this very important reason that His knowledge is the cause of things and our knowledge is caused by things, one can argue to the opposite point of view. It is true that speculative knowledge in us is caused by things; but practical knowledge in us is the cause of things. Nevertheless, the name *knowledge* is not predicated equivocally of both of these. Therefore, this argument does not take away the univocity of knowledge.

5. On the contrary, there is nothing common between the eternal and the corruptible except in name, as is said in *Meta*. X, quoting the Commentator as well as the Philosopher. But God's knowledge is eternal while ours is corruptible; this latter is evident, for example, by the fact that knowledge can be lost through forgetfulness, and knowledge can be gained through instruction and attention. Therefore knowledge is attributed equivocally to God and to us.

6. Moreover, when things are seen to be univocal on a certain point, there is a common likeness of them. But in all likenesses there is some kind of comparison. But comparison is attributed only to things that agree in some kind of nature. Since, therefore, no creature agrees with God in some kind of common nature, since that would make it (the common nature) prior to both of them, it seems that nothing can be said univocally of God and of a creature.

7. Moreover, nothing univocal can be in one case a substance and in another case an accident. But knowledge in us is an accident while in God it is His substance. Therefore it is to be predicated equivocally.

Solution:

I reply that something can be common to several things in three ways, namely, univocally, equivocally, or analogically. It is true that nothing can be predicated univocally of God and of a creature. The reason for this is that in treating reality one must consider two things, namely, the nature or the quiddity of a thing and its existence. It is necessary that in all univocal things there be a community according to nature and not according to existence, because one existence can be only in one thing. Therefore the character of humanity is not present in two men according to one and the same existence. Therefore whenever the form signified by a name is existence itself, it cannot have a univocal agreement, just as, therefore, being cannot be predicated univocally. Therefore, all those things which are predicated of God are by nature or from His own existence, since His act of being is His nature, and for this reason He is said by certain philosophers to be being not by essence, or knowing not by knowledge, and so on; thereby understanding that His essence is not really distinct from His existence, and so for every attribute, it follows that nothing can be predicated univocally of God and of creatures.

It is for this reason that some say that whatever is predicated of God and of a creature is said by pure equivocation. But this, too, cannot be, because in those things which are equivocal by chance or fortune (per *casum et fortunam*) it is not possible to know the one by means of the other as is true when the same name is found to be common when applied to two men. Since, therefore, we come to an understanding of God's knowledge through our own knowledge, it cannot be that it is entirely equivocal.

Therefore, one must say that knowledge is predicated analogically of God and of a creature, and so on for all other things of this kind. But there is a two-fold kind of analogy. Some things are in agreement by reason of one thing which is attributed to them by priority and posteriority. Now this kind of analogy cannot exist between God and creature just as there cannot be univocity. There is another kind of analogy according to which one thing imitates another insofar as that is possible; it cannot perfectly attain that likeness. This is the analogy between the creature and God.

To the first difficulty we say that a univocal effect is produced by an agent through its form only when the recipient is apt to receive the full power of the agent or can receive it according to its very nature. In this respect no creature is apt to receive knowledge from God in the way that knowledge is present in Him, just as no lower forms of body can receive heat in a univocal manner from the sun even though the sun acts by reason of its form.

To the second difficulty we say that God's knowledge is not a measure by which our knowledge is judged but rather that it exceeds our knowledge. Therefore it does not follow that it is of the same nature and is univocally the same as our knowledge but rather they are alike according to analogy.

To the third difficulty we say that more and less never take away the univocity or the unity of a species, but those things through which the greater and the less are caused can create a difference of species and take away univocity. Now this happens when the greater and less are caused not by different participation in one nature but rather by reason of a gradation according to different natures, as when an angel is said to be more intellectual than man.

To the fourth difficulty we say that the reason given by the Commentator is not per se sufficient to prove that univocity is destroyed unless one is dealing in a particular kind of matter. The knowledge which is the cause of things, as divine knowledge, cannot be univocally the same as knowledge caused by things. The reason for this has already been given.

The other reasons which seem to conclude that there was only equivocation are now to be answered.

To the fifth difficulty we answer that the argument is to be understood with respect to existence but not with respect to the common notion (*intentionem*) which is predicated. For the example of *body* which is used is predicated equivocally of corruptible and incorruptible things, even though the same notion or definition is found in both of them as long as one considers only the common idea of body.

To the sixth difficulty we say that there is no agreement in likeness on some common point between God and creature but that there is only an imitation. Therefore, the creature is said to be like God but the proposition is not convertible, as Dionysius says in his book *On Divine Names*, Chap. IX, Para. VI.

To the seventh difficulty we say that knowledge is not predicated of God according to a kind of genus, namely, as a quality or some accident, but only by reason of its specific diversity. This pertains to its perfection and in this respect is imitated by nature, as has been said.

7. Univocal, Equivocal, and Analogical Predication

St. Thomas, *On the Power of God*, q. 7, art. 7.*

See also *Summa Theologiae*, I, q. 13, art. 5: *Summa Contra Gentiles*, I, 32 ff.

The seventh point of inquiry is whether these terms are attributed to God and creatures univocally or equivocally.

1. Measure and the thing measured must be in the same genus. Now God's goodness is the measure of all created goodness, and the same applies to his wisdom. Therefore they are said of creatures univocally.

2. Things are like which have a common form. Now the creature can be likened to God, according to Genesis i, 26, *Let us make man to our own image*

---

* Translated by Dominican Fathers of the English Province (Westminster, Md.: The Newman Press, 1952).

and likeness. Therefore there is a community of form between God and the creature. Now something can be predicated univocally of things that have a common form. Therefore something can be predicated univocally of God and the creature.

3. More or less makes no difference in the species. Now whereas God is called good and the creature also is called good, the difference seems to be that God is better than the creature. Therefore goodness in God and the creature is of the same species and consequently is predicated univocally of both.

4. There is no comparison possible between things of different genera, as the Philosopher proves (*Phys.* vii); thus we cannot compare the speed of alteration with the speed of local movement. But we compare God to the creature: thus we say that God is supremely good, and that the creature is good. Therefore God and the creature are in the same genus and consequently something can be predicated of them univocally.

5. Nothing can be known except through a homogeneous species: thus whiteness in a wall would not be known by its image in the eye unless the two were homogeneous. Now God by his goodness knows all beings, and so forth. Therefore God's goodness and the creature's are homogeneous: and consequently good is predicated univocally of God and the creature.

6. The house that the builder has in his mind and the material house are homogeneous. Now all creatures came from God as a work proceeds from the craftsman. Therefore goodness that is in God is homogeneous with the goodness that is in the creature: wherefore we come to the same conclusion as before.

7. Every equivocal agent is reduced to something univocal. Therefore the first agent which is God must be univocal. Now something is predicated univocally of a univocal agent and its proper effect. Therefore something is predicated univocally of God and the creature.

1. On the contrary the Philosopher says (*Metaph.* x, 7) that nothing except in name is common to the eternal and the temporal. Now God is eternal and creatures temporal. Therefore nothing but a name can be common to God and creatures: and consequently these terms are predicated equivocally of God and the creature.

2. Since the genus is the first part of a definition, a difference of genus causes equivocation: so that if a term be employed to signify something in different genera it will be equivocal. Now wisdom as attributed to a creature is in the genus of quality: wherefore seeing that it is not a quality in God, as we have shown, it would seem that this word *wisdom* is predicated equivocally of God and his creatures.

3. Nothing can be predicated except equivocally of things that are in no way alike. Now there is no likeness between creatures and God: for it is

written (Isa. xl, 18): *To whom then have you likened God?* Therefore seemingly nothing can be predicated univocally of God and creatures.

4. But it will be replied that although God cannot be said to be like a creature, a creature can be said to be like God.

On the contrary, it is written (Ps. lxxxii, 2): *O God, who shall be like to thee?* as if to say *None.*

5. A thing cannot be like a substance in respect of an accident. Now wisdom in a creature is an accident, and in God is the substance. Therefore man cannot be like God by his wisdom.

6. Since in a creature being is distinct from form or nature, nothing can be like being itself by its form or nature. Now these terms when predicated of a creature signify a form or nature: while God is his own very being. Therefore a creature cannot be like God by these things that are predicated of a creature: and thus the same conclusion follows as before.

7. God differs more from a creature than number from whiteness. But it is absurd to liken a number to whiteness or vice versa. Therefore still more absurd is it to liken a creature to God: and again the same conclusion follows.

8. Things that are like have some one thing in common: and things that have one thing in common have a common predicate. But nothing whatever can be predicated in common with God. Therefore there can be no likeness between God and the creature.

I answer that it is impossible for anything to be predicated univocally of God and a creature: this is made plain as follows. Every effect of an univocal agent is adequate to the agent's power: and no creature, being finite, can be adequate to the power of the first agent which is infinite. Wherefore it is impossible for a creature to receive a likeness to God univocally. Again it is clear that although the form in the agent and the form in the effect have a common meaning (*ratio*), the fact that they have different modes of existence precludes their univocal predication: thus though the material house is of the same type as the house in the mind of the builder, since the one is the type of the other; nevertheless *house* cannot be univocally predicated of both, because the form of the material house has its being in matter, whereas in the builder's mind it has immaterial being. Hence granted the impossibility that goodness in God and in the creature be of the same kind, nevertheless *good* would not be predicated of God univocally: since that which in God is immaterial and simple, is in the creature material and manifold. Moreover being is not predicated univocally of substance and accident, because substance is a being as subsisting in itself, while accident is that whose being is to be in something else. Wherefore it is evident that a different relation to being precludes an univocal predication of being. Now God's relation to being is different from that of any creature's: for he is his own being, which cannot be said of any creature. Hence in no way can it be predicated univocally of

God and a creature, and consequently neither can any of the other predicables among which is included even the first, *being:* for if there be diversity in the first, there must be diversity in the others: wherefore nothing is predicated univocally of substance and accident.

Others, however, took a different view, and held that nothing is predicated of God and a creatuure by analogy but by pure equivocation. This is the opinion of Rabbi Moses, as appears from his writings. This opinion, however, is false, because in all purely equivocal terms, which the Philosopher calls equivocal *by chance,* a term is predicated of a thing without any respect to something else: whereas all things predicated of God and creatures are predicated of God with a certain respect to creatures or vice versa, and this is clearly admitted in all the aforesaid explanations of the divine names. Wherefore they cannot be pure equivocations. Again, since all our knowledge of God is taken from creatures, if the agreement were purely nominal, we should know nothing about God except empty expressions to which nothing corresponds in reality. Moreover, it would follow that all the proofs advanced about God by philosophers are sophisms: for instance, if one were to argue that whatsoever is in potentiality is reduced to actuality by something actual and that therefore God is actual being, since all things are brought into being by him, there will be a fallacy of equivocation; and similarly in all other arguments. And again the effect must in some way be like its cause, wherefore nothing is predicated equivocally of cause and effect; for instance, *healthy* of medicine and an animal.

We must accordingly take a different view and hold that nothing is predicated univocally of God and the creature: but that those things which are attributed to them in common are predicated not equivocally but analogically. Now this kind of predication is twofold. The first is when one thing is predicated of two with respect to a third: thus being is predicated of quantity and quality with respect to substance. The other is when a thing is predicated of two by reason of a relationship between these two: thus being is predicated of substance and quantity. In the first kind of predication the two things must be preceded by something to which each of them bears some relation: thus substance has a respect to quantity and quality: whereas in the second kind of predication this is not necessary, but one of the two must precede the other. Wherefore since nothing precedes God, but he precedes the creature, the second kind of analogical predication is applicable to him but not the first.

Reply to the First Objection. This argument avails in the case of a measure to which the thing measured can be equal or commensurate: but God is not a measure of this kind since he infinitely surpasses all that is measured by him.

Reply to the Second Objection. The likeness of the creature to God falls short of univocal likeness in two respects. First it does not arise from the participation of one form, as two hot things are like by participation of one form, because what is affirmed of God and creatures is predicated of him essentially, but of creatures, by participation: so that a creature's likeness to God is as that of a hot thing to heat, not of a hot thing to one that is hotter. Secondly, because this very form of which the creature participates falls short of the nature of the thing which is God, just as the heat of fire falls short of the nature of the sun's power whereby it produces heat.

Reply to the Third Objection. More and less may be considered from three points of view, and predicated accordingly. First when it is only a question of the quantity of the thing participated: thus snow is said to be whiter than the wall, because whiteness is more perfect in the snow than in the wall, and yet it is of the same nature: and consequently such a difference of *more* or *less* does not cause a difference of species. Secondly when the one is predicated participatively and the other essentially: thus we might say that goodness is better than a good thing. Thirdly when the one same term is ascribed to one thing in a more eminent degree than to another, for instance, heat to the sun than to fire. These last two modes of *more* and *less* are incompatible with unity of species and univocal predication: and it is thus that a thing is predicated *more* and *less* of God and creatures, as already explained.

Reply to the Fourth Objection. When we say that God is better or that he is the sovereign good we compare him to creatures not as though he participated of the same generic nature as creatures, like the species of a genus, but as the principle of a genus.

Reply to the Fifth Objection. Inasmuch as an intelligible species has a higher mode of existence, the knowledge arising therefrom is the more perfect: for instance, the knowledge arising from the image of a stone in the mind is more perfect than that which results from the species in the senses. Hence God is able to know things most perfectly in his essence inasmuch as in his essence is the supereminent but not homogeneous likeness of things.

Reply to the Sixth Objection. There is a twofold likeness between God and creatures. One is the likeness of the creature to the divine mind, and thus the form understood by God and the thing itself are homogeneous, although they have not the same mode of being, since the form understood is only in the mind, while the form of the creature is in the thing. There is another likeness inasmuch as the divine essence itself is the supereminent but not homogeneous likeness of all things. It is by reason of this latter likeness that good and the like are predicated in common of God and creatures: but not by reason of the former, because when we say *God is good* we do not mean to define him from the fact that he understands the creature's goodness, since it has already been observed that not even the house in the mind of the builder is called a house in the same sense as the house in being.

Reply to the Seventh Objection. The equivocal agent must precede the univocal: because the latter's causality does not extend to the whole species (else it were its own cause) but only to an individual member of the species.

But the equivocal agent's causality extends to the entire species and consequently the first agent must be an equivocal agent.

1. *Reply to the First Argument* on the contrary side. The Philosopher refers to things that are common physically, not logically. Now things that have a different mode of existence have nothing in common in respect of that being which is considered by the physicist, but they may have some common 'intention' that the logician may consider. Moreover, even from the physicist's point of view the elemental and the heavenly body are not in the same genus: but in the view of the logician they are. However, the Philosopher does not mean to exclude analogical but only univocal community: since he wishes to prove that the corruptible and the incorruptible have not a common genus.

2. Difference of genus excludes univocation but not analogy. In proof of this, *healthy* is applied to urine in the genus of *sign*, but to medicine in the genus of *cause*.

3. In no sense is God said to be like the creature, but contrariwise: for as Dionysius says (*Div. Nom.* x), *likeness is not reciprocated between cause and effect, but only in co-ordinates*: thus a man is not said to be like his statue, but vice versa, the reason being that the form wherein the likeness consists is in the man before it is in the statue. Hence we do not say that God is like his creatures but vice versa.

4. According to Dionysius (*ibid.*) when it is said that no creature is like God this is to be understood as referring to effects which are imperfect and beyond all comparison fall short of their cause: nor does this refer to the quantity of the thing participated but to the other two modes, as explained above (Reply to Third Objection).

5. A thing cannot be like substance in respect of an accident, so that the likeness regards a form of the same kind: but there may be the likeness that is between cause and effect: since the first substance must needs be the cause of all accidents.

6. *The Sixth Argument* is answered in like manner.

7. Whiteness is not in the genus of number, nor is it the principle of a genus: wherefore they do not admit of comparison. Whereas God is the principle of every genus, and consequently all things are somewhat likened to him.

8. This argument refers to things that have a common genus or matter: which does not apply to God and the creature.

READINGS FOR CHAPTER IV.   SUBSTANCE AND ACCIDENTS

1. The Primacy of Substance. Its Priority to Accidents

A. Aristotle, *Metaphysics*, VII, ch. 1 and 2, 1028a10–1028b32.*

The term *being* is used in many senses, as we have explained in our discussions of the different meanings of words. For in one sense it signifies the whatness of a thing and this particular thing; and in another sense it signifies of what sort a thing is or how much or any one of the other things which are predicated in this way. But of all the senses in which being is used, it is evident that the first of these is the whatness of a thing, which indicates substance.

For when we state of what sort a thing is, we say that it is good or evil, and not that it is three cubits long or a man; but when we state what a thing is, we do not say that it is white or black or three cubits long, but that it is a man or a god. And other things are called beings because they belong to such[1] a being, for some are qualities of it, others quantities, others affections, and so on.

Hence one may even be puzzled whether each of the following terms, namely, *to walk, to be healthy* and *to sit,* is a being or a non-being. And it is similar in the case of other things such as these; for no one of them is fitted by nature to exist of itself or is capable of existing apart from substance. But if anything is a being, it is rather the thing that walks and sits and is healthy. Now these appear to be beings to a greater degree because there is some subject which underlies them; and this is substance and the individual, which appears in a definite category; for the term *good* or *sitting* is not used without this. Evidently then it is by reason of this that each of the other categories is a being. Hence the first kind of being, and not being of a special sort but being in an unqualified sense, will be substance.

Now there are several senses in which a thing is said to be first; but substance is first in every respect: in definition, in the order of knowing, and in time; for none of the other categories can exist separately, but only substance. And it is first in definition; because in the definition of each thing it is necessary to include the definition of substance. And we think that we

---

* Translations from Aristotle's *Metaphysics* and St. Thomas' *Commentary* by John P. Rowan, Ph.D.

[1] Reading *talis* for *taliter* in keeping with St. Thomas' citation: "*Sunt talis entis*" (c. 1251).

know each thing best when we know what it is, for example, what a man is or what fire is, rather than when we know of what sort it is or how much it is or where it is; for we know each of these things only when we know what the quality or quantity is.

And the question which was raised formerly and is raised now and always, and which always causes difficulty, is what being is, and this is the question what substance is. For some[2] say that is is one, and others more than one; and some[3] say that it is limited, and others,[4] unlimited. And for this reason we must investigate chiefly and primarily and solely, as we might say, what this kind of being is.

Aristotle, *Metaphysics*, VII, Chapter 2.

Now it seems that substance is found most evidently in bodies. Hence we say that animals and plants and their parts are substances, and also natural bodies, such as fire, water, earth and particular things of this kind, and all things which are either parts of these or composed of these, either of parts or of all, for example, the heaven and its parts, such as the stars, the moon and the sun. But whether these alone are substances, or other things also are, or none of these but certain other things, must be investigated.

Again, it seems to some[5] that the limits of a body, such as surface, line, point and unit, are substances to a greater degree than a body or solid. And some[6] are of the opinion that there is nothing of this sort apart from sensible substances, while others think that there are eternal substances which are more numerous and possess being to a greater degree. Thus Plato claimed that there are two kinds of substance: the separate Forms and the objects of mathematics, and a third kind: the substances of sensible bodies. And Speusippus[7] admitted still more kinds of substances, beginning with the unit; and he posited principles for each kind of substance: one for numbers, another for continuous quantities, and still another for the soul; and by proceeding in this way he increases the kinds of substance. And some[8] say that the separate Forms and numbers have the same nature, and that other things, such as lines and surfaces, depend on these; and so on until one comes to the substance of the heavens and sensible bodies.

Regarding these matters, then, it is necessary to investigate which statements are true and which are not; and what things are substances; and whether there are or are not any substances in addition to sensible ones; and how these

2 I.e., Parmenides (65:C 133), Melissus (65:C 140) and the Milesian philosophers (67:C 145).

3 I.e., the Pythagoreans (68:C 149) and Empedocles (68:C 148).

4 I.e., Anaxagoras (44:C 90) and Democritus (55:C 113).

5 I.e., the Pythagoreans.

6 I.e., the Pre-Socratics.

7 Reading *Speusippus* for *Leucippus*; see Bekker 1028 b 23. Speusippus was Plato's nephew and his successor as head of the Academy.

8 The disciples of Xenocrates, the successor of Speusippus.

exist; and whether there is any separable substance (and if so, why and how), or whether there is no such substance apart from sensible ones. This must be done after we have first described what substance is.

B. St. Thomas, *Commentary on the Metaphysics*, VII, lesson 1, Nos. 1245–1269.

[1245.] Having dismissed both accidental being and being which signifies the true from the principal study of this science, here the Philosopher begins to establish the truth about essential being (*ens per se*), which exists outside the mind and constitutes the principal object of study in this science. This is divided into two parts; for this science discusses both being as being and the first principles of being, as has been stated in Book VI. Thus in the first part he establishes the truth about being; and in the second, about the first principles of being. He does this in Book XII, where he says "The study."

But since being and unity accompany each other and come within the scope of the same study, as has been stated at the beginning of Book IV, the first part is therefore divided into two sections. In the first he establishes the truth about being as being; and in the second, about unity and those attributes which naturally accompany it. He does this in Book X, where he says "It was pointed out."

Now essential being, which exists outside the mind, is divided twofoldly, as has been stated in Book V; for it is divided, first, into the ten categories, and second, into the potential and the actual. Accordingly, the first part is divided into two sections. In the first he establishes the truth about being as divided into the ten categories; and in the second, about being as divided into the potential and the actual. He does this in Book IX, where he says "We have dealt."

[1246.] The first part is divided again into two sections. In the first he shows that in order to establish the truth about being as divided into the ten categories, it is necessary to establish the truth about substance; and in the second, he begins to do this, where he says "The term *substance*."

In regard to the first he does two things. First, he shows that it is necessary to settle the issue about substance. Second, he indicates the things that have to be discussed about substance, where he says "Now it seems."

In regard to the first he does two things. He shows that one who intends to treat being should investigate substances separately; and he does this, first, by giving an argument; and second, by considering what others have been accustomed to maintain, where he says "And the question."

Hence in the first part his aim is to give the following argument. That which is the first among the kinds of being, since it is being in an unqualified sense and not being with some qualification, clearly indicates the nature of being. But substance is being of this kind. Therefore to know the nature of being it suffices to establish the truth about substance.

In regard to the first he does two things. First, he shows that substance is the first kind of being; and second, he shows in what way it is said to be first, where he says "Now there are several." In regard to the first he does two things.

[1247.] First, he explains his thesis. He says that the term *being* is used in many senses (as has been stated in Book V where he distinguished the different senses in which terms of this kind are used); for in one sense being signifies the whatness of a thing and this particular thing, i.e., substance, inasmuch as by "the whatness of a thing" is meant the essence of a substance, and by "this particular thing," an individual substance; and the different senses of substance are reduced to these two, as has been stated in Book V. And in another sense it signifies quality or quantity or any one of the other categories. And since being is used in many senses, it is evident that being in the primary sense is the whatness of a thing, i.e., the being which signifies substance.

[1248.] "For when we state."

Second, he proves his thesis by using the following argument: in every class of things that which exists of itself and is a being in an unqualified sense is prior to that which exists by reason of something else and is a being in a qualified sense. But substance is a being in an unqualified sense and exists of itself, whereas all classes of beings other than substance are beings in a qualified sense and exist by reason of substance. Therefore substance is the primary kind of being.

[1249.] He makes the minor premise clear in two ways. He does this, first, by considering the way in which we speak or make predications. He says that it is evident from this that substance is the primary kind of being, because when we state of what sort a thing is we say that it is either good or evil; for this signifies quality, which differs from substance and quantity. Now three cubits long signifies quantity and man signifies substance. Therefore when we state of what sort a thing is, we do not say that it is three cubits long or a man. And when we state what a thing is, we do not say that it is white or hot, which signify quality, or three cubits long, which signifies quantity, but we say that it is a man or a god, which signifies substance.

[1250.] From this it is clear that terms signifying substance express what a thing is in an unqualified sense, whereas those signifying quality do not express what a thing is in an unqualified sense, but what sort of thing it is. The same is true of quantity and the other genera.

[1251.] From this it is clear that substance itself is said to be a being of itself, because terms which simply signify substance designate what this thing is. But other class of things are said to be beings, not because they have a quiddity of themselves (as though they were beings of themselves, since they do not express what a thing is in an unqualified sense), but because "they belong to such a being," i.e., because they have some connection with substance, which is a being of itself. For they do not signify quiddity, since some of them are clearly qualities of such a being, i.e., of substance, other quantities, other affections, or something of the sort signified by the other genera.

[1252.]   "Hence one might."

Second he proves the same point by means of an example. The other kinds of beings are beings only inasmuch as they are related to substance. Therefore, since other beings when signified in the abstract do not designate any connection with substance, the question can arise whether they are beings or non-beings, for example, whether to walk, to be healthy, and to sit, and any one of these things which are signified in the abstract, is a being or a non-being. And it is similar in the case of other things such as these, which are signified in the abstract, whether they designate some activity, as the foregoing do, or whether they do not, as is the case with whiteness and blackness.

[1253.]   Now accidents signified in the abstract seem to be non-beings, because no one of them is fitted by nature to exist of itself. In fact the being of each of them consists in their existing in something else, and no one of them is capable of existing apart from substance. Therefore when they are signified in the abstract as though they were beings of themselves and separate from substance, they seem to be non-beings. The reason is that words do not signify things directly according to the mode of being which they have in reality, but indirectly according to the mode in which we understand them; for concepts are the likenesses of things, and words the likenesses of concepts, as is stated in Book I of the Perihermenias.[1]

[1254.]   Moreover, even though the mode of being which accidents have is not one whereby they may exist of themselves but only in something else, still the intellect can understand them as though they existed of themselves; for it is capable by nature of separating things which are united in reality. Hence abstract names of accidents signify beings which inhere in something else, although they do not signify them as inhering. And non-beings would be signified by means of this kind, granted that they would not inhere in something else.

[1255.]   Further, since these accidents signified in the abstract appear to be non-beings, it seems rather to be the concrete names of accidents that signify beings. And "if anything is a being," it seems rather to be "the thing that walks and sits and is healthy," because some subject is determined by them by reason of the very meaning of the term, inasmuch as they designate something connected with a subject. Now this subject is substance. Therefore every term of this kind which signifies an accident in the concrete "appears in a definite category," i.e., it seems to involve the category of substance, not in such a way that the category of substance is a part of the

---

[1] Perihermenias or De Interpretatione, 1 (16 a 4). In St. Thomas' day this work was divided into two books, the second beginning at our chapter 10.

meaning of such terms (for white in the categorical sense indicated quality alone), but so that terms of this sort signify accidents as inhering in a substance. And we do not use the terms "good or sitting without this," i.e., without substance; for an accident signifies something connected with substance.

[1256.] Again, since accidents do not seem to be beings insofar as they are signified in themselves, but only insofar as they are signified in connection with substance, evidently it is by reason of this that each of the other beings is a being. And from this it also appears that substance is "the first kind of being and being in an unqualified sense and not being of a special sort," i.e., without some qualification, as is the case with accidents; for to be white is not to be in an unqualified sense but with some qualification. This is clear from the fact that when a thing begins to be white we do not say that it begins to be in an unqualified sense, but that it begins to be white. For when Socrates begins to be a man, he is said to begin to be in an unqualified sense. Hence it is obvious that being a man signifies being in an unqualified sense, but that being white signifies being with some qualification.

[1257.] "Now there are several."

Here he shows in what respect substance is said to be first. He says that since the term first is used in several senses, as has been explained in Book V, then substance is the first of all beings in three respects: in the order of knowing, in definition, and in time. He proves that it is first in time by this argument: none of the other categories is capable of existing apart from substance, but substance alone is capable of existing apart from the others; for no accident is found without a substance, but some substance is found without an accident. Thus it is clear that an accident does not exist whenever a substance does, but the reverse, and for this reason substance is prior in time.

[1258.] It is also evident that it is first in definition, because in the definition of any accident it is necessary to include the definition of substance; for just as nose is given in the definition of snub, so too the proper subject of any accident is given in the definition of that accident. Hence just as animal is prior to man in definition, because the definition of animal is given in that of man, in a similar fashion substance is prior to accidents in definition.

[1259.] It is evident too that substance is first in the order of knowing, for that is first in the order of knowing which is better known and explains a thing better. Now each thing is better known when its substance is known rather than when its quality or quantity is known; for we think we know each thing best when we know what man is or what fire is, rather than when we know of what sort it is or how much it is or where it is or when we know it according to any of the other categories. For this reason too we think that we know each of the things contained in the categories of accidents when we know what each is; for example, when we know what being this sort of thing is, we know quality; and when we know what being how much is, we know quantity. For just as the other categories have being only insofar as they inhere in a substance, in a similar way they can be known only insofar as they share to some extent in the mode according to which substance is known, and this is to know the whatness of a thing.

[1260.] "And the question."

Here he proves the same point, namely, that it is necessary to treat substance separately, by considering what other philosophers have been accustomed to maintain. He says that when one raises the question what being is (and this is a question which has always caused difficulty for philosophers both "formerly," i.e., in the past, and "now," i.e., in the present), this is nothing else than the question or problem what the substance of things is.

[1261.] For some men, such as Parmenides and Melissus, said that "this being," i.e., substance, is one and immobile, whereas others, such as the ancient philosophers of nature, who maintained that there is only one material principle of things, said that it is mobile. And they thought that matter alone is being and substance. Hence when they claimed that there is one being, because there is one material principle, they obviously understood by one being, one substance. Other men maintained that there are more beings than one, namely, those who posited many material principles, and, consequently, many substances of things. And some of this group held that these principles are limited in number, for example, Empedocles, who posited four elements; and others held that they are unlimited in number, for example, Anaxagoras, who posited an unlimited number of like parts, and Democritus, who posited an unlimited number of indivisible bodies.

[1262.] If, then, the other philosophers in treating of beings paid attention to substances alone, we too should investigate "what this kind of being is," i.e., what substance itself is. And this we must do, I say, chiefly, because this is our principal aim; and primarily, because by means of it the other kinds of being are known; and solely, as we might say, because by establishing what is true about substance by itself, one acquires a knowledge of all the other kinds of being. Thus in one sense he deals with substance separately, and in another sense not. He indicates this when he says "as we might say" or inasmuch as we might speak in this way, as we are accustomed to say of things which are not true in every respect.

[1263.] "Now it seems."

Here he indicates the things that have to be discussed about substance; and in regard to this he does two things. First, he gives the opinions that other men have held about substance. Second, he states that it is necessary to determine which of their opinions are true, where he says "Regarding these matters."

In regard to the first he does two things. First, he indicates the things that are evident about substance. He says that substantial being is found most obviously in bodies. Thus we say that animals and plants and their parts are substances, and also natural bodies such as fire, earth, water, "and particular things of this kind," i.e., such elemental bodies as earth and fire, according to the opinion of Heraclitus, and other intermediate entities, according to the opinions of others. We also say that all parts of the elements are substances, as well as the bodies composed of the elements, whether of some of the elements, as particular compounds, or "of all the elements," i.e., the whole of the various elements, as this whole sphere of active and passive beings; and as we also say that "a heaven," which is a natural body distinct from the elements, is a substance, and also its parts, such as the stars, the moon and the sun.

[1264.] But whether these sensible substances are the only substances, as the ancient philosophers of nature claimed, or whether there are also some substances which differ from these, as the Platonists claimed, or whether these too are not substances, but only certain things which differ from these, must be investigated.

[1265.] "Again, it seems."

Second, he describes the philosophers' opinions about those substances which are not evident. He says that it seems to some philosophers that the limits of bodies are the substances of things, i.e., that surface, line, point and unit are substances to a greater degree than a body or solid. And those who held this opinion differed in their views; because some, for example, the Pythagoreans, thought that no limits of this kind are separate from sensible bodies, while others thought that there are certain eternal beings which are separate from and more numerous than sensible things and have being to a greater degree. I say "have being to a greater degree," because they are incorruptible and immobile, whereas sensible bodies are corruptible and mobile; and "more numerous," because while sensible bodies belong only to one order, these separate beings belong to two, inasmuch as "Plato claimed that there are two kinds of separate substances," or two orders of separate substances, namely, the separate Forms or Ideas and the objects of mathematics; and he also posited a third order — the substances of sensible bodies.

[1266.] But Speusippus, who was Plato's nephew and his successor, posited many orders of substances, and in each order he also began with the unit, which he posited as the principle in each order of substance. But he posited one kind of unit as the principle of numbers, which he claimed to be the first substances after the Forms, and another as the principle of continuous quantities, which he claimed to be second substances; and finally he posited the substance of the soul. Hence by proceeding in this way he extended the order of substances right down to corruptible bodies.

[1267.] But some thinkers differed from Plato and Speusippus, because they did not distinguish between the Forms and the first order of mathematical objects, which is that of numbers. For they said that the Forms and numbers have the same nature, and that "all other things depend on these," i.e., are related successively to numbers, namely, lines and surfaces, right down to the first substance of the heavens and the other sensible bodies which belong to this last order.

[1268.] "Regarding these matters."

Here he explains what should be said about the foregoing opinions. He says that it is necessary to determine which of the above opinions are true and which are not; and what things are substances; and whether the objects of mathematics and the separate Forms are substances in addition to sensible ones, or not; and if they are substances, what mode of being they have; and if they are not substances in addition to sensible ones, whether there is any other separate substance, and (if so), why and how; or whether there is no substance in addition to sensible substances.

[1269.] For he will settle this issue below and in Book XII of this work.

Yet before this is done it is first necessary to posit and explain what it is that constitutes the substance of these sensible bodies in which substance is clearly[2] found. He does this in the present Book (568:C 1270) and in Book VIII, which follows.

[2] Reading *manifeste* for *manifesta*.

2. The Being of Accidents

A. Aristotle, *Metaphysics*, XII, ch. 1, 1069 a 18–1069 a 30

The study here is concerned with substance; for it is the principles and causes of substances which are being investigated.

For if the totality of things is a kind of whole, substance is its first part; and if things constitute a whole by reason of succession, substance is also first, and next quality, and then quantity.

But at the same time[1] the latter are not, so to speak, beings in an unqualified sense, but are qualities and motions of it. Otherwise the non-white and not-straight would be beings; for we say that they are, for example, "the not-white is."

Again, none of the other genera can exist separately.

And the ancient philosophers testify to this in practice; for it was of substance that they sought the principles, elements and causes. Present day thinkers,[2] however, maintain that universals are substances; for genera are universals, and they say that these are principles and substances to a greater degree, because they investigate the matter dialectically. But the ancient philosophers regarded particular things as substances, for example, fire and earth and not what is common to both, body.

[1] Reading *simul* (with the Greek text and the *versio recens* of Parma).
[2] The Platonists.

B. St. Thomas, *Commentary on the Metaphysics*, XII, lesson 1,
nos. 2416–2423.

[2416.] Having summarized in the preceding book the points which were
previously discussed about imperfect being, both in this work and
in the *Physics*,[1] the Philosopher's aim in this book is to summarize the points
discussed about being in its unqualified sense, i.e., about substance, both in
Book VII and in Book VIII of this work and in Book I of the *Physics*,[2] and
to add any points which are missing in order to make his study of substances complete.

This is divided into two parts. In the first he shows that this science is
chiefly concerned with the study of substances. In the second he settles the
matter about the classes of substances, where he says, "Now there are three."

In regard to the first he does two things. First, he states his thesis, saying
that in this science "the study," i.e., the principal inquiry, has to do with
substances. For since this science, inasmuch as it is the first and the one
which is called wisdom, investigates the first principles of beings, the
principles and causes of substances must constitute its main object of study;
for these are the first principles of beings. The way in which principle and
cause differ has been stated in Book V.

[2417.] "For if the totality."

Then he proves his thesis in four ways. The first proof is as follows: since
substance is prior to the other kinds of beings, the first science should be
one that is chiefly concerned with the primary kind of being. He shows
that substance is the primary kind of being by using an analogous case in
the realm of sensible things, in which order is found in two ways. In one
way, order is found among sensible things insofar as the parts of any whole
are related to each other, for example in an animal the first part is the heart,
and in a house, the foundation. In another way, order is found among sensible
things in so far as some succeed others and one thing is not constituted from
them either by continuity or contact; and it is in this sense that one speaks
of the first and second line of an army. Hence, just as there is some first
part in any whole, and also some first entity among things that succeed
one another, in a similar way substance is the first of all other beings. This
is what he means when he says, "For if the totality," i.e., if the universe
of beings is a kind of whole, substance is its first part, just as the foundation
is the first part of a house. And if beings are like things that succeed one
another, substance will again be first, and then quantity, and then quality,
and then the other genera.

[2418.] But Averroes, failing to consider that this statement is analogical,
because he considered it impossible for anyone to think that all the

---

[1] *Physics*, II, 1–3.
[2] *Physics*, I, 1–6.

other genera[3] of existing things should be parts of one continuous whole, departs from the obvious sense of the text and gives a different explanation. He says that by these two orders Aristotle meant the twofold relationship which can be conceived to exist between beings. The first of these is that beings are like things having one nature and one genus, which would be true if being were their common genus or whatever way it might be common to them. And he says that this is what Aristotle means when he says, "If the totality of things be a kind of a whole." The second is that beings are related as things which have nothing in common. And he says that this is what Aristotle means when he says, "And if things constitute a whole by reason of succession." For in either case it follows that substance is prior to other beings.

[2419.] "But at the same time."

Then he proves the same point in a second way. He says that quantity and quality and the like are not beings in an unqualified sense, as will be said below. For being is spoken of in a sense as something having being. But it is substance alone which subsists. However, accidents are called beings, not because they are, but rather because by them something is; for example, whiteness is said to be because its subject is white. Hence, Aristotle says that accidents are not called beings in an unqualified sense, but beings of a being, for example, quality and motion.

[2420.] Nor is it surprising that accidents are called beings even though they are not beings in an unqualified sense, because even privations and negations are called beings in a sense, as the not-white and not-straight. For we say that the not-white is, not because the not-white has being, but because some subject is deprived of whiteness. Accidents and privations have this in common, then, that being is predicated of both by reason of their subject. But they differ in this respect, that while a subject has being of some kind by reason of accidents, it does not have being of any kind by reason of privations, but rather is deficient in being.

[2421.] Therefore, since accidents are not beings in an unqualified sense, but only substances are, this science, which considers being as being, does not make accidents the chief object of its study, but substances.

[2422.] "Again, none."

Then he proves his thesis in a third way, i.e., the fact that other beings cannot exist apart from substance. For accidents can only exist in a subject, and therefore the study of accidents is included in that of substance.

[2423.] "And the ancient."

Then he proves his thesis in a fourth way. He says that the ancient philosophers also testify to the fact that the investigations of the philosopher have to do with substances; because in seeking the causes of being they seek

---

[3] Reading *genera* for *genere*.

the causes only of substances. And certain modern thinkers also did this, but in a different way; for they did not seek principles, causes and elements in the same way, but differently. For the modern thinkers, i.e., the Platonists, say that universals are substances to a greater degree than particular things; for they say that genera, which are universals, are principles and causes of substances to a greater degree than particular things. And they said this because they investigated things from the viewpoint of dialectics. For they thought that universals, which are separate according to their mode of definition from sensible things, would also be separate in reality, and that they would be the principles of particular things. But the ancient philosophers, such as Democritus and Empedocles, claimed that the substances and principles of things are particular entities, such as fire and earth, but not this common principle, body.

3. The Definition of Person

St. Thomas, *Summa Theologiae*, I, q. 29, art. 1.*

We proceed thus to the First Article: —

Objection 1. It would seem that the definition of person given by Boethius is insufficient — that is, *a person is an individual substance of a rational nature.*[1] For nothing singular can be subject to definition. But *person* signifies something singular. Therefore person is improperly defined.

Obj. 2. Further, substance, as placed above in the definition of person, is either first substance or second substance. If it is the former, the word *individual* is superfluous, because first substance is individual substance; if it stands for second substance, the added word *individual* is false, for there is a contradiction in terms, since second substances are called *genera* or *species*. Therefore this definition is incorrect.

Obj. 3. Further, a term of intention must not be included in the definition of a thing. For to define a man as a *species of animal* would not be a correct definition, since *man* is the name of a thing, and *species* is a name of an intention. Therefore, since person is the name of a thing (for it signifies a substance of a rational nature), the word *individual* which is an intentional name comes improperly into the definition.

Obj. 4. Further, *Nature is the principle of motion and rest, in those things in which it is essentially, and not accidentally,* as Aristotle says.[2] But *person* is found in immovable things, as in God, and in the angels. Therefore the word *nature* ought not to enter into the definition of person, but the word should rather be *essence.*

---

* Anton C. Pegis, *Basic Writings of St. Thomas Aquinas* (New York: Random House, 1945).
[1] *De Duab. Nat.,* III (PL 64, 1343).
[2] *Phys.,* II, I (192 b 21).

Obj. 5. Further, the separated soul is an individual substance of a rational nature; but it is not a person. Therefore person is not properly defined as above.

I answer that, Although universal and particular exist in every genus, nevertheless, in a certain special way the individual belongs to the genus of substance. For substance is individuated through itself, whereas the accidents are individuated by the subject, which is the substance. For this particular whiteness is called *this* because it exists in this particular subject. And so it is reasonable that the individuals of the genus substance should have a special name of their own; for they are called *hypostases,*[3] or first substances.

Further still, in a more special and perfect way, the particular and the individual are found in rational substances, which have dominion over their own actions, and which are not only made to act, as are others, but act of themselves; for actions belong to singulars. Therefore, individuals of a rational nature even have a special name among other substances; and this name is *person.*

Thus the term *individual substance* is placed in the definition of person, as signifying the singular in the genus of substance; and the term *rational nature* is added, as signifying the singular in the class of rational substances.

Reply Obj. 1. Although this or that singular may not be definable, yet what belongs to the general idea of singular can be defined; and so the Philosopher gives a definition of first substance.[4] This is also the way in which Boethius defines person.

Reply Obj. 2. In the opinion of some, the term *substance* in the definition of person stands for first substance, which is the hypostasis;[5] nor is the term *individual* superfluously added, inasmuch as by the name of hypostasis or first substance the idea of universality and of part is excluded. For we do not say that man-in-general is an hypostasis, nor that the hand is, since it is only a part. But when *individual* is added, the idea of assumptibility is excluded from person; for the human nature in Christ is not a person, since it is assumed by a greater — that is, by the Word of God. It is, however, better to say that substance is here taken in a general sense, as divided into first and second, and that when *individual* is added, it is restricted to first substance.

Reply Obj. 3. Since substantial differences are unknown to us, or at least unnamed by us, it is sometimes necessary to use accidental differences in their place; as, for example, we may say that fire is a simple, hot, and dry body: for proper accidents are the effects of substantial forms, and make them known. Likewise, terms expressive of intention can be used in defining

---

[3] Cf. Boethius, *De Duab. Nat.,* III (PL 64, 1344).
[4] *Cat.,* V (2 a II).
[5] Richard of St. Victor, *De Trin.,* IV, 4; 20 (PL 196, 932; 943); Alex of Hales, *Summa Theol.,* II, no. 387 (I, 571).

realities if used to signify things which are unnamed. And so the term *individual* is placed in the definition of person to signify the mode of subsistence which belongs to particular substances.

Reply Obj. 4. According to the Philosopher, the term *nature* was first used to signify *the generation of living things*, which is called nativity.[6] And because this kind of generation comes from an intrinsic principle, this term is extended to signify *the intrinsic principle of any kind of movement*. In this sense he defines *nature*.[7] And since this kind of principle is either formal or material, both matter and form are commonly called nature. And as the essence of anything is completed by the form, for this reason the essence of anything, signified by the definition, is commonly called nature. And here nature is taken in that sense. Hence Boethius says that *nature is the specific difference giving its form to each thing;*[8] for the specific difference completes the definition, and is derived from the proper form of a thing. So in the definition of *person*, which means the singular in a determined *genus*, it was more correct for Boethius to use the term *nature* than *essence*, because the latter is taken from being, which is most common.

Reply Obj. 5. The soul is a part of the human species; and so, although it may exist in a separate state, yet since it retains its capacity for union, it cannot be called an individual substance, which is the hypostasis or first substance, as neither can the hand, nor any other part of man. Hence neither the definition nor the name of person belongs to it.

---

[6] *Metaph.*, IV, 4 (1014 b 16).
[7] Aristotle, *Phys.*, II, I (192b 14).
[8] *De Duab. Nat.*, I (PL 64, 1432).

4. Substance, Essence, and Subsistence

Whether Person is the Same as Hypostasis, Subsistence,
and Essence?

St. Thomas Aquinas, *Summa Theologiae*, I, a. 29, art. 2.*

We proceed thus to the Second Article: —

Objection 1. It would seem that person is the same as *hypostasis*, *subsistence*, and *essence*. For Boethius says that the Greeks called the individual substance of a rational nature by the name *hypostasis*.[1] But this with us signifies person. Therefore person is altogether the same as *hypostasis*.

Obj. 2. Further, as we say there are three persons in God, so we say there are three subsistences in God; which implies that *person* and *subsistence* have the same meaning. Therefore *person* and *subsistence* mean the same.

---

* Pegis, *op. cit.*
[1] *De Duab. Nat.*, III (PL 64, 1344).

Obj. 3. Further, Boethius says that οὐσία which means essence, signifies a being composed of matter and form.[2] Now, that which is composed of matter and form is the individual substance and is called *hypostasis* and *person.* Therefore all the aforesaid names seem to have the same meaning.

Obj. 4. On the contrary, Boethius says that *genera and species only subsist; whereas individuals not only subsist, but also substand.*[3] But subsistences are so called from subsisting, as substance or hypostasis is so called from substanding. Therefore, since genera and species are not hypostases or persons, these are not the same as subsistences.

Obj. 5. Further, Boethius says that matter is called hypostasis, and form is called οὐσίωσις — that is, subsistence.[4] But neither form nor matter can be called person. Therefore person differs from the others.

I answer that, According to the Philosopher, substance is twofold.[5] In one sense, it means *the quiddity of a thing,* signified by the definition, and thus we say that the definition signifies the substance of a thing; in which sense substance is called by the Greeks οὐσία, which we may call *essence.* In another sense, substance means a *subject* or *suppositum* which subsists in the genus of substance. To this, taken in a general sense, can be applied a name expressive of an intention; and thus it is called the *suppositum.* It is also called by three names signifying a reality — that is, a *thing of nature, subsistence,* and *hypostasis,* according to a threefold consideration of the substance thus named. For, as it exists in itself and not in another, it is called *subsistence;* for we say that those things subsist which exist in themselves, and not in another. As it underlies the accidents, it is called *hypostasis* or *substance.* What these three names signify in common in the whole genus of substances, this name *person* signifies in the genus of rational substances.

Reply Obj. 1. Among the Greeks, the term *hypostasis,* taken in the strict interpretation of the term, signifies any individual of the genus substance; but in the usual way of speaking, it means the individual of a rational nature, by reason of the excellence of that nature.

Reply Obj. 2. As we speak in the plural of *three persons* in God, and *three subsistences,* so the Greeks say *three hypostases.* But because the word *substance,* which, properly speaking, corresponds in meaning to *hypostasis,* is used among us in an equivocal sense (since it sometimes means the essence, and sometimes the hypostasis), in order to avoid any occasion of error, it was thought preferable to use *subsistence* for hypostasis, rather than *substance.*

---

[2] *In Cat. Arist.,* I (PL 64, 184).
[3] *De Duab. Nat.,* III (PL 64, 1344).
[4] *In Cat. Arist.,* I De subst. (PL 64, 182). Cf. St. Albert, *Sent.,* I, d. xxiii, a. 4, arg. I (XXV 591).
[5] *Metaph.,* IV, 8 (1017 b 23).

Reply Obj. 3. Strictly speaking, the essence is what is expressed by the definition. Now, the definition comprises the principles of the species, but not the individual principles. Hence in things composed of matter and form, the essence signifies not only the form, nor only the matter, but what is composed of matter and the common form, as the principles of the species. But what is composed of this matter and this form has the nature of hypostasis and person. For soul, flesh, and bone belong to the nature of this man. Therefore hypostasis and person add the individual principles to the notion of essence; nor are these identified with the essence in things composed of matter and form, as we said above when considering the divine simplicity.[6]

Reply Obj. 4. Boethius says that genera and species subsist,[7] inasmuch as it belongs to some individual things to subsist; for which the reason is that they belong to genera and species comprised in the predicament of substance, and not because species and genera themselves subsist, except in the opinion of Plato, who asserted that the species of things subsisted separately from singular things.[8] To substand, however, belongs to the same individual things in relation to accidents, which are outside the essence of genera and species.

Reply Obj. 5. The individual composed of matter and form substands in relation to accident from the very nature of matter. Hence Boethius says: *A simple form cannot be a subject.*[9] Its self-subsistence, however, is derived from the nature of its form, which does not enter an already subsisting thing, but gives actual existence to the matter, and so enables the individual to subsist. On this account, therefore, he ascribes hypostasis to matter, and οὐσίωσις or subsistence, to the form, because the matter is the principle of substanding, and the form is the principle of subsisting.

---

[6] Q. 3, a. 4.
[7] In Porphyrium I (PL 64, 85).
[8] Cf. ibid.
[9] De Trin., II, 2 (PL 64, 1250).

READINGS FOR CHAPTER V. POTENCY AND ACT; ESSENCE AND EXISTENCE

1. The Division of Potency Into Active and Passive. The Nature of Incapacity and Privation

A. Aristotle, *Metaphysics*, IX, ch. 1, 1045 b 27–1046 a 35.*

We have dealt then with the primary kind of being and the one to which all the other categories of being are referred, namely, substance. For it is in reference to the concept of substance that the other categories are called beings, i.e., quantity, quality, and others which are spoken of in this way; for all involve the concept of substance, as we have stated in our first discussions. And since being is used in one sense of quiddity or quantity or quality, and in another sense of potency and actuality and activity, let us now establish the truth about potency and actuality. And first let us consider potency in the most proper sense of the term, although not the one most useful for our present purpose; for potency and actuality are found in more things than those which are referred merely to motion. But when we have spoken about this sense of potency we shall, in our discussions about actuality, also explain the other senses of potency.

That the terms *potency* and *can* are used in many senses we have made evident elsewhere. And all of those senses of potency which are equivocal may be dismissed; for some senses of potency or power are merely figurative, as in geometry. And we say that things are possible or impossible because they either are or are not in some particular way. But all those potencies belonging to the same species are principles and are referred to one primary kind of potency, which is the principle of change in some other thing inasmuch as it is other. For one kind is a potency for being acted upon, which is, in the patient itself, the principle of its being passively moved by another inasmuch as it is other; and another kind of potency is the state of insusceptibility to change for the worse and to corruption by some other thing inasmuch as it is other, i.e., by a principle of change. And the intelligible character of the primary kind of potency is found in all of these terms. Again, these potencies are said to be potencies either just for acting or for being acted upon, or for acting or being acted upon well, so that in these latter kinds of potencies the notes of the prior kind are somehow present.

It is evident, then, that in one sense the potency for acting and for being acted upon is one; for a thing is potential both because it itself has the potency for being acted upon, and because something else can be acted

* Translation of Aristotle's *Metaphysics* and St. Thomas' *Commentary* are by John P. Rowan, Ph.D.

upon by it. And in another sense these potencies are different; for the one is in the patient, since it is because it has a principle, and because matter is a principle, that the patient is acted upon and changed by something else. For what is oily is capable of being burnt, and what is yielding in some way is capable of being broken (and the supposit is capable of being expressed);[1] and the same is true in other cases. And another kind of potency is in the agent, as the potency to heat and the potency to build — the former in the thing capable of heating, and the latter in the person capable of building. Hence inasmuch as a thing is by nature a unity, it cannot be acted upon by itself; for it is one thing and not also something else.

And incapacity or impossibility is the privation contrary to such potency, so that every potency and incapacity belong to the same subject and refer to the same attribute. And there are various kinds of privation; for there is one kind of privation when a thing does not have some attribute which it is naturally disposed to have, either in general, or when it is naturally disposed to have it. And this is so either in a particular way, for example, completely, or even in any way at all. And in some cases if things are naturally disposed to have some attribute and do not have it as a result of force, we say that they are deprived of it.

B. St. Thomas, *Commentary on the Metaphysics*, IX, lesson 1, nos. 1768–1785.

[1768.] Having established the truth about being as divided into the ten categories, the Philosopher's aim here is to establish the truth about being as divided into potency and actuality.

This is divided into two parts. In the first he links up this discussion with the foregoing one, and explains what he intends to do in this book. In the second he carries out his announced plan, where he says, "That the terms."

He accordingly points out, first, that he has already discussed above the primary kind of being to which all the other categories of being are referred, namely, substance. And he explains that all the other categories are referred to substance as the primary kind of being, because all other beings — quantity, quality, and the like — involve the concept of substance. For being is said of quantity because it is the measure of substance; and of quality because it is a certain disposition of substance; and the same thing applies in the case of the other categories. This is evident from the fact that all accidents involve the concept of substance, since in the definition of any accident it is necessary to include its proper subject; for example, in the definition of snub it is necessary to include nose. This was made clear at the beginning of Book VII.

---

[1] The equivalent of this statement is not found in the Greek text, although it does occur in St. Thomas' reading. See C 1782.

[1769.] But being is variously divided. One division is based on its designation as *whatness* (i.e., substance), quantity, or quality, which is
its division into the ten categories. Another is its division into potency and
actuality or activity, from which the word *actuality* (or *act*) is derived, as is
explained later on. And for this reason it is now necessary to deal with potency
and actuality.

[1770.] It is first necessary to speak of potency in its most proper sense,
although not the one which is most useful for our present purpose.
For potency and actuality are referred in most cases to things in motion,
because motion is the actuality of a being in potency. But the principal aim
of this branch of science is to consider potency and actuality, not insofar
as they are found in mobile beings, but insofar as they accompany being
in general. Hence potency and actuality are also found in immobile beings,
for example, in intellectual ones.

[1771.] And when we shall have spoken about the potency found in mobile
things, and about its corresponding actuality, we will also be able
to explain potency and actuality insofar as they are found in the intelligible
things classed as separate substances, which are treated later on. This order
is a fitting one, since sensible things, which are in motion, are more evident
to us, and therefore by means of them we may attain a knowledge of the
substances of immobile things.

[1772.] From this consideration the meaning of another text also becomes
evident, which says, "And potency in the proper sense is not the only
one which is useful for our present purpose," because even though the potency
which is present in mobile things is potency in its most proper sense, this is
still not the only sense in which potency is used, as was explained. And it is
useful for our present purpose, not as though it were the principal object of
our investigation, but because we may attain a knowledge of the other kinds
of potency from it.

[1773.] "That the terms."

Then he deals with potency and actuality; and this is divided into three
parts. In the first he discusses potency; and in the second, actuality, where
he says, "Since we have dealt"; and in the third, the relationshop of actuality
to potency, where he says, "Since we have established."

The first is divided into two parts. In the first of these he discusses
potency itself. In the second he discusses potency in relation to the things
in which it is found, where he says, "And since some."

The first is divided into two parts. In the first he deals with potency; and
in the second, with incapacity, where he says, "And incapacity." In regard
to the first he does two things. First, he explains the different senses of
potency. Second, he makes evident a truth about potency from the things
previously laid down, where he says, "It is evident."

He accordingly says, first, that it has been shown elsewhere, i.e., in Book V of this work, that the words *potency* and *can* have a multiplicity of meanings. But in some cases this multiplicity is a multiplicity of equivocation, and in others it is a multiplicity of analogy. For some things are said to be capable or incapable because they have some principle within themselves, and this refers to those senses in which all potencies are said to be such not equivocally but analogously. But other things are not said to be capable or able because of some principle which they have within themselves; and in their case the term potency is used equivocally.

[1774.]   Therefore, with regard to those senses in which the term potency is used equivocally, he says that these must be dismissed for the present. For the term potency is referred to some things, not because of some principle which they have, but in a figurative sense, as is done in geometry; for the square of a line is called its power (*potentia*), and a line is said to be capable of becoming its square. And similarly in the case of numbers it can be said that the number three is capable of becoming the number nine, which is its square; because when the number three is multiplied by itself the number nine results, for three times three make nine; and when a line, which is the root of a square, is multiplied by itself, a square results. And the same thing applies in the case of numbers. Hence the root of a square bears some likeness to the matter from which a thing is made; and for this reason the root is said to be capable of becoming its square as matter is capable of becoming a thing.

[1775.]   And similarly in the considerations of logic we say that some things are possible or impossible, not because of some potency, but because they either are or are not in some way; for those things are called possible whose opposites can be true, whereas those are called impossible whose opposites cannot be true. This difference depends on the relationship of predicate to subject, because sometimes the predicate is repugnant to the subject, as in the case of impossible things, and sometimes it is not, as in the case of possible things.

[1776.]   Passing over these senses of potency, then, we must consider those potencies which are reduced to one species, because each of these is a principle. And all potencies spoken of in this sense are reduced to some principle from which all the others derive their meaning; and this is an active principle, which is the source of change in some other thing inasmuch as it is other. He says this because it is possible for an active principle to be at the same time in the mobile or patient, as when something moves itself; although it is not mover and moved, or agent and patient, in the same respect. Hence the principle designated as active potency is said to be a principle of change in some other thing inasmuch as it is other; because, even though an active principle can be found in the same thing as a passive principle, this still does not happen insofar as it is the same, but insofar as it is other.

[1777.] That the other potencies are reduced to this principle which is called active potency is evident; for in one sense passive potency means the principle by which one thing is moved by some other thing inasmuch as it is other. He says this because, even if the same thing might be acted upon by itself, this still does not happen insofar as it is the same, but insofar as it is other. Now this potency is reduced to a first active potency, because when anything undergoes change this is caused by an agent. And for this reason passive potency is also reduced to active potency.

[1778.] In another sense potency means a certain state of insusceptibility (or impossibility) "to change for the worse," i.e., a disposition whereby a thing is such that it cannot undergo change for the worse; i.e., that it cannot undergo corruption as a result of some other thing "inasmuch as it is other," namely, by a principle of change which is an active principle.

[1779.] Now it is evident that both of these senses of potency imply something within us which is referred to the undergoing of a change. For in the one sense the term designates a principle by reason of which someone cannot be acted upon; and in the other sense it designates a principle by reason of which someone can be acted upon. Hence, since the state of being acted upon depends on action, the definition "of the primary kind of potency," namely, active potency, must be given in the definition of both senses of potency. Thus these two senses of potency are reduced to the first, namely, to active potency, as to something prior.

[1780.] Again, in another sense potencies are spoken of not only in relation to action and being acted upon but in relation to what is done well in each case. For example, we say that someone is capable of walking, not because he can walk in any way at all, but because he can walk well; and in an opposite sense we say of one who limps that he cannot walk. Similarly, we say that wood is capable of being burned because it can be burned easily; but we say that green wood is incapable of being burned because it cannot be burned easily. Hence it is clear that in the definitions of those potencies which are described as potencies for acting and being acted upon well, there are included the concepts of those primary potencies which were described as potencies for acting and being acted upon without qualification; for example, to act is included in to act well, and to be acted upon is included in to be acted upon well. Hence it is obvious that all of these senses of potency are reduced to one primary sense, namely, to active potency; and therefore it is also evident that this multiplicity is not the multiplicity of equivocation but of analogy.

[1781.] "It is evident, then."

From what has been said he now indicates something that is true about the foregoing potencies. He says that in one sense the potency for acting and that for being acted upon are one, and in another sense they are not. They are one potency if the relationship of the one to the other is considered;

for one is spoken of in reference to the other. For a thing can be said to have a potency for being acted upon, either because it has of itself a potency by which it may be potency if the relationship of the one to the other is considered; for one is spoken of in reference to the other. For a thing can be said to have a potency for being acted upon, either because it has of itself a potency by which it may be acted upon, or because it has a potency by which something else may be acted upon by it. And in this second sense active potency is the same as passive potency; for by reason of the fact that a thing has active potency it has a power by which something else may be acted upon by it.

[1782.]   However, if these two potencies — active and passive — are taken in reference to the subject in which they are found, then in this sense active and passive potency are different; for passive potency exists in a patient, since a patient is acted upon by reason of some principle existing within itself; and matter is of this sort. Now passive potency is nothing but the principle by which one thing is acted upon by another; for example, to be burned is to undergo a change, and the material principle by reason of which a thing is capable of being burned is the oily or the fat. Hence the potency itself is present as a passive principle in the thing capable of being burned. And similarly what yields to the thing touching it so that it receives an impression from it, as wax or something of this sort, is capable of doing so inasmuch as it is impressionable. "And the supposit," i.e., the male, is the proper subject of the modification resulting in an eunuch.[1] The same is true of other things which are acted upon insofar as they have within themselves a principle for being acted upon, which is called passive potency. But active potency is in the agent, as heat in the thing which heats, and the art of building in the builder.

[1783.]   And since active potency and passive potency are present in different things, it is obvious that nothing is acted upon by itself inasmuch as it is naturally disposed to act or to be acted upon. However, it is possible for something to be acted upon by itself accidentally, as a physician heals himself not inasmuch as he is a physician but inasmuch as he is ill. But in this case a thing is not acted upon by itself, because, properly speaking, one of the aforesaid principles is present in one and the same thing, and not the other. For the principle of being acted upon is not present in the one having the principle of action except accidentally, as has been said (744:C 1782).

[1784].   "And incapacity."

Here he establishes the truth about incapacity, saying that incapacity which is the contrary of the aforesaid potency or capacity, or impossibility, which is referred to incapacity of this sort, is the privation of the aforesaid potency. However, he says this to distinguish it from the impossible

---

[1] The reading which St. Thomas is following here has *eunuchizari* in place of *enuntiabile* in the Latin version of the Cathala-Spiazzi edition.

which signifies some mode of falsity, which is not referred to any incapacity, just as the possible is also not referred to any potency. For since privation and possession belong to the same subject and refer to the same attribute, potency and incapacity must belong to the same subject and refer to the same attribute. Hence there are as many senses of incapacity as there are of potency, to which it is opposed.

[1785.] But it must be noted that the term *privation* is used in many senses. For in one sense whatever does not have some attribute can be said to be deprived of it, as when we say that a stone is deprived of sight because it does not have sight; and in another sense a thing is said to be deprived only of what it can have and does not have. And this may happen in two ways: in one way when the thing does not have it at all, as if we say that a dog is deprived of sight when he cannot see at all. And, in another way, if it does not have it when it is naturally disosed to have it. Hence a dog is not said to be deprived of sight before the ninth day. This sense of privation is again divided. For in one sense a thing is said to be deprived of some attribute because it does not have it in a particular way, namely, completely and well; as when we say that someone who does not see well is blind. And in another sense a thing is said to be deprived of some attribute when it does not have it in any way at all; for example, we say that a person is deprived of sight who does not have sight at all. But sometimes force is included in the notion of privation, and then we say that some things are deprived of certain attributes when those which they are naturally disposed to have are removed by force.

2. Various Views on the Nature of Potency

A. Aristotle, *Metaphysics*, IX, ch. 3 and 4, 1046 b 29–1047 b 30.
Chapter 3

There are some, such as the members of the Megaric school, who say that a thing has a potency for acting only when it is acting, and that when it is not acting it does not have this potency; for example, one who is not building does not have the power of building, but only one who is building when he is building; and it is the same in other cases.

It is not difficult to see the absurd consequences of this position. For it is evident, according to this view, that a man will not be a builder if he is not building; because to be a builder is to be able to build. The same is true in the case of the other arts. Therefore, if it is impossible to have such arts if one has not at some time learnt and acquired them, and if it is impossible not to have them if one has not at some time lost them (either through forgetfulness or through some change or through the passage of time; for this cannot occur as a result of the object being destroyed, since it always exists), when one will have ceased to use an art he will not have it; and yet he will be able to build forthwith, thus somehow getting it back again.

And the same thing will be true in the case of non-living things; for neither the cold nor the hot nor the sweet nor the bitter nor any sensible thing will exist in any way at all, if they are not being sensed. Hence they will have to maintain the theory that Protagoras did.

In fact nothing will have senses unless it is sensing or acting. Therefore, if that is blind which does not have the power of sight, though it is designed by nature to have it, and when it is designed by nature to have it, and so long as it exists, the same persons will be blind many times during the day; and deaf as well.

Further, if what is deprived of a potency is incapable, it will be impossible for that to come into being which has not yet been generated; but he who says that what cannot possibly be generated either is or will be, is in error; for this is what impossible or incapable means. Hence these theories do away with both motion and generation; for what is standing will always stand, and what is sitting will always sit, because if it is sitting it will not get up, since it is impossible for anything to get up which has no possibility of doing so.

Therefore, if it is impossible to maintain this, it is evident that potency and actuality are different. But these views make potency and actuality the same, and for this reason it is no small thing which they seek to destroy. Hence it is possible for a thing to be capable of being and yet not be, and for a thing not to be and yet be capable of being. And it is similar in the case of the other categories; for example, a thing may be capable of walking and yet not walk, and be capable of not walking and yet walk.

Moreover, a thing has a potency if there is nothing impossible in its having the actuality of that of which it is said to have the potency. I mean, for example, that if a thing is capable of sitting, and it turns out to be sitting, there will be nothing impossible in its having a sitting position; and it is similar if it is capable of being moved or of moving something, or of standing or causing a thing to stand, or of being or coming to be, or of not being or not coming to be.

And the word *actuality*, which is combined with entelechy, is extended chiefly from motion to other things; for act seems to be identified mainly with motion. And for this reason they do not assign motion to non-existent things, but they do assign the other categories. For example, non-existent things are considered the objects of intellect and desire but not to be in motion. And the reason is that they would have to exist actually even though they did not exist actually; for some non-existent things are potential. Yet they do not exist, because they do not exist in complete actuality.

Chapter 4

Now if what has been called potential or possible is such because something follows from it, it is evident that it cannot be true to say that a thing is possible but will not be, because things which cannot possibly be would then disappear. An example would be if someone, thinking that nothing is impossible, were to affirm that it is possible for the diagonal of a square to be commensurate, even though it is not commensurate; because nothing prevents a thing that is capable of being or of coming to be from not being or not coming to be. But this conclusion necessarily follows from the things laid down above. And if we suppose that which is not, but is capable[1] of being, to be or to have come into being, nothing would be impossible. But in this case something impossible will occur; for it is impossible that a diagonal be commensurate.[2] For to be false and to be impossible are not the same; for while it is false that you are now standing, it is not impossible.

And at the same time it is evident that if, when A exists, B must exist, then, if A is possible, B must be possible; for if it is not necessary that B be possible, there is nothing to prevent its not being possible. Therefore, let A be possible. And if A is possible, then when A is possible, if A is assumed to exist, nothing impossible follows, but B necessarily exists. But this was supposed to be impossible. Therefore, let B be impossible. Then if B must be impossible, A must be so. But the first was supposed to be impossible; therefore so also is the second. Hence, if A is possible, B will be possible also, i.e., if they are so related that if, when A exists, B must exist. Therefore, if when A and B are so related, B is not possible, then A and B will not be related in the way supposed. On the other hand, if, when A is possible, B must be possible, then if A exists, B must exist. For to say that B must be possible if A is possible, means that if A exists both when it exists and inasmuch as it is possible for it to exist, then B must also exist and exist in that way.

B. St. Thomas, *Commentary on the Metaphysics*, IX, lesson 3, nos. 1795–1814.

[1795.] Having compared one kind of potency with another in the above discussion, here the Philosopher begins to explain how potency and actuality are found in the same subject. This is divided into two parts. In the first he rejects the false opinions of some men. In the second he establishes the truth, where he says, "And since among."

The first is divided into two parts. In the first part he rejects the opinion of those who said that a thing is possible or potential only when it is in a state of actuality. In the second part he rejects the opinion of those who maintain the reverse of this: that all things are potential or possible, even though they are not in a state of actuality, where he says, "Now if what."

In regard to the first he does two things. First, he rejects the erroneous opinion referred to. Second, he explains what it is to be potential or possible, and what it is to be actual, where he says, "Moreover, a thing."

---

[1] Reading *aliquid ens possibile* . . . ; the term *possibile* has been omitted from the Latin version of the Cathala-Spiazzi edition.

[2] This statement has been omitted from the Cathala-Spiazzi version; but see Greek text, 1047 b 12. The statement is also presupposed by the commentary, see C 1808.

In regard to the first he does three things. First, he gives this opinion. Second, he destroys it, where he says, "It is not difficult." Third, he draws his intended conclusion, where he says, "Therefore, if it."

He accordingly says, first, that some said that a thing is in a state of potency or capability only when it is acting; for example, a man who is not actually building is incapable of building, but he is capable of building only when he is actually building; and they speak in a similar way about other things. The reason for this position seems to be that they thought that all things come about necessarily because of some connection between causes. Thus if all things come about necessarily, it follows that those things which do not, are impossible.

[1796.]   "It is not difficult."

Then he raises arguments against the aforesaid opinion, and these reduce it to its absurd consequences. The first is as follows: to be building is to have the power or capability of building. Therefore, if no one has the power or capability of acting except when he is acting, no one is a builder except when he is building. And the same thing will be true of the other arts; for all arts are certain capabilities or potencies, as has been pointed out. It follows, then, that no one will have an art except when he is exercising it.

[1797.]   But this is shown to be impossible if two assumptions are made. The first is this: if someone did not at first have an art it would be impossible for him to have it later unless he had learned it or acquired it in some way, i.e., by discovery.

[1798.]   The second assumption is that if someone had an art it would be impossible for him not to have the same art later, unless he lost it in some way, either through forgetfulness or through some illness or through the passage of a long time during which the knowledge was not exercised; for this is the cause of forgetfulness. Now it cannot be that someone should lose an art as a result of the destruction of its object, as it sometimes happens[1] that true knowledge is lost when a thing is changed; for example, when someone makes a true judgment that Socrates is sitting, his true judgment is destroyed when Socrates stands up. But this cannot be said about an art; for an art is not a knowledge of what exists, but of what is to be made; and so long as the matter from which an art can produce something continues to exist, the object of that art always exists. Hence an art cannot be lost when its object is destroyed, except in the ways mentioned.

[1799.]   Now from these two assumptions the Philosopher argues as follows: if a man does not have an art except when he is exercising it, then when he begins to exercise it he has it anew. Therefore he must either have learned it or acquired it in some other way. And similarly when he ceases to exercise an art it follows that he lacks that art, and thus he loses the art which he had at first either through forgetfulness or through some

---
[1] Reading *contingit* for *convenit*.

change or through the passage of time. But both of these are clearly false; and therefore it is not true that someone has a potency only when he is acting.

[1800.] "And the same."

Here he gives the second argument, which now has to do with the irrational principles present in non-living things, namely, hot and cold, sweet and bitter, and other qualities of this kind, which are active principles changing the senses and thus are potencies. Now if potency is present in a thing only when it is acting, it follows that nothing is hot or cold, sweet or bitter, and so forth, except when it is being sensed through a change in the senses. But this is clearly false; for if it were true it would follow that Protagoras' opinion would be true, since he said that all the properties and natures of things have existence only in being sensed and in being thought. And from this it would follow that contradictories would be true at the same time, since different men have contradictory opinions about the same thing. Now the Philosopher argued dialectically against this position in Book IV. Therefore it is false that potency exists only when there is actuality.

[1801.] "In fact nothing."

Here he gives the fourth argument, which is as follows: sense is a kind of potency. Therefore, if potency exists only when there is actuality, it follows that a man has sensory power only when he is sensing, for example, the power of sight or hearing. But one who does not have the power of sight when he is naturally disposed to have it is blind; and one who does not have the power of hearing is deaf. Hence he will be blind and deaf many times on the same day. But this is clearly false, for a blind man does not afterwards regain sight nor a deaf man hearing.

[1802.] "Further, if what."

Here he gives the fourth argument, which is as follows: it is impossible for a thing to act which does not have the power to act. Therefore, if one has a potency or power only when he is acting, it follows that when he is not acting it is impossible for him to act. But whoever says that something incapable of happening either is or will be, is mistaken. This is evident from the meaning of the word *impossible*; for the impossible is said to be false because it cannot happen. It follows, then, that something which is not is incapable of coming to be in any way. And thus potency so understood will do away with motion and generation; because one who is standing will always stand, and one who is sitting will always sit. For if anyone is sitting, he will never stand afterwards, because so long as he is not standing he does not have the power to stand. Hence it is impossible for him to stand, and consequently it is impossible for him to get up. Similarly what is not white will be incapable of being white, and thus could not be made white. The same holds true in the case of all other things.

[1803.]   "Therefore, if."

He draws his intended conclusion, saying that, if the absurdities mentioned above cannot be admitted, it is obvious that potency and actuality are different. But those who hold the foregoing position make potency and actuality the same insofar as they say that something has potency only when it is in a state of actuality. And from this it is evident that they wish to remove from nature something of no little importance, for they eliminate motion and generation, as has been stated. Hence, since this cannot be admitted, it is obvious that something is capable of being which yet is not, and that something is capable of not being which yet is. And "it is similar in the case of the other categories," or predicaments; because it is possible from someone who is not walking to walk, and conversely it is possible from someone who is walking not to walk.

[1804.]   "Moreover, a thing."

Here he explains what it is to be potential and what it is to be actual. First, he explains what it is to be potential. He says that that is said to be potential from which nothing impossible follows when it is assumed to be actual; for example, if one were to say that it is possible for someone to sit if nothing impossible follows when he is assumed to sit. And the same holds true of being moved and of moving something, and other cases of this kind.

[1805.]   "And the word *actuality*."

Second, he explains what it is to be actual. He says that the word *actuality* is used to signify entelechy and perfection, namely, the form, and other things of this kind, as any action at all is derived properly from motion, so far as the origin of the word is concerned. For since words are signs of intellectual conceptions, we first give names to those things which we first understand, even though they may be subsequent in the order of nature. Now of all acts which are perceived by us in a sensible way, motion is the best known and most evident to us; and therefore the word actuality was first referred to motion, and from motion the word was extended to other things.

[1806.]   And for this reason motion is not attributed to nonexistent things, although certain of the other categories mentioned above are attributed to nonexistent things; for we say that nonexistent things are intelligible, or thinkable, or even desirable, but we do not say that they are moved. For, since to be moved means to be actual, it follows that things which do not exist actually would exist actually; but this is obviously false. or even if some nonexistent things are potential, they are still not said to be, since they are not actual.

[1807.] "Now if what."

Having destroyed the opinion of those who claim that nothing is possible except when it is actual, the Philosopher now destroys the opposite opinion of those who claim that all things are possible; and in regard to this he does two things. First, he destroys this opinion. Second, he establishes a truth about the succession of possible things, where he says, "And at the same."

He accordingly says, first, that, if it is true that a thing is said to be possible because something follows from it, inasmuch as the possible has been defined as that from which nothing impossible follows if it is assumed to exist, it is evident that the statements of some thinkers that anything is possible even if it never will be, cannot be true; since as a result of this position impossible things will be eliminated. For example, if one were to say that the diagonal of a square can be commensurate with a side, even though it is not commensurate with it (and one might speak in the same way about other impossible things), and not think that it is impossible for the diameter of a square to be commensurate with a side, those who maintain this position, I say, speak truly in one sense and in another not.

[1808.] For there are some things which nothing will prevent us from designating as capable or possible of coming to be, even though they never will be or ever come to be; but this cannot be said of all things. Yet according to the doctrine laid down above, and which it is not necessary for us to assume, only those things are capable of being or coming to be, even though they are not, from which nothing impossible follows when they are posited. However, when it is posited that the diagonal of a square is commensurate, an impossible conclusion follows. Thus it cannot be said that it is possible for the diagonal to be commensurate; for it is not only false but impossible.

[1809.] Now some things are false only but not impossible, as that Socrates sits or that he stands. For to be false and to be impossible are not the same; for example, it is false that you are now standing, but it is not impossible. Therefore the foregoing opinion is true of some things, because some are possible even though they are false. However, it is not true of all things, because some are both false and impossible.

[1810.] "And at the same."

And since he had said that a thing is judged possible because nothing impossible follows from it, he indicates the way in which there are possible consequents. He says that not only is the aforesaid position destroyed by the definition of the possible given above, but it is also evident at the same time that if the antecedent of a conditional proposition is possible, the consequent will also be possible; so that if this conditional proposition, "If when A is, B is," is true, then if A is possible, B must be possible.

[1811.]   Now in order to understand this we must note that the word
          possible is used in two senses. It is used, first, in contradistinction to
the necessary, as when we call those things possible which are capable
either of being or not being. And when possible is taken in this way, the
foregoing remarks do not apply. For nothing prevents the antecedent from
being capable of being or not being, even though the consequent is necessary, as is clear in this hypothesis, "If Socrates laughs, he is a man."

[1812.]   The word possible is used in a second sense inasmuch as it is
          common both to those things which are necessary and to those
which are capable of being or not being, according as the possible is
distinguished from the impossible. And the Philosopher is speaking of the
possible in this way here when he says that the consequent must be possible
if the antecedent was possible.

[1813.]   For let it be assumed that this conditional proposition is true:
          If A is, then B is; and let it be assumed that the antecedent, A,
is possible. Then it is necessary that B either be possible or not. Now if it
is necessary, then the assumption follows. But if it is not necessary, nothing
prevents the opposite from being assumed, namely, that B is not possible.
But this cannot stand; for A is assumed to be possible, and when it is
assumed to be possible, it is at the same time assumed that nothing impossible follows from it; for the possible was defined above as that from which
nothing impossible follows. But B follows from A, as was assumed, and B
was assumed to be impossible; for to be impossible is the same as not to
be possible. Therefore A will not be possible if B, which was held to be
impossible, follows from it. Therefore let B be assumed to be impossible,
and if it is impossible and if A is given B must exist, then both the first and
the second, namely, A and B, will be impossible.

[1814.]   In which place it must be noted that the following proposition is
          correct: if the consequent is impossible, the antecedent is impos-
sible; but the reverse is not true. For nothing prevents something necessary
from being a consequence of the impossible, as in this conditional proposition. "If man is an ass, he is an animal." Therefore what the Philosopher
says here must not be understood as meaning that, if the first, i.e., the
antecedent, were impossible, then the second, i.e., the consequent, would
also be impossible. But it must be understood to mean that if the consequent
is impossible, both will be impossible. Therefore it is obvious that, if A and
B are so related that when A is, B must be, it necessarily follows that, if A
is possible, B will be possible; and if B is not possible when A is possible,
then A and B are not related in the way supposed, namely, that B follows
from A. But it is necessary that when A is possible, B must be possible, if
when A exists it is necessary that B exist. Therefore when I say "If A is,
B is," this means that B must be possible if A is possible, in the sense that it
is possible for B to exist at the same time and in the way in which A is
possible; for it is not possible that it should exist at any time and in any way.

3. Actuality and Its Various Meanings

A. Aristotle, *Metaphysics*, IX, ch. 6, 1048 a 25–1048 b 36.

Since we have dealt with the kind of potency which is related to motion, let us now settle the issue about actuality; both what it is and what kind of thing it is. For in making our distinctions it will become evident at the same time, with regard to the potential, that we speak of the potential not only as that which is disposed by nature to move something else or be moved by something else, either in an unqualified sense or in some special way, but that we also use the word in a different sense. And for this reason we will also come upon these points in making our investigations.

Now actuality is the existence of a thing not in the sense in which we say that a thing exists potentially, as when we say that Mercury is potentially in the wood, and a half in the whole, because it can be separated from it; and as we also say that one who is not theorizing is a man of science if he is able to theorize; but the opposite of this exists actually.

What we mean becomes evident in particular cases by induction, and we should not look for the definition (boundaries) of every thing, but perceive what is proportional; for it is as one who is building to the thing capable of being built, and as one who is awake to one who is asleep, and as one who sees to one whose eyes are closed but who has the power of sight, and as that which is separated out of matter to matter, and as that which has been worked on to that which has not; and let actuality be defined by one member of this division and potency by the other.

However, things are not all said to be actual in the same way, but proportionally, as this is in that or to that; indeed, some are as motion to potency, and others as substance to some matter.

But the infinite and the void and all other such things are said to exist potentially and actually in a different sense from that which applies to many beings; for example, from that which sees or walks or is visible. For these things can be verified, and verified without qualification; for what is visible is so designated sometimes because it is being seen, and sometimes because it is capable of being seen. But the infinite does not exist potentially in the sense that it will ever have actual separate existence, but it exists potentially only in knowledge. For since the process of division never comes to an end, this shows that this actuality exists potentially, but not so that it ever exists separately.[1] Therefore, regarding actuality, both what it is and what kind of thing it is will be evident to us from these and similar considerations.

---

[1] At this point the Latin version of Aristotle omits a translation of the Greek text. See Bekker 1048 b 18–1048 b 35.

B. St. Thomas, *Commentary on the Metaphysics*, IX, lesson 5,
nos. 1823–1831.

[1823.] Having drawn his conclusion about potency, Aristotle now establishes the truth about actuality; and this is divided into two parts.
In the first he establishes what actuality is. In the second he establishes
what is true when something is in potency to actuality, where he says,
"However, we must."

In regard to the first he does two things. First, he links this up with the
preceding discussion. He says that since we have dealt with the kind of
potency which is found in mobile things, i.e., the kind which is an active
or passive principle of motion, we must now explain what actuality is and
how it is related to potency; because when we will have distinguished the
kinds of actuality, the truth about potency will become evident from this
at the same time. For actuality is found not only in mobile things but also
in immobile ones.

[1824]. And since potency is referred to actuality, it is evident from this
that capability or potency taken in reference to action is attributed
not only to something that is naturally disposed to move something else
actively or be moved by something else passively, either in an unqualified
sense inasmuch as potency is referred alike to acting and being acted upon,
or in some special way inasmuch as potency is referred to what is able to
act or be acted upon well; but capability or potency is also referred to that
actuality which is devoid of motion. For although the word actuality is
derived from motion, as was explained above, it is still not motion alone
that is designated as actuality. Hence, neither is potency referred only to
motion. It is therefore necessary to inquire about these things in our
investigations.

[1825.] "Now actuality."

Second he establishes the truth about actuality. First, he shows what
actuality is; and second, how it is used in a different sense in the case of
different things, where he says, "However, things."

In regard to the first he does two things. First, he shows what actuality is.
He says that a thing is actual when it exists but not in the way in which
it exists when it is potential. For we say that the image of Mercury is in
the wood potentially and not actually before the wood is carved; but once it
has been carved the image of Mercury is then said to be in the wood actually.
And in the same way we say that any part of a continuous whole is in that
whole, because any part (for example, the middle one) is present potentially
inasmuch as it is possible for it to be separated from the whole by dividing
the whole; but after the whole has been divided, that part will now be
present actually. The same thing is true of one who has a science and is not

speculating, for he is capable of speculating even though he is not actually doing so; but to be speculating or contemplating is to be in a state of actuality.

[1826.] "What we mean."

Here he answers an implied question; for someone could ask him to explain what actuality is by giving its definition. And he answers by saying that it is possible to show what we mean (i.e., by actuality) in the case of singular things by proceeding inductively from examples, "and we should not look for the boundaries of everything," i.e., the definition. For simple notions cannot be defined, since an infinite regress in definitions is impossible. But actuality is one of these first simple notions. Hence it cannot be defined.

[1827.] And he says that we can see what actuality is by means of the proportion existing between two things. For example, we may take the proportion of one who is building to the thing capable of being built; and of one who is awake to one asleep; and of one who sees to one whose eyes are closed, since he has the power of sight; and "of that which is separated out of matter," i.e., what is formed by means of the operation of art or of nature, and thus is separated out of unformed matter, to what is not separated out of unformed matter.[1] And similarly we may take the proportion[2] of what has been prepared to what has not been prepared, or of what has been worked on to what has not been worked on. But in each of these opposed pairs one member will be actual and the other potential. And thus by proceeding from particular cases we can come to an understanding in a proportional way of what actuality and potency are.

[1828.] "However, things."

Then he shows that the term actuality is used in different sense; and he gives two different senses in which it is used. First, actuality means action, or operation. And with a view to introducing the different senses of actuality he says, first, that we do not say that all things are actual in the same way but in different ones; and this difference can be considered according to different proportions. For a proportion can be taken in this sense, as when we say that, just as this is in that, so another thing is in something else; for example, just as sight is in the eye, so hearing is in the ear. And the relation of substance (i.e., of form) to matter is taken according to this kind of proportion; for form is said to be in matter.

[1829.] There is another kind of proportion inasmuch as we say that, just as this is related to that, so another thing is related to something else; for example, just as the power of sight is related to the act of seeing,

---

[1] In completing the proportion the Cathala-Spiazzi edition adds "*ad illud quod non est segregatum a materia informi.*" See Spiazzi edition, p. 437, n. 1.
[2] Reading *proportionem* for *per separationem* in keeping with the sense of the text.

so too the power of hearing is related to the act of hearing. And the relation of motion to motive power or of any operation to an operative potency is taken according to this kind of proportion.

[1830.] "But the infinite."

Second, he gives the other sense in which the word actuality is used. He says that the infinite and the empty or the void, and all things of this kind, are said to exist potentially and actually in a different sense from many other beings; for example, what sees and what walks and what is visible. For it is fitting that things of this kind should sometimes exist in an unqualified sense either only potentially or only actually; for example, the visible is actual only when it is seen, and it is potential only when it is capable of being seen but is not actually being seen.

[1831.]   But the infinite is not said to exist potentially in the sense that it may sometimes have separate actual existence alone; but in the case of the infinite, actuality and potentiality are distinguished only in thought and in knowledge. For example, in the case of the infinite in the sense of the infinitely divisible, actuality and potentiality are said to exist at the same time, because the capacity of the infinite for being divided never comes to an end; for when it is actually divided it is still potentially further divisible. However, it is never actually separated from potentiality in such a way that the whole is sometimes actually divided and is incapable of any further division. And the same thing is true of the void; for it is possible for a place to be emptied of this body, but not so as to be a complete void, for it continues to be filled by another body; and thus in the void potentiality always continues to be joined to actuality. The same thing is true of motion and time and other things of this kind which do not have complete being. Then at the end he makes a summary of what has been said. This is evident in the text.

4. Potency and Actuality Compared

A.   Aristotle, *Metaphysics*, IX, ch. 8, 1049 b 4–1050 a 3.

Since we have established the different senses in which the term *prior* is used, it is evident that actuality is prior to potency. And by potency I mean not only that definite kind which is said to be a principle of change in another thing, inasmuch as it is other, but in general every principle of motion or rest. For nature also belongs to the same thing, since it is in the same genus as potency; for it is a principle of motion, although not in another thing but in something inasmuch as it is the same. Therefore actuality is prior to all such potency both in intelligibility and in substance; and in time it is prior in one sense, and in another it is not.

It is evident, then, that actuality is prior to potency in intelligibility; for what is potential in a primary sense is potential because it is possible for it to become actual. I mean, for example, that it is what is capable of building that can build, and what is capable of theorizing that can theorize,[1] and what is capable of being seen that can be seen. And the same reasoning also applies in the case of other things; and therefore it is necessary that the conception or knowledge of the one should precede that of the other.

And actuality is prior to potency in time in the sense that an actuality which is specifically but not numerically the same as a potency is prior to it. I mean that the matter and the seed and the thing capable of seeing, which are a man and grain and seeing potentially but not yet actually, are prior in time to this man and to grain and to the act of seeing which exist actually. But prior to these are other actually existing things from which these have been produced; for what is actual is always produced from something potential by means of something which is actual. Thus man comes from man and musician from musician; for there is always some primary mover, and a mover is already something actual. And in our discussions about substance it was stated that everything which comes to be is produced from something, and this is specifically the same as itself.

And for this reason it seems to be impossible that anyone should be a builder who has not built something, or that anyone should be a harpist who has not played the harp. And the same holds true of all others who are learning; for one who is learning to play the harp learns to play it by playing it. And the same holds true in other cases.

From this arose the sophistical argument that one who does not have a science will be doing the thing which is the object of this science; for one who is learning a science does not have it.

But since some part of what is coming to be has come to be, and in general some part of what is being moved has been moved (as became evident in our discussions on motion[2]), perhaps one who is learning a science must have some part of that science. Hence it is also clear from[3] this that actuality is prior to potency both in the process of generation and in time.

B. St. Thomas, *Commentary on the Metaphysics*, IX, lesson 7, nos. 1844–1855.

[1844.] Having established the truth about potency and actuality, the Philosopher now compares one with the other; and this is divided into three parts. In the first part he compares them from the viewpoint of priority and posteriority; in the second, in terms of being better or worse, where he says, "Furthermore, that"; and in the third in reference to knowledge of the true and the false, where he says, "And it is."

---

[1] The Greek text reads ὁρατικὸν τὸ ὁρᾶν, i.e., "what is capable of seeing is what can see." The Latin version should read *visivum* for *speculatorem* and *videre* for *speculari*. St. Thomas follows the reading of the Latin version given in the Cathala-Spiazzi edition; see: C 1846.

[2] *Physica*, VI, 6 (236b 33).

[3] Reading *ex* for *et*.

In regard to the first he does two things. First, he explains his aim, saying that, since it has been established above, in Book V, that the term prior is used in different senses, it is evident that actuality is prior to potency in different ways. And we are now speaking of potency not only inasmuch as it is a principle of motion in some other thing as other, as active potency was defined above, but universally of every principle, whether it be a principle that causes motion or a principle of immobility or rest or a principle of action devoid of motion[1] (e.g. understanding), because nature also seems to belong to the same thing as potency.

[1845.] For nature is in the same genus as potency itself, because each is a principle of motion, although nature is not a principle of motion in some other thing but in the thing in which it is present as such, as is made clear in Book II of the *Physics*.[2] However, nature is a principle not only of motion but also of immobility. Hence actuality is prior to all such potency both in intelligibility and in substance. And in one sense it is also prior in time, and in another it is not.

[1846.] "It is evident."

Second he proves his thesis. First, he shows that actuality is prior to potency in intelligibility. Second, he shows how it is prior in time, and how it is not, where he says, "And actuality." Third, he shows how it is prior in substance, where he says, "But actuality."

The first is proved as follows: anything that must be used in defining something else is prior to it in intelligibility, as animal is prior to man and subject to accident. But potency or capability can only be defined by means of actuality, because the first characteristic of the capable consists in the possibility of its acting or being actual. For example, a builder is defined as one who can build, and a theorist as one who can theorize, and the visible as what can be seen; and the same is true in other cases. The concept of actuality must therefore be prior to the concept of potency, and the knowledge of actuality prior to the knowledge of potency. Hence Aristotle explained above what potency is by defining it in reference to actuality, but he could not define actuality by means of something else but only made it known inductively.

[1847.] "And actuality."

Then he shows how actuality is prior to potency in time, and how it is not. In regard to this he does two things. First, he makes this clear in the case of passive potencies; and second, in the case of certain active potencies, where he says, "And for this reason."

He accordingly says, first, that actuality is prior to potency in time in the sense that in the same species the agent, or what is actual, is prior to

---

[1] Reading *motu* (with the former Cathala edition) for *motus*.
[2] *Physica*, II, 1 (192 b 23).

what is potential; but in numerically one and the same thing what is potential is prior in time to what is actual.

[1848.] This is shown as follows: if we take this man who is now actually a man, prior to him in time there was a matter which was potentially a man. And similarly seed, which is potentially grain, was prior in time to what is actually grain. And "the thing capable of seeing,"[3] i.e., having the power of sight, was prior in time to the thing actually seeing. And prior in time to the things having potential being there were certain things having actual being, namely, agents, by which former have been brought to actuality. For what exists potentially must always be brought[4] to actuality by an agent, which is an actual being. Hence what is potentially a man becomes actually a man as a result of the man who generates him, who is an actual being; and similarly one who is potentially musical becomes actually musical by learning from a teacher who is actually musical. And thus in the case of anything potential there is always some first thing which moves it, and this mover is actual. It follows, then, that even though the same thing numerically exists potentially prior in time to existing actually, there is still also some actual being of the same species which is prior in time to the one that exists potentially.

[1849.] And because someone could be perplexed about some of the statements which he had made, he therefore adds that these have been explained above; for it was pointed out in the foregoing discussions about substance — in Book VII — that everything which comes to be comes from something as matter, and by something as an agent. And it was also stated above that this agent is specifically the same as the thing which comes to be. This was made clear in the case of univocal generations, but in the case of equivocal generations there must also be some likeness between the generator and the thing generated, as was shown elsewhere.

[1850.] "And for this reason."

He explains the temporal sequence of actuality and potency in the case of certain active potencies; and in regard to this he does three things. First, he explains what he intends to do. For it was said above that there are certain operative potencies whose very actions must be understood to be performed or exercised beforehand, as those acquired by practice or instruction. And with regard to these he says that in those things which are numerically the same, actuality is also prior to potency. For it seems impossible that anyone should become a builder who has not first built something; or that anyone should become a harpist who has not first played the harp.

[1851.] He draws this conclusion from the points laid down above; for it was said above that one who is potentially musical becomes actually

---

[3] St. Thomas reads *visivum* in place of *visibile* in the Latin version.
[4] Reading *fiat* for *sit*.

musical as a result of someone who is actually musical — meaning that he learns from him; and the same thing holds true of other actions. Now one could not learn an art of this kind unless he himself performed the actions associated with it; for one learns to play the harp by playing it. This is also true of the other arts. It has been shown, then, that it is impossible to have potencies of this sort unless their actions are also first present in one and the same subject numerically.

[1852.] "From this arose."

Second, he raises a sophistical objection against the above view. He says that "a sophistical argument arose," i.e., an apparently cogent syllogism which contradicts the truth, and it runs as follows: one who is learning an art exercises the action of that art. But one who is learning an art does not have that art. Hence one who does not have a science or an art is doing the thing which is the object of that science or art. This seems to be contrary to the truth.

[1853.] "But since some."

Third, he answers this objection by stating a position which was discussed and proved in the *Physics*, Book VI; for there he proved that being moved is always prior to having been moved, because of the division of motion. For whenever any part of a motion is given, since it is divisible, we must be able to pick out some part of it which has already been completed, while the part of the motion given is going on. Therefore whatever is being moved has already been partly moved.

[1854.] And by the same argument, whatever is coming to be has already partly come to be; for even though the process of producing a substance, with reference to the introduction of the substantial form, is indivisible, still if we take the preceding alteration whose terminus is generation, the process is divisible, and the whole process can be called a production. Therefore, since what is coming to be has partly come to be, then what is coming to be can possess to some degree the activity of the thing in which the production is terminated. For example, what is becoming hot can heat something to some degree, but not as perfectly as something that has already become hot. Hence, since to learn is to become scientific, the one learning must already have, as it were, some part of a science or an art. It is not absurd, then, if he should exercise the action of an art to some degree; for he does not do it as perfectly as one who already has the art.

[1855.] But in reason itself there are also naturally inherent certain seeds or principles of the sciences and virtues, through which a man can pass to some degree into the activity of a science or a virtue before he has the habit of a science or a virtue; and when this has been acquired he acts perfectly, whereas at first he acted imperfectly. Lastly he summarizes the above discussion, as is evident in the text.

5. Priority of Actuality over Potency in Substance

A.   Aristotle, *Metaphysics*, IX, ch. 8, 1050 a 4–1050 b 6.

But actuality is also prior in substance; (1) because those things which are subsequent in generation are prior in form and substance; for example, man is prior to boy, and human being to seed; for the one already has its form, but the other has not.

And (2) because everything which come to be moves toward a principle, namely, its goal (or end). For that for the sake of which a thing comes to be is a principle; and generation is for the sake of that goal. And actuality is the goal, and it is for the sake of this that potency is acquired.

For animals do not see in order that they may have the power of sight, but they have the power of sight in order that they may see.

And similarly men have the science of building in order that they may build, and they have theoretical knowledge in order that they may speculate; but they do not speculate in order that they may have theoretical knowledge, unless they are learning by practice. And these latter do not speculate (in a perfect way), but either to some degree or because they do not need to speculate.

Further, matter is in potency up to the time at which it attains its form; but when it exists actually, it then possesses its form. And the same holds true in the case of other things, even of those whose goal is motion. And for this reason, just as those who are teaching think that they have reached their goal when they exhibit their student performing, so it is with nature.

For if this were not so, Pauson's Mercury would exist again; because it would not be more evident whether scientific knowledge is internal or external, as is the case with the figure of Mercury. For the activity is the goal, and the actuality is the activity. And for this reason the term actuality is used in reference to activity and is extended to completeness.

But while in the case of some things the ultimate effect is the use, as, for example, in the case of sight the ultimate effect is the act of seeing, and no other work besides this results from the power of sight, still from some potencies something else is produced; for example, the art of building produces a house in addition to the act of building. Yet in neither case is the act any less or any more the end of the potency; for the act of building is in the thing being built, and it comes into being and exists simultaneously with the house. Therefore, in those cases in which the result is something other than the use, the actuality is in the thing being produced; for example, the act of building is in the thing being built, and the act of weaving in the thing being woven. The same holds true in all other cases. And in general motion is in the thing being moved. But in the case of those things in which nothing else is produced besides the activity, the activity is present in these, as the act of seeing is in the one seeing, and the act of speculating in the one speculating, and life in the soul. Accordingly, happiness is in the soul, for it is a kind of life.

It is evident, then, that substance or form is actuality. Hence is is clear according to this argument that actuality is prior to potency in substance. And, as we have said (780), one actuality is always prior to another in time right back to that actuality which is always the first principle of motion.

B. St. Thomas, *Commentary on the Metaphysics*, IX, lesson 8, nos. 1856–1866.

[1856.] Having shown that actuality is prior to potency in intelligibility and in one sense in time, the Philosopher now shows that it is prior in substance. This was the third way given above in which actuality is prior to potency.

This is divided into two parts. In the first part he proves his thesis by arguments taken from things which are sometimes potential and sometimes actual. In the second part he proves his thesis by comparing eternal things, which are always actual, with mobile things, which are sometimes actual and sometimes potential, where he says, "But actuality."

And since to be prior in substance is to be prior in perfection, and since perfection is attributed to two things, namely to the form and to the goal (or end), therefore in the first part he uses two arguments to prove his thesis. The first of these pertains to the form, and the second to the goal, and this is given at the words, "And (2) actuality."

He accordingly says, first, that actuality is prior to potency not only in intelligibility and in time "but in substance," i.e., in perfection; for the form by which something is perfected is customarily signified by the term *substance*. This first part is made clear by this argument: those things which are subsequent in generation are "prior in substance and form," i.e., in perfection, because the process of generation always goes from what is imperfect to what is perfect; for example, in the process of generation man is subsequent to boy, because man comes from boy; and human being is subsequent to seed. The reason is that man and human being already have a perfect form, whereas boy and seed do not yet have such a form. Hence, since in numerically one and the same subject actuality is subsequent to potency both in generation and in time, as is evident from the above, it follows that actuality is prior to potency in substance and in intelligibility.

[1857.] "And (2) because."

Here he proves the same point by an argument involving the goal of activity and here he does three things. First, he proposes his argument. Second, he explains one of the principles assumed in his argument, where he says, "For animals." Third, he settles an issue which could cause difficulty in the above argument, where he says, "But while."

He accordingly says, first, that everything which comes to be when it moves towards its goal moves towards a principle. For a goal, or that for the sake of which a thing comes to be, is a principle, because it is the first thing intended by an agent, since it is that for the sake of which generation takes place. But actuality is the goal of potency, and therefore actuality is prior to potency, and is one of its principles.

[1858.] "For animals."

He now explains the position which he maintained above, namely, that actuality is the goal of potency. He makes this clear, first, in the case of natural active potencies. He says that animals do not see in order that they may have the power of sight, but they rather have the power of sight in order that they may see. Thus it is clear that potency exists for the sake of actuality and not vice versa.

[1859.] "And similarly."

Second, he makes the same thing clear in the case of rational potencies. He says that men have the power of building in order that they may build; and they have "theoretical knowledge," or speculative science, in order that they may speculate. However, they do not speculate in order that they may have theoretical knowledge, unless they are learning and meditating about those matters which belong to a speculative science in order that they may acquire it. And these do not speculate perfectly but to some degree and imperfectly, as has been said above, because speculation is not undertaken because of some need, but for the sake of using science already acquired. But there is speculation on the part of those who are learning because they need to acquire science.

[1860.] "Further, matter."

Third he makes the same point clear in the case of passive potencies. He says that matter is in potency until it receives a form or specifying principle, but then it is first in a state of actuality when it receives its form. And this is what occurs in the case of all other things which are moved for the sake of a goal. Hence, just as those who are teaching think they have attained their goal when they exhibit their pupil whom they have instructed performing those activities which belong to his art, in a similar fashion nature attains its goal when it attains actuality. Hence it is made evident in the case of natural motion that actuality is the goal of potency.

[1861.] "For if this were not."

Fourth, he proves his thesis by an argument from the untenable consequences. He says that if a thing's perfection and goal do not consist in actuality, there would then seem to be no difference between someone wise, as Mercury was, and someone foolish, as Pauson was. For if the perfection of science were not in the one acting, Mercury would not have exhibited it in his own science, if he had "internal scientific knowledge," i.e., in reference to its internal activity, "or external," i.e., in reference to its external activity, as neither would Pauson.[1] For it is by means of the actual use of scientific knowledge, and not by means of the potency or power, that one is shown to have a science; because activity is the goal of a science, and activity is a kind of actuality. And for this reason the term actuality is derived from activity, as has been stated above (758:C 1805), and from this it was extended to form, which is called completeness or perfection.

[1862.] "But while."

He explains a point which could cause a difficulty in the foregoing argument. For since he had said that some product is the goal of activity, one could think that this is true in all cases. But he denies this, saying that the ultimate goal or end of some active potencies consists in the mere use of those potencies, and not in something produced by their activity; for example, the ultimate goal of the power of sight is the act of seeing, and there is no product resulting from the power of sight in addition to this activity. But in the case of some active potencies something else is produced in addition to the activity; for example, the art of building also produces a house in addition to the activity of building.

[1863.]   However, this difference does not cause actuality to be the goal of
            potency to a lesser degree in the case of some of these potencies
and to a greater degree in the case of others; because the activity is in the thing produced, as the act of building in the thing being built; and it comes into being and exists simultaneously with the house. Hence if the house, or the thing built, is the goal, this does not exclude actuality from being the goal of potency.

[1864.]   Now it is necessary to consider such a difference among the afore-
            said potencies, because when something else is produced besides
the actuality of a potency, which is activity, the activity of such potencies is in the thing being produced and is their actuality, just as the act of building is in the thing being built, and the act of weaving in the thing being woven, and in general motion in the being moved. And this is true, because when some product results from the activity of a potency, the activity perfects the thing being produced and not the one performing it. Hence it is in the thing being produced as an actuality and perfection of it, but not in the one who is acting.

[1865.]   But when nothing else is produced in addition to the activity of
            the potency, the actuality then exists in the agent as its perfec-
tion and does not pass over into something external in order to perfect it; for example, the act of seeing is in the one seeing as his perfection, and

---

[1] St. Thomas appears to be misinterpreting the example which Aristotle uses. The point at issue is not whether Mercury is wise and Pauson foolish, but whether the figure of Mercury (Hermes), which the sculptor, Pauson, gave to the stone, is an internal or external attribute of the stone.

the act of speculating is in the one speculating, and life is in the soul (if we understand by life vital activity). Hence it has been shown that happiness also consists in an activity of the kind which exists in the one acting, and not of the kind which passes over into something external; for happiness is a good of the one who is happy, namely, his perfect life. Hence just as life is in one who lives, in a similar fashion happiness is in one who is happy. Thus it is evident that happiness does not consist either in building or in any activity of the kind which passes over into something external, but it consists in understanding and willing.

[1866]. "Hence, it is evident."

Lastly he retraces his steps in order to draw the main conclusion which he has in mind. He says that it has been shown from the above discussion that a thing's substance or form or specifying principle is a kind of actuality; and from this it is evident that actuality is prior to potency in substance or form. And it is prior in time, as has been stated above, because the actuality whereby the generator or mover or maker is actual must always exist first before the other actuality by which the thing generated or produced becomes actual after being potential. And this goes on until one comes to the first mover, which is actuality alone; for whatever passes from potency to actuality requires a prior actuality in the agent, which brings it to actuality.

6. The Priority of Actuality in Incorruptible Things

A.   Aristotle, *Metaphysics*, IX, ch. 8, 1050 b 6–1051 a 3.

But actuality is prior to potency in a more fundamental sense; for eternal things are prior in substance to corruptible ones, and nothing eternal is potential.

The reason of this is that every potency is at the same time a potency for opposite determinations. For what is incapable of existing does not exist in any way; and it is possible for everything that is capable of existing not to exist actually. Therefore whatever is capable of existing may either be or not be, and thus the same thing is capable both of being and of not being. But what is capable of not being may possibly not be; and what may possibly not be is corruptible: either absolutely, or in the sense in which it is said to be possible for it not to be, either according to place or to quantity or to quality. And the term *absolutely* means *in reference to substance*.

Therefore nothing that is incorruptible in an absolute sense is potential in an absolute sense. But there is nothing that hinders it from being so in other respects, for example, in reference to quality or to place. Therefore all incorruptible things are actual.

And none of those things which exist necessarily are potential. In fact such things are the first; for if they did not exist, nothing would exist.

Nor is eternal motion potential, if there be such a thing; and if anything is moved eternally, it is not moved potentially except in reference to *whence* and *whether*. And nothing prevents the matter of this sort of thing from existing.

And for this reason the sun and the stars and the entire heaven are always active, and there is no need to fear, as the natural philosophers do,[1] that they may at some time stand still. Nor do they tire in their activity; for in them there is no potency for opposite determinations, as there is in corruptible things, so that the continuity of their motion should be tiresome. For the cause of this is that their substance is matter and potency and not actuality.

Moreover, incorruptible things are imitated by those which are in a state of change, such as fire and earth; for these latter things are always active, since they have motion in themselves and of themselves.

But all other potencies which have been defined are potencies for opposite determinations; for what is capable of moving something else in this way is also capable of not moving it in this way, i.e., all those things which act by reason. And irrational potencies will also be potencies for opposite determination by being absent or not.

If, then, there are any natures or substances such as those thinkers who in their theories proclaim the Ideas to be, there will be something much more scientific than science itself, and something much more mobile than motion itself; for the former will rather be the actualities and the latter the potencies of these. Hence it is evident that actuality is prior to potency and to every principle of change.

> B. St. Thomas, *Commentary on the Metaphysics*, IX, lesson 9, nos. 1867–1882.

[1867.] Aristotle proved above that actuality is prior to potency in substance, definition and perfection, by arguments drawn from corruptible things themselves; but here he proves the same point by comparing eternal things with corruptible ones.

This part is divided into two members. In the first he proves his thesis; and in the second, by the thesis thus proved, he rejects a certain statement made by Plato, where he says, "If, then."

In regard to the first he does two things. First, he proves his thesis. This he does by the following argument: eternal things are compared to corruptible ones as actuality to potency; for eternal things as such are not in potency, whereas corruptible things as such are in potency. But eternal

---

[1] See *De Coelo*, II, 1 (284 a 24–26).

things are prior to corruptible ones in substance and perfection; for this is evident (784:C 1856). Hence actuality is prior to potency both in substance and perfection. He says that his thesis is proved in a more proper way by this argument, because actuality and potency are not considered in the same subject but in different ones, and this makes the proof more evident.

[1868.] "The reason."

Second, he proves one assumption which he made, namely, that nothing eternal is in potency; and in regard to this he does two things. First, he gives an argument to prove this, and it runs as follows: every potency is at one and the same time a potency for opposite determinations. Now he does not say this about active potency, for it has already been shown that irrational potencies are not potencies for opposite determinations; but he is speaking here of passive potency, inasmuch as a thing is capable of being and not being either absolutely or in a qualified sense.

[1869.] Now the claim which he made he proves by an argument to the contrary: because where such potency does not exist neither of the opposite determinations is possible; for what is incapable of being never exists in any way. For if a thing is incapable of being, it is impossible for it to be, and it is necessary for it not to be. But what is capable of being may possibly not be actual. Hence it is evident that what is capable of being may either be or not be; and thus the potency is at one and the same time a potency for opposite determinations, because the same thing is in potency both to being and non-being.

[1870.] But what is capable of not being may possibly not be, for these two statements are equivalent ones. Moreover, what may possibly not be is corruptible either absolutely or in a qualified sense inasmuch as it is said to be possible for it not to be. For example, if it is possible for some body not to be in place, that body is corruptible as far as place is concerned; and the same applies to quantity and quality. But that is corruptible in an absolute sense which is capable of not existing substantially. Therefore it follows that everything potential inasmuch as it is potential is corruptible.

[1871.] "Therefore nothing."

Second, he draws from the foregoing the conclusion at which he aims; and in regard to this he does three things. First, he concludes to this thesis about eternal things, inferring from the observations made above that if everything potential is corruptible, it follows that nothing which is incorruptible in an absolute sense is a potential being, provided that we understand incorruptible things in an absolute sense and potential being in an absolute sense in reference to substance.

[1872.] But nothing prevents something that is incorruptible in an absolute sense from being potential in a qualified sense, in reference either to quantity or to place. For example, the moon is in a state of potency to being illuminated by the sun; and when the sun is in the east it is in a state of potency with regard to being in the west. It is evident from what has been said, then, that all eternal things as such are actual.

[1873.] "And none."

Second, he comes to the same conclusion about necessary things as he did about eternal things, because even in corruptible things there are certain necessary aspects; for example, man is an animal, and every whole is greater than its part. Hence he says that nothing necessary is potential; for necessary things are always actual and incapable of being or not being. And those things which are necessary are the first of all things, because if they ceased to exist, none of the others would exist; for example, if essential predicates, which are referred to a subject necessarily, were taken away, accidental predicates, which can be present and not present in some subject, could not be present in any subject. It follows, then, that actuality is prior to potency.

[1874.] "Nor is."

Third, he comes to the same conclusion about eternal motion as he did about eternal substances; and in regard to this he does three things. First, from what has been said above he concludes to his thesis. He says that, if some motion is eternal, that motion is not potential; nor is anything that is moved eternally in a state of potency to motion, but it is in a state of potency to this or to that place, i.e., inasmuch as it goes from this place to that place. For since motion is the actuality of something in potency, everything which is being moved must be in potency to the goal of that motion, not however as regards motion itself, but as regards some place to which it tends by its motion.

[1875.] And since what is being moved must have matter, he adds that nothing prevents a thing which is being moved by an eternal motion from having matter; because, even though it is not in potency to motion in an absolute sense, it is nevertheless in potency to this or to that place.

[1876.] "And for this."

Second, he draws a corollary from the above discussion. For since what is being moved by an eternal motion is not in potency to motion itself (and the motion of the heavens is eternal according to the discussion in Book VIII of the *Physics*[1]), it follows that the sun and the moon and the stars and the entire heaven are always active, because they are always being moved and are acting by means of their motion.

[1877.] Nor is it to be feared that at some time the motion of the heavens may cease, as "some of the natural philosophers feared it would," namely, Empedocles and his followers, who held that at times the world is destroyed by discord and is restored again by friendship. Hence he says that this is not to be feared, because they are not potentially immobile.

---

[1] *Physica*, VIII, 1 (252 b 5).

[1878.] And for this reason too incorruptible things insofar as they are
being moved do not tire in their activity, because "the potency for
opposite determinations" is not found in them, namely, the ability to be both
moved and not moved, as is found in corruptible things, which have these as
a result of motion. And thus in this way continuous motion becomes laborious
for them. For corruptible things labor insofar as they are moved, and the
reason is that they are in a state of potency both for being and not being
moved, and it is not proper to them by reason of their substantial nature always to be undergoing motion. Hence we see that the more laborious any
motion is the nearer also does the nature of the thing come to immobility;
for example, in the case of animals it is evident that motion in an upward
direction is more laborious.

[1879.] Now what he says here about the continuity of celestial motion
is in keeping with the nature of a celestial body, which we know
by experience. But this is not prejudicial to the divine will, on which the
motion and being of the heavens depend.

[1880.] "Moreover, incorruptible things."

Third, he compares corruptible bodies with incorruptible ones from the
viewpoint of activity. First, he does this insofar as they are alike. He says
that the bodies of those things whose being involves change resemble incorruptible bodies insofar as they are always acting; for example, fire, which of
itself always produces heat, and earth, which of itself always produces proper
and natural activities. And this is true, because they have motion and their
own proper activity of themselves — inasmuch, namely, as their forms are
principles of such motions and activities.

[1881.] "But all the other."

Second, he compares them insofar as they are unlike. He says that in contrast with eternal things, which are always actual, the other potencies of
mobile things, about which the truth has been established above, are all
potencies for opposite determinations. But this is verified in a different way;
for rational potencies are potencies capable of opposite determinations because they can move in this way or not, as has been said above (747:C 1789);
whereas irrational potencies, though acting in one way, are themselves also
potencies of opposite determinations in view of the fact that they can be
present in a subject or not; for example, an animal can lose its power of
vision.

[1882.] "If, then."

As a result of what has been said he rejects a doctrine of Plato. For Plato
claimed that there are certain separate Forms, which he held to have being
in the highest degree, as if one were to maintain that there is a separate
science, which he called *science-in-itself*; and he said that this is foremost in
the class of knowable entities. And similarly he maintained that *motion-in-
itself* is foremost in the class of mobile things. But according to the points

made clear above, something else besides science-in-itself will be first in the class of knowable things; for it was shown that actuality is prior to potency in perfection, and science itself is a kind of potency. Hence speculation, which is the activity of science, will be more perfect than science is; and the same will apply in the case of other things of this kind. Lastly he summarizes his discussion, saying that actuality is prior to potency and to every principle of motion.

7. Essence and Existence

St. Thomas, *On Being and Essence.**

Introduction

A small mistake in the beginning is a great one in the end, according to the Philosopher in the first book of the *De Caelo et Mundo.*[1] Moreover, as Avicenna declares early in his *Metaphysics,*[2] what the intellect first conceives is being and essence. Consequently, lest we fall into error through ignorance of them, we ought to state, with a view to disclosing the difficulty they involve: (1) what is meant by the terms *being* and *essence*; (2) how they are found in diverse things; and (3) how they are related to the intentions[3] of logic, namely, genus, species and difference.

* Translated by Armand Maurer, C.B.S. (Toronto: Pontifical Institute of Mediaeval Studies, 1949).
[1] I, 5, 271b–13.
[2] I, 6, fol. 72rb.
[3] *Intentio.* The mental word or concept which is the internally expressed conformity of the intellect to its object. By means of it the intellect tends toward what it knows. The intentions of logic are second intentions. Unlike first intentions, they do not directly represent some real thing, but they are formed by the intellect when it reflects upon itself and the way it understands. See St. Thomas, *Qu. Disp. De Potentia,* 7, 9 c.

Chapter I

Now, we ought to acquire knowledge of the simple from the composite and arrive at what is prior from what is posterior, so that, beginning with easier matters, we may advance more suitably in knowledge. For this reason we ought to go from the meaning of being to the meaning of essence.[1]

It should be known that being of itself is spoken of in two ways,[2] as the

[1] Being (*ens*) is the existing thing (*id quod habet esse*), including both essence and the act of existing. It is thus complex or composite. Essence is one of its components, and its notion is disengaged only after we know being. Being is also posterior to essence, not in time, but in nature, since what is composite is naturally posterior to its constitutive principles. See Cajetan, *Commentaria in De Ente et Essentia, Prooemium,* 8, p. 20.
[2] *Ens per se dicitur dupliciter.* In the first sense, *ens per se* is divided into the categories of substance and the nine accidents. This is real being, which either actually or possibly exists in nature. In distinction to *ens per se, ens per accidens,* or accidental

Philosopher says in the fifth book of the Metaphysics.³ In the first way it is divided into the ten categories; in the second way it signifies the truth of propositions. The difference between the two is that in the second sense we can call everything being about which we can form an affirmative proposition, even though it may posit nothing in reality. Thus, affirmation is opposed to negation, and blindness is in the eye. But, in the first sense, only that can be called being which posits something in reality. In this sense of the word, then, blindness and the like are not beings.

So, the term essence is not taken from being in the second sense of the word. For, as is clear in the case of privations, in that sense we call some things beings which do not have an essence. Essence is rather taken from being in the first sense. That is the reason why the Commentator declares in the same place⁴ that being in the first sense of the word is that which signifies the essence of a thing.

And because, as we have said,⁵ being in this sense is divided into the ten categories, essence must signify something common to all natures, through which natures different beings are placed in different genera and species. For example, humanity is the essence of man, and so with other things.

Moreover, since that by which a thing is constituted in its proper genus or species is what is signified by the definition expressing what the thing is, philosophers have taken to using the word quiddity for the word essence. The Philosopher frequently calls this the what a thing was to be,⁶ in other words, that by which a thing is a what. It is also called form,⁷ inasmuch as form

---

being, is a composition of beings in diverse categories. E.g., man and whiteness are entia per se. White man is ens per accidens.

Being in the second sense signifies the truth of propositions, e.g., when we judge, Socrates is blind, the copula is does not signify a real being, but a composition made in the mind in conformity with the object.

Cajetan points out three differences between these two meanings of being. (1) Being in the first sense is predicated only of things existing in the ten categories, while being in the second sense is predicated of everything that can be the subject of an affirmative proposition. (2) Being in the first sense is a composite, including both essence and the act of existing, while in the second sense there are some beings which do not have an essence (e.g., negations, chimera). (3) It follows from this that the name essence is taken from being in the first sense. See Cajetan, op. cit., cap. 1, n. 9, pp. 21, 22; St. Thomas, In V Meta., lect. 9, ed. Cathala, No. 885–896.

³ V, 7, 1017 a 22–35.

⁴ Averroes, In V Meta., 7, t. c. 14, fol. 55ᵛa56.

⁵ See above, p. 298.

⁶ Quod quid erat esse. A literal translation of Aristotle's: TO TI HN EINAI. See Aristotle, Post. Anal. 22, 82 b 38; De Anima III, 6, 430 b 28; Meta., VII, 3, 1028 b 34. W. D. Ross paraphrases the expression: "The answer to the question, what was it to be so-and-so" (Aristotle's Metaphysics, ed. Ross, Vol. I, p. 127). When we ask the question, — What is this thing? — the complete answer is the statement of its definition, or that which the nature tends to fulfill. For example, if the thing in question is a man, the answer is: He is a rational animal. The definition thus expresses what a thing is, its whatness or the what a thing was to be. The past tense of the verb (was) does not express past time. It expresses absolutely the direction of the tendency of a being's nature.

⁷ Form, as used here, is the whole essence; it does not signify that form which,

signifies the determination[8] of each thing, as Avicenna says in the second book of his *Metaphysics*.[9] Furthermore, it is called by another name, namely, *nature*, using nature in the first of the four senses given by Boethius in the treatise *De Duabus Naturis*.[10] In this sense every being which the intellect can in any way grasp is called a nature; for a thing is intelligible only by its definition and essence. Thus the Philosopher, too, declares in the fifth book of the *Metaphysics*[11] that every substance is a nature. In this sense of the word, however, nature seems to mean the thing's essence as ordered to its proper activity, for nothing is without its proper activity. The term *quiddity*, on the other hand, is derived from what the definition signifies, while essence means that through which and in which a being has its act of existing (*esse*).[12]

Now, being is predicated absolutely and primarily of substances; it is predicated secondarily and as in a qualified sense of accidents. For this reason essence is truly and properly in substances, but in accidents it is present in a certain manner and in a qualified sense.

Some substances, furthermore, are simple and some composite, and essence is in both. But, in simple substances it is present more truly and excellently, inasmuch as they also have the act of existing (*esse*) in a more excellent way; for they are the cause of composite substances — at least this is true of God, the first of the simple substances. But, because the essences of the simple substances are more hidden from us, we ought to begin with the essences of composite substances, so that, beginning with easier matters, we may advance more suitably in knowledge.

---

with matter, composes a material substance. These two meanings of *form* were expressed by medieval writers as *form of the whole* (*forma totius*) and *form of the part* (*forma partis*). The former is the whole essence, including in the case of a material substance both form and matter, e.g., humanity. The latter is a part of the essence, uniting with matter to make up the complete essence. See St. Thomas, *In VII Meta.*, lect. 9, No. 1467–1469. See also, below, pp. 305–306.

8 *Certitudo*. The Arabian expression which the medieval translator rendered by this Latin word has the meaning of perfection or complete determination. On the one hand, it signifies the objective truth of the thing; on the other, the precise and clear knowledge of it. See A.-M. Goichon, *La Distinction de l'essence et de l'existence d'apres Ibn Sina* (Avicenne), p. 34, note 7.

9 II, 2, fol. 76ʳa; cf. III, 5, fol. 80ʳb; I, 6, fol. 72ᵛa.

10 *Liber de Persona et Duabus Naturis*, I; PL, 64, 1341BC.

11 V, 4, 1014 b 35.

12 This does not mean that the essence confers *esse* on the substance, but that it is *in and by means of* the essence that the substance receives *esse*. See E. Gilson, *Le Thomisme*, p. 61, note 1. The word *esse*, which is here rendered *act of existing*, cannot be adequately translated into English. It is the *to be* of a thing, its supreme dynamic energy or actuality. According to St. Thomas, *esse* is other than essence (*De Potentia*, 7, 2, ad 9ᵐ). To translate *esse* by a noun is to reify it and to conceive it as if it were a substance or abstract essence. *Esse*, however, is a verb, and it designates, not an essence or substance, but the act which is the *to be* of the substance. For the Angelic Doctor, *esse* is what is most central in the existing thing. It is at once the metaphysical core of the thing's being and the ultimate reason for its intelligibility. See E. Gilson, *God and Philosophy*, p. 63 ff; *Le Thomisme*, p. 43 ff; J. Maritain, *A Preface to Metaphysics*, p. 19 ff; J. de Finance, *Etre et Agir*, p. 111 ff.

8. The Relation of Essence to Genus, Species, and Difference

St. Thomas, *On Being and Essence*, ch. III.*

Now that we have seen what the word *essence* means in composite substances, we must observe how it is related to the notions[1] of genus, species and difference.

Since that which has the nature of a genus, species or difference is predicated of this particular designated thing, the *essence*, expressed as a part (for instance, by the word *humanity* or *animality*), cannot possibly have the nature of a universal, that is, of a genus or species. Thus, Avicenna declares[2] that rationality is not a difference, but the originative source of a difference. For the same reason humanity is not a species nor animality a genus. Similarly, we cannot say that essence has the nature of a genus or species, if, as the Platonists held,[3] essence is something existing outside particular things, because then the genus and species would not be predicated of the particular individual. For we cannot say that Socrates is something separated from himself. What is more, something separated would be of no help in knowing the particular being. We conclude, therefore, that the essence has the nature of a genus or species insofar as it is expressed after the manner of a whole, for instance by the word *man or animal*, as containing implicitly and indistinctly everything that is in the individual.

If nature or essence is understood in this sense, we can consider it in two ways. First, we can consider it according to its proper meaning, which is to consider it absolutely. In this sense, nothing is true of it except what belongs to it as such; whatever else is attributed to it, the attribution is *false*. For example, to man as man belong rational, animal and whatever else his definition includes, whereas white or black, or anything of this sort, which is not included in the concept of humanity, does not belong to man as man. If someone should ask, then, whether the nature so considered can be called *one* or *many*, neither should be granted, because both are outside the concept of humanity and both can be added to it. If plurality were included in the concept of humanity, it could never be one, although it is one inasmuch as it is present in Socrates. Similarly, if unity were contained in its

---

* Maurer, *op. cit.*

[1] *Ratio*. The word is used frequently in this chapter, and it has been translated by such words as *notion, nature, character*. The *ratio* of a thing is its essence or nature considered precisely as intelligible, that is, as capable of being grasped by the intellect, and constituting the foundation for concepts that may be formed of it. The *ratio* as understood (*ratio intellecta*) is the intention or concept. See St. Thomas, *In I Sent.*, 33, 1, 1, ad 3m, ed. Mandonnet, vol. 1, p. 767. See also J. Peghaire, *Intellectus et Ratio selon S. Thomas d'Aquin*, p. 14 ff.

[2] *Meta.*, V, 6, fol. 90rb.

[3] See Aristotle, *Meta.*, I, 9, 990 b 1–991 a 14.

concept, then Socrates' and Plato's nature would be one and the same, and it could not be multiplied in many individuals.

Nature or essence is considered in a second way with reference to the act of existing (esse) it has in this or that individual. When the nature is so considered, something is attributed to it accidentally by reason of the thing in which it exists; for instance, we say that man is white because Socrates is white, although being white does not pertain to man as man.

This nature has a twofold act of existing, one in individual things, the other in the mind; and according to both modes of existing, accidents accompany the nature. In individual beings, moreover, it has numerous acts of existing corresponding to the diversity of individuals. Yet, the nature itself, considered properly — that is to say, absolutely — demands none of these acts of existing. It is false to say that the nature of man as such exists in this individual man, because, if existing in this individual belonged to man as man, it would never exist outside this individual. Similarly, if it belonged to man as man not to exist in this individual, human nature would never exist in it. It is true to say, however, that it does not belong to man as man to exist in this or that individual, or in the intellect. Considered in itself, the nature of man thus clearly abstracts from every act of existing, but in such a way that none may be excluded from it. And it is the nature considered in this way that we predicate of all individual beings.

Yet, we cannot say that universality belongs to the nature so considered, because unity and community belong to the notion of a universal. Now, neither of these belongs to human nature considered absolutely. If community were included in the notion of man, in whatever being humanity were found, community would be found. This is false, because we do not find any community in Socrates; everything in him is individuated. So, too, we cannot say that human nature as it exists in individual men has the character of a genus or species. We do not find human nature in them with a unity such that it constitutes one essence belonging to all, which the character of universality requires.

Human nature, then, can have the character of a species only as it exists in the intellect. Human nature itself exists in the intellect in abstraction from all individual conditions, and it thus has a uniform relation to all individual men outside the intellect, being equally the likeness of all and leading to a knowledge of all insofar as they are men. And from the fact that the nature has such a relation to all individual men, the intellect forms the notion of species and attributes it to the nature. That is why the Commentator asserts, in his exposition on the first book of the *De Anima*,[4] that it is the intellect which causes universality in things. Avicenna also says this in his *Metaphysics*.[5] And although the nature existing in the intellect has the character of a universal from its relation to things outside the intellect, since it is one likeness of them all, nevertheless, as it exists in this or that intellect, it is a certain

---

[4] Averroes, *In De Anima*, I, l, t. c. 8, fol. 109^{v}b23.
[5] V, 1, fol. 87^{r}b; 87^{v}a–b.

particular species apprehended by the intellect. The Commentator was thus clearly in error in his exposition on the third book of the *De Anima*,[6] for he wanted to conclude that the intellect is one in all men from the universality of the form in the intellect. For, the universality of that form does not come from the existence which it has in the intellect, but from its relation to things whose likeness it is. In the same way, if a material statue represented a number of men, it is agreed that the statue's image or likeness would have an individual and proper act of existing as it existed in this particular matter, but it would have community inasmuch as it would be the common representative of many men.

Moreover, since it is human nature absolutely considered that is properly predicated of Socrates, and since it does not have the character of a species when absolutely considered but has it from the accidents following upon its existing in the intellect, therefore the word *species* is not predicated of Socrates, so that we may say, "Socrates is a species." This would necessarily be the case if the nature of species belonged to man as existing in Socrates or to man as considered in himself insofar as he is man. For we may predicate of Socrates everything which belongs to man as man. Yet, it belongs to the genus in virtue of its very nature to be predicated, since this is part of its definition. For predication is something accomplished by the intellect's act of combining and dividing, having for its foundation in reality the very unity of those things, one of which is said of the other. Hence, the notion of predicability can be included in the notion of the intention which is the genus, which is also made by an act of the intellect. However, that to which the intellect, when combining one thing with another, attributes the intention of predicability is not the intention itself of the genus, but rather that to which the intellect attributes the intention of the genus, for instance, what is signified by the word *animal*.

To conclude, then, it is evident in what way essence or nature is related to the notion of species. The notion of species is not among those things which belong to essence or nature according to its absolute consideration, nor among the accidents which accompany it according to the existence it has outside the intellect, for example, whiteness or blackness. But it is to be found among the accidents which accompany it according to the existence which it has in the intellect. And it is according to this existence in the intellect that essence or nature takes on the character of genus or difference.

9. Essence in Separate Substances

St. Thomas, *On Being and Essence*, ch. IV.*

It remains for us to see in what way essence is in separated substances, namely, in the soul, in the intelligences and in the First Cause.

---

* Maurer, *op. cit.*
6 Averroes, *In De Anima*, III, 1, t.c. 5, fol. 164ra21 ff.

Although everyone admits the simplicity of the first Cause, some try to introduce the composition of matter and form in the intelligences and in souls.[1] The originator of this doctrine seems to have been Avicebron, the author of the *Fons Vitae*.[2] But it is not in accord with what philosophers generally say,[3] since they call these substances separated from matter, and they prove that they are entirely immaterial. The strongest demonstration of this is from their power of understanding.[4] We see that forms are not actually intelligible unless they are separated from matter and material conditions; nor are they rendered actually intelligible except through the power of an intelligent substance which receives them within itself and produces them.[5] Every intelligent substance, then, must be in every way free from matter, neither having matter as a part of itself, nor being, like material forms, a form impressed on matter. Nor can it be asserted that not any matter whatsoever, but only corporeal matter, stands in the way of intelligibility. If corporeal matter alone stood in the way of intelligibility, then matter must impede intelligibility because of its corporeal form, since matter is called corporeal only when it exists under a corporeal form. But this is impossible, because a corporeal form itself, like other forms, is actually intelligible when abstracted from matter.

Hence there is in no way a composition of matter and form in a soul or an intelligence so that matter may be thought to exist in them as it does in corporeal substances. There is in them, however, a composition of form and act of existing (esse). Thus, in the commentary on the ninth proposition of the *Liber de causis*,[6] it is said that an intelligence is a being having form and act of existing; and form is understood here as the essence itself or the simple nature.

---

[1] The common doctrine of the Franciscans, with the exception of John of Rupella. See especially Alexander of Hales (?), *Summa Theologica*, I–II, Inq. II, tr. II, q. unica, n. 106 (Quaracchi, II, p. 135); St. Bonaventure, *In II Sent.*, Lib. II, Dist. III, P. 1, a. 1, q. 1 (Quaracchi, II, p. 91); Roger Bacon, *Liber Primus Communium Naturalium*, Pars IV, Dist. 3, c. 4 (*Opera*, Oxford, 1911, Fasc. III, p. 291). It was also taught by some Dominicans, such as Roland of Cremona, Peter of Tarantasia, Robert of Fishacre and Robert Kilwardby. See Dom. O. Lottin, "La composition hylemorphique des substances spirituelles. Les debuts de la controverse," *Revue neo-scolastique de philosophie*, 34 (1932), pp. 21–41; M.-D. Roland-Gosselin, *op. cit.*, p. 30, note 2.

[2] See Avencebrolis (Ibn Gebirol) *Fons Vitae*, ed. cit., III, 18,p. 118.

[3] See Aristotle, *De Anima*, III, 4, 429a 10–25; St. Albert, *In II Sent.*, Dist. 1A, a. 4, ed. cit., vol. 27, p. 14b.

[4] See Avicenna, *De Anima*, V, 2, fol. 22ᵛb; 23ʳb; St. Albert, *In II Sent.*, Dist. 19A, a. 1 sed contra 3, vol. 27, p. 329a.

[5] That is, the being endowed with intelligence gives to the form an intentional mode of existing within itself.

[6] O. Bardenhewer, *Die pseudo-aristotelische Schrift "Ueber das reine Gute" bekannt unter dem Namen "Liber de Causis,"* 8, p. 173. The *Liber de Causis* is a Latin translation of a neoplatonic work whose contents are taken from Proclus' *Elements of Theology*. The composition of form and being (esse) found in this work is not one between essence and act of existing in the Thomistic sense. St. Thomas accommodates the words of the *Liber de Causis* to his own doctrine. For this work, *esse* is simply the first and most fundamental determination of a thing, the first substratum of the essential forms, such as life and intelligence, which later determine it.

It is easy to see how this is so. Whatever things are so related to each other that one is the cause of the other's existing, the one which is the cause can exist without the other, but not conversely. Now, we find the relation of matter and form such that form makes matter exist. It is thus impossible that matter exist without some form. On the other hand, it is not impossible that some form exist without matter, for form as such does not depend on matter. If we find some forms which can exist only in matter, this happens to them because they are far removed from the First Principle, which is primary and pure act. So, those forms closest to the First Principle subsist in virtue of themselves without matter. For, as we have said,[7] not every kind of form requires matter, and the intelligences are forms of this sort. It is not necessary, then, that the essences or quiddities of these substances be other than form itself.

Accordingly, the essence of a composite substance differs from that of a simple substance in that the essence of the composite substance is not form alone, but includes form and matter. The essence of a simple substance, on the contrary, is form alone. Two other differences follow upon this. The first is that we can signify the essence of a composite substance as a whole or as a part. This happens, as we have said,[8] because of the designation of matter. We may not predicate, then, in just any way the essence of a composite thing of the composite thing itself. We cannot say, for instance, that man is his quiddity. But the essence of a simple being, which is its form, cannot be signified except as a whole, since nothing is there besides the form as receiving the form. Thus, no matter in what way the essence of a simple substance is considered, it may be predicated of the substance. That is why Avicenna says: "The quiddity of a simple thing is the simple thing itself because there is nothing else receiving it."[9]

The second difference is that the essences of composite beings are multiplied according to the division of designated matter, because they are received in it. That is why it happens that some beings are specifically the same and numerically diverse. But, since the essence of a simple substance is not received in matter, it cannot be multiplied in this way. Of necessity, therefore, we do not find among those substances many individuals of the same species; but, as Avicenna clearly states,[10] there are as many species among them as there are individuals.

Although substances of this kind are forms alone and immaterial, they are not in every way simple so as to be pure act. They do have an admixture of potency, which is evident from the following consideration. Whatever does not belong to the notion of an essence or quiddity comes from without and enters into composition with the essence, for no essence is intelligible without its parts. Now, every essence or quiddity can be understood without anything being known of its existing. I can know what a man or a phoenix is and still be ignorant whether it exists in reality. From this it is clear that the act of

---

[7] See above, p. 304.
[8] See above, p. 300.

[9] *Meta.*, V, 5, fol. 90^{r}a.
[10] *Ibid.*, fol. 87^{v}a.

existing is other than essence or quiddity, unless, perhaps, there is a being whose quiddity is its very act of existing.[11] And there can be only one such being, the First Being. For nothing can be multiplied except: (1) through the addition of some difference, as the generic nature is multiplied into species; or (2) by the form being received in different individuals; or (3) by one thing being separate and another thing being received in something — for instance, if there were a separated heat,[12] by reason of its very separation it would be different from heat which is not separated. But, should there exist some being which is simply the act of existing, so that the act of existing be itself subsistent, a difference cannot be added to this act of existing. Otherwise, it would not be purely and simply the act of existing, but the act of existing plus a certain form. Much less can matter be added to it, because then it would not be a subsistent, but a material, act of existing. So we conclude that there can only be one such being which is its very act of existing. With this exception, in every other thing its act of existing is other than its quiddity, nature or form. The intelligences' act of existing must therefore be over and above their form, and for that reason it has been said[13] that an intelligence is form and act of existing.

Now, whatever belongs to a being is either caused by the principles of its nature, as the capability of laughter in man, or it comes to it from some extrinsic principle, as light in the air from the sun's influence. But it is impossible that the act of existing be caused by a thing's form or its quiddity, (I say *caused* as by an efficient cause);[14] for then something would be the cause of itself and would bring itself into existence — which is impossible. Everything, then, which is such that its act of existing is other than its nature must needs have its act of existing from something else. And since every being which exists through another is reduced, as to its first cause, to one existing in virtue of itself, there must be some being which is the cause of the existing of all things because it itself is the act of existing alone. If that were not so, we would proceed to infinity among causes, since, as we have said,[15] every being which is not the act of existing alone has a cause of its existence. Evidently, then, an intelligence is form and act of existing, and it has its act

---

[11] The proof for the distinction between essence and the act of existing in every creature rests on the fact that the essence of a creature in no way implies its existence. Actual existence does not enter into its concept. For the distinction between essence and the act of existing, see St. Thomas, *Super Boetium de Hebdomadibus*, c. 2 (*Opuscula Omnia*, vol. 1, p. 175); *Qu. Disp. De Veritate*, 8, 8; *Contra Gentiles*, II, 52; *Summa Theologiae*, I, 44, 1. See also H. Renard, *The Philosophy of Being*, pp. 45–59; E. Gilson, *Le Thomisme*, pp. 43–68; J. de Finance, *Etre et Agir dans la philosophie de S. Thomas*, pp. 94–110.

[12] Such a separated heat would be a subsistent form, "heat-in-itself," separate from all hot things. St. Thomas, of course, is using this as a hypothetical example, and does not subscribe to the Platonic doctrine of separated forms.

[13] See above, p. 304, note 6.

[14] Although the form is not the efficient cause of the act of existing, it does give existence as a *formal cause*. In this sense it is said to make matter exist. See above, p. 300, note 12.

[15] In the preceding sentence. Cf. also *Summa Theologiae*, I, 44, 1.

of existing from the First Being which is simply the act of existing. This is the First Cause, God.

Now, every being receiving something from another is potential with respect to what it receives, and what is received in it is its act. The quiddity itself, then, or the form which is the intelligence must be potential with respect to the existence which it receives from God, and that existence (esse)[16] is received as an act. Potency and act are thus found in the intelligences, but not form and matter except in an equivocal sense. So, too, as the Commentator says in his exposition on the third book of the *De Anima*,[17] to suffer, to receive, to be a subject of, and all characteristics of this sort which seem to belong to things by reason of matter, belong equivocally to intellectual and corporeal substances.

Furthermore, since the quiddity of an intelligence is, as we have said,[18] the intelligence itself, its quiddity or essence is identical with itself, and the act of existing it receives from God is that whereby it subsists in the world of things. For that reason some assert[19] that a substance of this kind is composed of *that by which it is* (*quo est*) and *that which it is* (*quod est*), or, as Boethius says,[20] of *that which it is* (*quod est*) and its *act of existing* (*esse*). Since, then, both potency and act are in the intelligences, finding a multitude among them will not be difficult, whereas it would be impossible if there were no potency in them. Thus, the Commentator declares in his exposition on the third book of the *De Anima*[21] that, if we did not know the nature of the possible intellect, we could not find multitude among separated substances.

These substances are accordingly distinct from one another by reason of their degree of potency and act. A superior intelligence, closer to the First Being, has more act and less potency, and so on with the others. This grada-

---

[16] To avoid repeating the word act, *esse* (which has generally been translated act of existing) is here rendered *existence*.

[17] Averroes, *In De Anima* III, 2, t. c. 14, fol. 168ʳᵛb9.

[18] See above, p. 301.

[19] See Alexander of Hales (?), *Summa Theol.*, I–II, Inq. II, Tr. II, q. unica, n. 106 (Quaracchi, II, p. 135); St. Bonaventure, *In II Sent.*, Lib. II, Dist. III, P. I, a. 1, q. 1 (Quaracchi, II, p. 91); St. Albert, *In II Sent.*, Dist. I A, a. 4 (Vol. 27, p. 14). For these philosophers, however, *quod est* is the concrete subject (e.g., Peter). *Quo est* is the essence or abstract nature (e.g., *humanity*), not the act of existing. See M.-D. Roland-Gosselin, *op. cit.*, p. 167.

For William of Auvergne, *id quod est* designates the essence; *id quo est* or *esse* designates existence, conceived after the manner of Avicenna as an accident of the essence. See P. Duhem, *Le Systeme du Monde*, Vol. 5, pp. 300 ff; J. Reginald O'Donnell, "The Notion of Being in William of Auvergne," *Proceedings of the American Catholic Philosophical Association*, 21 (1946), 156–165.

[20] *De Hebd.*; PL 64, 1311C. Boethius, however, does not mean that there is a composition in creatures of essence and act of existing. The distinction between the Boethian *quod est* and *esse* is that between the concrete substance and the abstract nature or form in which it participates. See Hermann Brosch, *Der Seinsbegriff bei Boethius*, p. 65; M.-D. Roland-Gosselin, *op. cit.*, pp. 142 ff; L.-B. Geiger, "La Participation dans la philosophie de S. Thomas d'Aquin" pp. 36 ff.

[21] Averroes, *In De Anima*, III, 1, t. c. 5, fol. 166ʳa16.

tion terminates in the human soul which holds the lowest degree among intellectual substances. As the Commentator states in his exposition on the third book of the *De Anima*,[22] the possible intellect of the human soul bears the same relation to intelligible forms that prime matter, holding the lowest position in sensible existence, bears to sensible forms. That is why the Philosopher compares it to a blank tablet on which nothing is written.[23] Having more potency than the other intellectual substances, the human soul is so close to matter that a material thing is drawn to share in its own act of existing, so that from soul and body there results in the one composite one act of existing,[24] although insofar as it is the soul's act of existing it is not dependent on the body. Posterior to that form which is the soul, other forms are found still more potential and close to matter, to such a point that they do not exist without matter. Among these forms, too, we find an order and hierarchy, until we reach the primary forms of the elements, which are closest to matter. Being so close to matter, they operate only according to the exigencies of active and passive qualities and other dispositions which prepare matter to receive form.

---

[22] *Ibid.*, fol. 160ᵛb42.

[23] Aristotle, *De Anima*, III, 4, 430a1.

[24] The unity of man is consequently that of his act of existing. The soul does not have a complete nature; the body must be added to it for its completion. Still, the soul does have a complete act of existing. That spiritual act of existing belongs in full right to the soul, and it is communicated to the body so that there is one act of existing of the whole composite. See *Qu. Disp. De Anima*, 1, ad 1m; *Contra Gentiles*, II, 68. See also E. Gilson, *Le Thomisme*, p. 277.

READINGS FOR CHAPTER VI.
THE TRANSCENDENTALS

1. Relation of the Transcendentals to Being

St. Thomas, *Truth*, q. 1, art. 1.*

Question One   Article I

The Problem under Discussion Is Truth, and in the
First Article We Ask: What Is Truth?

Difficulties:

It seems that the true is exactly the same as being, for

1. Augustine says: "The true is that which is."¹ But that which is, is simply being. The true, therefore, means exactly the same as being.

2. It was said in reply that the true and being are the same materially but differ formally. — On the contrary the nature of a thing is signified by its definition; and the definition of the true, according to Augustine, is "that which is."² He rejects all other definitions. Now, since the true and being are materially the same, it seems that they are also formally the same.

3. Things which differ conceptually are so related to each other that one of them can be understood without the other. For this reason, Boethius says³ that the existence of God can be understood if for a moment we mentally separate His goodness from His existence. Being, however, can in no way be understood apart from the true, for being is known only insofar as it is true. Therefore, the true and being do not differ conceptually.

4. If the true is not the same as being, it must be a state of being. But it cannot be a state of being. It is not a state that entirely corrupts — otherwise, this would follow: "It is true. Therefore, it is non-being" — as it follows when we say: "This man is dead. Therefore, this is not a man."

Similarly, the true is not a state that limits. If it were, one could not say: "It is true. Therefore it is." For one cannot say that a thing is white simply because it has white teeth. Finally, the true is not a state which contracts or specifies being, for it is convertible with being. It follows, therefore, that the true and being are entirely the same.

* Translated by Robert W. Mulligan, S.J. (Chicago: Henry Regnery, 1952).
¹ St. Augustine, *Soliloquiorum libri duo*, II, 5.
² *Ibid.*
³ Boethius, *De hebdomadibus.*

5. Things in the same state are the same. But the true and being are in the same state. Therefore, they are the same. For Aristotle writes: "The state of a thing in its act of existence is the same as its state in truth."[4] Therefore, the true and being are entirely the same.

6. Things not the same differ in some respect. But the true and being differ in no respect. They do not differ essentially, for every being is true by its very essence. And they do not differ in any other ways, for they must belong to some common genus. Therefore, they are entirely the same.

7. If they were not entirely the same, the true would add something to being. But the true adds nothing to being, even though it has greater extension than being. This is borne out by the statement of the Philosopher that we define the true as: "That which affirms the existence of what is, and denies the existence of what is not."[5] Consequently, the true includes both being and non-being; since it does not add anything to being it seems to be entirely the same as being.

To the Contrary:

1. Useless repetition of the same thing is meaningless; so, if the true were the same as being, it would be meaningless to say: "Being is true." This, however, is hardly correct. Therefore, they are not the same.

2. Being and the good are convertible. The true and the good, however, are not interchangeable, for some things, such as fornication, are true but not good. The true, therefore, and being are not interchangeable. And so they are not the same.

3. In all creatures, as Boethius has pointed out, "to be is other than that which is."[6] Now, the true signifies the existence of things. Consequently, in creatures it is different from that which is. But that which is, is the same as being. Therefore, in creatures the true is different from being.

4. Things related as before and after must differ. But the true and being are related in the aforesaid manner; for, as is said in *The Causes:* "The first of all created things is the act of existence."[7] In a study of this work, a commentator writes as follows: "Everything else is predicated as a specification of being."[8] Consequently, everything else comes after being. Therefore, the true and being are not the same.

5. What are predicated of a cause and of the effects of the cause are more united in the cause than in its effects — and more so in God than in creatures. But in God four predicates — being, the one, the true, and the good — are appropriated as follows: being, to the essence; the one, to the Father; the true, to the Son; and the good, to the Holy Spirit.

Since the divine Persons are really and not merely conceptually distinct,

---

[4] Aristotle, *Metaphysics*, 993b27.
[5] *Ibid.*, 1011b27.
[6] Boethius, *De hebdomadibus.*

[7] *Liber de Causis*, IV.
[8] *Ibid.*, XV, XVII, XXXI.

these notions cannot be predicated of each other; if really distinct when verified of the divine Persons, the four notions in question are much more so when verified of creatures.

Reply:

When investigating the nature of anything, one should make the same kind of analysis as he makes when he reduces a proposition to certain self-evident principles. Otherwise, both types of knowledge will become involved in an infinite regress, and science and our knowledge of things will perish.

Now, as Avicenna says,[9] that which the intellect first conceives as, in a way, the most evident, and to which it reduces all its concepts, is being. Consequently, all the other conceptions of the intellect are had by additions to being. But nothing can be added to being as though it were something not included in being — in the way that a difference is added to a genus or an accident to a subject — for every reality is essentially a being. The Philosopher has shown this[10] by proving that being cannot be a genus. Yet, in this sense, some predicates may be said to add to being inasmuch as they express a mode of being not expressed by the term *being*. This happens in two ways.

First, the mode expressed is a certain special manner of being; for there are different grades of being according to which we speak when we speak of different levels of existence, and according to these grades different things are classified. Consequently, *substance* does not add a difference to being by signifying some reality added to it, but *substance* simply expresses a special manner of existing, namely, as a being in itself. The same is true of the other classes of existents.

Second, some are said to add to being because the mode they express is one that is common, and consequent upon every being. This mode can be taken in two ways: first, insofar as it follows upon every being considered absolutely; second, insofar as it follows upon every being considered in relation to another. In the first, the term is used in two ways, because it expresses something in the being either affirmatively or negatively. We can, however, find nothing that can be predicated of every being affirmatively and, at the same time, absolutely, with the exception of its essence by which the being is said to be. To express this, the term *thing* is used; for, according to Avicenna,[11] thing differs from being because being gets its name from to-be, but thing expresses the quiddity or essence of the being. There is, however, a negation consequent upon every being considered absolutely: its undividedness, and this is expressed by *one*. For the *one* is simply undivided being.

If the mode of being is taken in the second way — according to the relation of one being to another — we find a twofold use. The first is based on the

9 Avicenna, *Metaphysica*, I, 6; I, 4; I, 6.
10 Aristotle, *Metaphysics*, 993b23.
11 Avicenna, *Metaphysica*, I, 6.

distinction of one being from another, and this distinctness is expressed by the word *something*, which implies, as it were, *some other thing*. For, just as a being is said to be *one* insofar as it is without division in itself, so it is said to be *something* insofar as it is divided from others. The second division is based on the correspondence one being has with another. This is possible only if there is something which is such that it agrees with every being. Such a being is the soul, which, as is said in *The Soul*, "in some way is all things."[12] The soul, however, has both knowing and appetitive powers. Good expresses the correspondence of being to the appetitive power, for, and so we note in the *Ethics*, the good is "that which all desire."[13] *True* expresses the correspondence of being to the knowing power, for all knowing is produced by an assimilation of the knower to the thing known, so that assimilation is said to be the cause of knowledge. Similarly, the sense of sight knows a color by being informed with a species of the color.

The first reference of being to the intellect, therefore, consists in its agreement with the intellect. This agreement is called "the conformity of thing and intellect." In this conformity is fulfilled the formal constituent of the true, and this is what *the true* adds to being, namely, the conformity or equation of thing and intellect. As we said, the knowledge of a thing is a consequence of this conformity; therefore, it is an effect of truth, even though the fact that the thing is a being is prior to its truth.

Consequently, truth or the true has been defined in three ways. First of all, it is defined according to that which precedes truth and is the basis of truth. This is why Augustine writes: "The true is that which is,"[14] and Avicenna: "The truth of each thing is a property of the act of being which has been established for it."[15] Still others say "The true is the undividedness of the act of existence from that which is."[16]

Truth is also defined in another way — according to that in which its intelligible determination is formally completed. Thus, Isaac writes: "Truth is the conformity of thing and intellect,"[17] and Anselm: "Truth is a rectitude perceptible only by the mind."[18] This rectitude, of course, is said to be based on some conformity. The Philosopher says that in defining truth we say that truth is had when one affirms that "to be which is, and that not to be which is not."[19]

The third way of defining truth is according to the effect following upon it. Thus, Hilary says[20] that the true is that which manifests and proclaims

---

[12] Aristotle, *De Anima*, 431b21.
[13] Aristotle, *Nicomachean Ethics*, 1094a2.
[14] St. Augustine, *Soliloquiorum*, II, 5.
[15] Avicenna, *Metaphysica*, VIII, 6.
[16] St. Thomas speaks of this definition as one commonly used in the medieval schools. Cf. St. Anselm, *De Veritate*, II.
[17] Isaac Israel, *Liber de definicionibus*.
[18] St. Anselm, *De Veritate*, XI.
[19] Aristotle, *Metaphysics*, 1011b27.
[20] St. Hilary, *De Trinitate*, V.

existence. And Augustine says: "Truth is that by which that which is, is so shown,"[21] and also: "Truth is that according to which we judge about inferior things."[22]

Answers to Difficulties:

1. That definition of Augustine is given for the true as it has its foundation in reality and not as its formal nature is given complete expression by conformity of thing and intellect. An alternative answer would be that in the statement, "The true is that which is," the word *is* is not here understood as referring to the act of existing, but rather as the mark of the intellectual act of judging, signifying, that is, the affirmation of a proposition. The meaning would then be this: "The true is that which is — it is had when the existence of what is, is affirmed." If this is its meaning, then Augustine's definition agrees with that of the Philosopher mentioned above.

2. The answer is clear from what has been said.

3. "Something can be understood without another" can be taken in two ways. It can mean that something can be known while another remains unknown. Taken in this way, it is true that things which differ conceptually are such that one can be understood without the other. But there is another way that a thing can be understood without another: when it is known even though the other does not exist. Taken in this sense, being cannot be known without the true, for it cannot be known unless it agrees with or conforms to intellect. It is not necessary, however, that everyone who understands the formal notion of being should also understand the formal notion of the true — just as not everyone who understands being understands the agent intellect, even though nothing can be known without the agent intellect.

4. The true is a state of being even though it does not add any reality to being or express any special mode of existence. It is rather something that is generally found in every being, although it is not expressed by the word *being*. Consequently, it is not a state that corrupts, limits, or contracts.

5. In this objection, *condition* should not be understood as belonging to the genus of quality. It implies, rather, a certain order; for those which are the cause of the existence of other things are themselves beings most completely, and those which are the cause of the truth of other things are themselves true most completely. It is for this reason that the Philosopher concludes[23] that the rank of a thing in its existence corresponds to its rank in truth, so that when one finds that which is most fully being, he finds there also that which is most fully true. But this does not mean that being and the true are the same in concept. It means simply that in the degree in which a thing has being, in that degree it is capable of being proportioned to intellect. Consequently, the true is dependent upon the formal character of being.

---

[21] St. Augustine, *De Vera Religione*, XXXVI.
[22] *Ibid.*, XXXI.
[23] Aristotle, *Metaphysics*, 993b27–30.

6. There is a conceptual difference between the true and being since there is something in the notion of the true that is not in the concept of the existing — not in such a way, however, that there is something in the concept of being which is not in the concept of the true. They do not differ essentially nor are they distinguished from one another by opposing difference.

7. The true does not have a wider extension than being. Being is, in some way, predicated of non-being insofar as non-being is apprehended by the intellect. For, as the Philosopher says,[24] the negation or the privation of being may, in a sense, be called being. Avicenna supports this by pointing out[25] that one can form propositions only of beings, for that about which a proposition is formed must be apprehended by the intellect. Consequently, it is clear that everything true is being in some way.

Answers to Contrary Difficulties:

1. The reason why it is not tautological to call a being true is that something is expressed by the word *true* that is not expressed by the word *being*, and not that the two differ in reality.

2. Although fornication is evil, it possesses some being and can conform to intellect. Accordingly, the formal character of the true is found here. So it is clear that *true* is coextensive with *being*.

3. In the statement, "To be is other than that which is," the act of being is distinguished from that to which that act belongs. But the name of being is taken from the act of existence, not from that whose act it is. Hence, the argument does not follow.

4. The true comes after being in this respect, that the notion of the true differs from that of being in the manner we have described.

5. This argument has three flaws. First, although the Persons are really distinct, the things appropriated to each Person are only conceptually, and not really, distinct. Secondly, although the Persons are really distinct from each other, they are not really distinct from the essence; so, truth appropriated to the Person of the Son is not distinct from the act of existence He possesses through the divine essence. Thirdly, although being, the true, the one, and the good are more united in God than they are in created beings, it does not necessarily follow, from the fact that they are only conceptually distinct in God, that they are really distinct in created beings. This line of argument is valid only when it is applied to things which are not by their very nature one in reality, as wisdom and power, which, although one in God, are distinct in creatures. But being, the true, the one, and the good are such that by their very nature they are one in reality. Therefore, no matter where they are found, they are really one. Their unity in God, however, is more perfect than their unity in creatures.

---

[24] *Ibid.*, 1004a16; *Physics*, 193b20.
[25] Avicenna, *Metaphysica*, I, 6.

2. Transcendental Truth

St. Thomas, *Truth*, q. 1, art. 2.*

In the Second Article We Ask: Is Truth Found
Principally in the Intellect or in Things?

Difficulties:

It seems that it is found principally in things, for

1. It was pointed out that the true is convertible with being. But being is found more principally in things than in the soul. The true, therefore, is principally outside the soul.

2. Things are not in the soul through their essences but, as pointed out by the Philosopher,[1] through species. If, therefore, truth is found principally in the soul, truth will not be the essence of a thing but merely its likeness or species; and the true will be the species of a being existing outside the soul. But the species of a thing existing in the soul is not predicated of a thing outside the soul and is not convertible with it; for, if this were so, the true could not be converted with being — which is false.

3. That which is in something is based upon that in which it is. If truth, then, is principally in the soul, judgments about truth will have as their criterion the soul's estimation. This would revive that error of the ancient philosophers[2] who said that any opinion a person has in his intellect is true and that two contradictories can be true at the same time. This, of course, is absurd.

4. If truth is principally in the intellect, anything which pertains to the intellect should be included in the definition of truth. Augustine, however, sharply criticizes[3] such definitions, as, for example, "The true is that which is as it is seen." For, according to this definition, something would not be true if it were not seen. This is clearly false of rocks hidden deep in the earth. Augustine similarly criticizes[4] the following definition: "The true is that which is as it appears to the knower, provided he is willing and able to know." For, according to this definition, something would not be true unless the knower wished and were able to know. The same criticism can be leveled against other definitions that include any reference to intellect. Truth, therefore, is not principally in the intellect.

---

* Mulligan, *op. cit.*
[1] Aristotle, *De Anima*, 431b29.
[2] Democritus and Protagoras, according to Aristotle, *De Anima*, 404a28.
[3] St. Augustine, *Soliloquiorum*, II, 4–5.
[4] *Ibid.*

To the Contrary:

1. The Philosopher says: "The true and the false are not in things but in the mind."[5]

2. Truth is "the conformity of thing and intellect." But since this conformity can be only in the intellect, truth is only in the intellect.

Reply:

When a predicate is used primarily and secondarily of many things, it is not necessary that that which is the cause of the others receive the primary predication of the common term, but rather that in which the meaning of the common term is first fully verified. For example, *healthy* is primarily predicated of an animal, for it is in an animal that the nature of health is first found in its fullest sense. But inasmuch as medicine causes health, it is also said to be healthy. Therefore, since truth is predicated of many things in a primary and secondary sense, it ought to be primarily predicated of that in which its full meaning is primarily found.

Now, the fulfillment of any motion is found in the term of the motion; and, since the term of the motion of a cognitive power is the soul, the known must be in the knower after the manner of the knower. But the motion of an appetitive power terminates in things. For this reason the Philosopher speaks[6] of a sort of circle formed by the acts of the soul: for a thing outside the soul moves the intellect, and the thing known moves the appetite, which tends to reach the things from which the motion originally started. Since good, as mentioned previously,[7] expresses a relation to appetite, and true, a relation to the intellect, the Philosopher says,[8] that good and evil are in things, but true and false are in the mind. A thing is not called true, however, unless it conforms to an intellect. The true, therefore, is found secondarily in things and primarily in intellect.

Note, however, that a thing is referred differently to the practical intellect than it is to the speculative intellect. Since the practical intellect causes things, it is a measure of what it causes. But, since the speculative intellect is receptive in regard to things, it is, in a certain sense, moved by things and consequently measured by them. It is clear, therefore, that, as is said in the *Metaphysics*,[9] natural things from which our intellect gets its scientific knowledge measure our intellect. Yet these things are themselves measured by the divine intellect, in which are all created things — just as all works of art find their origin in the intellect of an artist. The divine intellect, therefore, measures and is not measured; a natural thing both measures and is measured; but our intellect is measured, and measures only artifacts, not natural things.

---

5 Aristotle, *Metaphysics*, 1027b26.
6 Aristotle, *De Anima*, 433b21–30.
9 *Ibid.*, 1053a33; 1057a9–13.

7 Q. 1, art. 1, reply.
8 Aristotle, *Metaphysics*, 1027b26.

A natural thing, therefore, being placed between two intellects, is called *true* insofar as it conforms to either. It is said to be true with respect to its conformity with the divine intellect insofar as it fulfills the end to which it was ordained by the divine intellect. This is clear from the writings of Anselm[10] and Augustine,[11] as well as from the definition of Avicenna, previously cited: "The truth of anything is a property of the act of being which has been established for it."[12] With respect to its conformity with a human intellect, a thing is said to be true insofar as it is such as to cause a true estimate about itself; and a thing is said to be false if, as Aristotle says, "by nature it is such that it seems to be what it is not, or seems to possess qualities which it does not possess."[13]

In a natural thing, truth is found especially in the first, rather than in the second, sense; for its reference to the divine intellect comes before its reference to a human intellect. Even if there were no human intellects, things could be said to be true because of their relation to the divine intellect. But if, by an impossible supposition, intellect did not exist and things did continue to exist, then the essentials of truth would in no way remain.

Answers to Difficulties:

1. As is clear from the discussion, *true* is predicated primarily of a true intellect and secondarily of a thing conformed with intellect. *True* taken in either sense, however, is interchangeable with being, but in different ways. Used of things, it can be interchanged with being through a judgment asserting merely material identity, for every being is conformed with the divine intellect and can be conformed with a human intellect. The converse of this is also true.

But if *true* is understood as used of the intellect, then it can be converted with being outside the soul — not as denominating the same subject, but as expressing conformity. For every true act of understanding is referred to a being, and every being corresponds to a true act of understanding.

2. The solution of the second argument is clear from the solution of the first.

3. What is in another does not depend on that other unless it is caused by the principles of that other. For example, even though light is in the air, it is caused by something extrinsic, the sun; and it is based on the motion of the sun rather than on air. In the same way, truth which is in the soul but caused by things does not depend on what one thinks but on the existence of things. For from the fact that a thing is or is not, a statement of an intellect is said to be true or false.

----

[10] St. Anselm, *De Veritate*, VII.
[11] St. Augustine, *De Vera Religione*, XXXI.
[12] Avicenna, *Metaphysica*, VIII, 6.
[13] Aristotle, *Metaphysics*, 1024b22–24.

4. Augustine is speaking of a thing's being seen by the human intellect. Truth, of course, does not depend on this, for many things exist that are not known by our intellects. There is nothing, however, that the divine intellect does not actually know, and nothing that the human intellect does not know potentially, for the agent intellect is said to be that "by which we become all things."[14] For this reason, one can place in the definition of a true thing its actually being seen by the divine intellect, but not its being seen by a human intellect — except potentially, as is clear from our earlier discussion.

[14] Aristotle, De Anima, 430a14.

3. The Transcendental One

St. Thomas, Summa Theologiae, I, q. 11, art. 1.*

Whether One Adds Anything To Being?

We proceed thus to the First Article: —

Objection 1. It seems that one adds something to being. For everything is in a determinate genus by addition to being, which encompasses all genera. But one is in a determinate genus, for it is the principle of number, which is a species of quantity. Therefore one adds something to being.

Obj. 2. Further, that which divides something common is by addition to it. But being is divided by one and by many. Therefore one adds something to being.

Obj. 3. Further, if one does not add to being, one and being must have the same meaning. But it would be nugatory to call being by the name of being: therefore it would be equally so to call being one. Now this is false. Therefore one adds something to being.

On the contrary, Dionysius says: Nothing which exists is not in some way one,[1] which would be false if one were an addition to being, in the sense of limiting it. Therefore one is not an addition to being.

I answer that, One does not add any reality to being, but is only the negation of division; for one means undivided being. This is the very reason why one is convertible with being. For every being is either simple or composite. But what is simple is undivided, both actually and potentially; whereas what is composite has not being while its parts are divided, but after they make up and compose it. Hence it is manifest that the being of anything consists in indivision; and hence it is that everything guards its unity as it guards its being.

---

* Anton C. Pegis, Basic Writings of St. Thomas (New York: Random House, 1945).
[1] De Div. Nom., V, 2 (PG 3, 977).

Reply Obj. 1. Some, thinking that the *one* convertible with *being* is the same as the *one* which is the principle of number, were divided into contrary opinions. Pythagoras and Plato, seeing that the *one* convertible with *being* did not add any reality to *being*, but signified the substance of *being* as undivided, thought that the same applied to the *one* which is the principle of number.[2] And because number is composed of unities, they thought that numbers were the substances of all things. Avicenna, however, on the contrary, considering that the *one* which is the principle of number added a reality to the substance of being (otherwise number made of unities would not be a species of quantity), thought that the *one* convertible with *being* added a reality to the substance of beings; as *white* adds to *man*.[3] This, however, is manifestly false, inasmuch as each thing is *one* by its substance. For if a thing were *one* by anything else but by its substance, since this again would be *one*, supposing it were again *one* by another thing, we should be driven on to infinity. Hence we must adhere to the former statement; therefore we must say that the *one* which is convertible with *being* does not add a reality to *being*; but that the *one* which is the principle of number does add a reality to *being*, belonging to the genus of quantity.

Reply Obj. 2. There is nothing to prevent a thing, which in one way is divided, from being in another way undivided, as what is divided in number may be undivided in species; thus it may be that a thing is in one way *one*, and in another way *many*. Still, if it is absolutely undivided, either because it is so according to what belongs to its essence (though it may be divided as regards what is outside its essence, as what is one in subject may have many accidents), or because it is undivided actually, and divided potentially (as what is *one* in the whole, and is *many* in its parts), in which case a thing will be *one* absolutely, and *many* accidentally. On the other hand, if it be undivided accidentally, and divided absolutely, as if it were divided in essence and undivided in idea or in principle or cause, it will be *many* absolutely, and *one* accidentally; as what are *many* in number, and *one* in species, or *one* in principle. This is the way in which being is divided by *one* and by *many*; as it were by *one* absolutely, and by *many* accidentally. For multitude itself would not be contained under *being* unless it were in some way contained under *one*. Thus Dionysius says that *there is no kind of multitude that is not in a way one. But what are many in their parts are one in their whole; and what are many in accidents are one in subject; and what are many in number are one in species; and what are many in species are one in genus; and what are many in processions are one in principle.*[4]

Reply Obj. 3. It does not follow that it is nugatory to say *being* is *one*; since *one* adds something to *being* logically.

[2] Cf. Aristotle, *Metaph.*, I, 5 (987a 13; a 19); I 6 (987b 23). Cf. also St. Thomas *In Metaph.*, I, lect. 7 and 8. *Destruct.*, III (IX, 25ʳa).
[3] *Metaph.*, III, 3 (79r). Cf. also Averroes, *Destruct.*
[4] *De Div. Nom.*, XIII, 2 (PG 3, 980).

4. The One and the Many

St. Thomas, *Summa Theologiae*, I, q. 11, art. 2.*

Whether One and Many Are Opposed to Each Other?

We proceed thus to the Second Article: —

Objection 1. It seems that one and many are not mutually opposed. For no opposite is predicated of its opposite. But every multitude is in a certain way one, as appears from the preceding article. Therefore one is not opposed to multitude.

Obj. 2. Further, no opposite is constituted by its opposite. But *multitude* is constituted by one. Therefore it is not opposed to *multitude*.

Obj. 3. Further, each thing has one opposite. But the opposite of *many* is few. Therefore, the opposite is not *one*.

Obj. 4. Further, if one is opposed to *multitude*, it is opposed as the undivided is to the divided, and is thus opposed to it as privation is to habit. But this appears to be incongruous; because it would follow that one comes after *multitude*, and is defined by it; whereas, on the contrary, *multitude* is defined by one. Hence there would be a vicious circle in the definition; which is inadmissible. Therefore one and many are opposed to each other.

I answer that, One is opposed to many, but in various ways. The One which is the principle of number is opposed to *multitude* which is number as the measure is to the thing measured. For one implies the idea of a primary measure; and number is *multitude* measured by one, as is clear from *Metaph.* x.[1] But the one which is convertible with being is opposed to multitude by way of privation; as the undivided is to the divided.

Reply Obj. 1. No privation entirely takes away the being of a thing, inasmuch as privation means *negation in the subject*, according to the Philosopher.[2] Nevertheless, every privation takes away some being; and so in being, by reason of its community, the privation of being has its foundation in being; which is not the case in privations of special forms, as of sight, or of whiteness, and the like. And what applies to being applies also to one and to good, which are convertible with being, for the privation of good is founded in some good; likewise the removal of unity is founded in some one thing. Hence it happens that multitude is some one thing, and evil is some good thing, and non-being is some kind of being. Nevertheless, opposite is not predicated of opposite, since one is absolute, and the other is relative; for what is relatively being (i.e., in potency) is non-being absolutely, i.e., actually; or what is being absolutely in the genus of substance,

---

* Pegis, op. cit.
[1] Aristotle, *Metaph.*, IX, I (1052b 18); 6 (1057a 3).
[2] *Op. cit.*, III, 2 (1004a 15); cf. *Cat.*, X (12a 26).

is nonbeing relatively as regards some accidental being. In the same way, what is relatively good is absolutely bad, or vice versa; likewise, what is absolutely one is relatively many, and vice versa.

Reply Obj. 2. A whole is twofold. In one sense it is homogeneous, composed of like parts; in another sense it is heterogeneous, composed of dissimilar parts; Now in every homogeneous whole, the whole is made up of parts having the form of the whole, as, for instance, every part of water is water; and such is the constitution of a continuous thing made up of its parts. In every heterogeneous whole, however, every part is wanting in the form belonging to the whole; as, for instance, no part of a house is a house, nor is any part of man a man. Now multitude is such a kind of whole. Therefore, inasmuch as its part has not the form of the multitude, the latter is composed of unities, as a house is composed of not houses; not, indeed, as if unities constituted multitude so far as they are undivided, in which way they are opposed to multitude, but so far as they have being; as also the parts of a house make up the house by the fact that they are beings, not by the fact that they are not houses.

Reply Obj. 3. Many is taken in two ways: absolutely, and in that sense it is opposed to one; in another way, as importing some kind of excess, in which sense it is opposed to few. Hence, in the first sense two are many; but not in the second sense.

Reply Obj. 4. One is opposed to many privatively, inasmuch as the idea of many involves division. Hence division must be prior to unity, not absolutely in itself, but according to our way of apprehension. For we apprehend simple things by composite things; and hence we define a point to be, what has no part, or the beginning of a line. Multitude also, in idea, follows on one; because we do not understand divided things to convey the idea of multitude except by the fact that we attribute unity to every member. Hence one is placed in the definition of multitude; but multitude is not placed in the definition of one. But division comes to be understood from the very negation of being: so what first comes to the intellect is being; secondly, that this being is not that being, and thus we apprehend division as a consequence; thirdly, comes the notion of one; fourthly, the notion of multitude.

5. Unity and Number

St. Thomas, On the Power of God, q. 9, art. 7.*

Are Numeral Terms Predicated Of The Divine Persons?

The seventh point of inquiry is as to how numeral terms are predicated of the divine Persons, whether positively or only negatively: and it would seem that they are predicated positively.

---

* Translated by Dominican Fathers of the English Province (Westminster, Md.: The Newman Press, 1952).

1. If they signify nothing positive in God, then by affirming three Persons we do not speak of something that is in God. Therefore by denying three Persons one would not deny anything that is in God: and consequently one would not say that which is untrue nor would one be a heretic.

2. According to Dionysius (*Div. Nom.*)[1] things are predicated of God in three ways: negatively, eminently and causally. Now in whichever of these three senses numeral terms are predicated of God they must needs have a positive signification. This is evident if they be predicated eminently or causally: and likewise if they be predicated negatively. For as the same Dionysius says (*Coel. Hier.* ii; *Div. Nom.* iv, xi) we do not deny things of God as though he lacked them altogether, but because they are not appropriate to him in the same way as they are to us. Therefore in any way numeral terms must have a positive meaning as applied to God.

3. Whatsoever is predicated of God and creatures is affirmed in a more eminent sense of God than of creatures. Now numeral terms are predicated of creatures positively. Therefore with much more reason are they thus predicated of God.

4. Plurality and unity as implied by the numeral terms when predicated of God are not mere mental concepts, for thus there would not be three Persons in God save logically, which belongs to the heresy of Sabellius. Therefore they must be something really in God, and consequently predicated of him positively.

5. As unity is in the genus of quantity, so is good in the genus of quality. Now in God there is neither quantity nor quality nor any accident, and yet goodness is predicated of God not negatively but positively. Therefore unity is predicated of him in the same way, and consequently plurality which is based on unity.

6. There are four transcendentals, namely being, unity, truth and goodness. Now three of these, to wit being, truth and goodness, are predicated of God positively. Therefore unity is also consequently plurality.

7. Number and magnitude are two species of quantity, namely discrete and continuous quantity. Now magnitude is predicated of God positively (Ps. cxlvi, 5): *Great is our Lord and great is his power.* Therefore multitude and unity are also.

8. Creatures are like God inasmuch as they bear a trace of the Godhead. Now according to Augustine (*De Trin.* vi, 10) every creature bears a trace of the divine Trinity, inasmuch as it is *one particular thing, informed by a species, and has a certain order.* Therefore the creature is one in its likeness to God. Now *one* is predicated of a creature positively: and therefore of God also.

---

[1] *Myst. Theol.* i.

9. If *one* be predicated of God in a privative sense, it follows that it removes something, and this can only be plurality. Now it does not remove plurality, since if there be one *Person* it does not follow that there are not more. Therefore *one* is not said of God by way of remotion: and consequently neither is number.

10. Privation constitutes nothing: whereas unity constitutes number. Therefore the latter is not predicated in a privative sense.

11. There is no privation in God, since all privation is a defect. Now *one* is predicated of God. Therefore it does not denote a privation.

12. Augustine says (*De Trin.* v, 5) that whatsoever is predicated of God indicates either substance or relation. And Boethius (*De Trin.* iv) says that whatsoever is predicated of God refers to the substance except relative terms. If then numeral terms are predicated of God they must denote either the substance or a relation, and consequently must be predicated positively.

13. One and being are convertible terms and are apparently synonymous. Now being is predicated of God positively. Therefore one is also and consequently number.

14. If *one* be predicated of God by way of remotion, it must remove number as being contrary thereto. But this cannot be the case, since number is constituted by units: and one contrary is not made up of the other. Therefore *one* is not predicated of God by way of remotion.

15. If *one* indicates the removal of number, it follows that *one* is opposed to number as privation to habit. Now habit is naturally prior to privation: as well as logically, since privation cannot be defined except in reference to habit. Therefore number will precede unity both naturally and logically: which is apparently absurd.

16. If one and number are predicated of God by way of remotion, then *one* removes *number* and *number* removes *unity*. But this cannot be admitted, since it would lead to a vicious circle, namely that unity is where there is not number, and number where there is not unity, and we should be none the wiser. Therefore we must not say that *one* and *number* are said of God privatively.

17. Since *one* and *many* are as measure and measured it would seem that they are opposed to each other relatively. Now when terms are relatively opposite both are predicated positively. Therefore both unity and number are predicated of God positively.

1. On the contrary, Dionysius says (*Div. Nom.* iv, 13): *That Unity with Trinity in which we worship the supreme Godhead is not the same unity or trinity with which we or any other living being are acquainted.* Therefore seemingly numeral terms are predicated of God by way of remotion.

2. Augustine says (*De Trin.* viii, 4): *The poor human tongue sought how to express the Three, and it called them substances or persons: not intending to imply that they are different, yet desirous to avoid saying that there is only one.* Hence in speaking of God these numeral terms are employed negatively rather than positively.

3. One and many, i.e. number are in the genus of quantity. Now there is no quantity in God, seeing that quantity is an accident and a disposition of matter. Therefore numeral terms indicate nothing positive in God.

4. To this it will be replied that although quantity as to its generic nature or considered as an accident cannot be in God, yet in its specific nature a certain kind of quantity may be predicated of God, even as a certain kind of quality such as knowledge or justice.

On the contrary only those species of quality can be predicated of God which in their specific nature contain no imperfection, such as knowledge, justice, equity, but not ignorance or whiteness. But all quantity by its specific nature implies imperfection: because since a thing that has quantity is divisible, the various species of quantity are distinguished according to various kinds of division: thus plurality is quantity divisible into non-continuous parts: a line is quantity divisible as to one dimension: while a surface is divisible as to two, and a body as to three. Now division is incompatible with the perfection of divine simplicity. Therefore no quantity as to its specific nature can be predicated of God.

5. But it will be argued that distinction according to the relations which cause the number of Persons in God, does not imply perfection in him.

On the contrary every division or distinction causes plurality of some kind. Now not every kind of plurality is that number which is a species of quantity, inasmuch as *many* and *one* pervade all the genera. Hence not any division or distinction suffices to set up number which is a species of quantity, but only quantitative division, and such is not relative division.

6. But it will be objected that every plurality is a species of quantity, and every division suffices to cause a species of quantity.

On the contrary, given substance, quantity does not necessarily follow, inasmuch as substance can be without accident. Now given substantial forms only, there follows distinction in substances. Therefore not every distinction causes number, which is an accident and a species of quantity.

7. Discreteness that causes number which is a species of quantity is opposed to continuity. Now discreteness is opposed to continuity because it consists in division of the continuous. Therefore only division of the continuous, which division is impossible in God, causes number that is a species of quantity: so that such a number cannot be predicated of God.

8. Every substance is one. Either then it is one by its essence, or by

something else. If by something else, since this again must be one, it must be one either of itself or by something else, and this again by something else. But this cannot go on indefinitely: and hence we must stop somewhere. And it were better to stop at the beginning, so that substance be one of itself. Therefore unity is not something added to substance: and thus seemingly it does not signify anything positively.

9. But it will be argued that a substance is one not by itself but by accidental unity: and unity is one essentially, since the primary notions are named after themselves: thus goodness is good, truth is true and likewise unity is one. — On the contrary these are named after themselves because they are primary forms; whereas second forms are not named after themselves: thus whiteness is not white. Now things which result from addition to others are not primary. Therefore unity and goodness are not additional to substance.

10. According to the Philosopher (*Metaph.* v) a thing is one insofar as it is undivided. Now to be undivided is nothing positive but only removes something. Therefore unity is predicated of God not positively but negatively: and the same applies to number which is composed of units.

I answer that about unity and number there are various points which have given rise to various opinions among philosophers. As regards unity it is to be observed that it is the principle of number and that it is convertible with being: and as regards plurality it belongs to a species of quantity called number; moreover, it pervades all the genera like unity, which apparently is opposed to number.

Accordingly some philosophers failed to distinguish between unity which is convertible with being, and unity which is the principle of number, and thought that in neither sense does unity add anything to substance, and that in either sense it denotes the substance of a thing. From this it followed that number which is composed of unities is the substance of all things: and this was the opinion of Pythagoras and Plato.

On the other hand others who failed to distinguish between unity that is convertible with being and unity that is the principle of number held the contrary opinion that in any sense unity adds a certain accidental being to substance: and that in consequence all number is an accident pertaining to the genus of quantity. This was the opinion of Avicenna: and apparently all the teachers of old followed him: for they did not understand by one and many anything else but something pertaining to discrete quantity.

There were others who, considering that there cannot be quantity of any kind in God, maintained that words signifying one or many have no positive signification, when attributed to God, but only remove something from him. For they cannot ascribe to him save what they signify, to wit discrete quantity, and this can nowise be in God. Hence according to these one is predicated of God in order to remove the plurality of discrete quantity; and terms signifying plurality are said of God in order to remove that unity which is the principle of discrete quantity. Apparently this was the view of the Master (I., D. xxiv): and granted the principle on which his opinion is based, namely that all multitude signifies discrete quantity, and all unity is the principle of such quantity, this opinion would seem of all the most reasonable. For Dionysius (*Coel. Hier.* ii) says that we are nearer the truth when we speak of God in the negative, and that all our affirmations about him are figurative. For we know not what God is, but rather what he is not, as Damascene says (*De Fid. Orth.* i, 4). Hence Rabbi Moses says that whatever we affirm about God is to be taken as removing something from him rather than as placing something in him. Thus we say that God is a living being in order to remove from him that mode of being which inanimate beings have, and not in order to ascribe life to him; since life and such terms are employed to denote certain forms and perfections of creatures which are far distant from God. And yet this is not altogether true, for as Dionysius says (*Div. Nom.* xii) wisdom and life and the like are not removed from God as though they were not in him; but because he has them in a higher degree than mind can conceive or words express: and from that divine perfection created perfections come down in an imperfect likeness to it. Wherefore things are said of God according to Dionysius (*Myst. Theol.* i: *Coel. Hier.* ii: *Div. Nom.* ii) not only negatively and causally but also eminently. Still whatever the truth may be with regard to spiritual perfections it is certain that material dispositions are altogether to be removed from God. Wherefore since quantity is a disposition of matter, if numeral terms signify nothing outside the genus of quantity it follows that they are not to be said of God except as removing what they signify, according to the Master's opinion (*loc. cit.*), and although in his opinion unity removes plurality and plurality unity, this does not involve a vicious circle, because the unity and plurality removed from God are in the genus of quantity, neither of which can be ascribed to God. So that the unity ascribed to God which removes plurality is not removed, but that other unity which cannot be said of God.

Some, however, through not understanding how affirmative expressions can be predicated of God for the purpose of negation, and not conceiving unity and plurality except as included in the genus of discrete quantity, which they dared not ascribe to God, said that numeral terms are not predicated of God as though they expressed an idea with an objective reality, but as official expressions positing something in God, namely a kind of syncategorematic distinction, all of which is clearly absurd, since nothing of the kind can be had from the meaning of these terms.

Wherefore others, though holding that unity and multitude are only in the genus of quantity, said that these terms denote something positive in God. They say in effect that it is not unreasonable to ascribe some kind of quantity to God, although the genus is not to be attributed to him: even as certain species of quality, as wisdom and justice are predicated of God, although there cannot be quality in God. But as indicated in an objection (5) there is no comparison: because all the species of quantity from their specific nature are imperfect, but not all species of quality. Moreover quantity properly speaking is a disposition of matter: so that all the species of quantity are mathematical entities which cannot exist apart from sensible matter, except time and place which are natural entities and which are better described as adjuncts of sensible matter. It is evident then that no species of quantity can be attributed to spiritual things otherwise than metaphorically. Whereas quality follows the form, wherefore certain qualities are altogether immaterial and can be ascribed to spiritual things. Accordingly the above opinions were based on the supposition that the *one* which is convertible with *being* is the same with that which is the principle of number, and that there is no plurality but number that is a species of quantity. Now this is clearly false. For since division causes plurality and indivision unity, we must judge of *one* and *many* according to the various kinds of division. Now there is a kind of division which altogether transcends the genus of quantity, and this is division according to formal opposition which has nothing to do with quantity. Hence the plurality resulting from such a division, and the unity which excludes such a division, must needs be more universal and comprehensive than the genus of quantity. Again there is a division of quantity which does not transcend the genus of quantity. Wherefore the plurality consequent to this division and the unity which excludes it are in the genus of quantity. This latter unity is an accidental addition to the thing of which it is predicated, in that it measures it: otherwise the number arising from this unity would not be an accident nor the species of a genus. Whereas the unity that is convertible with being, adds nothing to being except the negation of division, not that it signifies indivision only, but substance with indivision: for *one* is the same as individual being. In like manner the plurality that corresponds to this unity adds nothing to the *many things* except distinction, which consists in each one not being the other: and this they have not from anything added to them but from their proper forms. It is clear then that *one* which is convertible with *being*, posits *being* but adds nothing except the negation of division. And the *number* corresponding to it adds this to the things described as *many*, that each of them is *one* and that each of them is not the other, wherein is the essence of distinction. Accordingly then, while *one* adds to *being* one negation inasmuch as a thing is undivided in itself; *plurality* adds two negations, inasmuch as a certain thing is undivided in itself, and distinct from another; i.e., one of them is not the other.

I say then that in speaking of God we do not predicate the unity and plurality which belong to the genus of quantity, but the *one* which is convertible with being and the corresponding plurality. Wherefore *one* and *many* predicate in God that which they signify: but they add nothing besides distinction and indistinction, which is the same as to add negations as explained above. Hence we grant that as regards what they add to the things of which they are predicated, they are attributed to God by way of removal; but insofar as in their signification they include the things of which they are said they are predicated of God positively. We must now reply to the objections on both sides.

Reply to the First Objection. To speak of three Persons in God is to indicate a distinction of Persons: and to deny this is heresy. But this distinction adds nothing to the distinct Persons.

Reply to the Second Objection. It is true that while we remove certain things from God we understand at the same time that these things are predicated of God eminently and causally: but some things are denied of God absolutely and in no way predicated of him; as for instance, God is not a body. In this way according to the Master's opinion it might be said that numeral quantity is altogether denied of God: and in like manner according to our own opinion when we say: *The divine essence is one,* we altogether deny that God's essence is divided.

Reply to the Third Objection. In created things numeral terms posit nothing in addition to the things to which they are affixed, except insofar as they signify something in the genus of discrete quantity: in this way they are not predicated of God, and this pertains to his perfection.

Reply to the Fourth Objection. It is true that the unity and plurality signified by numeral terms predicated of God are not purely subjective but are really in God: and yet it does not follow that they signify something positive besides the things to which they are attributed.

Reply to the Fifth Objection. The good that is a kind of quality is not the good that is convertible with being. The latter adds nothing real to being, whereas the former adds a quality in respect of which a man is said to be good. The same applies to unity, as already explained; yet there is this difference that good in either sense can be predicated of God, whereas unity cannot: because as already explained the comparison between quantity and quality fails.

Reply to the Sixth Objection. Of these primary notions being is the first, wherefore it must be predicated positively: because negation or privation cannot be the first thing conceived by the intellect, since we cannot understand a negation or privation unless we first understand what is denied or lacking. But the other three must add something that is not a contraction of being: for if they contracted being they would no longer be primary notions. Now this is impossible unless that which they add were purely logical, and this is either a negation which is added by unity as already stated, or relation to something which by its very nature is universally referable to being: and this is either the intellect to which the true bears a relation, or the appetite to which the good bears a relation, for the good is what all things seek (*Ethic.* i, I).

Reply to the Seventh Objection. According to the Philosopher (*Metaph.* x) we speak of a *number* of things in two senses: first absolutely, and then number is the opposite of one: secondly comparatively, as denoting excess in relation to a smaller number, and then number is opposed to a *few*. In like manner magnitude may be taken in two ways: first absolutely, in the sense of a continuous quantity which is called a magnitude: secondly comparatively, as denoting excess in relation to a smaller quantity. In the first sense magnitude is not predicated of God but in the second, and denotes his eminence over all creatures.

Reply to the Eighth Objection. The unity that pertains to the trace of God in his creatures is the one that is convertible with being. As we have already stated this posits something, namely *being*, to which it adds nothing but a negation.

Reply to the Ninth Objection. One opposite does not exclude the other except from the subject of which it is predicated. For supposing that Socrates is white it does not follow that nothing is black, but that he is not black. Wherefore if the person of the Father is one it follows that there are not several persons of the Father, but not that there is not more than one Person in God.

Reply to the Tenth Objection. One is not a constituent of a number, on the side of privation, but inasmuch as it posits *being*.

Reply to the Eleventh Objection. Privation may be taken in three ways (*Metaph.* v, text. 27). First strictly, when a thing lacks that which by nature it should have, and when by nature it should have it: thus to lack sight is in a man privation of sight. Secondly in an extended sense, when a thing lacks that which is due not to its specific but to its generic nature: thus lack of sight may be called a privation of sight in a mole. Thirdly in a very broad sense, when a thing lacks that which may be naturally due to anything else but not to it, nor to any other member of its genus: thus lack of sight may be called a privation in a plant. This last kind of privation is a mean between real privation and simple negation, and has something in common with both. With real privation in that it is the negation of something in a subject, so that it cannot be predicated simply of non-being; and with simple negation, in that it does not require aptitude in the subject. It is in this way that *one* denotes privation, and in this sense it can be predicated of God, like other things that can be predicated of God in the same way, as, for instance, *invisible, immense* and so forth.

Reply to the Twelfth Objection. Numerical terms add nothing to God besides the subject of which they are predicated. Hence when they are predicated of essentials they signify the essence, and when they are predicated of personal properties they signify the relations.

Reply to the Thirteenth Objection. One and being are convertible as to their supposits: yet *one* adds logically the privation of division and thus they are not synonymous, because synonyms are words which signify the same thing from the same point of view.

Reply to the Fourteenth Objection. One may be considered in two ways. First as to what it posits, and thus it is a constituent of number: secondly as to the negation which it adds, and thus it is opposed to number privatively.

Reply to the Fifteenth Objection. According to the Philosopher (*Metaph.* x), number precedes unity objectively, as the whole precedes its parts and the composite precedes the simple: but unity precedes number naturally and logically. But this seemingly is not sufficient in order that unity be opposed to number privatively. For privation logically is an afterthought, since in order to understand a privation we must first understand its opposite whence its definition is taken: unless perhaps this refer merely to the definition of the term, insofar as *one* has a privative signification, while *number* has a positive meaning: since we name things according as we know them. Wherefore in order that a term have a privative signification it suffices that the thing signified come in any way whatsoever to our knowledge as an afterthought: although this is not enough to make the thing itself privative, unless it come afterwards logically. It would be better then to say that division is the cause of number and precedes it logically; and that *one* since it is undivided being is predicated privatively in relation to division, but not in relation to multitude. Hence division logically precedes being but number follows it: and this is proved as follows. The first object of the intellect is *being*; the second is the negation of being. From these two there follows thirdly the understanding of distinction (since from the fact that we understand that this thing is and that it is not that thing we realize that these two are distinct): and it follows fourthly that the intellect apprehends the idea of unity, in that it understands that this thing is not divided in itself; and fifthly the intellect apprehends number, in that it understands this as distinct from that and each as one in itself. For however much things are conceived as distinct from one another, there is no idea of number unless each be conceived as one. Wherefore there is not a vicious circle in the definitions of unity and number. And this suffices for the *Reply to the Sixteenth Objection.*

Reply to the Seventeenth Objection. The *one* which is a principle of number is compared to *many* as measure to the thing measured: and unity in this sense adds something positive to substance, as stated in the Article.

After what we have said the arguments on the other side present no difficulty to those who realize that they contain a certain amount of truth. We must, however, take notice of one point advanced in these objections, namely that these primary notions, essence, unity, truth and goodness denominate themselves inasmuch as one, true and good are consequent to being. Now seeing that *being* is the first object of the intellect, it follows that every other object of the intellect is conceived as a being, and therefore as one, true and good. Wherefore since the intellect apprehends essence, unity, truth and goodness in the abstract, it follows that being and the other three concretes must be predicated of them. Thus it is that they denominate themselves, whereas things that are not convertible with being do not.

6. The Transcendental Good

St. Thomas, *Truth*, q. 21, art. 1.*

The Question Concerns Good, and in the First Article
We Ask: Does Good Add Anything to Being?

Difficulties:

It seems that it does, for

1. Everything is a being essentially. But a creature is good not essentially but by participation. Good, therefore, really adds something to being.

2. Since good includes being in its very notion, and yet good is rationally distinct from being, the formal character of good must add something to that of being. But it cannot be said to add a negation to being, as does the one, which adds undividedness, because the whole character of good consists in something positive. Hence it adds something to being positively, and thus it seems to add to being in reality.

3. The answer was given that it adds a relation to an end. — On the contrary, in this case good would be nothing but related being. But related being pertains to a definite category of being, which is called "relation" or "to something." Good would therefore be in a definite category. But this is contrary to what the Philosopher says, placing good in all the categories.

4. As can be gathered from the words of Dionysius, good tends to pour out itself and existence. A thing is good, therefore, by the fact that it is diffusive. But to pour out or diffuse implies an action, and an action proceeds from the essence through the mediation of a power. A thing is therefore said to be good by reason of a power added to the essence, and so good really adds something to being.

5. The farther we get from the first being, which is one and simple, the more we find difference in things. But in God being and good are really one, being distinguished only conceptually. In creatures, therefore, they are distinguished more than conceptually; and so, since there is no distinction beyond the conceptual except the real, they are distinguished really.

6. Accidentals really add something to the essence. But goodness is accidental to the creature; otherwise it could not be lost. Good therefore really adds something to being.

7. Whatever is predicated as informing something else really adds something to it, since nothing is informed by itself. Good, however, is predicated as informing, as is said in *The Causes*. It therefore adds something to being.

---

* Translated by Robert W. Schmidt, S.J. (Chicago: Henry Regnery Company, 1953).

8. Nothing is determined by itself. But good determines being. It therefore adds something to being.

9. The answer was given that good determines being in concept. — On the contrary, corresponding to that concept there is either something in reality or nothing. If nothing, it follows that the concept is void and useless; but if there is something corresponding in reality, the point is established: good really adds something to being.

10. A relation is specified according to the term in respect to which it is predicated. But good implies a relation to a definite sort of being, an end. Good therefore implies a specified relation. Every specified being, however, really adds something to being in general. Hence good really adds something to being.

11. Good and being are interchangeable, like man and "capable of laughter." But though "capable of laughter" is interchangeable with man, it nevertheless really adds something to man, namely, a property. But a property is classed as an accident. Similarly, therefore, good really adds something to being.

To the Contrary:

1. Augustine says: "Inasmuch as God is good, we are; but inasmuch as we are, we are good." It therefore seems that good does not add anything to being.

2. Whenever things are so related that one adds something to the other either really or conceptually, one can be understood without the other. But being cannot be understood without good. Hence good does not add anything to being either really or conceptually. Proof of the minor: God can make more than man can understand. But God cannot make a being that is not good, because by the very fact of its being from good it is good, as Boethius makes clear. Therefore neither can the intellect understand it.

Reply:

Something can be added to something else in three ways. (1) It adds some reality which is outside the essence of the thing to which it is said to be added. For instance, white adds something to body, since the essence of whiteness is something beyond that of body. (2) One thing is added to the other as limiting and determining it. Man, for instance, adds something to animal — not indeed in such a way that there is in man some reality which is completely outside the essence of animal; otherwise it would be necessary to say that it is not the whole of man which is animal but only a part. Animal is limited by man because what is contained in the notion of man determinately and actually, is only implicitly and, as it were, potentially contained in the notion of animal. It belongs to the notion of man that he have a rational soul; to the notion of animal, that it have a soul, without its being determined to rational or nonrational. And yet that determination by reason of which man is said to add something to animal is founded in reality. (3) Something is said to add to something else in concept only. This occurs when something which is nothing in reality but only in thought, belongs to the notion of one thing and not to the notion of the other, whether that to which it is said to be added is limited by it or not. Thus *blind* adds something to man, i.e., blindness, which is not a being in nature but merely a being in the thought of one who knows privations. By it man is limited, for not every man is blind. But when we say "a blind mole," no limitation is placed by what is added.

It is not possible, however, for something to add anything to being in general in the first way, though in that way there can be an addition to some particular sort of being; for there is no real being which is outside the essence of being in general, though some reality may be outside the essence of *this* being. But in the second way certain things are found to add to being, since being is narrowed down in the ten categories, each of which adds something to being — not, of course, an accident or difference which is outside the essence of being, but a definite manner of being which is founded upon the very existence of the thing. It is not in this way, however, that good adds something to being, since good itself, like being, is divided into the ten categories, as is made clear in the *Ethics*.

Good must, accordingly, either add nothing to being or add something merely in concept. For if it added something real, being would have to be narrowed down by the character of good to a special genus. But since being is what is first conceived by the intellect, as Avicenna says, every other noun must either be a synonym of being or add something at least conceptually. The former cannot be said of good, since it is not nonsense to call a being good. Thus good, by the fact of its not limiting being, must add to it something merely conceptual.

What is merely conceptual, however, can be of only two kinds: negation and a certain kind of relation. Every absolute positing signifies something existing in reality. Thus to being, the first intellectual conception, *one* adds what is merely conceptual — a negation; for it means undivided being. But *true* and *good*, being predicated positively, cannot add anything except a relation which is merely conceptual. A relation is merely conceptual, according to the Philosopher, when by it something is said to be related which is not dependent upon that to which it is referred, but vice versa; for a relation is a sort of dependence. An example is had in intellectual knowledge and its object, as also in sense and the sensible object. Knowledge depends upon its object, but not the other way about. The relation by which knowledge is referred to its object is accordingly real, but the relation by which the object is referred to the knowledge is only conceptual. According to the Philosopher the object of knowledge is said to be related, not because it is itself referred, but because something else is referred to it. The same holds true of all other things which stand to one another as measure and thing measured or as perfective and perfectible.

The true and the good must therefore add to the concept of being a relationship of that which perfects. But in any being there are two aspects to be considered, the formal character of its species and the act of being by which it subsists in that species. And so a being can be perfective in two ways. (1) It can be so just according to its specific character. In this way the intellect is perfected by a being, for it perceives the formal character of the being. But the being is still not in it according to its natural existence. It is this mode of perfecting which the true adds to being. For the true is in the mind, as the Philosopher says, and every being is called true inasmuch as it is conformed or conformable to intellect. For this reason all who correctly define *true* put intellect in its definition. (2) A being is perfective of another not only according to its specific character but also according to the existence which it has in reality. In this fashion the good is perfective; for the good is in things, as the Philosopher says. Inasmuch as one being by reason of its act of existing is such as to perfect and complete another, it stands to that other as an end. And hence it is that all who rightly define *good* put in its notion something about its status as an end. The Philosopher accordingly says that they excellently defined good who said that it is "that which all things desire."

First of all and principally, therefore, a being capable of perfecting another after the manner of an end is called good; but secondarily something is called good which leads to an end (as the useful is said to be good), or which naturally follows upon an end (as not only that which has health is called healthy, but also anything which causes, preserves, or signifies health).

Answers to Difficulties:

1. Since being is predicated absolutely and good adds to it the status of a final cause, the essence of a thing considered absolutely suffices for the thing to be called a being on its account, but not thereby to be called good. Just as in the case of the other kinds of causes the status of a secondary cause depends upon that of the primary cause, but that of the primary cause depends upon no other; so also in the case of final causes secondary ends share in the status of final cause from their relation to the last end, but the last end has this status of itself.

And so it is that the essence of God, who is the last end of creatures, suffices for God to be called good by reason of it; but when the essence of a creature is given, the thing is not yet called good except from the relation to God by reason of which it has the character of a final cause. In this sense it is said that a creature is not good essentially but by participation. For from one point of view this is so inasmuch as the essence itself, in our understanding of it, is considered as something other than that relation to God by which it is considered a final cause and is directed to God as its end. But from another point of view a creature does not exist without a relation to God's goodness. This is Boethius' meaning.

2. It is not only negation that expresses what is merely conceptual but also a certain type of relation, as has been said.

3. Every real relation is in a definite category, but non-real relations can run through all being.

4. Though, according to the proper use of the word, *to pour out* seems to imply the operation of an efficient cause, yet taken broadly it can imply the status of any cause, as do *to influence, to make,* etc. When good is said to be of its very notion diffusive, however, diffusion is not to be understood as implying the operation of an efficient cause but rather the status of a final cause. Nor is such diffusion brought about through the mediation of any added power. Good expresses the diffusion of a final cause and not that of an agent, both because the latter, as efficient, is not the measure and perfection of the thing caused but rather its beginning, and also because the effect participates in the efficient cause only in an assimilation of its form, whereas a thing is dependent upon its end in its whole existence. It is in this that the character of good was held to consist.

5. Things can be really one in God in two ways. (1) Their unity may be merely from that in which they are, and not from their own formal characters. In this way knowledge and power are one; for knowledge is not really the same as power by reason of its being knowledge, but by reason of its being divine. Now things which are really one in God in this way are found to differ really in creatures.

(2) The things which are said to be really one in God may be so by their very formal characters. In this way good and being are really one in God, because it is of the very notion of good that it does not differ in reality from being. Hence, wherever good and being are found, they are really identical.

6. Just as there is essential being and accidental being, so also there is essential good and accidental good; and a thing loses its goodness in just the same way as it loses its substantial or accidental act of being.

7. From the relationship mentioned above it comes about that good is said to inform or determine being conceptually.

8. The answer is clear from what has just been said.

9. To that concept something does correspond in reality (a real dependence of that which is a means to an end upon the end itself), as there also does in other conceptual relations.

10. Although *good* expresses a special status, that of an end, nevertheless that status belongs to any being whatsoever and does not put anything real into being. Hence the conclusion does not follow.

11. "Capable of laughter," though interchanged with man, still adds to man a distinct reality which is over and above man's essence. But nothing can be added to being in this way, as has been said.

Answers to Contrary Difficulties:

1. We grant this, because good as such does not really add anything to being.

2. This argues that nothing is added even conceptually. To this it must be said that a thing can be understood without another in two ways. (1) This occurs by way of enunciating, when one thing is understood to be without the other. Whatever the intellect can understand without another in this sense, God can make without the other. But being cannot be so understood without good, i.e., so that the intellect understands that something is a being and is not good. (2) Something can be understood without another by way of defining, so that the intellect understands one without at the same time understanding the other. Thus animal is understood without man or any of the other species. In this sense being can be understood without good. Yet it does not follow that God can make a being without good, because the very notion of making is to bring into existence.

7. The Relation of the Good to Being

St. Thomas, *Truth*, q. 21, art. 2.*

In the Second Article We Ask: Are Being and Good
Interchangeable as to Their Real Subjects?

Difficulties:

It seems that they are not, for

1. Opposites are capable of occurring in regard to the same thing. But good and evil are opposites. Now evil is not capable of being in all things; for, as Avicenna says, beyond the sphere of the moon there is no evil. It seems, then, that neither is good found in all beings. And so good is not interchangeable with being.

2. Predicates such that one extends to more things than another are not interchangeable with one another. But, as Maximus the commentator says, good extends to more things than being; for it extends to non-beings, which are called into being by good. Therefore good and being are not interchangeable.

3. Good is a perfection of which the apprehension is enjoyable, as Algazel says. But not every being has perfection, for prime matter has none. Not every being, therefore, is good.

4. In mathematics being is found but not good, as appears from what the Philosopher says. Being and good are therefore not interchangeable.

---
* Schmidt, op. *cit.*

5. In *The Causes* it is said that the first of created things is the act of being. But according to the Philosopher "the prior is that from which there is a sequence which cannot be reversed." The sequence from being to good therefore cannot be reversed; and so good and being are not interchangeable.

6. What is divided is not interchangeable with any one of the things into which it is divided, as animal is not interchangeable with rational. But being is divided into good and evil, since many beings are called evil. Therefore good and being are not interchangeable.

7. Even a privation, according to the Philosopher, is called a being in a certain sense. But it cannot in any sense be called good; otherwise evil, consisting essentially in a privation, would be good. Good and being are therefore not interchangeable.

8. According to Boethius all things are said to be good by reason of the fact that they are from the good, namely God. But God's goodness is His very wisdom and justice. By the same reasoning, then, all things which are from God would be wise and just. But this is false. So too, then, is the first, viz., that all things are good.

To the Contrary:

1. Nothing tends except to what is like itself. But, as Boethius says, "every being tends to good." Then every being is good, and nothing can be good unless it in some way is. Consequently good and being are interchangeable.

2. Only what is good can be from the good. But every being proceeds from the divine goodness. Therefore every being is good; and so the conclusion must be the same as above.

Reply:

Since the essence of good consists in this, that something perfects another as an end, whatever is found to have the character of an end also has that of good. Now two things are essential to an end: it must be sought or desired by things which have not yet attained the end, and it must be loved by the things which share the end, and be, as it were, enjoyable to them. For it is essentially the same to tend to an end and in some sense to repose in that end. Thus by the same natural tendency a stone moves toward the center (of the world) and comes to rest there.

These two properties are found to belong to the act of being. For whatever does not yet participate in the act of being tends toward it by a certain natural appetite. In this way matter tends to form, according to the Philosopher. But everything which already has being naturally loves its being and with all its strength preserves it. Boethius accordingly says: "Divine providence has given to the things created by it this greatest of reasons for remaining, namely, that they naturally desire to remain to the best of their ability. Therefore you cannot in the least doubt that all beings naturally seek permanence in perduring and avoid destruction."

Existence itself, therefore, has the essential note of goodness. Just as it is impossible, then, for anything to be a being which does not have existence, so too it is necessary that every being be good by the very fact of its having existence, even though in many beings many other aspects of goodness are added over and above the act of existing by which they subsist.

Since, moreover, good includes the note of being, as is clear from what has been said, it is impossible for anything to be good which is not a being. Thus we are left with the conclusion that good and being are interchangeable.

Answers to Difficulties:

1. Good and evil are opposed as privation and possession or habit. But privation does not have to be in every being in which habit is found; and so evil does not have to be in everything in which there is good. Furthermore, in the case of contraries as long as one is really in a certain thing, the other is not capable of being in the same thing, as the Philosopher says. Good, however, is really in every being whatever, since it is called good from its own real act of existing.

2. Good extends to non-beings not attributively but causally, inasmuch as non-beings tend to good. And so we can call non-beings things which are in potency and not in act. But the act of being does not have causality except perhaps after the manner of an exemplary cause. This sort of causality, however, extends only to the things which actually participate in being.

3. Just as prime matter is a being in potency and not in act, so it is perfect in potency and not in act and good potentially and not actually.

4. The things which a mathematician studies are good according to the existence which they have in reality. The very existence of a line or of a number, for instance, is good. But the mathematician does not study them according to their existence but only according to their specific formal character. For he studies them abstractly, though they are not abstract in their existence but only in their notion. It was said above that good is not consequent upon the specific character except according to the existence which it has in some real thing. And so the note of goodness does not belong to a line or number as they fall within the purview of the mathematician, even though a line and a number are good.

5. Being is not called prior to good in the sense of *prior* employed in the objection, but in another sense, as the absolute is prior to the relative.

6. A thing can be called good both from its act of existing and from some added property or state. Thus a man is said to be good both as existing and as being just and chaste or destined for beatitude. By reason of the first goodness being is interchanged with good, and conversely. But by reason of the second, good is a division of being.

7. Privation is not called a reality but only a conceptual being. In this

sense it is a good for reason, for to know a privation or anything of the sort is good. Even knowledge of evil, as Boethius points out, cannot be lacking in good.

8. According to Boethius a thing is called good from its very existence, but is called just by reason of some action of its own. Existence, however, is communicated to everything that comes forth from God. But not all things share in that activity to which justice is referred. For although in God to act and to be are the same thing, and thus His justice is His goodness, nevertheless in creatures to act and to be are distinct. Hence existence can be communicated to something to which activity is not; and even in those beings to which both are communicated, to act is not the same as to be. Hence also men who are good and just are indeed good because they exist, but not just because they exist, but rather because they have a certain habit directed to action. And the same can be said of wisdom and other things of the sort.

Or a different answer can be taken from the same Boethius: The just and the wise and other things of this kind are special goods since they are special perfections; but good designates something perfect in an unqualified sense. From the perfect God, therefore, things come forth perfect, but not with the same degree of perfection with which God is perfect, because what is made does not exist in the manner of the agent but in that of the product. Nor do all things which receive perfection from God receive it in the same measure. And so, just as it is common to God and all creatures to be perfect in an absolute sense, but not to be perfect in this or that particular way, so also does it belong to God and to all creatures to be good; but the particular goodness which is wisdom or that which is justice does not have to be common to all. Some goods belong to God alone, as eternity and omnipotence: but some others, to certain creatures as well as to God, as wisdom and justice and the like.

8. The Nature of Evil

St. Thomas, *Summa Theologiae*, I, q. 48, art. 1.*

Whether Evil is a Nature?

We must now consider the distinction of things in particular. And firstly the distinction of good and evil; then the distinction of spiritual and corporeal creatures.[1] Concerning the first, we inquire into evil and its cause.[2]

We proceed thus to the First Article: —

Objection 1. It would seem that evil is a nature. For every genus is a nature. But evil is a genus, for the Philosopher says that *good and evil are not in a genus, but are genera of other things.*[3] Therefore evil is a nature.

---

* Pegis, *op. cit.*
[1] Q. 50.
[2] Q. 49.
[3] Aristotle, *Cat.*, XI (14a 23).

Obj. 2. Further, every difference which constitutes a species is a nature. But evil is a difference constituting a species in the field of morals; for a bad habit differs in species from a good habit, as does liberality from illiberality. Therefore evil signifies a nature.

Obj. 3. Further, each extreme of two contraries is a nature. But evil and good are not opposed as privation and habit, but as contraries, as the Philosopher shows by the fact that between good and evil there is an intermediate position, and from evil there can be a return to good.[4] Therefore evil signifies a nature.

Obj. 4. Further, what is not, acts not. But evil acts, for it corrupts good. Therefore evil is a being and a nature.

Obj. 5. Further, nothing belongs to the perfection of the universe except what is a being and a nature. But evil belongs to the perfection of the universe of things, for Augustine says that *the admirable beauty of the universe is made up of all things. In which even what is called evil, well ordered and in its place, makes better known the greatness of the good.*[5] Therefore evil is a nature.

On the contrary, Dionysius says that *Evil is neither a being nor a good.*[6]

I answer that, One opposite is known through the other, as darkness is known through light. Hence, what evil is must be known from the nature of good. Now, we have said above that good is everything that is appetible;[7] and thus, since every nature desires its own being and its own perfection, it must be said also that the being and the perfection of any nature is good. Hence it is impossible that evil signifies any being, or any form or nature. Therefore, by the name *evil* there must be signified some absence of good. And this is what is meant by saying that *evil is neither a being nor a good.* For since being, as such, is good, the absence of being involves the absence of good.

Reply Obj. 1. Aristotle speaks there according to the opinion of the Pythagoreans, who thought that evil was a kind of nature, and therefore they asserted the existence of good and evil as genera.[8] For Aristotle, especially in his logical works, was in the habit of bringing forward examples that in his time were probable in the opinion of some philosophers. Or, it may be said that, as the Philosopher says, *the first kind of contrariety is habit and privation,*[9] being verified in all contraries; for one contrary is always imperfect in relation to another, as black in relation to white, and bitter in relation to sweet. And in this way good and evil are said to be genera, not absolutely, but in regard to contraries; because, just as every form has the nature of good, so every privation, as such, has the nature of evil.

---

[4] *Op. cit.,* X (12a 22; b 26).
[5] *Enchir.,* X (PL 40, 236).
[6] *De Div. Nom.,* IV, 20 (PG 3, 717).

[7] Q. 5, a. I.
[8] Aristotle, *Metaph.,* I, 5 (986a 33).
[9] *Metaph.,* IX, 4 (1055a 33).

Reply Obj. 2. Good and evil are not constitutive differences except in moral matters, which receive their species from the end, which is the object of the will, the source of all morality. And because good has the nature of an end, for this reason good and evil are specific differences in moral matters — the good in itself, but evil as the absence of the due end. Yet neither does the absence of the due end by itself constitute a species in moral matters, except as the absence is joined to an undue end; just as we do not find the privation of the substantial form in natural things, unless it is joined to another form. Thus, therefore, the evil which is a constitutive difference in morals is a certain good joined to the privation of another good; just as the end proposed by the intemperate man is not the privation of the good of reason, but the delight of sense against the order of reason. Hence evil is not as such a constitutive difference, but by reason of the good that is annexed.

Reply Obj. 3. The answer to this objection appears from the above. For the Philosopher there speaks of good and evil in morality. Now in that respect, between good and evil there is something intermediate; as good is considered something rightly ordered, and evil a thing not only out of right order, but also injurious to another. Hence the Philosopher says that a *prodigal man is foolish, but not evil.*[10] And from this evil in morality, there may be a return to good, but not from any sort of evil; for from blindness there is no return to sight, although blindness is an evil.

Reply Obj. 4. A thing is said to act in a threefold sense. In one way, *formally*, as when we say that whiteness makes white; and in that sense evil considered even as a privation is said to corrupt good, for it is itself a corruption or privation of good. In another sense, a thing is said to act *effectively*, as when a painter makes a wall white. Thirdly, it is said in the sense of the *final cause*, as the end is said to effect by moving the efficient cause. But in these last two ways evil does not effect anything of itself, that is, as a privation, but by virtue of the good annexed to it. For every action comes from some form; and everything which is desired as an end is a perfection. Therefore, as Dionysius says, evil does not act, nor is it desired, except by virtue of some good joined to it: while of itself it is nothing definite, and outside the scope of our will and intention.[11]

Reply Obj. 5. As was said above, the parts of the universe are ordered to each other, according as one acts on the other, and according as one is the end and exemplar of the other.[12] But, as was said above, this can happen to evil only as joined to some good. Hence evil neither belongs to the perfection of the universe, nor comes under the order of the universe, except accidentally, that is, by reason of some good joined to it.

---

[10] *Eth.,* IV, 1 (1121a 25).
[11] *De Div. Nom.,* IV, 20; 32 (PG 3, 720; 733).
[12] Q. 2, a. 3; q. 19, a. 5, ad 2; q. 21, a. 1, ad 3; q. 44, a. 3.

9. The Presence of Evil in Things

St. Thomas, *Summa Theologiae*, I, q. 48, art. 2.*

Objection 1. It would seem that evil is not found in things. For whatever is found in things is either something, or a privation of something, which is a *non-being*. But Dionysius says that evil is distant from the existent, and even more distant from the non-existent.[1] Therefore evil is not at all found in things.

Obj. 2. Further *being* and *thing* are convertible. If, therefore, evil is a being in things, it follows that evil is a thing; which is contrary to what has been said.

Obj. 3. Further, the whiter white is *the white unmixed with black*, as the Philosopher says.[2] Therefore the good unmixed with evil is the greater good. But God always makes what is better much more than nature does. Therefore in things made by God there is no evil.

On the contrary, On the above assumptions, all prohibitions and penalties would cease, for they are concerned only with evils.

I answer that, As was said above, the perfection of the universe requires that there should be inequality in things, so that every grade of goodness may be realized.[3] Now, one grade of goodness is that of the good which cannot fail. Another grade of goodness is that of the good which can fail in goodness. These grades of goodness are to be found in being itself; for there are some things which cannot lose their being, as incorruptible things, while there are some which can lose it, as corruptible things. As, therefore, the perfection of the universe requires that there should be not only incorruptible beings, but also corruptible beings, so the perfection of the universe requires that there should be some which can fail in goodness and which sometimes do fail. Now it is in this that evil consists, namely, in the fact that a thing fails in goodness. Hence it is clear that evil in found in things in the way that corruption also is found; for corruption itself is an evil.

Reply Obj. 1. Evil is distant both from being absolutely and from *non-being* absolutely, because it is neither a habit nor a pure negation, but a privation.

Reply Obj. 2. As the Philosopher says, *being* (*ens*) is said in two ways.[4] In one way, it is considered as signifying the entity of a thing, according as it is divided by the ten categories. In that sense it is convertible with *thing*, and thus no privation is a being, and neither therefore is evil a being. In another sense, *being* is said to be that which signifies the truth of a proposi-

---

* Pegis, *op. cit.*

[1] *De Div. Nom.*, IV, 19 (PG 3, 716).   [3] Q. 47, a. 2.

[2] *Top.*, III, 5 (119a 27).   [4] Aristotle, *Metaph.*, IV, 7 (1017a 22).

tion which consists in composition, revealed by the verb *is*. In this sense, being is what answers to the question, *Does it exist?* It is in this sense that we speak of blindness as being in the eye; or of any other privation. In this way even evil can be called a being. Through ignorance of this distinction, some considering that things may be evil, or that evil is said to be in things, believed that evil was a positive thing in itself.[5]

Reply Obj. 3. God and nature and any other agent make what is better in the whole, but not what is better in every single part, except in relation to the whole, as was said above.[6] And the whole itself, which is the universe of creatures, is all the better and more perfect if there be some things in it which can fail in goodness, and which do sometimes fail, without God preventing it. This happens, firstly, because *it belongs to Providence, not to destroy, but to save nature,* as Dionysius says.[7] But it belongs to nature that what may fail should sometimes fail. It happens, secondly, because, as Augustine says, *God is so powerful that He can even make good out of evil.*[8] Hence many good things would be taken away if God permitted no evil to exist; for fire would not be generated if air was not corrupted, nor would the life of a lion be preserved unless the ass were killed. Neither would avenging justice nor the patience of a sufferer be praised if there were no injustice.

---

[5] Cf. a. 1, ad I; below, q. 49, a. 3.   [7] *De Div. Nom.,* IV, 3 (PG 3, 733).
[6] Q. 47, a. 2, ad 1.   [8] *Enchir.,* XI.

10. The Cause of Evil

St. Thomas, *Summa Theologiae,* I, q. 49, art. 1.*

Whether Good Can Be The Cause Of Evil?

We proceed thus to the First Article: —

Objection 1. It would seem that good cannot be the cause of evil. For it is said (*Matt.* vii. 18): *A good tree cannot bring forth evil fruit.*

Obj. 2. Further, one contrary cannot be the cause of another. But evil is the contrary to good. Therefore good cannot be the cause of evil.

Obj. 3. Further, a deficient effect can proceed only from a deficient cause. But supposing that evil has a cause, it is a deficient effect; and therefore it has a deficient cause. But everything deficient is an evil. Therefore the cause of evil can be only evil.

Obj. 4. Further, Dionysius says that evil has no cause.[1] Therefore good is not the cause of evil.

---

* Pegis, *op. cit.*
[1] *Op. cit.,* IV, 30 (PG 3, 732).

On the contrary, Augustine says: *There is no possible source of evil except good.*[2]

I answer that, It must be said that every evil in some way has a cause. For evil is the absence of the good which is natural and due to a thing. But that anything fall short of its natural and due disposition can come only from some cause drawing it out of its proper disposition. For a heavy thing is not moved upwards except by some impelling force; nor does an agent fail in its action except from some impediment. But only good can be a cause; because nothing can be a cause except inasmuch as it is a being, and every being, as such, is good. And if we consider the special kinds of causes, we see that the agent, the form and the end imply some kind of perfection which belongs to the notion of good. Even matter, as a potentiality to good, has the nature of good.

Now that good is the cause of evil by way of the material cause was shown above.[3] For it was shown that good is the subject of evil. But evil has no formal cause, but is rather a privation of form. So, too, neither has it a final cause, but is rather a privation of order to the proper end; since it is not only the end which has the nature of good, but also the useful, which is ordered to the end. Evil, however, has a cause by way of an agent, not directly, but accidentally.

In proof of this, we must know that evil is caused in action otherwise than in the effect. In action, evil is caused by reason of the defect of some principle of action, either of the principal or the instrumental agent. Thus, the defect in the movement of an animal may happen by reason of the weakness of the motive power, as in the case of children, or by reason only of the ineptitude of the instrument, as in the lame. On the other hand, evil is caused in a thing, but not in the proper effect of the agent, sometimes by the power of the agent, sometimes by reason of a defect, either of the agent or of the matter. It is caused by reason of the power or perfection of the agent when there necessarily follows on the form intended by the agent the privation of another form; as, for instance, when on the form of fire there follows the privation of the form of air or of water. Therefore, as the more perfect the fire is in strength, so much the more perfectly does it impress its own form, so also the more perfectly does it corrupt the contrary. Hence that evil and corruption befall air and water comes from the perfection of the fire, but accidentally; because fire does not aim at the privation of the form of water, but at the introduction of its own form, though by doing this it also accidentally causes the other. But if there is a defect in the proper effect of the fire — as, for instance, that it fails to heat — this comes either by defect of the action, which implies the defect of some principle, as was said above, or by the indisposition of the matter, which does not receive the action of the fire acting on it. But the fact itself that it is a deficient

---

[2] *Contra Julian.,* I, 9 (PL 44, 670).
[3] Q. 48, a. 3.

being is accidental to good to which it belongs essentially to act. Hence it is true that evil in no way has any but an accidental cause. Thus good is the cause of evil.

Reply Obj. 1. As Augustine says, *The Lord calls an evil will an evil tree, and a good will a good tree.*[4] Now, a good will does not produce a morally bad act, since it is from the good will itself that a moral act is judged to be good. Nevertheless the movement itself of an evil will is caused by the rational creature, which is good; and thus good is the cause of evil.

Reply Obj. 2. Good does not cause that evil which is contrary to itself, but some other evil. Thus, the goodness of the fire causes evil to the water, and man, good in his nature, causes a morally evil act. Furthermore, as was explained above, this is by accident.[5] Moreover, it does happen sometimes that one contrary causes another by accident: for instance, the exterior surrounding cold heats inasmuch as the heat is confined by it.

Reply Obj. 3. Evil has a deficient cause in voluntary beings otherwise than in natural things. For the natural agent produces the same kind of effect as it is itself, unless it is impeded by some exterior thing; and this amounts to some defect in it. Hence evil never follows in the effect unless some other evil pre-exists in the agent or in the matter, as was said above. But in voluntary beings the defect of the action comes from an actually deficient will inasmuch as it does not actually subject itself to its proper rule. This defect, however, is not a fault; but fault follows upon it from the fact that the will acts with this defect.

Reply Obj. 4. Evil has no direct cause, but only an accidental cause, as was said above.

---

[4] *Contra Julian.*, I, 9 (PL 44, 672).   [5] Q. 19, a. 9.

11. God and Evil

St. Thomas, *Summa Theologiae*, I, q. 49, art. 2.*

Whether The Highest Good, God, Is The Cause Of Evil?

We proceed thus to the Second Article: —

Objection 1. It would seem that the highest good, God, is the cause of evil. For it is said (*Isa.* xlv 5, 1): *I am the Lord, and there is no other God, forming the light, and creating darkness, making peace, and creating evil.* It is also said (*Amos* iii. 6), *Shall there be evil in a city, which the Lord hath not done?*

Obj. 2. Further, the effect of the secondary cause is reduced to the first cause. But good is the cause of evil, as was said above. Therefore, since God is the cause of every good, as was shown above,[1] it follows that also every evil is from God.

---

* Pegis, *op. cit.*
[1] Q. 2, a. 3; q. 6, a. 1 and 4.

Obj. 3. Further, as is said by the Philosopher, the cause of both the safety and danger of the ship is the same.[2] But God is the cause of the safety of all things. Therefore He is the cause of all perdition and of all evil.

On the contrary, Augustine says that, *God is not the author of evil, because He is not the cause of tending to non-being.*[3]

I answer that, As appears from what was said, the evil which consists in the defect of action is always caused by the defect of the agent. But in God there is no defect, but the highest perfection, as was shown above.[4] Hence, the evil which consists in defect of action, or which is caused by defect of the agent, is not reduced to God as to its cause.

But the evil which consists in the corruption of some things is reduced to God as the cause. And this appears as regards both natural things and voluntary things. For it was said that some agent, inasmuch as it produces by its power a form which is followed by corruption and defect, causes by its power that corruption and defect. But it is manifest that the form which God chiefly intends in created things is the good of the order of the universe. Now, the order of the universe requires, as was said above, that there should be some things that can, and sometimes do, fail.[5] And thus God, by causing in things the good of the order of the universe, consequently and, as it were by accident, causes the corruptions of things, according to *I Kings* ii. 6: *The Lord killeth and maketh alive.* But when we read that *God hath not made death* (*Wis.* i. 13), the sense is that God does not will death for its own sake. Nevertheless, the order of justice belongs to the order of the universe; and this requires that penalty should be dealt out to sinners. And so God is the author of the evil which is penalty, but not of the evil which is fault, by reason of what is said above.

Reply Obj. 1. These passages refer to the evil of penalty, and not to the evil of fault.

Reply Obj. 2. The effect of the deficient secondary cause is reduced to the first non-deficient cause as regards what it has of being and perfection, but not as regards what it has of defect; just as whatever there is of motion in the act of limping is caused by the motive power, whereas what is unbalanced in it does not come from the motive power, but from the curvature of the leg. So, too, whatever there is of being and action in a bad action is reduced to God as the cause; whereas whatever defect is in it is not caused by God, but by the deficient secondary cause.

Reply Obj. 3. The sinking of a ship is attributed to the sailor as the cause, from the fact that he does not fulfill what the safety of the ship requires; but God does not fail in doing what is necessary for safety. Hence there is no parity.

---

[2] Aristotle, *Phys.*, II, 3 (195a 3).
[3] *Lib.* 83, *Quaest.*, q. 21 (PL 40, 16).
[4] Q. 4, a. 1.
[5] Q. 22, a. 2, ad 2; q. 48, a. 2,

READINGS FOR CHAPTER VII. THE METAPHYSICAL PRINCIPLES OF KNOWLEDGE AND THE CAUSES OF BEING

1. The Meaning of the Term "Principle"

A. Aristotle, *Metaphysics*, V, ch. 1, 1012b 34–1013a 23.*

Five Senses of the Term Principle. The Common Definition of Principle.

In one sense the term principle (beginning or starting point) means that from which someone first moves something; for example, in the case of a line or a journey, if the motion is from here, this is the principle, but if the motion is in the opposite direction, this is something different. In another sense principle means that from which a thing best comes into being, as the starting point of instruction; for sometimes it is not from what is first or from the starting point of a subject that one must begin, but from that from which one learns most readily. Again, principle means that first inherent thing from which something is brought into being, as the keel of a ship and the foundation of a house, and as some suppose the heart to be the principle in animals, and others the brain, and others anything else of the sort. In another sense it means that non-inherent first thing from which something comes into being; and that from which motion and change naturally first begins, as a child comes from its father and mother, and a fight from abusive language. In another sense principle means that according to whose will moveable things are moved and changeable things are changed; for example, in states, princely, magistral, imperial, or tyrannical power are all principles. And so also are the arts, especially the architectonic arts, called principles. And that from which a thing can first be known is also called a principle of that thing, as the postulates of demonstrations. And causes are also spoken of in the same number of senses, for all causes are principles.

Therefore, it is common to all principles to be the first thing from which a thing either is, comes to be, or is known. And of these some are intrinsic and others extrinsic. And for this reason nature is a principle, and so also is an element, and mind, purpose, substance, and the final cause; for good and evil[1] are the principle both of the knowledge and motion of many things.

---

* Aristotle's *Metaphysics* and St. Thomas' *Commentary* translated by John P. Rowan, Ph.D.
[1] The Greek text reads τὸ καλόν, i.e., "the beautiful."

B. St. Thomas, *Commentary on the Metaphysics*, V, lesson 1,
nos. 749–762.

[749.] Having established in the preceding book the things which pertain
to the consideration of this science, the Philosopher begins here to
establish the truth about the things which this science considers.

And since the attributes considered in this science are common to all
things, they are not predicated of different things univocally but in a prior
and subsequent way, as is stated in Book IV. Therefore, first, he distinguishes
the meanings of the terms which fall under the investigation of this science.
Second, he begins to deal with the things which fall under the investigation
of this science. He does this in the sixth book, which begins: "The
principles."

Now since it is the office of each science to consider both its subject and
the properties and causes of its subject, this fifth book is therefore divided
into three parts. In the first he establishes the different senses of the terms
that signify causes; in the second, the different senses of the terms that
signify the subject of this science or its parts, where he says, "In another
sense"; and in the third, the different senses of the terms that signify the
properties of being as being, where he says, "A thing."

The first part is divided into two members. First, he distinguishes the
different senses in which the term *cause* is used. Second, he discusses the
meaning of a term that signifies something associated with a cause, namely,
the *necessary*; for a cause is that in reference to which something else follows
of necessity. He treats this where he says, "That is said."

The first part is divided into two members. First, he distinguishes the
different senses of the terms that signify cause in a general way. Second
(413:C 808), he gives the meaning of a term that signifies a special kind
of cause, i.e., the term *nature*. This begins at the words "In one sense nature."

[750.] The first part is divided into three members. First, he gives the
different meanings of the term *principle*; second, of the term *cause*,
where he says, "In one sense the term *cause*"; and third, of the term
element, where he says, "An element."

He follows this order because the term principle is more common than
the term cause, for something may be a principle and not be a cause; for
example, the principle of motion is said to be the point from which motion
begins. Again, a cause is found in more things than an element is, for only
an intrinsic cause can be called an element.

In regard to this he does two things. First, he gives the meanings of the
term principle. Second, he reduces all of these to one common notion, where
he says, "Therefore, it is common."

[751.] Now it must be noted that, although a principle and cause are the
same in reality, they nevertheless differ conceptually. For the term principle implies an order or sequence, whereas the term cause implies some influ-

ence on the being of the thing caused. Now an order of priority and posteriority is found in different things; but according to what is first known by us order is found in local motion, because that kind of motion is more evident to the senses. Further, order is found in three classes of things, one of which is naturally associated with the others, i.e., continuous quantity, motion and time. For in so far as there is priority and posteriority in continuous quantity there is priority and posteriority in motion, and insofar as there is priority and posteriority in motion there is priority and posteriority in time, as is stated in Book IV of the *Physics*.[1] Therefore, because a principle is described as what is first[2] in any order, and the order which is considered according to priority and posteriority in continuous quantity is first known to us (and things are named by us insofar as they are known to us), for this reason the term principle, properly considered, designates what is first in a continuous quantity over which motion passes. Hence he says that a principle is described as "that from which someone first moves something," i.e., any part of a continuous quantity from which local motion begins. Or, according to another reading, "Some part of a thing from which motion will first begin," i.e., some part of a thing from which something first begins to be moved; for example, in the case of a line and of any kind of journey the principle is the point from which motion begins. But the opposite or contrary point is "what is different or other than this," i.e., the end or terminus. And it is to be noted that a principle of motion and a principle of time belong to this class for the reason just given.

[752.]   But because motion does not always begin from the starting point of a continuous quantity, but from that part from which the motion of each thing begins most readily, he therefore gives a second meaning of principle, saying that we speak of a principle of motion in another way "as that from which a thing best comes into being," i.e., the point from which each thing begins to be moved most easily. He makes this clear by an example, for in the disciplines one does not always begin to learn from something that is a beginning in an absolute sense and by nature, but from that from which one "is able to learn" most readily, i.e., from those things which are better known to us, though they are sometimes more remote by their nature.

[753.]   Now this sense of principle differs from the first. For in the first sense a principle of motion gets its name from the starting point of continuous quantity, whereas here the principle of continuous quantity gets its name from the starting point of motion. Hence in the case of those motions which are over circular continuous quantities and which have no starting point, the principle is also considered to be that point from which the mobile body is best or most fittingly moved according to its nature. For example, in the case of the first mobile (the first sphere), the starting point is from

---

[1] *Physica*, IV, 11 (219a 14).
[2] Reading *Quia igitur principium dicitur quod est primum in aliquo*. . . . In the previous Marietti ed. (as well as the Parma) the *est* is present, though not the *primum*.

the east. The same thing is true of our own movements; for a man does not always start to move from the beginning of a road but sometimes from the middle or from any point at all from which it is convenient for him to start moving.

[754.]   Now from the order considered in local motion we come to know the order in other motions. And in this way we come to the meanings of principle based upon the starting point of generation or coming to be of things. But this is taken in two ways; for such a principle is either "inherent" or intrinsic, or "non-inherent" or extrinsic.

[755.]   In the first way, then, a principle means that part of a thing which first comes into being and from which the generation of the thing proceeds; for example, in the case of a ship the first thing to come into being is the base or keel, which is in a sense the foundation on which the whole superstructure of the ship is raised. And similarly in the case of a house the first thing that comes into being is the foundation. And in the case of an animal the first thing that comes into being, according to some, is the heart, and according to others, the brain or some such member of the body. For an animal is distinguished from a non-animal by reason of sensation and motion. Now the principle of motion appears to be in the heart, and sensory operations are more evident in the brain. Hence those who considered an animal from the viewpoint of motion held that the heart is the principle in the generation of an animal. But those who considered an animal only from the viewpoint of sensation held that the brain is this principle, although the first principle of sensation is also in the heart even if the operation of the senses are completed in the brain. And those who considered an animal from the viewpoint of operation, or according to some of its activities, held that the organ which is naturally disposed for that operation, as the liver or some other such part, is the first to be generated in an animal. But in the Philosopher's opinion the first part is the heart, because all of the soul's powers are diffused throughout the body by means of the heart.

[756.]   In the second way, a principle means that from which a thing's process of generation begins but which is outside the thing. This is made clear in the case of three kinds of things. First, in that of natural things, in which the principle of generation is said to be the first thing from which motion naturally begins in those things which come to be through motion (as those which come to be through alteration or through some similar kind of motion; for example, a man is said to become large or white); or that from which a complete change begins (as in the case of those things which are not a result of motion but which come into being through mutation alone). This is evident in the case of substantial generation; for example, a child comes from its father and mother, who are its principles, and a fight comes from abusive language, which moves the souls of men to quarrel.

[757.]   Second, this is also made clear in matters of human conduct, whether
          ethical or political, in which that by whose will or intention others
are moved or changed is said to be their principle. Thus those who hold
civil, imperial, or even tyrannical power in states are said to have the
principal places. For it is by means of their will that all things come to pass
and are put into motion in states. Now men are said to have civil power
who are put in command of particular offices in states, as judges and persons
of this kind. And those are said to have imperial power who govern everyone
without exception, as kings. And those hold tyrannical power who through
violence and disregard for law keep royal power within their grip for their
own benefit.

[758.]   As a third example he points to things made by art; for the arts in like
          manner are also said to be principles of artificial things, because
the motion necessary for producing an artifact begins from an art. And of
these arts the architectonic, which "derive their name" from the word
principle, i.e., those called principal arts, are said to be principles in the
highest degree. For those arts which govern subordinate arts are called architectonic arts, as the art of the navigator governs the art of the shipwright,
and the military art governs the art of horsemanship.

[759.]   Again, in likeness to the order considered in external motions a
          certain order may also be observed in our apprehensions of things;
and especially in so far as our act of understanding, by proceeding from
principles to conclusions, bears a certain likeness to motion. Therefore, in
another way a principle means that from which a thing first becomes known,
as we say that "postulates," i.e., axioms and assumptions, are the principles
of demonstrations.

[760.]   And in these senses causes are also said to be principles; "for all
          causes are principles." For the motion that terminates in the being
of a thing begins from some cause, as has been pointed out above.

[761.]   "Therefore, it is common."

Then he reduces all the foregoing senses of principle to a single common
notion. He says that there is something common in all of the foregoing
senses inasmuch as that is said to be a principle which comes first either
with reference to a thing's being (as the first part of a thing is said to be
its principle), or with reference to its coming to be (as the first mover
is said to be a principle), or with reference to our knowing it.

[762.]   But while all principles agree in this respect, as has been stated,
          they nevertheless differ, because some are intrinsic and others are
extrinsic, as is clear from the above. Hence nature and element, which are
intrinsic, can be principles: nature, as that from which motion begins; and
element, as the first part in a thing's generation. "And mind," i.e., intellect,
and "purpose," i.e., man's intention, are said to be principles as extrinsic

ones. Further, "a thing's substance," i.e., its form, which is its principle of being, is called an intrinsic principle, since a thing has being by its form. Again, according to what has been said, that for the sake of which something comes to be is said to be one of its principles. For the good, which has the character of an end in the case of pursuing, and evil, in that of shunning, are principles of the knowledge and motion of many things, for example, of all things which are done for the sake of an end. For in the realm of nature, in that of moral acts, and in that of artifacts, demonstrations make special use of the final cause.

2. The Defense of the First Principle

A. Aristotle, *Metaphysics*, IV, chs. 3 and 4, 1005 b 8–1006 a 18.

First Philosophy Must Examine the First Principle of Demonstration. The Nature of This Principle. The Errors about it.

Chapter 3

And it is fitting that the person who is best informed about each class of things should be able to state the firmest principles of his subject. Hence he who understands beings as beings should be able to state the firmest principles of all things. This person is the philosopher.

And the firmest of all principles is that about which it is impossible to make a mistake; for such a principle must be both the best known (for all men make mistakes about things which they do not know), and not hypothetical. For the principle which everyone must have who understands anything about beings is not hypothetical; and that which everyone must know who knows anything must be had by him when he comes to his subject. It is evident, then, that such a principle is the firmest of all.

And let us next state what this principle is. It is, that the same attribute cannot both belong and not belong to the same subject at the same time and in the same respect; and any other qualifications that have to be laid down with a view to meeting dialectical difficulties. Now this is the firmest of all principles, since it answers to the definition given; for it is impossible for anyone to think that the same thing both is and is not, although some are of the opinion that Heraclitus speaks in this way; for what a man says he does not necessarily accept. But if it is impossible for contraries to belong simultaneously to the same subject (and let us then suppose that the same things are established here as in the usual proposition[1]), and if one opinion which is the contradictory of another is contrary to it, evidently the same man at the same time cannot think that the same thing can both be and not be; for one who is mistaken on this point will have contrary opinions at the same time. And it is for this reason that all who make demonstrations

---

[1] Reading *propositione* for *positione.*

reduce their argument to this ultimate position. For this is by nature the starting point of all the other axioms.

Chapter 4

Now as we have said, there are some who claimed that the same thing can both be and not be, and who thought that this is so. And many of those who treat of nature adopt this theory. But now we take it to be impossible for a thing both to be and not be at the same time, and by means of this we have shown that this is the firmest of all principles.

But some deem it fitting that even this principle should be demonstrated, and they do this through want of education. For not to know of what things one should seek demonstration and of what things one should not shows want of education. For it is altogether impossible that there should be demonstration of all things, for there would then be an infinite regress, so that there would still be no demonstration. But if there are some things of which it is not necessary to seek demonstration, these people cannot say what principle they think to be more such.

But even in this case it is possible to show by refutation that this view is impossible, if only an opponent will say something. But if he says nothing, it is ridiculous to look for an argument against one who does not have an argument as such; for such a man is really like a plant. Now I say that demonstration by refutation is different from demonstration (in the strict sense), because he who would demonstrate this principle in the strict sense would seem to beg the question.[2] But when someone argues for the sake of convincing another there will be refutation, not demonstration.

B. St. Thomas, *Commentary on the Metaphysics*, IV, lesson 6, nos. 596–610.

[596.] He shows here that it is the first philosopher who is chiefly concerned with the first principle of demonstration; and in regard to this he does two things. First, he shows that it is the business of the first philosopher to consider this principle; and second, he begins to examine this principle, where he says, "The starting-point."

In regard to the first he does three things. First, he shows that it is the office of this science to consider the first principle of demonstration. Second, he indicates what this principle is, where he says, "And the firmest." Third, he rejects certain errors regarding this same principle, where he says, "Now as we have said."

In regard to the first point he uses the following argument. In every class of things that man is best informed who knows the most certain principles, because the certitude of knowing depends on the certitude of principles. But the first philosopher is best informed and most certain in

---

[2] Reading . . . *demonstraret, videretur quaerere quod a principio erat* (with the *versio recens* of Parma) for . . . *demonstrat quidem in principio*.

his knowledge; for this was one of the conditions of wisdom, as was made clear in the prologue of this work, namely, that he who knows the causes of things has the most certain knowledge. Hence the philosopher ought to consider the most certain and firmest principles of beings, which he considers as the subject-genus proper to himself.

[597.] "And the firmest."

Then he shows what the firmest or most certain principle is; and in regard to this he does two things. First, he states the conditions of the most certain principle; and then, he shows how they fit a single principle, where he says, "And let us."

He accordingly gives, first, the three conditions for the firmest principle. The first is that no one can make a mistake or be in error regarding it. And this is evident, because since men only make mistakes about those things which they do not know, then that principle about which no one can make a mistake must be the one which is best known.

[598.] The second condition is that it must "not be hypothetical," i.e., it must not be held as a supposition, as those things which are maintained through some kind of common agreement. Hence another translation reads, "And they do not hold a subordinate place," i.e., those principles which are most certain do not hold a subordinate place. And this is true, because whatever is necessary for understanding anything at all about being "is not hypothetical," i.e., it is not a supposition but must be self-evident. And this is true, because whatever is necessary for understanding anything at all must be known by anyone who knows other things.

[599.] The third condition is that it is not acquired by demonstration or by some similar method, but comes in a sense by nature to the one having it inasmuch as it is naturally known and not acquired. For first principles become known through the natural light of the agent intellect, and they are not acquired by any process of reasoning but by their terms becoming known. This comes about by reason of the fact that memory is derived from sensible things, experience from memory, and knowledge of those terms from experience. And when they are known, common propositions of this kind, which are the principles of the arts and sciences, become known. Hence it is evident that the most certain or firmest principle should be such that there can be no error regarding it, that it is not hypothetical, and that it comes naturally to the one having it.

[600.] "And let us next."

Then he indicates the principle to which the above definition applies. He says that it is proper to this principle, as the one which is firmest, that it should be as follows: it is impossible for the same attribute both to belong and not belong to the same subject at the same time. And it is necessary to add "in the same respect," and any other qualifications that have to be given regarding this principle, as well as any that can be laid down "with a view to meeting dialectical difficulties," since without these qualifications there would seem to be a contradiction when there is none.

[601.] That this principle must meet the conditions given above he shows as follows: it is impossible for anyone to think, or hold as an opinion, that the same thing both is and is not at the same time, although some believe that Heraclitus was of this opinion. But while it is true that Heraclitus spoke in this way, he could not think that this is true; for it is not necessary that one should mentally accept or hold as an opinion everything that he says.

[602.] But if one were to say that it is possible for someone to think that the same thing both is and is not at the same time, this absurd consequence follows: contraries could belong to the same subject at the same time. And "let us suppose that the same things are established," or shown, here as in the usual proposition established in our logical treaties. For it was shown at the end of the Perihermenias[1] that contrary opinions are not those which have to do with contraries but those which have to do with contradictories, properly speaking. For when one person thinks that Socrates is white and another thinks that he is black, these are not contrary opinions in the primary and proper sense; but contrary opinions are had when one person thinks that Socrates is white and another thinks that he is not white.

[603.] Therefore, if someone thinks that two contradictories are true at the same time by thinking that the same thing both is and is not at the same time, he will have contrary opinions at the same time; and thus contraries will belong to the same thing at the same time. But this is impossible. It is impossible, then, for anyone to be mistaken in his own mind about these things and to think that the same thing both is and is not at the same time. And it is for this reason that all demonstrations reduce their propositions to this proposition as the ultimate opinion common to all; for this proposition is by nature the starting point and axiom of all axioms.

[604.] The other two conditions are therefore evident; because insofar as those making demonstrations reduce all their arguments to this principle as the ultimate one by referring them to it, evidently this principle is not based on an assumption. Indeed, insofar as it is by nature a starting point it clearly comes to the one having it and is not acquired.

[605.] Now for the purpose of making this evident it must be noted that, since the intellect has two operations, one by which it knows quiddities, which is called the understanding of indivisibles, and another by which it combines and separates, there is something first in both operations. In the first operation the first thing that the intellect conceives is

---
[1] De Interpretatione, 14 (23b 23).

being, and in this operation nothing else can be conceived unless being is understood. And because this principle — it is impossible for a thing to be and not be at the same time — depends on the understanding of being (just as this principle — every whole is greater than one of its parts — depends on the understanding of whole and part), then this principle is by nature also the first in the second operation of the intellect, i.e., in the act of combining and separating. And no one can understand anything by this intellectual operation unless this principle is understood. For just as a whole and its parts are understood only by understanding being, in a similar way this principle — every whole is greater than one of its parts — is understood only when the firmest principle is understood.

[606.] "Now as we have said."

Then he shows how some men erred regarding this principle; and in regard to this he does two things. First, he touches on the error of those who rejected the foregoing principle; and second, he deals with those who wished to demonstrate it, where he says, "But some."

He accordingly says that some men, as was stated above about Heraclitus, said that the same thing can both be and not be at the same time, and that it is possible to hold this opinion; and many of the philosophers of nature adopted this position, as will be made clear below. But we do not now hold this principle to be true on the basis of a supposition, i.e., the principle that the same thing cannot both be and not be, but we show that it is certain because of its very truth. For from the fact that a thing cannot both be and not be it follows that contraries cannot belong to the same subject, as will be said below. And from the fact that contraries cannot belong to a subject at the same time it follows that a man cannot have contrary opinions and, consequently, that he cannot think that contradictories are true, as has been shown.

[607.] "But some."

Then he mentions the error of certain men who wished to demonstrate the above-mentioned principle; and in regard to this he does two things. First, he shows that it cannot be demonstrated in the strict sense; and second, that it can be demonstrated in a way, where he says, "But it is possible."

Thus he says, first, that certain men deem it fitting, i.e., desire, to demonstrate this principle, and they do this "through want of education," i.e., through lack of learning or instruction. For there is want of education when a man does not know of what things one should seek demonstration and of what not; for not all things can be demonstrated. For if all things were demonstrable, then, since the same thing is not demonstrated through itself but through something else, demonstrations would either be circular (although this cannot be true, because the same thing would be both better known and less well known, as is clear in Book I of the *Posterior Analytics*[2]), or they would have to proceed to infinity. But if there were an infinite regress in demonstrations, demonstration would be impossible; because the certainty of the conclusion of any demonstration is tested by reducing it to the first principle of demonstration. But this would not be the case if demonstration proceeded to infinity in an upward direction. It is clear, then, that not all things are demonstrable. And if some things are not demonstrable these men cannot say that any principle is more indemonstrable than the above-mentioned one.

[608.] "But it is possible."

Here he shows that the above-mentioned principle can be demonstrated in a way. He says that it may be demonstrated by disproof. In Greek the word is ἐλεγχή, which is better translated as *by refutation*; for an ἐλεγχή is a syllogism establishing the contradictory of a proposition, and so is introduced to refute some false position. And on these grounds it can thus be shown that it is impossible for the same thing both to be and not be. But this kind of argument can be employed only if the one denying that principle because of some difficulty "says something," i.e., if he signifies something by means of a word. But if he says nothing, it is ridiculous to look for an argument against one who refuses to offer an argument by refusing to speak; for in this dispute such a one who signifies nothing will be like a plant. For even brute animals signify something by means of such signs.

[609.] For it is a different thing to give a strict demonstration of this principle and to demonstrate it argumentatively or by refutation. For if anyone wished to give a strict demonstration of this principle, he would seem to be begging the question, because any principle that he could take in order to demonstrate it would be one of those that would depend on the truth of this principle, as is clear from what has been said above. But when such demonstration, i.e., demonstration in the strict sense, is impossible, there will then be disproof or refutation but not demonstration.

[610.] Another text states this better by saying "But when one argues for the sake of convincing another, there will then be refutation but not demonstration," i.e., when a process of this kind from a less well known to a better known principle is employed for the sake of convincing another man who denies this, there will then be disproof or refutation but not demonstration, i.e., it will be possible to have a syllogism which contradicts his view, since what is less known absolutely is admitted by his opponent, and thus it will be possible to proceed to demonstrate the above-mentioned principle so far as the man is concerned, but not in the strict sense.

<hr>

[2] *Analytica Posteriora*, I, 2 (72 a 30); 3 (72 b 5 ff.).

3. The Principle of Contradiction

A.   Aristotle, *Metaphysics*, XI, chs. 5 and 6, 1061 b 34–1062 b 19.

Chapter 5

There is a principle in existing things about which it is impossible to make a mistake, but of which one must always do the contrary, I mean acknowledge it as true, namely, that the same thing cannot both be and not be at one and the same time; and the same thing is also true of other things which are opposed in this way.

And while there is no demonstration in the strict sense of such principles, one may employ an argument *ad hominem*; for it is impossible to construct a syllogism from a more certain principle than this one. But this would be necessary if there were demonstration of it in the strict sense.

Now he who wants to prove to an opponent who makes opposite statements to his own that he is wrong must take some such principle which will be the same as this one, namely, that the same thing cannot both be and not be at the same time, but shall not seem to be the same. For this will be the only method of demonstration that can be used against one who says that opposite statements can be truly made about the same subject.

Accordingly, those who are to join in some discussion must understand each other to some extent. And if this does not happen, how will they join in a common discussion? Therefore each of the terms used must signify something, and not many things but only one. But if a term does signify many things, it must be made clear to which of these it refers. Hence, one who says that this is and is not, totally denies what he affirms, and thus denies that the term signifies what it signifies. But this is impossible. Hence, if *to be this* has some meaning, the contradictory cannot be said to be true of the same subject.

Again, if a term signifies something and this is affirmed to be true, it must necessarily be so; and what is necessarily so cannot not be. Hence opposite affirmations and negations cannot be true of the same object.

Again, if the affirmation is in no way truer than the negation, it will not be truer to say that something is a man than to say that it is not a man. And it would also seem that it is more or not less true to say that a man is not a horse than to say that he is not a man. Hence one will also be right in saying that the same thing is a horse; for it was assumed that opposite statements are equally true. Therefore it follows that the same thing is a man and a horse, or any other animal. Hence, while there is no demonstration in the strict sense of these principles, there is still demonstration *ad hominem* against one who makes these assumptions.

And perhaps if one had questioned Heraclitus himself in this way, he would quickly have forced him to admit that opposite statements can never be true of the same subjects. But he adopted this view without understanding his own statement. And in general if what he said is true, not even this statement will be true — I mean that the same thing can both be and not be at one and the same time. For just as when they are separated the affirmation will not be truer than the negation, in a similar way when both are combined and taken together as though they were one affirmation, the negation will not be truer than the whole statement regarded as an affirmation.

Again, if it is possible to affirm nothing truly, even this statement — that no affirmation is true — will be false. But if there is a true affirmation, this will refute what is said by those who raise such objections and completely destroy discussion.

Chapter 6

The statement made by Protagoras is similar to those mentioned; for he said that man is the measure of all things,[1] meaning simply that whatever appears so to anyone is just as it appears to him. But if this is true, it follows that the same thing is and is not, and is good and evil, and that other statements involving opposites are true; because often a particular thing appears to be good to some and just the opposite to others, and that which appears to each man is the measure.

B. St. Thomas, *Commentary on the Metaphysics*, XI, lesson 5,[2] nos. 2211–2224.

[2211.] Having shown that a study of the common principles of demonstration belongs chiefly to the consideration of this philosophical science, the Philosopher now deals with the first of these principles. For just as all beings must be referred to one first being, in a similar fashion all principles of demonstration must be referred to some principle which pertains in a more basic way to the consideration of this philosophical science. This principle is that the same thing cannot both be and not be at the same time. It is the first principle because its terms, *being* and *non-being*, are the first to be apprehended by the intellect.

[2212.] This part is divided into two members. In the first he establishes the truth of this principle. In the second he rejects an error, where he says, "Now he who."

In reference to the first part he does two things regarding this principle. First he says that there is a principle of demonstration that pertains to beings "about which it is impossible to make a mistake" (i.e., so far as its meaning is concerned), but of which we "must always do the contrary,"

---

[1] Frag. 1.
[2] This lesson is a shorter form of Lessons 6–9, Book IV, ch. 4.

namely, acknowledge it as true. This principle is that the same thing cannot both be and not be at one and the same time, granted of course that the other conditions which it is customary to give in the case of a contradiction are fulfilled, namely, in the same respect, in an unqualified sense, and the like. For no one can think that this principle is false; because if someone were to think that contradictories may be true at the same time, he would then have contrary opinions at the same time; for contrary opinions deal with contraries. For example, the opinion of someone that "Socrates is sitting" is contrary to the opinion that "Socrates is not sitting."

[2213.] "And while."

Second, he says that while there cannot be demonstration in the strict sense of the above mentioned principle and other similar ones, one may offer an argument *ad hominem* in support of it. That it cannot be demonstrated in the strict sense he proves thus: no one can prove this principle by constructing a syllogism from some principle which it is better known. But such would be necessary if that principle were to be demonstrated in the strict sense. However, this principle can be demonstrated by using an *ad hominem* argument against one who admits that some other statement is true, although it be less known.

[2214.] "Now he who."

Then he rejects the opinion of those who deny this principle; and this is divided into two parts. First, he argues against those who deny this principle. Second, he shows how one can meet this opinion, where he says, "Now this difficulty."

In regard to the first he does two things. First, he argues against those who unqualifiedly deny this principle. Second, he turns his attention to certain particular opinions, where he says, "And perhaps."

In regard to the first he does two things. First, he gives the method of arguing against this error. He says that in arguing against some opponent who claims that contradictory propositions are true, one who wants to show that this opinion is false ought to take some such principle which is the same as this one — that the same thing cannot both be and not be at the same time — but does not seem to be the same. For if it seemed to be the same it would not be admitted by an opponent. But if it were not the same, he could not prove his thesis; because a principle of this kind cannot be demonstrated from some principle which is better known. Hence, only in this way can demonstration be made against those who say that contradictories may be true of the same subject, namely, so that the proposition which is taken is the same as the conclusion but does not seem to be the same.

[2215.] "Accordingly."

Second, he begins to argue dialectically against the above mentioned error; and in regard to this he gives three arguments. First, he argues as follows: if two men are to join in a discussion in such a way that one may communicate his own reasoning to the other by means of a dispute, each must understand something that the other is saying. For if this were not the case no statement would be understood by both of them; and thus an argument with an opponent would be pointless.

[2216.] However, if one of them is to understand what the other is saying, each of the terms used must be understood according to its proper meaning, and must therefore signify some one thing and not many things. And if it should signify many, it will be necessary to make clear which of the many things it signifies, otherwise one would not know what the other person wants to say.

[2217.] Now granted that a term signifies one thing, it is evident that one who says both that *this is* and that *this is not*, for example, that Socrates is a man and that he is not a man, denies the one thing which he attributed to Socrates, namely, that he is a man, when he adds that he is not a man; and thus he denies what he first signified. Hence it follows that a word does not signify what it signifies. But this is impossible. Consequently, if a term signifies some definite thing, the contradictory cannot be truly affirmed of the same subject.

[2218.] "Again, if a term."

Then he gives the second argument, which runs as follows: if a term signifies some attribute, and the attribute signified by the term is truly affirmed of the same subject of which the term is first predicated, this attribute must belong to the subject of which the term is predicated so long as the proposition is true. For this conditional proposition, "If Socrates is a man, Socrates is a man," is clearly true. Now every true conditional proposition is a necessary one. Hence, if the consequent is true, the antecedent must be true. But what is necessary cannot sometimes not be, because to be necessary and to be incapable of not being are equivalent. Therefore so long as the proposition "Socrates is a man" is true, the proposition "Socrates is not a man" cannot be true. Thus it is evident that opposite affirmations and negations cannot be true of the same subject at the same time.

[2219.] "Again, if the affirmation."

Then he gives the third argument, which is as follows: if an affirmation is not truer than the negation opposed to it, one who says that Socrates is a man does not speak with greater truth than one who says that Socrates is not a man. But it is evident that one who says that a man is not a horse speaks either with greater or no less truth than one who says that a man is not a man. Hence, according to this argument, he who says that a man is not a horse will speak with equal or no less truth. But if contradictory opposites are true at the same time, for example, if the proposition "Man is not a horse" is true, and the proposition "Man is a horse" is also true, then it follows that a man is a horse and also any other animal.

[2220.]   But because someone could criticize the foregoing arguments on the grounds that the things assumed in them are less known than the intended conclusion, he therefore answers this by saying that no one of the foregoing arguments is demonstrative in the strict sense, although there can be an argument *ad hominem* against an opponent who gives this argument, because the things assumed must be admitted to be true even though they are less known absolutely than what he denies.

[2221.]   "And perhaps."

Then he rejects the above error by considering certain particular thinkers. He does this, first, with regard to Heraclitus; and second, with regard to Protagoras, where he says, "The statement."

Now Heraclitus posited two things: first, that an affirmation and a negation may be true at the same time (and from this it would follow that every proposition, affirmative as well as negative, is true); and second, that there may be an intermediate between affirmation and negation (and from this it would follow that neither an affirmation nor negation can be true. Consequently every proposition is false).

[2222.]   First, he raises an argument against Heraclitus' first position; and second, against his second position, where he says, "Again, if it is possible."

He accordingly says, first, that by giving an *ad hominem* argument in this way one may easily bring even Heraclitus, who was the author of this statement, to admit that opposite propositions may not be true of the same subject. For he seems to have accepted the opinion that they may be true of the same subject because he did not understand his own statement. And he would be forced to deny his statement in the following way: if what he said is true, namely, that one and the same thing can both be and not be at one and the same time, it follows that this very statement will not be true; for if an affirmation and a negation are taken separately, an affirmation is not truer than a negation; and if an affirmation and a negation are taken together in such a way that one affirmation results from them, the negation will not be less true of the whole statement made up of the affirmation and negation than of the opposite affirmation. For it is clearly possible that some copulative proposition is true, just as for some simple proposition it is possible to take its negation. And whether the copulative proposition be composed of two affirmative propositions, as when we say "Socrates is sitting and arguing," or of two negative propositions, as when we say "It is true that Socrates is not a stone or an ass," or of an affirmative proposition and a negative proposition, as when we say "It is true that Socrates is sitting and not arguing," nevertheless a copulative proposition is always taken to be true because one affirmative proposition is true. And he who says that it is false takes the negation in a sense of the whole copulative proposition. Hence he who says that it is true that man is and is not at the same time, takes this as a kind of affirmation; and he who says that this is not true, takes the negation of this. Hence, if an affirmation and a negation are true at the same time, it follows that the negation which states that this is not true, i.e., that an affirmation and a negation are true at the same time, is equally true. For if any negation is true at the same time as the affirmation opposed to it, every negation must be true at the same time as the affirmation opposed to it; for the reasoning is the same in all cases.

[2223.]   "Again, if it is possible."

Then he introduces an argument against the second position of Heraclitus: that no affirmation is true. For if it is possible to affirm that nothing is true, and if one who says that no affirmation is true does affirm something, namely, that it is true that no affirmation is true, then this statement will be false. And if some affirmative statement is true, the opinion of people such as those who oppose all statements will be rejected. And those who adopt this position destroy the whole debate, because if nothing is true, nothing can be conceded on which an argument may be based. And if an affirmation and a negation are true at the same time, it will be impossible to signify anything by a word, as was said above, and then the argument will cease.

[2224.]   "The statement."

Here he considers the opinion of Protagoras. He says that the statement made by Protagoras is similar to the one made by Heraclitus and by others who claim that an affirmation and a negation are true at the same time. For Protogoras says that man is the measure of all things, i.e., according to the intellect and the senses, as has been explained in Book IX, as if the being of a thing depended upon intellectual and sensory apprehension. And one who says that man is the measure of all things merely says that whatever appears so to anyone is true. But if this is maintained, it follows that the same thing both is and is not, and is both good and evil at the same time. The same thing is also true of other opposites, because often something seems to be good to some men and seems to be just the opposite to others, and the way things seem or appear is the measure of all things according to the opinion of Protagoras; i.e., inasmuch as a thing is true to the extent that it appears to anyone.

4. Causes in General

A.   Aristotle, *Metaphysics*, V, ch. 2, 1013 a 24–1013 b 16.*

The Four Classes of Causes. Several Causes of the Same Effect.

Causes May Be Causes of Each Other. Contraries Have the Same Cause.

In one sense the term cause means that from which, as something intrinsic, a thing comes to be, as the bronze of a statue and the silver of a goblet, and the genera of these. In another sense it means the form and pattern of a thing, i.e., the intelligible expression of the quiddity and its genera (for example, the ratio of 2:1 and number in general are the cause of the octave chord) and the parts which are included in the intelligible expression. Again, that from which the first beginning of change or rest comes is a cause, for example, an adviser is a cause, and a father is the cause of a child, and in general a maker is a cause of the thing made and a changer the cause of the thing changed. Further, a thing is a cause inasmuch as it is an end, i.e., that for the sake of which something is done; for example, health is the cause of walking. For if we ask why one walks, we answer that he does so in order to be healthy, and in saying this we think we have given the cause. And whatever occurs on the way to the end under the motion of something else is also a cause. For example, reducing, purging, drugs and instruments are causes of health; for all of these exist for the sake of the end, although they differ from each other inasmuch as some are instruments and others are processes. These, then, are nearly all the ways in which causes are spoken of.

And since there are several senses in which causes are spoken of, it turns out that there are many causes of the same thing, and not in an accidental way. For example, both the maker of a statue and the bronze are causes of a statue not in any other respect but insofar as it is a statue. However, they are not causes in the same way, but the one as matter and the other as the source of motion.

And there are things which are causes of each other. Pain, for example is a cause of health and health is a cause of pain, although not in the same way, but one as an end and the other as a source of motion.

Further, the same thing is sometimes the cause of contraries; for that which when present is the cause of some particular thing, this when absent we sometimes blame for the contrary. Thus the cause of the loss of a ship is the absence of the pilot whose presence is the cause of the ship's safety. And both of these — the absence and the presence — are moving causes.

---

* Rowan translation.

B. St. Thomas, Commentary on the Metaphysics, V, lesson 2,
nos. 763–776.

[763.] Here the Philosopher distinguishes the various ways in which the
term cause is used; and in regard to this he does two things. First,
he enumerates the classes of causes. Second, he gives the modes of causes,
where he says, "Now the modes."

In regard to the first part he does two things. First he enumerates the
different classes of causes. Second, he reduces them to four, where he says,
"All the things."

In regard to the first part he does two things. First he enumerates the
different classes of causes. Second, he clarifies certain things about the classes
of causes, where he says, "And since."

He accordingly says, first, that in one sense the term cause means that
from which a thing comes to be and is "something intrinsic," i.e., something
existing within the thing. This is said to distinguish it from a privation and
also from a contrary. For a thing is said to come from a privation or from a
contrary as from something which is not intrinsic; for example, white is
said to come from black or from the not-white. But a statue comes from
bronze and a goblet from silver as from something which is intrinsic; for
the nature bronze is not destroyed when a statue comes into being, nor is
the nature silver destroyed when a goblet comes into being. Therefore
the bronze of a statue and the silver of a goblet are causes in the sense of
matter. He adds "and the genera of these," because of whatever thing matter
is the species, matter is also the genus. For example, if the matter of a
statue is bronze, its matter will also be metal, compound and body. The
same holds true of other things.

[764.] In another sense cause means the form and pattern of a thing,
i.e., its exemplar; and this is the formal cause, which is related to a
thing in two ways. In one way it stands as the intrinsic form of a thing,
and in this respect it is called its formal principle. In another way it stands
as something which is extrinsic to a thing but is that in likeness to which
a thing is made, and in this respect an exemplar is also called the form of
a thing. It is in this sense that Plato held the Ideas to be forms. Moreover,
because it is from its form that each thing acquires its nature, whether
of its genus or of its species, and the nature of its genus or of its species
is what is signified by its definition, which expresses a thing's quiddity, the
form is therefore the intelligible expression of a thing's quiddity, i.e., the
definition by which a thing's quiddity is known. For even though certain
material parts are given in a definition, the principal part of a definition
must still come from a thing's form. Therefore the reason why the form
is a cause is that it completes the intelligible expression of a thing's quiddity.
And just as the genus of a particular matter is also matter, in a similar way
the genera of forms are the forms of things; for example, the form of the

octave chord is the ratio of 2:1. For when two notes stand to each other in the ratio of 2:1, the interval between them is one octave. Hence twoness is its form; for the ratio of 2:1 derives its meaning from twoness. And because number is the genus of twoness, therefore generally speaking number is also the form of the octave, so that we may say that the octave chord involves the ratio of one number to another. And not only is the whole definition related to the thing defined as its form, but so also are the parts of the definition, namely, those which are given directly in the definition. For just as two-footed animal capable of walking is the form of man, so also is animal, capable of walking and two-footed. But sometimes matter is given indirectly in the definition, as when the soul is said to be the act of a physical organic body having life potentially.

[765.]   In a third sense cause means that from which the first beginning of change or rest comes, i.e., the moving or efficient cause. He says "of change or rest," because motion and rest which are natural are traced back to the same cause, and the same is true of motion and rest which are a result of force. For the cause by which something is moved to a place is the same as the one by which it is made to rest there. "An adviser" is an example of this kind of cause, for it is as a result of an adviser that motion begins in the one who acts upon his advice for the sake of safeguarding something. And in a similar way "a father is the cause of a child." In these two examples Aristotle touches upon the two principles of motion from which all things come to be, namely, purpose in the case of an adviser, and nature in the case of a father. And in general every maker is a cause of the thing made and every changer a cause of the thing changed.

[766.]   Moreover, it must be noted that according to Avicenna there are four modes of efficient cause, namely, the perfective, dispositive, auxiliary and advisory. An efficient cause is said to be perfective inasmuch as it causes the final perfection of a thing, as the one who induces a substantial form in natural things or artificial forms in things made by art, as a builder induces the form of a house.

[767.]   An efficient cause is said to be dispositive if it does not induce the final form that perfects a thing but only prepares the matter for that form, as one who hews timbers and stones is said to build a house. This cause is not properly said to be the efficient cause of a house, because what he produces is only potentially a house. But he will be more properly an efficient cause if he induces the ultimate disposition on which the form necessarily follows; for example, man generates man without causing his intellect, which comes from an extrinsic cause.

[768.]   And an efficient cause is said to be auxiliary insofar as it contributes to the principal effect. Yet it differs from the principal efficient cause in this respect, that the principal efficient cause acts for its own end, whereas an auxiliary cause acts for an end which is not its own. For example, one who assists a king in war acts for the king's end. And this is the way in which a secondary cause is disposed for a primary cause. For in the case of all efficient causes which are directly subordinated to each other, a secondary cause acts because of the end of a primary cause; for example, the military art acts because of the end of the political art.

[769.] And an advisory cause differs from a principal efficient cause inasmuch as it specifies the end and form of the activity. This is the way in which the first agent, by his intellect, is related to every secondary agent, whether it be natural or intellectual. For in every case a first intellectual agent gives to a secondary agent its end and its form of activity; for example, the naval architect gives these to the shipwright, and the first intelligence does the same thing for everything in the natural world.

[770.] Further, to this genus of cause is reduced everything that makes anything to be in any manner whatsoever, not only as regards substantial being, but also as regards accidental being, which occurs in every kind of motion. Hence he says not only that the maker is the cause of the thing made, but also that the changer is the cause of the thing changed.

[771.] In a fourth sense cause means a thing's end, i.e., that for the sake of which something is done, as health is the cause of walking. And since it is less evident that the end is a cause in view of the fact that it comes into being last of all (which is also the reason why this cause was overlooked by the earlier philosophers, as was pointed out in Book I), he therefore gives a special proof that an end is a cause. For to ask why or for what reason is to ask about a cause, because when we are asked why or for what reason someone walks, we reply properly by answering that he does so in order to be healthy. And when we answer in this way we think that we are stating a cause. Hence it is evident that the end is a cause. Moreover, not only the ultimate reason for which an agent acts is said to be an end with respect to those things which precede it, but everything that is intermediate between the first agent and the ultimate end is also said to be an end with respect to the preceding agents. And similarly those things are said to be causes from which motion arises in subsequent things. For example, between the art of medicine, which is the first efficient cause in this order, and health, which is the ultimate end, there are these intermediates: *reducing*, which is the most proximate cause of health in those who have a superfluity of humors; purging, by means of which reducing is brought about; drugs, i.e., laxative medicine, by means of which purging is accomplished; and "instruments," i.e., the instruments by which medicine or drugs are prepared and administered. And all such things exist for the sake of the end, although one of them is the end of another. For reducing is the end of purging, and purging is the end of purgatives. However, those intermediates differ from each other in that some are instruments, i.e., the instruments by means of which medicine is prepared and administered (and the administered medicine itself is something which nature employs as an instrument); and some — purging and reducing — are processes, i.e., operations or activities.

[772.]   He concludes, then, that "these are the ways in which causes are spoken of," i.e., the four ways; and he adds "nearly all" because of the modes of causes which he gives below. Or he also adds this because the same classes of causes are not found for the same reason in all things.

[773.]   "And since. "

Then he indicates certain points which follow from the things said above about the causes, and there are four of these. The first is that, since the term *cause* is used in many senses, there may be several causes of one thing not accidentally but properly. For the fact that there are many causes of one thing accidentally presents no difficulty, because many things may be accidents of something that is the proper cause of some effect, and all of these can be said to be accidental causes of that effect. But that there are several proper causes of one thing becomes evident from the fact that causes are spoken of in various ways. For the maker of a statue is a proper cause and not an accidental cause of a statue, and so also is the bronze, but not in the same way. For it is impossible that there should be many proper causes of the same thing within the same genus and in the same order, although there can be many causes providing that one is proximate and another remote; or that neither of them is of itself a sufficient cause, but both together. An example would be many men rowing a boat. Now in the case in point these two things are causes of a statue in different ways: the bronze as matter, and the artist as efficient cause.

[774.]   "'And there are."

Then he sets down the second fact that may be drawn from the foregoing discussion. He says that it may also happen that any two things may be the cause of each other, although this is impossible in the same class of cause. But it is evident that this may happen when causes are spoken of in different senses. For example, the pain resulting from a wound is a cause of health as an efficient cause or source of motion, whereas health is the cause of pain as an end. For it is impossible that a thing should be both a cause and something caused. Another text states this better, saying that "exercise is the cause of physical fitness," i.e., of the good disposition caused by moderate exercise, which promotes digestion and uses up superfluous humors.

[775.]   Now it must be borne in mind that, although four causes are given above, two of these are related to one another, and so also are the other two. The efficient cause is related to the final cause, and the material cause is related to the formal cause. The efficient cause is related to the final cause, because the efficient cause is the starting point of motion, and the final cause is its terminus. There is a similar relationship between matter and form. For form gives being, and matter receives it. Hence the efficient cause is the cause of the final cause, and the final cause is the cause of the efficient cause. The efficient cause is the cause of the final cause inasmuch at it makes the final cause be, because by causing motion the efficient cause brings about the final cause. But the final cause is the cause of the efficient cause, not in the sense that it makes it be, but inasmuch as it is the reason for the causality of the efficient cause. For an efficient cause is a cause inasmuch as it acts, and it acts only because of the final cause. Hence the efficient cause derives its casuality from the final cause. And form and matter are mutual causes of being: form is a cause of matter inasmuch as it gives actual being to matter, and matter is a cause of form inasmuch as it keeps a form in being. And I say that both of these together are causes of being either in an unqualified sense or with some qualification. For substantial form gives being absolutely to matter, whereas accidental form, inasmuch as it is a form, gives being in a qualified sense. And matter sometimes does not keep a form in being in an unqualified sense but according as it is the form of this particular thing and has being in this particular thing. This is what happens in the case of the human body in relation to the rational soul.

[776.] "Further, the same thing."

Then he gives the third conclusion that may be drawn from the foregoing discussion. He says that the same thing can be the cause of contraries. This would also seem to be difficult or impossible if it were related to both in the same way. But it is the cause of each in a different way. For that which when present is the cause of some particular thing, when absent "we accuse," i.e., we blame it, "for the contrary." For example, it is evident that by his presence the pilot is the cause of a ship's safety, and we say that his absence is the cause of the ship's loss. And lest someone might think that this is to be attributed to different classes of causes, just as the preceding two were, he therefore adds that both of these may be reduced to the same class of cause — the moving cause. For the opposite of a cause is the cause of an opposite effect in the same line of causality as that in which the original cause was the cause of its effect.

5. Four Classes of Causes

A.   Aristotle, *Metaphysics*, V, ch. 2, 1013b 16–1014a 25.*

All Causes Reduced to Four Classes.

All the causes mentioned fall under one of the four classes which are most evident. For the elements of syllables, the matter of things made by art, fire and earth and all such elements of bodies, the parts of a whole, and the premises of a conclusion, are all causes in the sense of that from which things are made. But of these some are causes as a subject, for example, parts, and others as the essence, for example, the whole, the composition and the species; whereas the seed, the physician, the adviser, and in general every agent, are all sources of change or of rest. But the others are causes as the end and the good of other things. For that for the sake of which other things come to be is the greatest good and the end of other things. And it makes no

---
* Rowan translation.

difference whether we say that it is a good or an apparent good. These, then, are the causes, and this the number of their classes.

Now the modes of causes are many in number, but these become fewer when summarized. For causes are spoken of in many senses; and of those which belong to the same class, some are prior and some subsequent. For example, both the physician and one possessing an art are causes of health, and both the ratio of 2:1 and number are causes of the octave chord; and always those classes which contain singulars. Further, a thing may be a cause in the sense of an accident, and the classes which contain these; for example, in one sense the cause of a statue is Polyclitus and in another a sculptor, because it is accidental that a sculptor should be Polyclitus. And the universals which contain accidents are causes; for example, a man is the cause of a statue, and even generally an animal, because Polyclitus is a man and an animal. And of accidental causes some are more remote and some more proximate than others. Thus what is white and what is musical might be said to be the causes of a statue, and not just Polyclitus or man. Again, in addition to all of these, i.e., both proper causes and accidental causes, some are said to be causes potentially and some actually, as a builder and one who is building. And the distinctions which have been made will apply in like manner to the effects of these causes, for example, to this statue, or to a statue, or to an image generally, or to this bronze, or to bronze, or to matter in general. And the same applies to accidental effects. Again, both proper and accidental causes may be spoken of together, so that the cause of a statue may be referred to as neither Polyclitus nor a sculptor but the sculptor Polyclitus. But while all these varieties of causes are six in number, each is spoken of in two ways; for causes are either singular or generic; either proper or accidental, or generically accidental; or they are spoken of in combination or without qualification; and again they are either active or potential causes. But they differ in this respect, that active causes, i.e., singular causes, exist or cease to exist simultaneously with their effects, as this particular one who is healing with this particular person who is being healed, and as this particular builder with this particular thing which is being built. But this is not always true of potential causes; for the builder and the thing built do not cease to exist at the same time.

B. St. Thomas, *Commentary on the Metaphysics*, V, lesson 3, nos. 777–794.

[777.] Here the philosopher reduces all causes to the classes of causes mentioned above, saying that all those things which are called causes fall into one of the four classes mentioned above. For "elements," i.e., letters, are said to be the causes of syllables; and the matter of artificial things is said to be their cause; and fire and earth and all simple bodies of this kind are said to be causes of compounds. And parts are said to be the causes of a whole, and "premises," i.e., propositions previously set down from which conclusions are drawn, are said to be the causes of the conclusion. And in all of these cases cause has a single formal aspect according as cause means that from which a thing is produced, and this is the formal aspect of material cause.

[778.] Now it must be noted that propositions are said to constitute the matter of a conclusion, not inasmuch as they exist under such a form, or according to their force (for in this way they would rather have the formal aspect of an efficient cause), but with reference to the terms of which they are composed. For a conclusion is constituted of the terms contained in the premises, i.e., of the major and minor terms.

[779.] And of those things of which something is composed, some are like a subject, for example, parts and the other things mentioned above, whereas some are like the essence, for example, the whole, the composition and the species, which have the character of a form whereby a thing's essence is made complete. For it must be borne in mind that sometimes one thing is the matter of something else in an unqualified sense (for example, silver of a goblet), and then the form corresponding to such a matter can be called the species. But sometimes many things taken together constitute the matter of a thing; and this may occur in three ways. For sometimes things are united merely by their arrangement, as the men in an army or the houses in a city; and then the whole has the role of a form which is designated by the term army or city. And sometimes things are united not just by arrangement alone but by contact and a bond, as is evident in the parts of a house; and then their composition has the role of a form. And sometimes the alteration of the component parts is added to the above, as occurs in the case of a compound; and then the compound state itself is the form, and this is still a kind of composition. And a thing's essence is derived from any one of these three — the composition, species, or whole — as becomes clear when an army, a house, or a goblet is defined. Thus we have two classes of cause.

[780.] But the seed, the physician and the adviser, and in general every agent, are called causes for a different reason, namely, because they are the sources of motion and rest. Hence this is now a different class of cause because of a different formal aspect of causality. He puts seed in this class of cause because he is of the opinion that the seed has active power, whereas as woman's menstrual fluid has the role of the matter of the offspring.

[781.] There is a fourth formal aspect of causality inasmuch as some things are said to be causes in the sense of the end and good of other things. For that for the sake of which something else comes to be is the greatest good "and the end" of other things, i.e., it is naturally disposed to be their end. But because someone could raise the objection that an end is not always a good, since certain agents sometimes inordinately set up an evil as their end, he therefore replies that it makes no difference to his thesis whether we speak of what is good without qualification or of an apparent good. For one who acts does so, properly speaking, because of a good, for this is what he has in mind. And one acts for the sake of an evil accidentally inasmuch as he happens to think that it is good. For no one acts for the sake of something with evil in view.

[782.]   Moreover, it must be noted that, even though the end is the last thing to come into being in some cases, it is always prior in causality. Hence it is called the cause of causes, because it is the cause of the causality of all causes. For it is the cause of efficient causality, as has already been pointed out; and the efficient cause is the cause of the causality of both the matter and the form, because by its motion it causes matter to be receptive of form and makes form exist in matter. Therefore the final cause is also the cause of the causality of both the matter and the form. Hence in those cases in which something is done for an end (as occurs in the realm of natural things, in that of moral matters, and in that of art), the most forceful demonstrations are derived from the final cause. Therefore he concludes that the foregoing are causes, and that causes are distinguished into this number of classes.

[783.]   "Now the modes."

Then he distinguishes between the modes of causes. And causes are distinguished into classes and into modes. For the division of causes into classes is based on different formal aspects of causality, and is therefore equivalently a division based on essential differences, which constitute species. But the division of causes into modes is based on the different relationships between causes and things caused, and therefore pertains to those causes which have the same formal aspect of causality. An example of this is the division of causes into proper and accidental causes, and into remote and proximate causes. Therefore this division is equivalently a division based on accidental differences, which do not constitute different species.

[784.]   He accordingly says that there are many modes of causes, but these are found to be fewer in number when "summarized," i.e., when brought together under one head. For even though proper causes and accidental causes are two modes, they are still reduced to one head insofar as both may be considered from the same point of view. The same thing is true of the other different modes. For many different modes of causes are spoken of, not only with reference to the different species of causes but also with reference to causes of the same species, namely, those which are reduced to one class of cause.

[785.]   For one cause is said to be prior and another subsequent; and causes are prior or subsequent in two ways. In one way, when there are many distinct causes which are related to each other, one of which is primary and remote, and another secondary and proximate (as in the case of efficient causes man generates man as a proximate and subsequent cause, but the sun as a prior and remote cause); and the same thing can be considered in the case of the other classes of causes. In another way, when the cause is numerically one and the same but is considered according to the sequence which reason sets up between the universal and the particular; for the universal is naturally prior and the particular subsequent.

[786.] But he omits the first way and considers the second. For in the second way the effect is the immediate result of both causes, i.e., of both the prior and subsequent cause; but this cannot happen in the first way. Hence he says that the cause of health is both the physician and one possessing an art, who belong to the class of efficient cause: one possessing an art as a universal and prior cause, and the physician as a particular, or special, and subsequent cause. The same thing is true of the formal cause, since this cause may also be considered in two ways; for example, for an octave chord "double," or the ratio of 2:1, or the number two, is a formal cause as one that is special and subsequent, whereas number, or the ratio of one number to another or to the unit, is like a universal and prior cause. And in this way too "always those classes which contain singulars," i.e., universals, are said to be prior causes.

[787.] Causes are distinguished in another way inasmuch as one thing is said to be a proper cause and another an accidental cause. For just as proper causes are divided into universal and particular, or into prior and subsequent, so also are accidental causes. Therefore, not only accidental causes themselves are called such, but so also are the classes which contain these. For example, a sculptor is the proper cause of a statue, and Polyclitus is an accidental cause inasmuch as he happens to be a sculptor. And just as Polyclitus is an accidental cause of a statue, in a similar way all universals "which contain accidents," i.e., accidental causes, are said to be accidental causes, for example, man and animal, which contain under themselves Polyclitus, who is a man and an animal.

[788.] And just as some proper causes are proximate and some remote, as was pointed out above, so also is this the case with accidental causes. For Polyclitus is a more proximate cause of a statue than the white or the musical. For an accidental mode of predication is more remote when an accident is predicated of an accident than when an accident is predicated of a subject. For one accident is predicated of another only because both are predicated of a subject. Hence when something pertaining to one accident is predicated of another, as when something pertaining to a builder is predicated of the musical, this mode of predication is more remote than one in which something is predicated of the subject of an accident, as when something pertaining to a builder is predicated of Polyclitus.

[789.] Now it must be borne in mind that one thing can be said to be the accidental cause of something else in two ways: in one way, from the viewpoint of the cause; because whatever is accidental to a cause is itself called an accidental cause, for example, when we say that something white is the cause of a horse. In another way, from the viewpoint of the effect; i.e., inasmuch as one thing is said to be an accidental cause of something else because it is an accident of the proper effect. This can happen in three ways. In one way a thing is an accident of the proper effect because it has a necessary connection with the effect. Thus that which removes an obstacle is said to be a mover accidentally. This is the case whether that accident be a contrary, as when bile prevents coolness (and thus scammony is said to produce coolness accidentally, not because it causes coolness, but because it removes the obstacle preventing coolness, i.e., bile, which is its contrary); or even if it is not a contrary, as when a pillar hinders the movement of an adjacent stone, so that one who removes a pillar is said to move the stone accidentally. In a second way, something is an accident of the proper effect when the accident is connected with the effect neither necessarily nor in the majority of cases but seldom, as the discovery of a treasure is connected with digging in the soil. It is in this way that fortune and chance are said to be accidental causes. In a third way things are accidents of the effect when they have no connection except perhaps in the mind, as when someone says that he is the cause of an earthquake because an earthquake took place when he entered a house.

[790.] And besides the distinction of all things into causes in themselves or proper causes and accidental causes, there is a third division of causes inasmuch as some things are causes potentially and some actually, i.e., actively. For example, the cause of building is a builder in a state of potency (for this designates his habit or office), or one who is actually building.

[791.] And the same distinctions which apply to causes can apply to the effects of which these causes are the causes. For effects, whether particular or universal, can be divided into prior and subsequent, as if we were to say that a sculptor is the cause of this statue, which is subsequent; or of a statue, which is more universal and prior; or of an image, which is still more universal. And similarly something is the formal cause of this particular bronze; or of bronze, which is more universal; or of matter, which is still more universal. The same things can be said of accidental effects, i.e., of things produced by accident. For a sculptor who is the cause of a statue is also the cause of the heaviness, whiteness or redness which are in it as accidents from the matter and are not caused by this agent.

[792.] Again, he gives a fourth division of causes, namely, the division into simple causes and composite causes. A cause is said to be simple when, for example, in the case of a statue, the proper cause alone is considered, as a sculptor, or when an accidental cause alone is considered, as Polyclitus. But a cause is said to be composite when both are taken together, for example, when we say that the cause of a statue is the sculptor Polyclitus.

[793.] There is moreover another way in which causes are said to be composite, i.e., when several causes act together to produce one effect, for example, when many men act together in order to row a boat, or when many stones combine in order to constitute the matter of a house. But he omits the latter way because no one of these things taken in itself is the cause, but a part of the cause.

[794.] And having given these different modes of causes he brings out their number, saying that these modes of causes are six in number, and that each of these have two alternatives so that twelve result. For these six modes are either singular or generic (or, as he called them above, prior and subsequent); either proper or accidental (to which the genus of accident is also reduced, for the genus to which an accident belongs is an accidental cause); and again, either composite or simple. Now these six modes are further divided by potency and actuality and thus are twelve in number. Now all these modes must be divided by potency and actuality for this reason, that potency and actuality distinguish the connection between cause and effect. For active causes are at one and the same time particulars and cease to exist along with their effects; for example, this act of healing ceases with this act of recovering health, and this act of building with this thing being built; for a thing cannot be being built unless something is actually building. But potential causes do not always cease to exist when their effects cease; for example, a house and a builder do not cease to exist at one and the same time. In some cases, however, it does happen that when the activity of the efficient cause ceases the substance of the effect ceases. This occurs in the case of those things whose being consists in coming to be, or whose cause is not only the cause of their coming to be but also of their being. For example, when the sun's illumination is removed from the atmosphere, light ceases to be. He says "singular causes" because acts belong to singular things, as was stated at the beginning of this discussion (410:C 783).

READINGS FOR CHAPTER VIII. THE ORIGIN AND END OF ALL

1. Evidence of God's Existence

St. Thomas, *Summa Theologiae*, I, q. 2, art. 1.*

We proceed thus to the First Article: —

Obj. 1. It seems that the existence of God is self-evident. For those things are said to be self-evident to us the knowledge of which exists naturally in us, as we can see in regard to first principles. But as Damascene says, *the knowledge of God is naturally implanted in all*.[1] Therefore the existence of God is self-evident.

Obj. 2. Further, those things are said to be self-evident which are known as soon as the terms are known, which the Philosopher says is true of the first principles of demonstration.[2] Thus, when the nature of a whole and of a part is known, it is at once recognized that every whole is greater than its part. But as soon as the signification of the name *God* is understood, it is at once seen that God exists. For by this name is signified that thing than which nothing greater can be conceived. But that which exists actually and mentally is greater than that which exists only mentally. Therefore, since as soon as the name *God* is understood it exists mentally, it also follows that is exists actually. Therefore the proposition *God exists* is self-evident.

Obj. 3. Further, the existence of truth is self-evident. For whoever denies the existence of truth grants that truth does not exist: and, if truth does not exist, then the proposition *Truth does not exist* is true: and if there is anything true, there must be truth. But God is truth itself: *I am the way, the truth, and the life* (Jo. xiv. 6). Therefore *God exists* is self-evident.

On the contrary, No one can mentally admit the opposite of what is self-evident, as the Philosopher states concerning the first principles of demonstration.[3] But the opposite of the proposition *God is* can be mentally admitted: *The fool said in his heart, There is no God* (Ps. lii. I). Therefore, that God exists is not self-evident.

---

* Anton C. Pegis, *The Basic Writings of St. Thomas Aquinas* (New York: Random House, 1945).

[1] *De Fide Orth.*, I, I; 3 (PG 94, 789; 793).

[2] *Post. Anal.*, I, 3 (72b 18).

[3] *Metaph.*, III, 3 (1005b II); *Post. Anal.*, I, 10 (76b 23).

I answer that, A thing can be self-evident in either of two ways: on the one hand, self-evident in itself, though not to us; on the other, self-evident in itself, and to us. A proposition is self-evident because the predicate is included in the essence of the subject: e.g., *Man is an animal*, for animal is contained in the essence of man. If, therefore, the essence of the predicate and subject be known to all, the proposition will be self-evident to all; as is clear with regard to the first principles of demonstration, the terms of which are certain common notions that no one is ignorant of, such as being and non-being, whole and part, and the like. If, however, there are some to whom the essence of the predicate and subject is unknown, the proposition will be self-evident in itself, but not to those who do not know the meaning of the predicate and subject of the proposition. Therefore, it happens, as Boethius says, that there are some notions of the mind which are common and self-evident only to the learned, as that incorporeal substances are not in space.[4] Therefore I say that this proposition, *God exists*, of itself is self-evident, for the predicate is the same as the subject, because God is His own existence as will be hereafter shown.[5] Now because we do not know the essence of God, the proposition is not self-evident to us, but needs to be demonstrated by things that are more known to us, though less known in their nature — namely, by His effects.

Reply Obj. 1. To know that God exists in a general and confused way is implanted in us by nature, inasmuch as God is man's beatitude. For man naturally desires happiness, and what is naturally desired by man is naturally known by him. This, however, is not to know absolutely that God exists; just as to know that someone is approaching is not the same as to know that Peter is approaching, even though it is Peter who is approaching; for there are many who imagine that man's perfect good, which is happiness, consists in riches, and others in pleasures, and others in something else.

Reply Obj. 2. Perhaps not everyone who hears this name *God* understands it to signify something than which nothing greater can be thought, seeing that some have believed God to be a body.[6] Yet, granted that everyone understands that by this name *God* is signified something than which nothing greater can be thought, nevertheless, it does not therefore follow that he understands that what the name signifies exists actually, but only that it exists mentally. Nor can it be argued that it actually exists, unless it be admitted that there actually exists something than which nothing greater can be thought; and this precisely is not admitted by those who hold that God does not exist.

Reply Obj. 3. The existence of truth in general is self-evident, but the existence of a Primal Truth is not self-evident to us.

---

[4] *De Hebdom.* (PL 64, 1311).

[5] Q. 3, a. 4.

[6] Cf. *C. G.*, I, 20. Cf. also Aristotle, *Phys.*, I, 4 (18 7a 12); St. Augustine, *De Civit. Dei*, VIII, 2; 5 (PL 41, 226; 239); *De Haeres.*, 46, 50, 86 (PL 42, 35; 39; 46); *De Genesi ad Litt.*, X, 25 (PL 34, 427); Maimonides, *Guide*, I, 53 (p. 72).

2. Demonstrability of God's Existence

St. Thomas, *Summa Theologiae*, I, q. 2, art. 2.*

We proceed thus to the Second Article: —

Obj. 1. It seems that the existence of God cannot be demonstrated. For it is an article of faith that God exists. But what is of faith cannot be demonstrated, because a demonstration produces scientific knowledge, whereas faith is of the unseen, as is clear from the Apostle (*Heb.* xi. 1). Therefore it cannot be demonstrated that God exists.

Obj. 2. Further, essence is the middle term of demonstration. But we cannot know in what God's essence consists, but solely in what it does not consist, as Damascene says.[1] Therefore we cannot demonstrate that God exists.

Obj. 3. Further, if the existence of God were demonstrated, this could only be from His effects. But His effects are not proportioned to Him, since He is infinite and His effects are finite, and between the finite and infinite there is no proportion. Therefore, since a cause cannot be demonstrated by an effect not proportioned to it, it seems that the existence of God cannot be demonstrated.

On the contrary, The Apostle says: *The invisible things of Him are clearly seen, being understood by the things that are made* (*Rom.* i. 20). But this would not be unless the existence of God could be demonstrated through the things that are made; for the first thing we must know of anything is, whether it exists.

I answer that, Demonstration can be made in two ways: One is through the cause, and is called *propter quid,* and this is to argue from what is prior absolutely. The other is through the effect, and is called a demonstration *quia;* this is to argue from what is prior relatively only to us. When an effect is better known to us than its cause, from the effect we proceed to the knowledge of the cause. And from every effect the existence of its proper cause can be demonstrated, so long as its effects are better known to us; because, since every effect depends upon its cause, if the effect exists, the cause must pre-exist. Hence the existence of God, insofar as it is not self-evident to us, can be demonstrated from those of His effects which are known to us.

Reply Obj. 1. The existence of God and other like truths about God, which can be known by natural reason, are not articles of faith, but are preambles to the articles; for faith presupposes natural knowledge, even as grace presupposes nature and perfection the perfectible. Nevertheless, there is nothing to prevent a man, who cannot grasp a proof, from accepting, as a

---

* Pegis, *op. cit.*
1 *De Fide Orth.,* I, 4 (PG 94, 800).

matter of faith, something which in itself is capable of being scientifically known and demonstrated.

Reply Obj. 2. When the existence of a cause is demonstrated from an effect, this effect takes the place of the definition of the cause in proving the cause's existence. This is especially the case in regard to God, because, in order to prove the existence of anything, it is necessary to accept as a middle term the meaning of the name, and not its essence, for the question of its essence follows on the question of its existence. Now the names given to God are derived from His effects, as will be later shown.[2] Consequently, in demonstrating the existence of God from His effects, we may take for the middle term the meaning of the name *God*.

Reply Obj. 3. From effects not proportioned to the cause no perfect knowledge of that cause can be obtained. Yet from every effect the existence of the cause can be clearly demonstrated, and so we can demonstrate the existence of God from His effects; though from them we cannot know God perfectly as He is in His essence.

[2] Q. 13, a. 1.

3. The Demonstration of God's Existence

St. Thomas, *Summa Theologiae*, I, q. 2, art. 3.*

We proceed thus to the Third Article: —

Obj. 1. It seems that God does not exist; because if one of two contraries be infinite, the other would be altogether destroyed. But the name *God* means that He is infinite goodness. If, therefore, God existed, there would be no evil discoverable; but there is evil in the world. Therefore God does not exist.

Obj. 2. Further, it is superfluous to suppose that what can be accounted for by a few principles has been produced by many. But it seems that everything we see in the world can be accounted for by other principles, supposing God did not exist. For all natural things can be reduced to one principle, which is nature; and all voluntary things can be reduced to one principle, which is human reason, or will. Therefore there is no need to suppose God's existence.

On the contrary, It is said in the person of God: *I am Who am* (*Exod.* iii, 14).

I answer that, The existence of God can be proved in five ways.

The first and more manifest way is the argument from motion. It is certain, and evident to our senses, that in the world some things are in motion. Now whatever is moved is moved by another, for nothing can be moved except it is in potentiality to that towards which it is moved; whereas a thing moves inasmuch as it is in act. For motion is nothing else than the reduction

* Pegis, *op. cit.*

of something from potentiality to actuality. But nothing can be reduced from potentiality to actuality except by something in a state of actuality. Thus that which is actually hot, as fire, makes wood, which is potentially hot, to be actually hot, and thereby moves and changes it. Now it is not possible that the same thing should be at once in actuality and potentiality in the same respect, but only in different respects. For what is actually hot cannot simultaneously be potentially hot; but it is simultaneously potentially cold. It is therefore impossible that in the same respect and in the same way a thing should be both mover and moved, i.e., that it should move itself. Therefore, whatever is moved must be moved by another. If that by which it is moved be itself moved, then this also must needs be moved by another, and that by another again. But this cannot go on to infinity, because then there would be no first mover, and, consequently, no other mover, seeing that subsequent movers move only inasmuch as they are moved by the first mover; as the staff moves only because it is moved by the hand. Therefore it is necessary to arrive at a first mover, moved by no other; and this everyone understands to be God.

The second way is from the nature of efficient cause. In the world of sensible things we find there is an order of efficient causes. There is no case known (neither is it, indeed, possible) in which a thing is found to be the efficient cause of itself; for so it would be prior to itself, which is impossible. Now in efficient causes it is not possible to go on to infinity, because in all efficient causes following in order, the first is the cause of the intermediate cause, and the intermediate is the cause of the ultimate cause, whether the intermediate cause be several, or one only. Now to take away the cause is to take away the effect. Therefore, if there be no first cause among efficient causes, there will be no ultimate, nor any intermediate, cause. But if in efficient causes it is possible to go on to infinity, there will be no first efficient cause, neither will there be an ultimate effect, nor any intermediate efficient causes; all of which is plainly false. Therefore it is necessary to admit a first efficient cause, to which everyone gives the name of God.

The third way is taken from possibility and necessity, and runs thus. We find in nature things that are possible to be and not to be, since they are found to be generated, and to be corrupted, and consequently, it is possible for them to be and not to be. But it is impossible for these always to exist, for that which can not-be at some time is not. Therefore, if everything can not-be, then at one time there was nothing in existence. Now if this were true, even now there would be nothing in existence, because that which does not exist begins to exist only through something already existing. Therefore, if at one time nothing was in existence, it would have been impossible for anything to have begun to exist; and thus even now nothing would be in existence — which is absurd. Therefore, not all beings are merely possible, but there must exist something the existence of which is necessary. But every necessary thing either has its necessity caused by another, or not. Now it is impossible to go on to infinity in necessary things which have their necessity caused by another, as has been already proved in regard to efficient causes. Therefore we cannot but admit the existence of some being having of itself its own necessity, and not receiving it from another, but rather causing in others their necessity. This all men speak of as God.

The fourth way is taken from the gradation to be found in things. Among beings there are some more and some less good, true, noble, and the like. But more and less are predicated of different things according as they resemble in their different ways something which is the maximum, as a thing is said to be hotter according as it more nearly resembles that which is hottest; so that there is something which is truest, something best, something noblest, and, consequently, something which is most being, for those things that are greatest in truth are greatest in being, as it is written in Metaph. ii.[1] Now the maximum in any genus is the cause of all in that genus, as fire, which is the maximum of heat, is the cause of all hot things, as is said in the same book.[2] Therefore there must also be something which is to all beings the cause of their being, goodness, and every other perfection; and this we call God.

The fifth way is taken from the governance of the world. We see that things which lack knowledge, such as natural bodies, act for an end, and this is evident from their acting always, or nearly always, in the same way, so as to obtain the best result. Hence it is plain that they achieve their end, not fortuitously, but designedly. Now whatever lacks knowledge cannot move towards an end, unless it be directed by some being endowed with knowledge and intelligence; as the arrow is directed by the archer. Therefore some intelligent being exists by whom all natural things are directed to their end; and this being we call God.

Reply Obj. 1. As Augustine says: Since God is the highest good, He would not allow any evil to exist in His works, unless His omnipotence and goodness were such as to bring good even out of evil.[3] This is part of the infinite goodness of God, that He should allow evil to exist, and out of it produce good.

Reply Obj. 2. Since nature works for a determinate end under the direction of a higher agent, whatever is done by nature must be traced back to God as to its first cause. So likewise whatever is done voluntarily must be traced back to some higher cause other than human reason and will, since these can change and fail; for all things that are changeable and capable of defect must be traced back to an immovable and self-necessary first principle, as has been shown.

---

[1] Metaph. Ia, I (993b 30).   [2] Ibid. (993b 25).   [3] Enchir., XI (PL 40, 236).

4. Difficulties in Demonstrating God's Existence

St. Thomas, Summa Contra Gentiles, I, ch. 12.*

(1)   There are others who hold a certain opinion, contrary to the position mentioned above, through which the efforts of those seeking to prove

---

* Anton C. Pegis, On the Truth of the Catholic Faith, Book One: God (New York: Doubleday Image, 1955).

the existence of God would likewise be rendered futile. For they say that we cannot arrive at the existence of God through the reason; it is received by way of faith and revelation alone.

(2)   What led some persons to hold this view was the weakness of the arguments which had been brought forth by others to prove that God exists.

(3)   Nevertheless, the present error might erroneously find support in its behalf in the words of some philosophers who show that in God essence and being are identical, that is, that that which answers to the question *what is it?* is identical with that which answers to the question *is it?* Now, following the way of the reason we cannot arrive at a knowledge of what God is. Hence, it seems likewise impossible to demonstrate by the reason that God exists.

(4)   Furthermore, according to the logic of the Philosopher, as a principle to demonstrate whether a thing is we must take the signification of the name of that thing;[1] and, again according to the Philosopher, the meaning signified by a name is its definition.[2] If this be so, if we set aside a knowledge of the divine essence or quiddity, no means will be available whereby to demonstrate that God exists.

(5)   Again, if, as is shown in the *Posterior Analytics*,[3] the knowledge of the principles of demonstration takes its origin from sense, whatever transcends all sense and sensibles seems to be indemonstrable. That God exists appears to be a proposition of this sort and is therefore indemonstrable.

(6)   The falsity of this opinion is shown to us, first, from the art of demonstration which teaches us to arrive at causes from their effects. Then, it is shown to us from the order of the sciences. For, as it is said in the *Metaphysics*,[4] if there is no knowable substance higher than sensible substance, there will be no science higher than physics. It is shown, thirdly, from the pursuit of the philosophers, who have striven to demonstrate that God exists. Finally, it is shown to us by the truth in the words of the Apostle Paul: "For the invisible things of God . . . are clearly seen, being understood by the things that are made" (Rom. 1:20).

(7)   Nor, contrary to the first argument, is there any problem in the fact that in God essence and being are identical. For this is understood of the being by which God subsists in Himself. But we do not know of what sort this being is, just as we do not know the divine essence. The reference is not to the being that signifies the composition of intellect. For thus the existence of God does fall under demonstration; this happens when our mind is led from demonstrative arguments to form such a proposition of God whereby it expresses that He exists.

---

[1] Aristotle, *Posterior Analytics*, II, 9 (93b 23).
[2] Aristotle, *Metaphysics*, IV, 7 (1012a 23–24).
[3] Aristotle, *Posterior Analytics*, I, 18 (81a 38).
[4] Aristotle, *Metaphysics*, IV, 3 (1005a 18).

(8)   Now, in arguments proving the existence of God, it is not necessary to assume the divine essence or quiddity as the middle term of the demonstration. This was the second view proposed above. In place of the quiddity, an effect is taken as the middle term, as in demonstration quia.[5] It is from such effects that the meaning of the name God is taken. For all divine names are imposed either by removing the effects of God from Him or by relating God in some way to His effects.

(9)   It is thereby likewise evident that, although God transcends all sensible things and the sense itself, His effects, on which the demonstration proving His existence is based, are nevertheless sensible things. And thus, the origin of our knowledge in the sense applies also to those things that transcend the sense.

[5] That is, demonstrations proving *that* something is so — for example, *that* God exists.

5. The Argument From the Principle of Motion

St. Thomas, *Summa Contra Gentiles*, I, 13.*

(1)   We have now shown that the effort to demonstrate the existence of God is not a vain one. We shall therefore proceed to set forth the arguments by which both philosophers and Catholic teachers have proved that God exists.

(2)   We shall set forth the arguments by which Aristotle proceeds to prove that God exists. The aim of Aristotle is to do this in two ways, beginning with motion.

(3)   Of these ways the first is as follows.[1] Everything that is moved is moved by another. That some things are in motion — for example, the sun — is evident from sense. Therefore, it is moved by something else that moves it. This mover is itself either moved or not moved. If it is not, we have reached our conclusion — namely, that we must posit some unmoved mover. This we call God. If it is moved, it is moved by another mover. We must, consequently, either proceed to infinity, or we must arrive at some unmoved mover. Now, it is not possible to proceed to infinity. Hence, we must posit some prime unmoved mover.

(4)   In this proof, there are two propositions that need to be proved, namely, that *everything that is moved is moved by another*, and that *in movers and things moved one cannot proceed to infinity*.

(5)   The first of these propositions Aristotle proves in three ways. The first way is as follows. If something moves itself, it must have within itself

* Pegis, *On the Truth of the Catholic Faith*.
[1] Aristotle, *Physics*, VII, 1 (241b 24).

the principle of its own motion; otherwise, it is clearly moved by another. Furthermore, it must be primarily moved. This means that it must be moved by reason of itself, and not by reason of a part of itself, as happens when an animal is moved by the motion of its foot. For, in this sense, a whole would not be moved by itself, but a part, and one part, and one part would be moved by another. It is also necessary that a self-moving being be divisible and have parts, since, as it is proved in the *Physics*,[2] whatever is moved is divisible.

(6)   On the basis of these suppositions Aristotle argues as follows. That which is held to be moved by itself is primarily moved. For, if while one part was at rest, another part in it were moved, then the whole itself would not be primarily moved; it would be that part in it which is moved while another part is at rest. But nothing that is at rest because something else is at rest is moved by itself; for that being whose rest follows upon the rest of another must have its motion follow upon the motion of another. It is thus not moved by itself. Therefore, that which was posited as being moved by itself is not moved by itself. Consequently, everything that is moved must be moved by another.

(7)   Nor is it an objection to this argument if one might say that, when something is held to move itself, a part of it cannot be at rest; or, again, if one might say that a part is not subject to rest or motion except accidentally, which is the unfounded argument of Avicenna.[3] For, indeed, the force of Aristotle's argument lies in this: if something moves itself primarily and through itself, rather than through its parts, that it is moved cannot depend on another. But the moving of the divisible itself, like its being, depends on its parts; it cannot therefore move itself primarily and through itself. Hence, for the truth of the inferred conclusion it is not necessary to assume as an absolute truth that a part of a being moving itself is at rest. What must rather be true is this conditional proposition: *if the part were at rest, the whole would be at rest*. Now, this proposition would be true even though its antecedent be impossible. In the same way, the following conditional proposition is true: *if man is an ass, he is irrational*.

(8)   In the second way, Aristotle proves the proposition by induction.[4] Whatever is moved by accident is not moved by itself, since it is moved upon the motion of another. So, too, as is evident, what is moved by violence is not moved by itself. Nor are those beings moved by themselves that are moved by their nature as being moved from within; such is the case with animals, which evidently are moved by the soul. Nor, again, is this true of those beings, such as heavy and light bodies, which are moved through nature. For such beings are moved by the generating cause and the cause removing impediments. Now, whatever is moved is moved through itself or by accident. If it is moved through itself, then it is moved either violently or by nature; if

---

[2] Aristotle, *Physics*, VI, 4 (234b 10).
[3] Avicenna, *Sufficientia*, II, 1 (fol. 24ra).
[4] Aristotle, *Physics*, VIII, 4 (254b 8).

by nature, then either through itself, as the animal, or not through itself, as heavy and light bodies. Therefore, everything that is moved is moved by another.

(9) In the third way, Aristotle proves the proposition as follows.[5] The same thing cannot be at once in act and in potency with respect to the same thing. But everything that is moved is, as such, in potency. For motion is *the act of something that is in potency inasmuch as it is in potency.*[6] That which moves, however, is as such in act, for nothing acts except according as it is in act. Therefore, with respect to the same motion, nothing is both mover and moved. Thus, nothing moves itself.

(10) It is to be noted, however, that Plato, who held that every mover is moved,[7] understood the name *motion* in a wider sense than did Aristotle. For Aristotle understood motion strictly, according as it is the act of what exists in potency inasmuch as it is such. So understood, motion belongs only to divisible bodies, as it is proved in the *Physics.*[8] According to Plato, however, that which moves itself is not a body. Plato understood by motion any given operation, so that *to understand* and *to judge* are a kind of motion. Aristotle likewise touches upon this manner of speaking in the *De anima.*[9] Plato accordingly said that the first mover moves himself because he knows himself and wills or loves himself. In a way, this is not opposed to the reasons of Aristotle. There is no difference between reaching a first being that moves himself, as understood by Plato, and reaching a first being that is absolutely unmoved, as understood by Aristotle.

(11) The second proposition, namely, *that there is no procession to infinity among movers and things moved,* Aristotle proves in three ways.

(12) The first is as follows.[10] If among movers and things moved we proceed to infinity, all these infinite beings must be bodies. For whatever is moved is divisible and a body, as is proved in the *Physics.*[11] But every body that moves some thing moved is itself moved while moving it. Therefore, all these infinites are moved together while one of them is moved. But one of them, being finite, is moved in a finite time. Therefore, all those infinites are moved in a finite time. This, however, is impossible. It is, therefore, impossible that among movers and things moved one can proceed to infinity.

(13) Furthermore, that it is impossible for the above-mentioned infinites to be moved in a finite time Aristotle proves as follows. The mover and the thing moved must exist simultaneously. This Aristotle proves by induction in the various species of motion. But bodies cannot be simultaneous except through continuity or contiguity. Now, since, as has been proved, all the aforementioned movers and things moved are bodies, they must constitute by

5 Aristotle, *Physics,* VIII, 5 (257a 39).
6 Aristotle, *Physics,* III, 1 (201a 10).
7 Plato, *Phaedrus,* VI, 4 (234b 10).
8 Aristotle, *Physics,* VI, 4 (234b 10).
9 Aristotle, *De anima,* III, 7 (431a 6).
10 Aristotle, *Physics,* VII, 1 (241b 24).
11 Aristotle, *Physics,* VI, 4 (234b 10).

continuity or contiguity a sort of single mobile. In this way, one infinite is moved in a finite time. This is impossible, as is proved in the *Physics*.[12]

(14)   The *second* argument proving the same conclusion is the following.[13]

In an ordered series of movers and things moved (this is a series in which one is moved by another according to an order), it is necessarily the fact that, when the first mover is removed or ceases to move, no other mover will move or be moved. For the first mover is the cause of motion for all the others. But, if there are movers and things moved following an order to infinity, there will be no first mover, but all would be as intermediate movers. Therefore, none of the others will be able to be moved, and thus nothing in the world will be moved.

(15)   The *third* proof comes to the same conclusion, except that, by beginning with the superior, it has a reversed order. It is as follows. That which moves as an instrumental cause cannot move unless there be a principal moving cause. But, if we proceed to infinity among movers and things moved, all movers will be as instrumental causes, because they will be moved movers and there will be nothing as a principal mover. Therefore, nothing will be moved.

(16)   Such, then, is the proof of both propositions assumed by Aristotle in the first demonstrative way by which he proved that a first unmoved mover exists.

(17)   The second way is this. If every mover is moved, this proposition is true either by itself or by accident. If by accident, then it is not necessary, since what is true by accident is not necessary. It is something possible, therefore, that no mover is moved. But, if a mover is not moved, it does not move: as the adversary says: It is therefore possible that nothing is moved. For, if nothing moves, nothing is moved. This, however, Aristotle considers to be impossible — namely, that at any time there be no motion.[14] Therefore, the first proposition was not possible, since from a false possible, a false impossible does not follow. Hence, this proposition, *every mover is moved by another*, was not true by accident.

(18)   Again, if two things are accidentally joined in some being, and one of them is found without the other, it is probable that the other can be found without it. For example, *if white* and *musical* are found in Socrates, and in Plato we find *musical* but not *white*, it is probable that in some other being we can find the *white* without the *musical*. Therefore, if mover and thing moved are accidentally joined in some being, and the thing moved be found without the mover in some being, it is probable that the mover is found without that which is moved. Nor can the example of two things, of which one depends on the other, be brought as an objection against this. For the union we are speaking of is not essential, but accidental.

12 Aristotle, *Physics*, VII, 1 (241b 12); VI, 7 (237b 23 ff).
13 Aristotle, *Physics*, VIII, 5 (256a 12).
14 Aristotle, *Physics*, VIII, 5 (256b 4–13).

(19)   But, if the proposition that every mover is moved is true by itself,
       something impossible or awkward likewise follows. For the mover must
be moved either by the same kind of motion as that by which he moves, or
by another. If the same, a cause of alteration must itself be altered, and
further, a healing cause must itself be healed, and a teacher must himself be
taught and this with respect to the same knowledge. Now, this is impossible.
A teacher must have science, whereas he who is a learner of necessity does
not have it. So that, if the proposition were true, the same thing would be
possessed and not possessed by the same being — which is impossible.
If, however, the mover is moved by another species of motion, so that
(namely) the altering cause is moved according to place, and the cause
moving according to place is increased, and so forth, since the genera and
species of motion are finite in number, it will follow that we cannot proceed
to infinity. There will thus be a first mover, which is not moved by another.
Will someone say that there will be a recurrence so that when all the genera
and species of motion have been completed the series will be repeated and
return to the first motion? This would involve saying, for example, that a
mover according to place would be altered, the altering cause would be increased, and the increasing cause would be moved according to place. Yet
this whole view would arrive at the same conclusion as before: whatever
moves according to a certain species of motion is itself moved according to
the same species of motion, though mediately and not immediately.

(20)   It remains, therefore, that we must posit some first mover that is not
       moved by any exterior moving cause.

(21)   Granted this conclusion — namely, that there is a first mover that is
       not moved by an exterior moving cause — it yet does not follow that
this mover is absolutely unmoved. That is why Aristotle goes on to say that the
condition of the mover may be twofold.[15] The first mover can be absolutely
unmoved. If so, we have the conclusion we are seeking: there is a first unmoved mover. On the other hand, the first mover can be self-moved. This
may be argued, because that which is through itself is prior to what is through
another. Hence, among things moved as well, it seems reasonable that the
first moved is moved through itself and not by another.

(22)   But, on this basis, the same conclusion again follows.[16] For it cannot
       be said that, when a mover moves himself, the whole is moved by
the whole. Otherwise, the same difficulties would follow as before: one person
would both teach and be taught, and the same would be true among other
motions. It would also follow that a being would be both in potency and in
act; for a mover is, as such, in act, whereas the thing moved is in potency.
Consequently, one part of the self-moved mover is solely moving, and the
other part solely moved. We thus reach the same conclusion as before: there
exists an unmoved mover.

---

[15] Aristotle, *Physics*, VIII, 5 (256a 13).
[16] Aristotle, *Physics*, VIII, 5 (257b 2).

(23)   Nor can it be held that both parts of the self-moved mover are moved, so that one is moved by the other, or that one moves both itself and the other, or that the whole moves a part, or that a part moves the whole. All this would involve the return of the aforementioned difficulties: something would both move and be moved according to the same species of motion; something would be at once in potency and in act; and, furthermore, the whole would not be primarily moving itself, it would move through the motion of a part. The conclusion thus stands: one part of a self-moved mover must be unmoved and moving the other part.

(24)   But there is another point to consider. Among self-moved beings known to us, namely, animals, although the moving part, which is to say the soul, is unmoved through itself, it is yet moved by accident. That is why Aristotle further shows that the moving part of the first self-moving being is not moved either through itself or by accident.[17] For, since self-moving beings known to us, namely, animals, are corruptible, the moving part in them is moved by accident. But corruptible self-moving beings must be reduced to some first self-moving being that is everlasting. Therefore, some self-moving being must have a mover that is moved neither through itself nor by accident.

(25)   It is further evident that, according to the position of Aristotle, some self-moved being must be everlasting. For, if, as Aristotle supposes, motion is everlasting, the generation of self-moving beings (this means beings that are generable and corruptible) must be endless. But the cause of this endlessness cannot be one of the self-moving beings, since it does not always exist. Nor can the cause be all the self-moving beings together, both because they would be infinite and because they would not be simultaneous. There must therefore be some endlessly self-moving being, causing the endlessness of generation among these sublunary self-movers. Thus, the mover of the self-moving being is not moved, either through itself or by accident.

(26)   Again, we see that among beings that move themselves some initiate a new motion as a result of some motion. This new motion is other than the motion by which an animal moves itself, for example, digested food or altered air. By such a motion the self-moving mover is moved by accident. From this we may infer that no self-moved being is moved everlastingly whose mover is moved either by itself or by accident. But the first self-mover is everlastingly in motion; otherwise, motion could not be everlasting, since every other motion is caused by the motion of the self-moving first mover. The first self-moving being, therefore, is moved by a mover who is himself moved neither through himself nor by accident.

(27)   Nor is it against this argument that the movers of the lower spheres produce an everlasting motion and yet are said to be moved by accident. For they are said to be moved by accident, not on their own account,

---

[17] Aristotle, *Physics*, VIII, 6 (258b 15).

but on account of their movable subjects, which follow the motion of the higher sphere.

(28)   Now, God is not part of any self-moving mover. In his *Metaphysics*, therefore, Aristotle goes on from the mover who is a part of the self-moved mover to seek another mover — God — who is absolutely separate.[18] For, since everything moving itself is moved through appetite, the mover who is part of the self-moving being moves because of the appetite of some appetible object. This object is higher, in the order of motion, than the mover desiring it; for the one desiring is in a manner a moved mover, whereas an appetible object is an absolutely unmoved mover. There must, therefore, be an absolutely unmoved separate first mover. This is God.

(29)   Two considerations seem to invalidate these arguments. The first consideration is that, as arguments, they presuppose the eternity of motion, which Catholics consider to be false.

(30)   To this consideration the reply is as follows. The most efficacious way to prove that God exists is on the supposition that the world is eternal. Granted this supposition, that God exists is less manifest. For, if the world and motion have a first beginning, some cause must clearly be posited to account for this origin of the world and of motion. That which comes to be anew must take its origin from some innovating cause; since nothing brings itself from potency to act, or from non-being to being.

(31)   The second consideration is that the demonstrations given above presuppose that the first moved being, namely, a heavenly body, is self-moved. This means that it is animated, which many do not admit.

(32)   The reply to this consideration is that, if the prime mover is not held to be self-moved, then it must be moved immediately by something absolutely unmoved. Hence, even Aristotle himself proposed this conclusion as a disjunction: it is necessary either to arrive immediately at an unmoved separate first mover, or to arrive at a self-moved mover from whom, in turn, an unmoved separate first mover is reached.[19]

(33)   In *Metaphysics* II Aristotle also uses another argument to show that there is no infinite regress in efficient causes and that we must reach one first cause — God.[20] This way is as follows. In all ordered efficient causes, the first is the cause of the intermediate cause, whether one or many, and this is the cause of the last cause. But, when you suppress a cause, you suppress its effect. Therefore, if you suppress the first cause, the intermediate cause cannot be a cause. Now, if there were an infinite regress among efficient causes, no cause would be first. Therefore, all the other causes, which are intermediate, will be suppressed. But this is manifestly false. We must, therefore, posit that there exists a first efficient cause. This is God.

---

18 Aristotle, *Metaphysics*, XII, 7 (1072a 23).
19 Aristotle, *Physics*, VII, 5 (258a 1; b 4).
20 Aristotle, *Metaphysics*, Ia, 2 (994a 1).

(34)   Another argument may also be gathered from the words of Aristotle.

In *Metaphysics* II he shows that what is most true is also most a being.[21] But in *Metaphysics* IV he shows the existence of something supremely true from the observed fact that of two false things one is more false than the other, which means that one is more true than the other.[22] This comparison is based on the nearness to that which is absolutely and supremely true. From these Aristotelian texts we may further infer that there is something that is supremely being. This we call God.

(35)   Damascene proposes another argument for the same conclusion taken from the government of the world.[23] Averroes likewise hints at it.[24] The argument runs thus. Contrary and discordant things cannot, always or for the most part, be parts of one order except under someone's government, which enables all and each to tend to a definite end. But in the world we find that things of diverse natures come together under one order, and this not rarely or by chance, but always or for the most part. There must therefore be some being by whose providence the world is governed. This we call God.

---

[21] Aristotle, *Metaphysics*, Ia, 1 (993b 30).
[22] Aristotle, *Metaphysics*, IV, 4 (1008b 37).
[23] St. John Damascene, *De fide orthodoxa*, I, 3 (PG, 94, col. 796CD).
[24] Averroes, *In II Physicorum*, t.c. 75 (fol. 75ᵛ–76ʳ).

6. God's Universal Governance of All Things

St. Thomas, *Summa Theologiae*, I, q. 103, art. 1.*

We proceed thus to the First Article: —

Objection 1. It would seem that the world is not governed by anyone. For it belongs to those things to be governed, which move or work for an end. But natural things which make up the greater part of the world do not move, or work for an end; for they have no knowledge of their end. Therefore the world is not governed.

Obj. 2. Further, those things are governed which are moved towards some object. But the world does not appear to be so directed, but has stability in itself. Therefore it is not governed.

Obj. 3. Further, what is necessarily determined by its own nature to one particular thing, does not require any external principle of government. But the principal parts of the world are by a certain necessity determined to something particular in their actions and movements. Therefore the world does not require to be governed.

---

* Pegis, *Basic Writings of St. Thomas.*

On the contrary, It is written (Wisd. xiv. 3): *But Thou, O Father, governest all things by Thy Providence*. And Boëthius says (*De Consol.* iii): *Thou Who governest this universe by mandate eternal.*

I answer that, Certain ancient philosophers denied the government of the world, saying that all things happened by chance. But such an opinion can be refuted as impossible in two ways. First, by the observation of things themselves. For we observe that in nature things happen always or nearly always for the best; which would not be the case unless some sort of providence directed nature towards good as an end. And this is to govern. Therefore the unfailing order we observe in things is a sign of their being governed. For instance, if we were to enter a well-ordered house, we would gather from the order manifested in the house the notion of a governor, as Cicero says (*De Nat Deorum* ii.), quoting Aristotle.* Secondly, this is clear from a consideration of Divine goodness, which, as we have said above (Q. XLIV., A. 4; Q. LXV., A. 2), is the cause of the production of things in being. For *as it belongs to the best to produce the best*, it is not fitting that the supreme goodness of God should produce things without giving them their perfection. Now a thing's ultimate perfection consists in the attainment of its end. Therefore it belongs to the Divine goodness, as it brought things into being, so to lead them to their end. And this is to govern.

Reply Obj. 1. A thing moves or operates for an end in two ways. First, in moving itself to the end, as do man and other rational creatures; and such things have knowledge of their end, and of the means to the end. Secondly, a thing is said to move or operate for an end, as though moved or directed thereto by another, as an arrow is directed to the target by the archer, who knows the end unknown to the arrow. Hence, as the movement of the arrow towards a definite end shows clearly that it is directed by someone with knowledge, so the unvarying course of natural things which are without knowledge, shows clearly that the world is governed by some reason.

Reply Obj. 2. In all created things there is a stable element, even if this be only primary matter; and something belonging to movement, if under movement we include operation. And things need governing as to both, because even that which is stable, since it is created from nothing, would return to nothingness were it not sustained by a governing hand, as will be explained later (Q. CIV., A. 1).

Reply Obj. 3. The natural necessity inherent in those beings which are determined to a particular course is a kind of impression from God, directing them to their end; as the necessity whereby an arrow is moved so as to fly towards a certain point is an impression from the archer, and not from the arrow. But there is a difference, inasmuch as that which creatures receive from God is their nature, while that which natural things receive from man in addition to their nature is something violent. Therefore, just as the violent necessity in the movement of the arrow shows the action of the archer, so the natural necessity of things shows the government of Divine Providence.

---

* Cleanthes.

7. God's Continued Act of Creation

St. Thomas, *Summa Theologiae*, I, q. 104, art. 1.*

We proceed thus to the First Article: —

Objection 1. It would seem that creatures do not need to be kept in being by God. For what cannot not-be, does not need to be kept in being; just as that which cannot depart, does not need to be kept from departing. But some creatures by their very nature cannot not-be. Therefore not all creatures need to be kept in being by God. The middle proposition is proved thus. That which of itself is included in the nature of a thing is necessarily in that thing, and its contrary cannot be in it; thus a multiple of two must necessarily be even, and cannot possibly be an odd number. Now being follows necessarily upon a form, because everything is a being actually, so far as it has form. But some creatures are subsistent forms, as we have said of the angels (Q. L., AA. 2, 5): and thus to be is in them of themselves. The same reasoning applies to those creatures whose matter is in potentiality to one form only, as was explained above of heavenly bodies (Q. LXVI., A. 2). Hence such creatures as these have in their nature to be necessarily, and cannot not-be. For there can be no potentiality to not-being, either in the form which has being of itself, or in matter existing under a form which it cannot lose, since it is not in potentiality to any other form.

Obj. 2. Further, God is more powerful than any created agent. But a created agent, even after ceasing to act, can cause its effect to be preserved in being. Thus, the house continues to stand after the builder has ceased to build; and water remains hot for some time after the fire has ceased to heat. Much more, therefore, can God cause His creature to be kept in being, after He has ceased to create it.

Obj. 3. Further, nothing violent can occur, except it have some active cause. But tendency to not-being is unnatural and violent to any creature, since all creatures naturally desire to be. Therefore no creature can tend to not-being, except through some active cause of corruption. Now there are creatures of such a nature that nothing can cause them to be corrupted. Such are spiritual substances and heavenly bodies. Therefore such creatures cannot tend to not-being, even if God were to withdraw His action.

Obj. 4. Further, if God keeps creatures in being, this is done by some action. Now every action of an agent, if that action be efficacious, produces something in the effect. Therefore the conserving power of God must produce something in the creature. But this is not so, because this action does not give being to the creature, since being is not given to that which already is: nor does it add anything new to the creature, because either God would

---

* Pegis, *Basic Writings of St. Thomas.*

not keep the creature in being continually, or He would be continually adding something new to the creature, either of which is unreasonable. Therefore creatures are not kept in being by God.

On the contrary, It is written (Heb. i. 3): *Upholding all things by the word of His power.*

I answer that, Both reason and faith bind us to say that creatures are kept in being by God. To make this clear, we must consider that a thing is conserved by another in two ways. First, indirectly, and accidentally; thus a person is said to conserve anything by removing the cause of its corruption; as a man may be said to conserve a child, whom he guards from falling into the fire. In this way God conserves some things, but not all, for there are some things of such a nature that nothing can corrupt them, so that it is not necessary to keep them from corruption. Secondly, a thing is said to conserve another essentially and directly, namely, in so far as what is conserved depends on the conserver in such a way that it cannot exist without it. In this manner all creatures need to be conserved by God. For the being of every creature depends on God, so that not for a moment could it subsist, but would fall into nothingness, were it not kept in being by the operation of the Divine power, as Gregory says (*Moral.* xvi.).

This is made clear as follows: Every effect depends on its cause, so far as it is its cause. But we must observe that an agent may be the cause of the *becoming* of its effect, but not directly of its *being*. This may be seen both in artificial and in natural things. For the builder causes the house in its *becoming,* but he is not the direct cause of its *being*. For it is clear that the *being* of the house is a result of its form, which consists in the putting together and arrangement of the materials, and which results from the natural qualities of certain things. Thus a cook prepares the food by applying the natural activity of fire; and in the same way a builder constructs a house, by making use of cement, stones, and wood which are able to be put together in a certain order and to conserve it. Therefore the *being* of a house depends on the nature of these materials, just as its *becoming* depends on the action of the builder. The same principle applies to natural things. For if an agent is not the cause of a form as such, neither will it be directly the cause of the *being* which results from that form; but it will be the cause of the effect only in its *becoming.*

Now it is clear that of two things in the same species one cannot be essentially the cause of the other's form as such, since it would then be the cause of its own form, since both forms have the same nature; but it can be the cause of this form in as much as it is in matter — in other words, it may be the cause that *this matter* receives *this form.* And this is to be the cause of *becoming,* as when man begets man, and fire causes fire. Thus whenever a natural effect is such that it has an aptitude to receive from its active cause an impression specifically the same as in that active cause, then the *becoming* of the effect depends on the agent but not its *being.*

Sometimes, however, the effect has not this aptitude to receive the impression of its cause in the same way as it exists in the agent; as may be seen clearly in all agents which do not produce an effect of the same species as themselves. Thus, the heavenly bodies cause the generation of inferior bodies which differ from them in species. Such an agent can be the cause of a form as such, and not merely as being joined to this matter; and consequently, it is not merely the cause of *becoming* but also the cause of *being*.

Therefore as the becoming of a thing cannot continue when that action of the agent ceases which causes the *becoming* of the effect: so neither can the *being* of a thing continue after that action of the agent has ceased, which is the cause of the effect not only in *becoming* but also in *being*. This is why hot water retains heat after the cessation of the fire's action; while, on the contrary, the air does not continue to be lit up, even for a moment, when the sun ceases to act upon it. For water is a matter susceptive of the fire's heat in the same way as it exists in the fire. Therefore if it were to be reduced to the perfect form of fire, it would retain that form always; whereas if it has the form of fire imperfectly and inchoately, the heat will remain for a time only by reason of the imperfect participation of the principle of heat. On the other hand, air is not of such a nature as to receive light in the same way as it exists in the sun, namely, to receive the form of the sun, which is the principle of light. Therefore, since it has no root in the air, the light ceases with the action of the sun.

Now every creature may be compared to God as the air is to the sun which illumines it. For as the sun possesses light by its nature, and as the air is illumined by participating light from the sun, though not participating in the sun's nature, so God alone is Being by virtue of His own Essence (since His Essence is His being), whereas every creature has being by participation, so that its essence is not its being. Therefore, as Augustine says (Gen. ad lit, iv. 12): *If the ruling power of God were withdrawn from His creatures, their nature would at once cease, and all nature would collapse.* In the same work (viii. 12) he says: *As the air becomes light by the presence of the sun, so is man illumined by the presence of God, and in His absence returns at once to darkness.*

Reply Obj. 1. *Being* naturally results from the form of a creature, given the influence of the Divine action; just as light results from the diaphanous nature of the air, given the action of the sun. Hence, the potentiality to not-being in spiritual creatures and heavenly bodies is rather something in God, Who can withdraw His influence, than in the form or matter of those creatures.

Reply Obj. 2. God cannot communicate to a creature that it be conserved in being after the cessation of the Divine influence; as neither can He make it not to have received its being from Himself. For the creature needs to be conserved by God in so far as the being of an effect depends on the cause of its being. Hence there is no comparison with an agent that is not the cause of being but only of becoming.

Reply Obj. 3. This argument holds in regard to that conservation which consists in the removal of corruption: but all creatures do not need to be conserved thus, as stated above.

Reply Obj. 4. The conservation of things by God is not by a new action, but by a continuation of that action whereby He gives being, which action is without either motion or time; so also the preservation of light in the air is by the continual influence of the sun.

Index

Abstraction, from matter, 22 ff; function of, 25; modes of, 22 ff; orders of, 22 ff; third order of, 27 ff

Abstraction and separation, difference between, 26 ff

Accident, predicable and predicamental, 76 f

Accidental series of causes, 163 f

Accidents, being of, 75 f; existence of, 72 f; and metaphysics, 76 ff; mode of existence of, 78 ff; reality of, 80; related to substance, 81 f; and subject of metaphysics, 63

Accidents and substance, analogy of, 58, 77 ff

Act, analogous notion of, 89 ff; kinds of, 90 ff; limited by potency, 93 ff; meaning of, 88 ff; priority of, 91 ff

Act of existence, 100 ff

Act and potency, 83 ff; comparison of, 91 ff

Act of subsistence, 106 ff

Agens agit sibi simile, 101 ff

Agent acts for an end, 164 ff

Agent cause, 155

Analogical causes, 162

Analogical character of substance, 73 ff

Analogical effects, 162

Analogical predication, 40

Analogous notion of act, 89 ff

Analogous terms, foundations of, 48 ff

Analogy, distinction between mode of signification and what is signified, 43 ff; divisions of, 45 ff; the doctrine of, 41 ff; etymology of term, 41; in existence, 47; itself analogical, 45; and logic, 41; logical and metaphysical notions of, 45; metaphysical use of, 44; priority in, 42; in signification, 46 f; and the unity of metaphysics, 59

Analogy based on proper proportionality, 56 f

Analogy based on simple proportion, 53 f

Analogy of names, 43 f

Analogy of simple proportion, 50

Analogy of substance and accident, 58, 71 ff

Anderson, James F., translation of Summa Contra Gentiles, Book II, ix

Atheistic existentialism, 87 ff

Beauty, and clarity, 128 f; conditions of, 127 ff; and harmony, 129; and integrity, 128; transcendental, 125 ff

Being, accidental, 75 f; multiplicity in, 130 f; transcendental properties of, 109 ff; unity of, 112 f

Bourke, Vernon, translation of Summa Contra Gentiles, Book III, ix

Categories of being, 61 f; and logic, 61 f

Causal relationship in analogy, 56 ff

Causality, efficient, 18; principle of final, 164 ff

Cause, 152 ff; agent, 155; efficient, 154 f; final, 155 f; formal, 154; material, 154; nominal definition of, 152 f; primary and secondary, 158; principal and instrumental, 156; and principle, 153; proper and accidental, 157; universal and particular, 157

Cause of evil, 136 f

Causes, analogical, 162; the modes of, 156 ff; relationship of, 166; in series, 163 f; univocal, 162

Certainty, and metaphysics, 10 ff

Chance, 168 ff; causality in, 169 ff; and ignorance, 168; in nature, 169; and universal cause, 170

Chenu, M. D., O.P., on medieval commentators, vi

Clarity, in beauty, 128 f

Cognitive power, 20

Commentators, medieval, vi–vii

Common being, 36; knowledge of, 18; unity in, 40

Common good, 123 ff

Common matter, 98

Common sense, and metaphysics, 1; metaphysics of, 2

Contradiction, principle of, 143 ff, 147 ff

Contraries of transcendentals, 129 ff

Creatures, and universal effects, 162 f

Demonstration, and the first principles, 143; and metaphysics, 8

Demonstration of the existence of God, 176 ff; first way, 178 ff; second way, 183 ff; third way, 185 ff; fourth way, 195 ff; fifth way, 197 ff

Descartes, and possibilities, 88

Designated matter, 98 ff

Differences in speculative sciences, 21

Divine science, 23, 30, 38

Division of being, per se and per accidens, 63; substance and accident, 63

Effects, analogical, 162; univocal, 162

Efficient causality, 18; principle of, 158

Efficient cause, 154 f

Empiricism, and substance, 70

End, and causality, 164 ff

End of man, and knowledge, 6

Epistemology and metaphysics, 142

Equivocal predication, 40

Essence, composition in, 99; imperfection in, 191; meaning of, 96 ff; of natural substance, 97 f; a potency for existence, 188; principle of limitation, 193; and substance, 65; as substance, 65 f; synonyms for, 97

Essence and existence, 96 ff; real distinction between, 187 ff

Essential judgment, 18

Essentialistic concept of substance, 65

Evil, cause of, 136 f; and good, 134 ff; moral, 137 ff; subjects of, 135 f

Existence, as an accident, 75; of accidents, 78 ff; act of, 100 ff; and being, 65; imperfection of, 191; and the individual, 102 ff; perfection of, 100

Existence of God, first way of demonstration, 178 ff; second way of demonstration, 183 ff; third way of demonstration, 185 ff; fourth way of demonstration, 195 ff; fifth way of demonstration, 197 ff

Existence or "to be," a twofold meaning, 25

Existential judgment, 18

Existentialism, 101; atheistic, 87 ff; authentic, v

Experience and first principles, 143 f

Falsehood, truth and, 131 ff

Fifth way of demonstrating God's existence, 197 ff

Final causality, principle of, 164 ff

Final cause, 155 f

First Cause, 83; God as, 36

First philosophy, 23, 38; metaphysics as, 10

First principle(s), 141 ff; defense of, 147 ff; and experience, 143 f; of knowledge, 144; not demonstrated, 143; of science and metaphysics, 12 f

First substance, primary in order of existence, 66

First way of demonstrating God's existence, 178 ff

Formal cause, 154

Formal diversity of object, 21

Formal object, 19, 21; of a science, 18

Formal subject and formal object, relationship of, 19

Formal subject of metaphysics, 35

Formal subject of a science, 17

Foundations of analogy, 48 ff

Fourth way of demonstrating God's existence, 195 ff

Function of abstraction, 25

Genus, meanings of, 39 f

Gilson, Etienne, on abstraction, 24; and analogy, 56

God, as the First Cause, 36; knowledge of, 18

Good, common, 123 ff; diffusion of, 167 f; kinds of, 121 ff; relationship to existence, 120 f; transcendental, 120 ff

Good and evil, 134 ff

Habits or power, distinguishing of, 21

Happiness of man, and knowledge, 6

Harmony, in beauty, 129

Hegel, Georg, and contradiction, 141

Heraclitus, and contradiction, 148 f

Hume, David, and substance, 70

Identity, principle of, 144 ff; and tautology, 146

Individual, and existence, 102 ff

Individual substance, 65 f

Individuality, analogous character of, 104; and subsistence, 105 ff

Individuation, kinds of, 102 ff

Infinite series, possibility of, 182 f

Infinite series of causes, 163 f

Instrumental and principal cause, 156

Integrity, in beauty, 128

James, William, and pluralism, 113

Judgment, essential, 18; existential, 18

Kant, Immanuel, on existence of God, 184

Knowledge, of common being, 18; end of learning, 90; first principle of, 144; of God, 18

Learning, order of, 5, 15 f

Liberal knowledge, meaning of, 13; and metaphysics, 13 ff

Likeness of effect in cause, 161 ff

Limitation of act by potency, 93 ff

Locke, John, and substance, 70

Logic, and analogy, 41; and the categories, 61 f; and metaphysics, 26 ff

Logical order of transcendentals, 109 ff

McGlynn, James, S.J., translation of *Truth*, Vol. II, ix

Index

McInerny, Ralph, translation of the *Exposition of the Trinity of Boethius,* ix
Maritain, Jacques, on existentialism, v; and the principle of finality, 166
Marxism, and contradiction, 141
Material cause, 154
Material object, 21
Material substances, and metaphysics, 74
Materialistic conception of substances, 73 f
Mathematical abstraction, and separation, 24 ff
Matter, and substance, 74
Maurer, Armand, translation of *On Being and Essence,* ix
Meaning of essence, 96 ff
Medieval commentators, vi ff
Metaphorical proportionality, 54 f
Metaphysical being, classes of, 33
Metaphysics, and accidents, 76 ff; and the categories, 61 f; and certainty, 10 ff; and common sense, 1 f; and demonstration, 8; difficulty of, 4 f; as directive knowledge, 9 f; a distinct science, 37; as first philosophy, 10; and first principles, 12 f; formal subject of, 35; liberal knowledge, 13 ff; and logic, 26 ff; and material substances, 74; as natural theology, 36; object of, 25; and the order of learning, 15; and the philosophy of nature, 29 ff; prescientific, 1, 3; proper subject of, 33; and science, 7; as a science, 4; subject of, 25; a transphysics, 32; a universal science, 75; universality of, 12 f; value of studying, 6; and wisdom, 8 f; as wisdom, 36; and youth, 5
Metaphysics of St. Thomas, and that of Aristotle, 35
Meyerson, Emile, on metaphysics, 1
Modes of abstraction, 22 ff
Modes of causes, 156 ff
Moral evil, 137 ff
Motion, Aristotelian notion of, 180; mathematical notion of, 181
Mulligan, Robert W., S.J., translation of *Truth,* Vol. I, ix
Multiplicity, in number and in being, 130 f
Multiplicity and unity, 130 ff

Natural being, composition of, 97 f
Natural substances, essence of, 97 f
Natural theology, and metaphysics, 36; and revealed truth, 15 f; and sacred theology, 172 f
Negative judgment, act of, 24
Neo-Thomism, v

Number, multiplicity in, 130 f

Object, formal, 19, 21; formal diversity of, 21; material, 21; meanings of, 19; potential, 21
Object of metaphysics, and separation, 23 ff
Objective relationship, 20
O'Neil, Charles, translation of *Summa Contra Gentiles,* Book IV, ix
Ontological argument, 174 ff; Thomistic refutation of, 175
Operations of the intellect, and abstraction, 23
Order of learning, 5, 15 ff
Orders of abstraction, 22 ff
Orders of speculative sciences, 21 ff

Passive potency, 84
Pegis, Anton, *Basic Writings of St. Thomas Aquinas,* viii; translation of *Summa Contra Gentiles,* Book I, ix
Per accidens series, 182
Per se series, 182
Person, 106 ff; etymology of term, 107
Phenomenalism, and substance, 70 ff
Philosopher, etymology of name, 2
Philosophia perennis, v
Philosophy, first, 38; and wonder, 1
Philosophy of nature, and metaphysics, 29 ff; precedes metaphysics, 30
Pluralism, and William James, 113
Point of departure for metaphysics, 74
Possibility, 34, 87
Potency, denial of, 85 ff; etymology of word, 84; first meaning of, 87; limits act, 93 ff; and material cause, 95; meaning of, 84 ff; passive, 84; reality of, 85 ff
Potency and act, 83 ff; comparison of, 91 ff
Potential object, 21
Powers, specification of, 20 f
Predicable accident, 63, 76
Predicamental accident, 63, 76 f
Predication, univocal, equivocal, and analogical, 40
Prescientific metaphysics, 1, 3
Primary and secondary cause, 158
Principal cause, and instrumental cause, 156
Principle, first, not demonstrated, 143; and cause, 153; meaning of, 142
Principle of contradiction, 143 ff, 147 ff
Principle of efficient causality, 158 ff
Principle of final causality, 164 ff
Principle of identity, 144 ff; application of, 146

Principle of sufficient reason, 150 ff
Principle(s), first, 141 ff; first, defense of, 147 ff; of knowledge, 144
Priority, in analogy, 42
Priority of act, 91 ff
Priority of unity over multiplicity, 130
Proper and accidental cause, 157
Proper proportionality, analogy based on, 56; causal relationship in, 56 ff
Proper subject of metaphysics, 33
Properties of being, 109 ff
Proportion, analogy based on, 53 f; meanings of, 48
Proportion and proportionality in St. Thomas, 49 ff
Proportionality, analogy based on, 53 f; divisions of, 54; meaning of, 49; metaphorical, 54 f
Protagoras, on potency, 86
Psychology, and metaphysics, 30
Pythagoreans, 24

Real distinction between essence and existence, 187 ff
Reality of accidents, 80
Reality of substance, 68 ff
Relationship, of causes, 166; of essence and existence, 191; of formal subject and formal object, 19; of good and existence, 120 f
Relationships, based on proportion, 48; based on proportionality, 49
Revelation, necessity of, 173 f
Rowan, John, translation of *Commentary on the Metaphysics*, ix

Sacred Theology, and natural theology, 172 f
Schmidt, Robert W., translation of *Truth* Vol. III, ix
Science, development of, 17; divine, 23, 30, 38; formal object of, 18; formal subject of, 17; goal of, 18; meaning of, 4; and metaphysics, 7; metaphysics as, 4; nature of, 19; and other intellectual disciplines, 7; and the scientific method, 4
Scientific investigation, purpose of, 19
Second way of demonstrating God's existence, 183 ff
Separated substances, 25
Separation, and the object of metaphysics, 23 ff
Separation and abstraction, difference between, 26 ff
Series, *per accidens*, 182; *per se*, 182; possibility of infinite, 182 f

Series of causes, 163 f; infinite, 163 f
Signification in analogy, 46 f
Simple proportion, analogy of, 50
Sophists, and contradiction, 148
Specification of powers, 20
Speculation, objects of, 22 ff
Speculative sciences, how they differ, 21; orders of, 21 ff
Suarez, and chance events, 168
Subject, of evil, 135 f; of metaphysics, 25, 61 ff; of a science, 36
Subsistence, act of, 106 ff; and individuality, 105
Substance, as abstract universal, 66; and accidents, analogy of, 77 ff; analogical character of, 73 ff; cannot be demonstrated, 69 ff; definition of, 62 ff, 67; denial of, 73 f; as essence, 65 f; etymology of name, 70; individual, 65 f; materialistic conception of, 73 f; and matter, 74; phenomenalist rejection of, 70 ff; as primary genus, 66; primary kind of being, 63 f; primary subject of metaphysics, 61 ff; reality of, 68 ff; related to accidents, 81 f; twofold meaning of, 106; twofold notion of individuality in, 105; various notions of, 64 ff
Substance and accident, analogy of, 58, 77 ff
Sufficient reason, principle of, 150 ff

Tautology and identity, 146; and judgment, 146
Theology, and philosophy, 22; supernatural, 37
Third order of abstraction, 27 ff
Third way of demonstrating God's existence, 185 ff
Transcendental beauty, 125 ff
Transcendental good, 120 ff
Transcendental one, 111 ff; see Transcendental unity
Transcendental truth, 115 ff; basis of, 117 ff; and principle of sufficient reason, 151
Transcendental unity, and principle of identity, 146
Transcendentals, 109 ff; contraries to, 129 ff; logical order of, 109 ff
Truth, different meanings of, 119; and falsehood, 131 ff; transcendental, 115 ff; various notions of, 116
Twofold meaning of existence or "to be," 25

Unity and being, 112 ff
Unity in common being, 40

Unity of man's operations, 3
Unity of metaphysics, and analogy, 59
Unity and multiplicity, 130 ff
Universal effects, 162 f
Universal and particular cause, 157
Universality of metaphysical knowledge, 12 f
Univocal causes, 162
Univocal effects, 162

Univocal predication, 40

Value of studying metaphysics, 6

Wisdom, and metaphysics, 8 f, 36; and philosophy, 2
Wise man, characteristics of, 8 f

Youth, and metaphysics, 5

Index of Readings

Abstraction, divisions of, 225 ff; kinds of, 221 ff; in mathematics, 226 f
Accidental causes, 373 ff
Accidents, being of, 255 f, 259 ff
Act, 267 ff; and potency, 284 ff
Active potency, 270 f
Actuality, 281 ff; priority of, 289 ff
Analogy, 235 ff; of God and creatures, 235 ff; in substance and accidents, 247
Angels, composition in, 233; and philosophy, 232 f
Argument from motion, 383 ff
Art, and practical knowledge, 219

Being and good, 332 ff, 336 ff
Being and one, 318 f

Categories, 268; of being, 251 ff
Cause, accidental, 373 ff; definition of, 365 ff; of evil, 343 ff
Causes, 364 ff; classes of, 369 ff; divisions of, 365 ff; modes of, 372 ff
Certainty of metaphysics, 206
Composition in separate substances, 304 f
Conservation of the world, 392 ff
Contradiction, principle of, 358 ff

Defense of first principle(s), 352 ff, 355 f
Demonstrability of God's existence, 378 f
Demonstration, and first principle(s), 354
Demonstration of existence of God, 379 ff; difficulties in, 381 ff
Demonstration of first principle(s), 356 f
Demonstration of principle of contradiction, 360 ff
Distinction between essence and existence, 305 ff
Divine science, 228 ff
Division of causes, 365 ff
Division and number, 330

Efficient cause, 366, 371
Equivocal names, 236 f
Essence and existence, 298 ff; distinction between, 305 ff
Essence in separate substances, 303 ff
Essence and substance, 264 ff
Evil, as a cause, 341; cause of, 343 ff; and God, 345 f; and good, 338 f; nature of, 339 ff; in things, 342 f; in the universe, 341
Existence, and essence, 298 ff; modes of, 302

Final cause, 367, 371
First philosophy, 213 f
First principle(s), 347 ff; condition of, 354 f; defense of, 352 ff, 355 f; demonstration of, 356 f; meaning of, 352 ff
First substance, 263
Five ways of St. Thomas, 379 ff
Formal cause, 365

God, and evil, 345 f; existence of, 376 ff; and motion, 383 ff
God's conservation of the world, 392 ff
God's existence, demonstrability of, 378 ff
God's government of things, 390 ff
Good, and being, 332 f, 336 ff; and evil, 338 f; transcendental, 331 ff
Government of things, 390 ff

Heraclitus, and contradiction, 362 f
Hypostasis, 263 ff

Impossible, 279 ff
Incorruptible being, priority of, 293 ff
Individual substance, 263
Infinity, actual, 281; potential, 281

Liberal knowledge, 211 f; and metaphysics, 208 ff
Logical beings, and essence, 361 ff

Many, see One and the many
Material cause, 365, 370 f
Material substances, 258 f
Mathematical abstraction, 226 f
Matter, and principle of individuality, 227
Megaric school of philosophy, 273
Metaphysics, certainty of, 206; nature of, 200 ff; principles of, 347 ff; science of, 200 ff; subject of, 201; as universal science, 205 f; as wisdom, 202 ff
Modes of causes, 372 ff
Motion and God, 383 ff

Names, analogical, 236 ff; equivocal, 236 f; of metaphysics, 202
Natural substances, 252 ff
Number and division, 330
Number in God, 325 ff
Number and unity, 321 ff

One, and being, 318 f; and the many, 320 ff; principle of number, 325 ff; transcendental, 318 ff